D1068156

Miriam Cohen

A Daughter of Two Mothers

A True Story of
Separation and Reunion,
Loyalty and Love

FELDHEIM PUBLISHERS
JERUSALEM   NEW YORK

First published in Hebrew as *Yetomah L'Shtei Imahos*
by Feldheim Publishers (2003)

Translated into English by Sandy Bloom
Edited by Chana D. Sklar

Also by the author:
Behind the Walls (Jerusalem: Feldheim Publishers, 2006)

ISBN: 978-1-58330-932-2

FELDHEIM PUBLISHERS
POB 43163
Jerusalem, Israel

208 Airport Executive Park
Nanuet, NY 10954

10 9 8 7 6 5

www.feldheim.com

Printed in Israel

Contents

Preface

I HAD TO take care of some paperwork in a government office in Jerusalem. I wandered down a long hall lined with doors, looking for the office that I needed. Each door had a neat plaque with the name and position of the person who sat inside.

Without warning I passed a door that looked just like all the others, but with a sign that made my heart pound:

Dovid Fruchter—Director

Without so much as knocking, I walked into the office and halted opposite a large office desk. Behind the desk sat a young man, perhaps in his late twenties. Despite the fact that I had just barged in, he smiled politely and asked how he could help me.

I tried to compose myself, but my whole body was trembling. "Your name, Dovid Fruchter—whom are you named after?" I asked. Actually, I shouted.

Mr. Fruchter's smile disappeared, and he looked at me in astonishment. "Please tell me!" I pleaded. "You see...my father's name was Dovid Fruchter. I didn't know that any other family member had survived except for me." The last sentence came out in a whisper.

1

Although he was clearly taken aback, the man answered me courteously. "I am named after my mother's father, Dovid Aharon Goldberg. My father—he was Chaim Moshe Fruchter and he passed away a year and a half ago. As far as I know, he was also the only one of his family to survive the Holocaust. He did not talk about it much."

Mr. Fruchter seemed embarrassed; he sat opposite me quietly and seriously, and then noticed that I was still standing and trembling. He got up from his place, walked around the desk, approached me and offered me a chair. "Please sit down. Here, let me pour you a glass of water," he said pleasantly. "I am truly sorry. My father, *alav ha-shalom*, did not tell us anything about his family and I cannot help you," he added.

I drank the water, mumbled an apology and rushed home. I don't remember exactly what happened after that. All I can recall is that I found myself lying in my bed, crying uncontrollably. I hid my head in the pillow and tears inundated me, wave after wave, as the memories flooded back.

From that moment on, I spent entire days walking about as if in a dream. I did not function at home and did not accomplish much at work; I was immersed in another world. But somehow, I knew what I had to do: I had to write down the story of my life, if only to return myself to sanity.

My memories are interwoven with my mother's memories. We would sit at home in the evenings and talk by the light of the lantern. Mama had told me her own memories so many times—and I had asked over and over again—until those memories became my own. They blended together in my mind, and then became engraved in my heart. Maybe no one will believe that these stories really happened, but they did...

❦ 1 ❧
All Alone
[SEVLUS]

AFTER MAMA'S FIRST husband passed away, she was left with three children: her daughter Caroli, the Hungarian equivalent of her Jewish name Kreindy — which only Mama called her by; and the boys Izzy and Ari — that is, Yitzchak and Aharon.

Reb Elya Rubenstein, their father, died after a long and agonizing illness. The economic situation in the house was grave when he passed away. Every penny had been spent on doctors and medications, though nothing was able to save Reb Elya in the end, and Mama and her children lacked for food and basic necessities.

After her father's death, Caroli found a job in a shoe store where she earned a few pennies. Izzy also began to work — for a building contractor named Mr. Neufeld. Izzy didn't get paid for his work because Mr. Neufeld was teaching him the trade, but he went to live with his employer and received food and clothing. Mama consoled herself that at least her son was fortunate to get enough food, as befits a growing boy, and clothing as well. Izzy visited Mama frequently, and whenever he came, he was always well-dressed and looked good. Mrs. Neufeld would always send along something for Mama and the children.

Ari, the youngest, was still in school at the time. At first he learned in a *cheder*, but Mama had no money to pay for his studies so she was forced to stop sending him. Instead he went to the local public school, which did not charge tuition at all. Twice a year the pupils received new clothes, and every day they received a cup of milk and a slice of bread. There was one family that brought kosher food for the Jewish pupils, and in the afternoon the Rav would come and teach them everything a good Jew should know. Mama used to joke that it was thanks to the *goyim* (that is, the public school) — that Ari didn't grow up like a *goy*.

But it was not long before Caroli left the little town and moved to a larger city, Nagybocskó. Before she left, she told Mama that she would earn a lot more money in the new city and get herself on her feet, then bring Mama and the boys to her. Mama objected strenuously; why, she explained, Caroli-Kreindy would have to spend all the money she earned on rent, heating, laundry, and the like, and that would eat away all her earnings. In her heart, Mama did not want Kreindy to leave home and she had reason to worry.

Caroli was adamant, however. She settled down in the big city and only sent home an occasional letter, telling everyone that she was fine. She quickly forgot that she had wanted to send for her mother and brothers. She came home once a year, for Pesach. Caroli looked tall and beautiful in the elegant clothes that she wore, like a real lady, not like Kreindy, the daughter of Sheina Ruchel.

She also did not allow Mama to treat her like a daughter. She considered herself an important and respectable guest in her own house.

It was not long before Izzy also left home and went to

Nagybocskó. He had already mastered the building trade and in the new city he became a partner to a well-known contractor, an older man, who was pleased to have a young, energetic fellow join his business. The first thing that Izzy did in town was cut off his *payos* and exchange his traditional Jewish garb for modern, fashionable clothing.

It was no wonder that Mama shed countless tears for him: "Izzy, Izzy my son," she would tell him on his visits home, "don't ever forget that you are scion to an important, respectable Jewish family."

But Izzy paid no attention, and only replied, "I'm not a little boy anymore. Please don't call me Izzy; my name is Isidor. And about that so-called 'important, respectable family,' where were they when we had no food to eat and we went to bed hungry? Why should I take them into consideration? Did they ever consider our needs? Did they as much as glance in our direction when Tatte was so terribly ill? And after he died, did they take an interest in us? Yes, they reminded me not to forget to say *Kaddish*, but they forgot to ask if I had food to eat! They do not interest me, as I evidently do not interest them," he declared.

Mama continued to cry to him: "If you won't remember that you are a Jew and instead act like a *sheigetz*, the *goyim* will remind you that you are not one of them and it will end badly." Her words were prophetic, but she did not know it at the time.

Mama's last hope was her youngest, Ari. He finished his compulsory education and, despite all his many promises to his mother that he would stay with her and remain a good Jew, he, too, followed Izzy. He lived with his older brother, worked with him, and changed his ways like him.

Mama was left alone. She continued to work: In the summer she worked in the many vineyards that grew on the Carpathian Mountains. In the winter she sewed clothes for Mr. Gelernter's clothing business.

Some time after all this took place, she married my father, Dovid Fruchter.

❧ 2 ❧
Happy Days

[SEVLUS]

M Y FATHER, Dovid Fruchter, was an unusually good person. He possessed exceptional patience and knew how to calm Mama when she wept over the fate of her children who had left her. My father sent them letters begging them to return to their hometown of Sevlus and promising to support them and marry them off, find them respectable *shidduchim*.

But they—they were far away, pleased with their important positions, proud of being products of the big city. What did they have in common with Sevlus, a tiny village at the foot of the Carpathians? (Sevlus was a town with several names; the official name in Hungarian was "Nagyszőllős," but everyone called it "Sevlus," or even "Selish.")

Tatte earned a respectable salary and Mama stopped working. She returned to being a full-time homemaker, as she had been before her first husband became ill. True, it had been a long time ago, but she hadn't forgotten the profession.

In those days it was not a simple thing to be a housewife. Electrical appliances had not been invented yet, and the typical housewife was busy from sun-up to sun-down, drawing water using a pump in the yard, laundering the family's clothing by hand, cooking and baking on a primitive oven fueled by wood blocks or coals, even sewing all the clothes as well as the linens, and of course—embroidering the linens. After all, how could someone of that generation even consider sleeping on sheets that were not embroidered! And cooking, of course, was a project unto itself.

But Mama loved it. Finally, finally, the days she had so longed for had arrived; days of tranquility and peace after all she had endured, happy at last with her husband and her life. Mama used to tell me about that idyllic period over and over; she didn't cry over the past, but her voice was always wistful when she recalled Tatte and those good years they had together.

How short were those happy days! Even though Mama never forgot her older children and always regretted that they had left, she didn't allow that pain to ruin her newfound happiness. "True, it's sad that my children didn't want to return to us, that they viewed me as primitive and provincial, but I felt so fortunate and happy — I focused on the good I did have. I trust in Hashem," she always said.

One evening we sat near the warm heater, drinking tea. Outside it was dark, snowy, and very cold but in the house/store we lived in, it was warm and pleasant. We knew that no customers would come shopping in such freezing weather. Usually, people made their purchases in daylight hours and didn't leave their homes at night when it was so cold.

That night, I was sitting near the table and embroidering a tablecloth. Mama leaned her back against the stove, closed her eyes and began telling me the story of her life. Mama was a storyteller par excellence. She spoke so enthusiastically and vividly about the events she was retelling, that I could visualize it all happening. Mama talked a great deal about her life; she told me also stories from the *Tzena U'Rena* and stories of *tzaddikim* that she had heard. Her amazing memory and a special way of storytelling made the listener feel as if the story was happening then and there. I always sat spellbound when I listened to her.

It was on that cold night that Mama told me about her childhood. "You see, Leichu" — my name is Leah, but people have always called me by my nickname — "you see that even though I only have one hand, it is always busy. And when I had both hands, they were also always busy, always active." Even now, with her one hand, Mama was able to help me embroider and show me the correct stitches and especially how to unstitch when I made a mistake.

Mama told me about her faraway childhood, wonderful days full of joy. Her mother—my Bubby—was a happy woman who always found reasons to laugh. When Mama was ten years old and her younger brother was five, her mother gave birth to a little girl, and the happy life was over. Her mother became very sick and was paralyzed. From a happy and joyful person she became extremely irritable, as she was always in great pain, and my mother, at ten years old, took over the running of the house. In addition to household duties, she took care of the baby, her younger brother, and even her paralyzed mother.

Bubby's years of suffering did not last long and she died in the prime of life, leaving her little children and husband to fend for themselves. Mama did the best she could, and her father tried to help, but he was hardly home. He had a large store for building supplies and spent many hours trying to eke out a living. When he finally came home after a long work day, he was too exhausted to be of much help.

Mama spent a long time telling me about the difficulties she underwent starting from the tender age of ten when her mother became ill. A while after her mother died, her father remarried and Mama turned into the maid—looked down upon by the lady of the house, her stepmother. It was no wonder that Mama was thrilled when, at age sixteen-and-a-half, her father told her that she was engaged!

One night her father came home late. Mama was sound asleep, but her father woke her up to tell her the good news. "*Mazel tov*, Sheina Ruchel! You are engaged to a *bachur* by the name of Elya Rubinstein from the Pressburg yeshiva."

Mama was ecstatic, and it didn't bother her at all that she did not know her *chasan*. In those days, that is how *shidduchim* were arranged, and all of Mama's friends married young men chosen for them by their parents. She was only sorry that she would remain in Sevlus and not move to the big city of Pressburg where the yeshiva was, and which was the city that every girl her age dreamed about in those days.

Following her marriage, Mama continued to work for her stepmother. Even after Kreindy, her eldest, was born, she dutifully carried out her role as the stepmother's maid. This went on until Izzy's birth because her father demanded this, evidently on behalf of his wife.

After Izzy's birth, Mama's stepmother was not pleased that she could not continue to help her. Mama was forced to promise that she would come back to help when the children grew up a little. But when Izzy was three years old, Ari was born, and shortly afterwards Reb Elya became ill and died. Then, when Mama needed help so badly, her father died. Her stepmother, who was well-off financially, never even considered coming to Mama's aid.

And thus, on that cold and snowy evening, I learned a bit about my mother's life; a life in which much suffering and grief overpowered the joy and happiness.

❧ 3 ❧
The Sinister Building
[SEVLUS]

AFTER MAMA MARRIED Dovid Fruchter, my father, all the neighbors comforted her by saying, "Now you will have a good life." They said what they said and they were right, but unfortunately it was true for only a short time. Six months before I was born, my father was drafted into the Czechoslovakian army for half a year. (Although we spoke Hungarian and considered ourselves Hungarians, our city of Sevlus was in one of those regions of the world that kept being annexed to different countries. Originally it had been part of Hungary, but in 1920 it was taken away from Hungary and given over to Czechoslovakia.) A short time before I was born, my father was released from the army.

Tatte came home happily telling everyone the good news: He had received a permanent exemption! True, the exemption cost a lot of money and my parents sank into debt as a result. But, they agreed, it was worth it.

Three weeks later, I was born. They named me after Tatte's mother—Leah. Tatte's happiness knew no bounds. A wonderful baby daughter! He venerated his mother, always saying that she was a true *tzadekes* like Leah Imeinu. He was the one who gave me the nickname that stuck to me my entire life: "Leichu." Was there any other child in the world who could compare to his very own Leichu?

But the joy in our home did not last long, because Tatte had come home from the army with a terrible cough. When it did not improve, Mama kept begging him to go to the doctor and he kept making excuses. "Why should I go to the doctor when all he will do is prescribe a *guggel muggel*," he would say, referring to an old Jewish remedy of raw egg, honey and hot milk to alleviate coughs. "You can make me the best *guggel muggel* in the world, without a doctor's prescription!" Another time that Mama insisted he go to the doctor, he picked me up and said that the best medicine in the world was to kiss his very own Leichu three times.

Finally, Mama had enough of this and one day, she took me in her arms and persuaded Tatte to go for a walk with her. When Tatte found himself standing outside the doctor's home, he knew that he was bested. Tatte followed Mama into the adjacent office.

Once in the waiting room, they were amazed at all the people they knew who were waiting in line. There was Mr. Aaron, who was squirming nervously in his chair and groaning out loud, "*Oy, oy, oy.*"

Tatte inquired, "Mr. Aaron, what is hurting you so badly?"

"Don't ask, young man, don't ask. Only I know what hurts me, even the doctor doesn't know," moaned Mr. Aaron. "In fact, the doctor doesn't know a thing! *Oy, oy,* it hurts!"

"So why do you go to a doctor who doesn't know anything?" asked Tatte curiously. Mr. Aaron got angry at this remark and shouted at Tatte. At that point, Dr. Bergman came out of his office and walked over to Mr. Aaron.

"Now, now, Mr. Aaron," he said. "You know that my condition for seeing you is that you do not pick fights with the other patients in the waiting room." Mr. Aaron's response was a very loud groan.

"Yes, I know that you are in pain," soothed Dr. Bergman, "but I cannot treat people when there is this kind of noise in the background." Mr. Aaron reluctantly agreed to quiet down, and the doctor went back into his office.

Mrs. Gross, who was sitting next to her husband, tried to make funny faces at me so I would smile. But I was only an infant and I started to cry. Mr. Gross was annoyed at his wife for frightening the baby and exclaimed, "Why, that swollen eye of yours is enough to scare anyone, let alone a baby!" Mrs. Gross took offense and started to shout that Mr. Aaron was really the one who had scared me. Of course, Mr. Aaron denied the accusation vociferously, and when the three of them were busy arguing with one another, Tatte and Mama slipped into the doctor's office that had just been vacated. Luckily, no one in the waiting room noticed.

Tatte and Mama smiled understandingly at the doctor as he shook his head. "This performance repeats itself all the time, and the chief actor is Mr. Aaron!" the doctor sighed. "He shows up here every day like clockwork, even though he's as healthy as an ox, and he tries to act sick so that people will take pity on him and give him money." He sighed. "Everyone has his own hobbies." He turned to Mama. "And what's your hobby, Mrs. Fruchter? How is your adorable daughter feeling? Is she sick?"

Mama smiled. "No, doctor," she said. "Our Leah is fine, *Baruch Hashem* — she's not my first child, you know. I'm not a nervous first-time mother anymore. It's actually because of my husband Dovid that we are here today. Dovid has had a terrible cough ever since he came back from his army service. Can you please listen to his lungs?"

Tatte waved his hand. "I cough a little, and she makes a big deal out of it. I only came here today so that she would stop nudging me."

"I see," smiled Dr. Bergman. "Let me examine you so that we can pacify Mrs. Fruchter."

Dr. Bergman took out his stethoscope to examine Tatte. His smile disappeared immediately. He took a deep breath. "Mr. Fruchter, I am sorry to tell you this, but I don't like what I hear in your lungs."

"That's fine," joked Tatte. "I didn't come here to find favor in your eyes — what's important is that I find favor in Hashem's eyes — *she'emtza chen b'eini Elokim.*"

"And man — *v'adam,*" Dr. Bergman added, without missing a beat.

Mama asked the doctor for a more detailed explanation, but instead he insisted that Tatte take a specialized test in the large municipal clinic. "I can't give a diagnosis until you do as I say," he said firmly. Going to the city clinic was serious business, and even Tatte stopped making jokes. "You must do a special test in a new machine called an X-ray," he said. "This will give us a picture of your lungs, almost like a photograph. I'll be honest with you: Your lungs do not sound good, but I must send you to the special clinic to be sure. Yes, it is very expensive, but you have no choice."

Tatte and Mama came out of the office with worried looks on their faces. They were greeted in the waiting room with anger. "Why did you sneak into the doctor out of turn?" shouted Mrs. Gross, and Mr. Aaron joined in the criticism. But Tatte was not in the mood for this anymore, and they left as quietly as they could.

Tatte went to speak to the *Dayan* to ask what to do. The *Dayan*, who knew Dr. Bergman and trusted his expertise, told him to listen to the doctor, and do the special test as soon as possible.

The very next morning my parents left me with a neighbor and went to the municipal clinic. The clinic was situated in the center of town, on the main street of Sevlus. The road was paved with smooth, straight stones, and tall trees lined the sides of the roads. The wagons and carriages flew by quickly, their wooden wheels gliding over the smooth stones without bouncing — unlike the local roads that were paved with non-chiseled rocks. Even the horseshoes made a smooth, even, clickety-clack noise on the road.

The clinic itself was two stories high and situated behind a beautiful flowering garden. There were a number of sparkling windows in the building, with no curtains at all. As Tatte and Mama walked up the path leading up to the clinic, they instinctively slowed down. The building, and the front door, seemed so threatening. Slowly but surely, however, they approached the door. The doorman opened the door for them and directed them to a long hall. On one side, facing the street, was a row of windows and opposite the windows

The municipal clinic

was a row of grey doors. Under the windows were brown benches. In each corner of the corridor stood a shiny, enamel spittoon. It appeared that no one ever used them.

The benches were full of non-Jews — Tatte and Mama noticed one lone Jew in the entire waiting room. They sat down on the bench next to him.

A short time later, a clerk approached them with a large notebook. Mama gave him the referral from Dr. Bergman and the clerk wrote Tatte's name in the notebook, returned the note to Mama and told them to wait until they were called. Although there were many people waiting, it was very quiet. Everyone sat stiffly on the benches, without speaking or moving.

Tatte couldn't help but recall Dr. Bergman's waiting room, where everyone chatted with everyone else: Mr. Aaron moaned, Mrs. Gross complained. Everyone knew exactly what everyone else's problems were — who had a bad back, who suffered from a plantar wart on his foot. The people in Dr. Bergman's waiting room acted in the clinic just as they did at home, in the company of their friends. But in the gray hall with gray doors and brown benches and shiny, glittering white spittoons, the people were afraid to move. They all sat rooted to their spots; they all worried. They worried because of the medical problem that brought them to this forbidding place to begin with; they were intimidated by the clerks who milled around; they felt so terribly uncomfortable on the hard benches—and couldn't wait to finish and be out of this foreboding place.

Finally it was Tatte's turn. Mama got up and wanted to accompany her husband, but the clerk would not allow her. He pointed to her seat and made it clear that she was to wait outside until her husband returned. Mama waited alone, among all the non-Jews, making superhuman efforts not to cry. The building was so dank and frightening, and it seemed like an eternity until Tatte finally came out. The two of them hurried as fast as they could out of the "sinister building"—the municipal clinic.

Only after they were outside did Mama ask Tatte what had happened. Tatte told her that the results would be sent to Dr. Bergman the next day, but would only reach him a few days later.

They would have to wait an entire week before returning to the doctor for the results of the test.

❧ 4 ❧
The Diagnosis
[SEVLUS]

THAT WAS THE longest week of their lives. On the outside, everything went on as usual: Tatte went to the *beis midrash* every morning to daven, ate a quick breakfast at home and then left to work. In the late afternoons, when he returned home, he kept to his regular schedule as well: he ate supper, played with me for a while, and then went to daven. After Minchah and Maariv, he stayed in *shul* to hear the Rav's *shiur*, and then he returned home. Mama took care of the house, and me, as usual.

Yes, everything went on as usual on the surface, but the tension inside Mama and Tatte was unbearable. Both of them took pains not to mention anything at all connected to the doctor, the clinic, and their fears of the diagnosis. They even ignored Tatte's cough. True, he did not stop coughing, but he refused to acknowledge it. Years later when Mama told me the story I didn't really understand why they put on such an act, but I didn't ask any questions. Sometimes, there are things you simply cannot explain.

The dreaded day finally arrived. Tatte came home early from work, and my parents left me with a neighbor while they walked over to Dr. Bergman.

The waiting room that greeted them was a repeat of the previous week: packed full of people, all talking and arguing with one another. Mr. Aaron was there too, moaning and groaning as usual. Some of the patients talked a lot and loudly while others answered questions quietly. After all, everyone had to know why everyone else had come to the doctor. This was not only out of mere curiosity but out of a sense of partnership; Jews simply cared about one another.

When it was Tatte's turn, he and Mama entered together. No one told Mama to wait outside; here it was clear that whatever happened to Tatte involved Mama as well.

It was there, inside Dr. Bergman's office, that the bad news was delivered to them, the news that they had feared so much. It was there that the name of the dreaded malady was stated out loud, the one that they had not dared to even whisper: Tuberculosis. Evidently, Tatte had contracted the dreadful disease in the army.

Tuberculosis was the dreaded disease of that generation and many other generations before the advent of modern antibiotics. It was a terrible, threatening disease, a contagious disease, and worst of all—it was incurable.

Dr. Bergman had no consoling words for Tatte and Mama, and he told them bluntly, "I will not try to hide the truth from you. The disease is grim and painful and we have no cure. We don't even have medication to relieve the symptoms. All I can tell you is to try to take advantage of the time you have left."

Dr. Bergman went on to say that some people do manage to live with the disease for many years and with tolerable symptoms. "I can only say that I truly pray that Dovid will be one of the more fortunate sufferers of this disease," he said sincerely.

Tatte and Mama came home; their whole world had fallen apart in front of their eyes. The neighbors came to support, encourage, comfort, and to help. Everyone had advice to give, but most of their suggestions were totally impractical or useless. Some people told them to go to Switzerland, as the clear air in that country was considered beneficial for TB sufferers. But who could afford the trip to Switzerland—they might as well save up to go to the moon! Even after they had talked it over many times, the bottom line was this: no tuberculosis sufferer they had heard of who made the very expensive trip to the faraway country, ever came back healthy. So what was the point?

Tatte stated resolutely that in any case, he was not willing to leave his family. He would try to work for as long as possible, and afterwards—Hashem would have mercy! He insisted that he would remain with his beloved family until his dying day, whether that day was sooner or later.

And so Tatte maintained his regular schedule: davening, work, more prayers, and Torah study. He took the advice of friends and dutifully drank all kinds of potions and extracts from strange grasses and plants, but nothing helped. His cough only worsened, and slowly he became weaker and weaker until he had to stop working. Still, he insisted on davening in shul, so twice a day, he dragged himself to the *beis midrash*, back and forth.

Then the really difficult days arrived. When Tatte could no longer walk by himself, the neighbors came to assist him. In the mornings, Reb Elya Hershko, *Hy"d*, took him to shul. Tatte walked slowly, leaning on Reb Elya. Tatte could not even carry his own tallis and tefillin bag, so Reb Elya supported him with one hand and with his body, and in the other hand he carried both of their tallis-tefillin bags.

Every evening, a different neighbor would take Tatte to

Minchah-Maariv and to the *shiur*. But it was hard for Tatte to concentrate on the *shiur* and his loud, raspy cough bothered the other participants. The walk home from shul in the dark was also hard for him, and before long he had to stop. That's when the neighbors developed a rotation system to come to Tatte at home and daven with him (without a *minyan*) and learn Torah with him. This was true devotion: Men who had always prayed with a *minyan* gave up this privilege in order to stay with Tatte so that he would not feel so alone. Then, afterwards, Tatte would go back into bed and the men would sit next to him and learn. Mama always said that this was the biggest *chesed* of all.

There was one particular neighbor who stayed by Tatte's side through thick and thin, through all the months of Tatte's illness, and that was Reb Elya Hershko. He came every single day, and when Tatte could not manage to walk to shul even for Shacharis, Reb Elya would daven together with Tatte at home. When Tatte could not even get up from bed, Reb Elya would lay tefillin on Tatte. He never tired and never despaired.

◇◇

Reb Elya Hershko and his wife, Esther Bluma, and their four small children were murdered by the Nazis. May Hashem avenge their blood, together with the innocent blood of the rest of the righteous Jews of Sevlus, who were murdered al kiddush HaShem in the Holocaust.

◇◇

Tatte would not let himself be vanquished easily and valiantly fought his disease. Even when he had no energy to leave the house, he tried not to lie in bed all day. He tried to sit and learn Torah; he helped with the household work a little; he walked around the house — anything to stay out of bed. But as time went on he became weaker and weaker. His coughing fits became more frequent and stronger and they caused great pain in his chest and back. After each coughing fit he had to rest for a long time, and sometimes, after he rested and finally felt better, another coughing fit brought him back to bed. There were very few good days when his coughing was not too bad.

Mama had to go to work to support the family, so she returned to picking grapes in the vineyards. I remained at home with Tatte, and he tried to take care of me as best as he could. He would sit next to my crib and sing songs to me, until his coughing made him stop. Mama used to tell me, with tears in her eyes, "Leichu, if only you could have seen how happy your father was to sing to you and play with you. You were his whole world, and he loved you dearly."

When I was five months old, Tatte's condition deteriorated; by then he could not get out of bed. Reb Elya continued to come every day to lay tefillin for Tatte and learn with him; when Tatte could not even learn Torah with him, Reb Elya sat next to him and talked to him. When even that became too much for Tatte, Reb Elya held Tatte's hand and said *Tehillim*.

Mama described to me how Reb Elya used to say *Tehillim*: He would say each and every word slowly and out loud, as if they were precious stones that he could not bear to part with. You could hear his whole heart and soul in those *pirkei Tehillim*, she said. Tatte tried to whisper the holy words together with his friend, though he was not always successful. But you could see how his eyes, and his heart, followed every word with deep concentration.

Day by day, Tatte got weaker. When Mama was at work, kind women from the neighborhood would come to take care of me. They also made sure that Tatte drank his special milk, because everyone said that milk was very important for TB sufferers. Every morning, Mama would go to the cow shed to be present during the milking (so that the milk would not be considered *chalav akum*, as the dairy-farmer was a gentile). But the day came when even the simple act of drinking a cup of milk became too hard for Tatte. The kind women, Reb Elya, and of course Mama, took turns sitting next to Tatte and feeding him spoonfuls of milk.

❧ 5 ❧
Darkness
[SEVLUS]

ONE DAY TATTE felt a bit better and even managed to sip a little milk. He sat up in bed, and told Reb Elya that there was something important he wanted to ask him. Reb Elya, happy to see that Tatte was feeling better, hurried to rearrange the pillows so Tatte would be as comfortable as possible. "Yes," he said, "of course I promise to do as you ask, whatever it is."

"My request from you," said Tatte, "is this: When the time comes for me to move to the World of Truth, I implore you to continue helping my wife and child as much as you can."

"Why are you talking like that?" said Reb Elya. "Why, I see how you feel better already, and when you recuperate you will be able to go back to work and support your family. Why do you want me to promise such a thing?"

But Tatte would not be dissuaded and with tears in his eyes, Reb Elya did, indeed, promise.

Every one of the women who came in that day to help, was happy to see Tatte sitting up and looking much better. But Tatte made the same request from all of them, and they all complied.

Before Reb Elya left that day, Tatte asked him to bring him his Yom Kippur *machzor*. When Mama came home from work in the afternoon, she was overjoyed to see Tatte looking so well.

"Hello, Sheina Ruchel," Tatte said. "Please pick up Leichu and come sit next to me."

Mama was surprised but did as he asked. Tatte took the *machzor* and then placed one hand on my head. Then he began to recite *Birkas HaBanim*, the special blessing that parents give their children on *erev Yom Kippur*.

Mama was taken aback but did not say a word. Tatte started to talk to her about how to bring me up. Mama interrupted him, telling him that he was getting better and would be the one to bring me up, but he continued. "Sheina Ruchel," he said, "promise me that you will never allow yourself to be separated from our Leichu. Don't ever let her work for strangers, as Kreindy did." Tatte sighed, and continued, "Even if you are hungry, don't leave her; keep her close to you so that you can teach her about Torah and Yiddishkeit. When the day comes, make sure that our Leichu will be married to a *ben Torah*, a God-fearing, upright Jewish man. The Torah will fill their home with light, just like in our home—even if their financial state is poor.

"Sheina Ruchel," continued Tatte, "I entrust in your hands our most precious gift from Hashem: our little girl Leichu. I am giving you sole responsibility for the lofty task of bringing her up as a God-fearing *bas Yisrael*, in the path of our *Imahos*, Sarah, Rivkah, Rachel and Leah."

Mama wept bitterly. "Why are you talking this way? You're the one who will be my partner in her upbringing. We will help each other!"

Tatte did not reply. The conversation had been the longest one he had conducted for some time, and he had to rest to gather his strength. Then he made another request. "I have one more thing to ask of you, and that is—forgiveness."

"You have been a wonderful husband and father," said Mama. "What do I have to forgive you for?"

"Please forgive me for leaving you and our beloved Leichu. Please forgive me for leaving you a widow again." Mama cried but Tatte did not relent until she said that she forgave him with all her heart.

"Now, my dear wife, I want you to daven the *tefillah* of *Ne'ilah* with me."

My mother told me how I, the small infant, had been snuggled quietly in her arms the entire time. I had been extremely alert, my green eyes wide open. I did not cry even though it was time for me to eat, and I didn't even happily babble the way I usually did. It was as if I, too, understood the gravity of the situation and the importance of being as quiet as possible.

So Tatte and Mama davened the whole *Ne'ilah* prayer together: Tatte in a weak but audible voice, and Mama in a choked whisper. Mama stood up for *Shemoneh Esrei*, with me in her arms, while Tatte remained half-sitting up in bed, supported by the pillows. Mama told me that I did not disturb her at all, I only tried to wipe away her tears with my tiny hands.

As Mama concluded davening *Shemoneh Esrei*, Tatte motioned for her to sit next to him again, and he continued to daven. When he reached the paragraph that says "You give hand to transgressors, and Your right hand is stretched out to accept those who return [to You]," Tatte started to sob. "And may You accept us in Your presence through perfect repentance," he cried to his Father in Heaven. Meanwhile, Mama sat next to him, praying together with him, her tears flowing freely and soaking me while I lay there, nestled in her arms, looking up at her.

Tatte continued to weep. "Forgive us this day, now that the day has passed... Speedily open the gates... Have mercy upon Your creation and declare us not guilty, King of Justice...." Tatte stopped for a moment as he was having trouble breathing, and Mama quietly fed him a few tablespoons of milk, without talking, as if they were in the middle of davening in shul. Then Tatte continued: "Open the gate of prayer for us, even at the time of the gate's closing, even now that the day has passed." It seemed that the milk had given him strength; he raised his voice and sounded almost like the old Tatte, before the disease had weakened him so. "Have mercy..." His voice became progressively louder as he prayed. When he reached the final verses of "*Shema Yisrael*" and "*Hashem Hu HaElokim*," Tatte's voice was resounding and his head erect. He gasped for breath, then exclaimed forcefully, "*L'Shanah ha-ba'ah bi'Yerushalayim HaBenuyah!*" and reclined his head back on the pillow. He looked intently at Mama and me, put his hand on my head, and didn't say another word. He refused more milk, he just looked at us.

That night, Reb Elya arrived as usual. Mama and I were still sitting in the chair next to Tatte's bed. Mama got up to give Reb Elya the chair, and as soon as she stood up, I burst out crying. Mama remembered that I was long due for a feeding. When she started to feed me, I turned my eyes toward Tatte, and when she tried to put me down to sleep after she had changed my diaper, I cried again. Mama held me and sat down not far from Tatte and Reb Elya. Reb Elya said *Tehillim*—but this time he recited the words quietly, unlike his usual practice.

Finally Reb Elya rose to leave, and Tatte whispered two words to him: "*Chevrah Kadisha*."

Reb Elya said he would do as Tatte asked him, though he

felt it was unnecessary. "You look better by the minute," he said to Tatte. And it was true: Tatte looked better than he had been for a long time. The frightening paleness of his face had disappeared and his skin had returned to its healthy color. Even his eyes that had seemed to have shrunken into their sockets were now wide open.

Reb Elya returned with the *Chevrah Kadisha* and the head of the group said to Tatte, "I think we are unnecessary here, you are so full of life."

Tatte didn't answer. When the man suggested that Tatte say *Viduy* with them, he refused. Mama told them that he had prayed the entire *Neilah* prayer. Mama tried to take me to my bed again, but once more I started wailing. When she sat on the chair near Tatte, however, I quieted down instantly. Tatte reached out, grasped my tiny hand and did not release his grip. Occasionally his eyes closed, but he did not release his grip for a long time.

And then, he closed his eyes and his hand dropped. His entire body trembled, a brief shudder, and all at once his face became white, almost translucent. The men of the *Chevrah Kadisha* shouted *Shema Yisrael*, and Mama sat rooted to her seat like a statue. Only I started crying. The head of the group said quietly, *"Baruch Dayan HaEmes"* and only then did Mama start to cry and shout hysterically.

A member of the *Chevrah Kadisha* ran to call a neighbor over, and she guided Mama away from Tatte's bed.

And so my Tatte passed away.

❧ 6 ❧

A Swollen Hand

[SEVLUS]

I HAVE NOTHING of my father's, not even the shadow of a memory. Not a picture or a book, nothing to remind me of him. I don't even know what he looked like. His name, Dovid Fruchter, and my mother's memories, are all I know about my father.

Mama continued to work in the vineyards. Those vineyards dotted the slope of the Carpathian Mountains, and during grape-picking season many people came to Sevlus to work. Even many Sevlus residents took vacation from their regular occupations in order to pick grapes. It must have been worth their while, I suppose. Thus the vineyards were full of hordes of harvesters with pruning-shears in their hands. All the pickers carried large wicker baskets in which they collected the clusters of grapes that they picked. When the basket was full, they would gently spill its contents into a large wooden box. The supervisor would record how many wooden boxes each picker filled up, and pay their wages accordingly.

Mama took me with her. Tatte was no longer alive to babysit for me, and she had promised him before his death not to

29

leave me anywhere, but keep me next to her, always.

Every day, when we reached the vineyard, Mama would take two baskets. She would line one of the baskets with a blanket for me, and put me down near the grapes she was picking. Everything was green—the grapevines, the grapes and the soft grasses that grew between the vines.

Most of the pickers were non-Jewish women, dressed in colorful clothes. They were a jolly group, laughing among themselves the entire time, even breaking into cheerful song occasionally. Only Mama worked in total silence, sad and withdrawn. Her pain was so intense that she did not pay attention to the tumult around her, but she worked steadily and took care of me. I was a good girl, and only cried when I was hungry. Mama would put down her shears and feed me, then hug and kiss me and return me to my basket.

One day, during work, a large splinter became imbedded in Mama's hand. One of the workers pulled it out, but even after it was out, Mama's hand became swollen and painful. She decided that the pain would eventually subside, and that she'd just ignore it in the meanwhile. After all, the splinter had been removed.

Eventually, picking season was over. The grapes were sent to Tokai, city of wineries. Practically every home in Tokai had a small winery, and every vineyard-owner in the Carpathian Mountains sent his grapes to a specific Tokai winery.

At the end of the picking season, the owner of the vineyard would host a big party for all the workers. He served a lavish meal and hired musicians to liven up the festivities all the more so. Everyone sang and danced, and the owner paid the workers their wages.

Mama, of course, did not partake in the celebrations. The owner paid her wages before the party. Mama immediately told the man that he had grossly overpaid her, but the kindly owner insisted that he was just giving her what she deserved, according to the supervisor's ledgers. Mama did not argue; she needed the money desperately.

Mama remained at home one or two days after the end of the season. Her hand had become extremely swollen and painful, and she realized that she had to see a doctor. She later regretted that she had waited as long as she did.

My deceased father had a first cousin named Rivka Klar. Mama was very close to Rivka, so she naturally turned to her for advice. Mama did not want to go to Dr. Bergman, so Rivka suggested that she turn to Dr. Yaakov Lezman, a neighbor and friend of the family. Dr. Lezman was a very pleasant fellow and Mama had met him a number of times at the Klars'. In fact, Rivka's husband, Nachman Klar — who was a carpenter — had built a beehive for the doctor's bee-collecting hobby. When Dr. Lezman would come visiting, he always brought his young daughter with him. The little girl was orphaned of her mother,

Dr. Yaakov Lezman, Hy"d

and she would sit on her father's lap with her finger in her mouth, watching the Klar children playing games.

Dr. Lezman's clinic was the opposite of Dr. Bergman's: It was a tiny apartment with a small kitchen that served as a waiting room, and a bedroom that also served as the doctor's office. Mama entered the kitchen-cum-waiting room, and saw that one of the patients who was waiting there was stirring a pot so that the doctor's lunch would not burn. Another woman was busy washing the dishes. This set-up was unlike Dr. Bergman's elegant waiting room with matching chairs, curtains and pictures, but the human factor was similar. Here, too, everyone knew everyone else.

Everything was homey; the patients were the doctor's neighbors and friends who felt responsible to help him as much as they could, since the doctor had no wife and was struggling to raise his daughter alone. So in Dr. Lezman's waiting room, the patients did not gripe about their aches and pains, but instead chatted about recipes for their beloved doctor.

When Mama came in she felt a little out of place. She lived in a different neighborhood and was not acquainted with these people. But one of the patients immediately spotted her swollen hand and it was not long before the people in the waiting room were asking questions and giving all kinds of advice and suggestions. One of the women generously offered to hold little Leah when Mama's turn would come to see the doctor. Mama was happy to take her up on the offer.

The doctor examined her hand, though Mama was in so much pain that she could scarcely sit still for the examination. "I am so sorry that you did not come in earlier, Mrs. Fruchter," said Dr. Lezman. "Evidently a piece of the splinter is still embedded inside your hand. If you had come to me immediately I could have opened up the area to remove the splinter, but now your hand is infected." He sighed. "I am sorry to tell you that you must undergo surgery, regular surgery in a hospital."

Mama realized that this was serious. There were no antibiotics in those days to cure infections, and surgical operations were far more dangerous than in our time, but Mama had no choice. She could not help but scream when the doctor touched the swollen area and tried to move her hand. "I see that the nearby gland is very swollen, which means that the infection has already spread. You must go to the hospital in Budapest today for emergency surgery," he urged.

Mama explained to him that her little baby was waiting for her at that very moment in the kitchen. "I will be happy to watch your little girl together with my child," the doctor replied. "I know how to care for children; I have been taking care of my own daughter by myself." Mama was touched by this generous offer but explained that she couldn't accept it. "I promised my deceased husband on his deathbed that I would never leave my daughter," she explained. "I will go to Budapest tomorrow," she said, "and make all my travel arrangements today."

Mama left the doctor's office and walked over to Rivka Klar's house to tell her the news. "You must leave Leichu with me, of course," exclaimed Rivka. "It would be my pleasure to watch her while you take care of your hand in Budapest."

"Thank you so much for your offer, my dear Rivka. But I cannot accept. Just before Dovid died, he asked me to promise him that I would never be separated from Leichu. Not even for a short time, he said." Mama sighed. "I also have no idea how long this process will take in Budapest. I may end up staying there for an extended period of time, and I simply can't leave Leichu in Sevlus for so long."

Rivka tried to convince Mama, but she was not successful. Mama was to shed many tears in later years over this fateful decision and berate herself for not listening to reason and leaving me with the kindly Rivka Klar. But there was no way she could have prophesied the terrible results of this decision at the time, no way at all, and I never blamed her for it.

❧ 7 ❧

One Hand

[SEVLUS]

THE NEXT DAY, Mama left for Budapest on the train. She carried me in her healthy arm, and took a large bag of clothing for both of us that rested on her shoulder. She knew that Tatte had relatives in Budapest and relied on them to help her in her crisis: a newly widowed mother with a baby and a swollen hand. Tatte's relatives, the Goldman family, welcomed Mama warmly. They sat with Mama the entire day and told her stories about Tatte in his youth, and about his parents and the entire family. Late that afternoon, Mrs. Goldman escorted Mama to the emergency room of the hospital and talked to the doctors who examined her. An appointment for emergency surgery was scheduled for the very next day.

Mama's hand was in very bad shape and the doctors were doubtful of the chances of recovery. Remember that this took place in the 1920s — before antibiotics and before advancements in modern surgical procedures. During the examination Mama tried very hard to stifle her screams of pain in front of the doctors and in front of Mrs. Goldman, a relative of Tatte she never really knew. Mama was a private person and felt uncomfortable exposing her intense pain in front of these strangers, people who had never known her in her "good" days. Yes, the pain was unbearable but somehow Mama managed to allow only some faint groans to escape from her throat. After the examination was over, the chief physician told Mrs. Goldman that Mama was a courageous woman. He knew quite well what excruciating pain she was undergoing, and he appreciated Mama's efforts to cooperate with the doctors despite the great pain.

The next morning, Mama left me with the relatives who had welcomed her so lovingly and went to the hospital for the surgery. Unfortunately, it turned out that the misgivings of the doctors were justified: They made all sorts of attempts but were ultimately unsuccessful in saving Mama's hand. Mama had simply waited too long and the infection that had spread was life-threatening. There was no choice but to amputate at the elbow in order to save her life.

The surgery was long and complicated and Mama was left lying helpless in the hospital with high fever and terrible pain. The doctors gave her strong painkillers that numbed the pain somewhat, but put her to sleep. The Goldmans visited Mama daily, bringing along with them kosher food and reports of how adorable and smart I was. "Why, at the beginning Leichu looked around for you a bit, but she adjusted very quickly," they told her. "She is a quiet, delightful infant." The news about me gladdened Mama's soul and made her determined to get well.

Mama was finally released from the hospital, but her travails were far from over. She discussed her problem with the Goldmans: The doctors told her that she had to undergo treatments for several months until her arm would be sufficiently healed in order to attach a prosthesis. But the same treatments were considerably less expensive in Sevlus than in the big city of Budapest. As it was, Mama had borrowed money from her neighbors in Sevlus to pay for the surgery and had none left to cover the treatments. She was supposed to receive a small compensation sum from the army for Tatte's death, and she hoped that it would arrive soon so that she could pay for the treatments in Sevlus.

The Goldmans had a practical suggestion: Why not leave Leichu with them in the meanwhile? How could she travel home with a baby with only one hand? In fact, how could she take care of a baby with one arm, terrible pain, and frequent medical treatments?

At first Mama would not hear of such a thing. She had been heartsick at the thought of leaving me for two weeks during her hospitalization, and she couldn't imagine being separated for a longer period of time. But she saw that she could not hold me with one hand, even for a little while. The stump bled constantly and she used her good hand to press a bandage onto the stump and to constantly change the dressings. She needed help to change her bandages, and she realized with dismay that there were a lot of things that she could no longer do alone. How would she diaper her baby? She couldn't even cook cereal for me with one hand — that involved turning on the fire, stirring the cereal, turning off the fire and pouring the cereal into a glass bottle. She simple couldn't manage all that with one hand! And the stump bled all the time. How could she travel with me back to Sevlus? Every tiny task seemed like an impossible mission.

On the night before her trip, Mama asked the Goldmans to place me in bed with her. All night long she held me with one hand and cried. She envisioned Tatte just before his death when he begged her, "Promise me that you will never allow yourself to be separated from our Leichu. Even if you are hungry, don't ever leave her. You must be the one to raise

her." Yes, she had promised him. But who could have anticipated this sorry state of affairs, when she could not even hold
her own daughter? What was she supposed to do?

All night long, she reviewed the options in her head. If
only she had some money to pay a young girl to take care of
me! But she already had taken out loans that she could not
repay, loans that she took out for the surgery. How could she
assume even more debt, when she had no means of livelihood to repay the money? She was relying on the small compensation sum from the army to pay for her treatments and
for food until her arm would heal and she could find some
means of support.

But I, Leichu, slept peacefully all night long, oblivious to
my mother's torment.

The next morning, the Goldmans urged Mama to leave
me with them. "You must take care of yourself," they reassured her. "We will take good care of Leichu, have no fear.
Why, we love her dearly, and she has already gotten used to
us."

Mama realized that she had no choice, but it was with
a heavy heart that she parted from me. "As soon as I can, I
will come back for you, my precious daughter," she told me,
the smiling infant who remembered nothing of all this. "The
treatments will end soon, *b'ezras Hashem*, and I will take you
home with me." The words were a promise from the depths
of her hearts. Then she thanked the Goldmans and tearfully
wished us a final goodbye.

But many years were to pass before that dream became a
reality.

❧ 8 ❧
Leichu's Diary

[BUDAPEST]

TODAY I CELEBRATED my ninth birthday! I got a brand-new present from my aunt, Anya's[1] sister: a very thick notebook, almost like a real book.

I am very happy with my present and have decided to keep a diary. I don't really know how to keep a diary but Bezhee, my old nanny, once told me a story about girls who kept a diary, and if I'm not mistaken, she mentioned that she also kept a diary! So I opened my notebook and decided to write everything that I remember about myself.

Friday, 2 Nissan 5691, March 20, 1931

Dear Diary,

My name is Leichu (Leah) Feldman, daughter of Leibu (Yehudah Leib) and Minchu (Mina) Feldman. I am an only child, and I have a nanny named Briendy who also helps Anya in the house.

---

1. Anya is Hungarian for "mother".

We live on Flower Street No. 36. I attend the Jewish school on Panonya Street near Arpad Square. I am in fourth grade, and a very good student.

Our apartment on Flower Street is a large apartment in a big apartment building that is built around an inner courtyard. Many families live in the building. The Kantzuk family's apartment faces you when you enter the building. Their apartment is right in the entrance, because they are the doormen. Like all doormen in all apartment buildings, they guard our building and make sure that the yard and the stairwell are kept clean. They also check the strangers who enter the building and make sure that unwelcome people do not come in.

The apartments that face Flower Street are large, beautiful apartments. However, the inner apartments that face the courtyard are small and shabby; the people who live there don't have better alternatives. Most of those tenants rent their apartments; they don't own their apartments, like we do.

Many of our neighbors are *goyim*. There are only two Jewish families whose apartments face Flower Street. One is the Ullman family, an older couple whose married children live not far from here. There is also Mrs. Neufeld, an elderly woman who always seems angry. She has a companion who lives with her, and she is also old. Mrs. Neufeld does not speak to us at all, and Anya does not know why she is angry at us. But it seems to me that she's angry at all the tenants, and does not talk to anyone. In any case, I have never seen her talking to anyone. Every time I see her leave the building, Mrs. Kantzuk calls out "Goodbye," but Mrs. Neufeld never answers. I also curtsy to her and politely say, "Have a nice day," but she doesn't even look in my direction. My mother says that I must continue to mind my manners and greet her even if she never answers, because it does not take much effort for me to be polite.

We live in the most beautiful city in the world—that's what Bezhee always said — in Budapest. We live in the new part of the city called Pest, but we can see the tops of the towers in Buda from our apartment. The Danube River flows between the two sections of the city—Buda and Pest—and although there are sections of the river that are so wide that you can't see from one side to the other, in most places you can see the bank on the opposite side.

All along the river, on both sides, are large, beautiful gardens and parks. There are numerous bridges that cross over the river; some bridges are for pedestrians, others for trolley cars, while the biggest bridges can hold automobiles as well. Horse-drawn carriages travel on almost all the bridges too.

And now, my dear diary, I will write what I remember from the time I was little:

Bezhee, my nanny, is holding my hand and the two of us are walking up the stairs toward home. Bezhee is angry at me because I got my fancy outfit dirty. We were in the playground and after I finished swinging on the swings, I jumped on the grass with some other children. Bezhee bought me a large chocolate lollipop and I didn't even notice that the chocolate dripped all over my dress. But Bezhee noticed! She took the lollipop and threw it in the garbage. I tried to clean the stain with my embroidered handkerchief, but I only got the hanky dirty while the stain on my dress remained. Bezhee knew that it was really her fault, because she should have been watching me instead of chatting with her friends, so she grabbed my hand and we rushed home.

I was quiet the whole way home because I was afraid that anything I'd say would make Bezhee even angrier. Bezhee was surprised at my silence—I am usually very talkative.

At the entrance to the house I met Mrs. Kantzuk, the doorman's wife. She looked at me and clapped her hands dramatically, "Oh my, little lady, what will Anya say about your outfit!"

Her little dramatic play made me even more worried about what my mother would say, and I turned white. Bezhee defended me by shouting at Mrs. Kantzuk for minding business that was not hers and frightening the "young lady Leichu," as they called me. Mrs. Kantzuk apologized, but Bezhee ignored her and pulled me wildly toward the staircase.

Anya opened the door with a big smile. I was so worried. What would she say about the big stain on my dress? But I didn't have to worry, because she didn't seem to notice.

"Please go straight to Leichu's room, I have guests," she told us in a pleasant tone of voice. Then she turned to Bezhee, and added sharply, "Why did you return so early? I told you to stay in the park until six-thirty, and it is not even five o'clock yet!"

We went into my room and Bezhee quickly peeled off my stained outfit. I put on a simple housedress and Bezhee and I sat down together next to the small table and played board games.

Bezhee didn't talk or smile. I could tell by her movements and the expression on her face that she was nervous and angry. So I also remained quiet. Finally, when I couldn't stand it any longer, I whispered to her, "Tell, me, Bezhee, are you planning to leave me because I got my dress dirty?"

Bezhee looked up from the game and stared at me in amazement. Then she tried to calm me down. True, she was angry at me—so she said—but under no circumstances would she leave me, and I didn't have to worry so much; a little bit of anger never hurt anyone. In any event, Bezhee said, the gypsy laundress was coming the following day and she would wash my dress so that no one would ever know.

Later on, after the guests left, Anya let me eat some of the fancy cake that was left over and even let me take some chocolate. I ate a little bit, and then hid the rest in a napkin in my special drawer. I planned on giving the chocolate to the gypsy laundress. I always tried to hide sweets for her, and sometimes even real food.

I love her, that gypsy laundress. She would hide everything I gave her in the big pockets of her many skirts that she wore under the black skirt on top.

Chungarabi the gypsy also loves me. Whenever she would come to our house, Bezhee was free to do her housework in peace and quiet because I would sit, transfixed, on a small chair next to the gypsy laundress.

I heard so many stories from Chungarabi. At first I could not understand her well because she speaks Hungarian mixed with the gypsy language — Romany. But I began learning many words of her language and Chungarabi enjoyed teaching me; she was impressed at my skill in picking up her language. Eventually I was able to speak fluently.

Laundry days were holidays for me, though for Bezhee they were hard days indeed because Bezhee did most of the housework on those days. The only thing she didn't do was the cooking; Anya did that, or she bought prepared food from Guttmann's Restaurant. Sometimes we would go eat out in the restaurant too.

On laundry days, after Chungarabi finished all the laundry, she also washed the floors in every room of the house. Still, Bezhee had a lot of work on laundry day, and she didn't exactly love those days as I did.

Once in a while, usually before Pesach, Mrs. Kantzuk would come to clean our house thoroughly. On these occasions, Anya would take me out and Bezhee would stay behind with Mrs. Kantzuk. After many hours we would return home to a spotless, shining home—and Bezhee's sour face.

Now I will describe Chungarabi to you: She is a little shorter than my mother. Although she looks fat, I know that she is really very thin and only looks larger than she is because she wears so many layers of clothes. Chungarabi has dark skin and black eyes. I have big green eyes, but Chungarabi's eyes are black, small and wary. She has two black braids, very long, in which she braids colored ribbons and colored glass beads. Anya thinks those braids are ridiculous, even grotesque, but I really like the way Chungarabi decorates her hair. If I had braids I would also make them pretty the way she does. But unfortunately, my own hair is short and curly.

My hair causes me so many problems! I can never keep it neat. It is so curly that it just doesn't stay put; that's why Anya cuts my hair short. Even so, it is hard to comb; the teeth of my combs are forever breaking and I always have to get new ones. And I can't use a brush at all; it just doesn't penetrate the tangled layers of curls. Maybe that's why Chungarabi's hair seems so lovely to me, because her black hair is straight and you can make so many hairstyles out of it.

Chungarabi's hands are small and very wrinkled. Her face is also wrinkled. But Chungarabi is not old, so I think that her hands are wrinkled from doing so much laundry for everyone. In fact, she has a young daughter, and old ladies don't have young daughters, right?

Chungarabi is a happy, lively person. She is either telling me fascinating stories about the lives of gypsies, or singing gypsy songs. Sometimes the songs are sad and full of longing; sometimes they are happy and rhythmic. And sometimes, when Anya is not around, Chungarabi even dances a bit while she sings and she shakes her hands to and fro. All her bracelets and bangles shake too, making a cheerful, tinkling noise.

She even taught me some of her songs, and sometimes Chungarabi and I sing them together and even dance—but only when no one is around. Otherwise, Chungarabi sits and sings to herself quietly while she works. No wonder I am always happy when I am alone with her in the house.

I have much more to say about Chungarabi the gypsy and her stories, but I've already written lots this time and it's late.

So—goodnight, my dear diary. I will continue tomorrow.

❦ 9 ❦
What Is Hereditary?
[BUDAPEST]

L ET ME TELL you something about my fifth birthday party, the first party I really remember:

I am sitting next to Apa's[2] place at the head of the table. In front of me is a huge cream cake adorned with five lit candles. Anya invited so many guests — including children, and they're all sitting around the table. I wish I could get up and join the children at the other end of the table because in my seat next to Apa, everyone keeps looking at me.

Anya spent a full day cooking the festive meal in honor of my birthday. I snuck into the kitchen a few times and after Anya and Bezhee got tired of telling me to stay out, they let me stay in the kitchen and help. Bezhee gave me a small knife and a potato and told me to try to peel it.

Anya was shocked—giving a knife to a little girl! But Bezhee promised her that she'd stand next to me to watch over me, and said that it was time to teach Leichu to do some things around the house.

---

2. Apa is Hungarian for "father".

Anya, who had been busy near the oven, came to join us at the table, and the two of them watched as I peeled a potato with a knife. It was very hard work, peeling the potato, but I finally succeeded! Both Anya and Bezhee agreed that I was capable of peeling without cutting myself, but that one potato was enough. One shouldn't tempt fate too much, Anya said.

The potato was so small after I finished peeling it, and both of them laughed when I held it up to show them. Bezhee said that if someone needs a small potato, they don't peel a large potato to make a small potato, they just take a small one!

I understood what she meant, and I was very insulted. Anya saw the hurt look in my eyes and gave me a big hug, saying, "You are a wonderful, big girl, and you learn quickly; you did a great job peeling!" I peeked at Bezhee over Anya's shoulder and she smiled at me. Then I realized that they hadn't meant to make fun of me, they were just in a jolly, joking mood.

When my mother got ready to broil a goose liver that she had bought for the party, I ran out of the kitchen. They both knew that I couldn't stand liver, that even the smell of it made me nauseous. I wondered out loud why they were preparing it for a banquet in my honor. Bezhee explained to me that since liver was considered a delicacy, Anya just had to prepare it for such a festive meal. But she promised me that they would not force me to eat it. My parents had tried to force me to eat liver a few times, but each time my face turned red and I threw up. Finally the doctor told Anya that my body simply could not tolerate liver and they should stop trying to force me to eat it.

The doctor also said that in most cases, food allergies were hereditary. And Anya merely replied, "Who knows?

Anything is possible."

∾   ∾   ∾

On Shabbos I sat on Apa's knees and played with his pocket watch while he spoke about the *parashah*. He talked about a big golden table that was covered with bread and said that they didn't eat any of the bread right away, but waited a week—and the bread was fresh after a week, as if it had been baked that very day. I asked tons of questions. "Why did they wait a week to eat the bread? Why did they put all the bread on the table? Didn't they have a pantry?" Apa tried to explain to me, and I didn't understand. But then I asked him, "Why would you put a tablecloth on a golden table? Wouldn't the tablecloth cover all the gold and then no one would see it?" Apa burst out laughing. He laughed so hard, his whole body shook. And then, while he was still laughing, I asked him quickly, "What is hereditary?" That was the word the doctor had said to Anya.

Apa started to explain to me that "hereditary" refers to those traits that are passed down from parents to children.

"So why am I allergic to liver and you are not?"

Apa lowered me from his lap and said that he had to review the *parashah*. That's what he always did; when he couldn't answer a question of mine, he would start to learn from his *sefarim*. But I guess his books did not have the answer because even when he stopped learning, he did not answer my question. Maybe when I go to Bubby and Zaidy Shapiro, I'll ask Zaidy. He always treats me seriously and never laughs at my questions.

Anya bought me a new coat. The coat has a fur collar and the edges of the coat are lined with the same fur. The matching hat is also lined with fur. Anya was very proud of her purchase. When we came home from the store, she did not put the coat in the closet along with all the other coats. Instead, she hung it on a knob on the window so that she could show it off to everyone who entered the room.

I was dressed up in my new coat when I went with Anya to visit her parents, Bubby and Zaidy Shapiro. Bubby gave me a big hug — Bubby and Zaidy Shapiro were always happy to see me, not like Bubby and Zaidy Feldman who barely paid attention to me.

Zaidy wasn't home yet. He hadn't returned from the *beis midrash*. But Bubby was really impressed with my new coat. She made me turn this way and that way to admire it and when Anya told her how much it cost, she clapped her hands and said, "Really? You spent so much money? What does Leibu to say about that?"

Bubby took the coat off and hung it carefully on a hanger while she continued to stroke the fur and admire it. Then she said to Anya, "Minchu darling, I think Leibu is right; you went overboard this time." But Anya shook her head and answered with a shout, "She is the only thing I have! What is my money for, anyway?" Then she burst into tears.

Bubby gave me a chocolate candy and ran to Anya, guided her gently toward the couch and started to talk to her quietly in Yiddish. But my mother would not be comforted and continued to shout. "What should I do? He says we should get divorced. After ten years you are supposed to get divorced, and we have been married thirteen years already. I thought that Leichu would appease him, but see —it's all coming back to the surface again." Anya cried and cried, and even Bubby started to cry together with her while they continued whispering in Yiddish.

I stared at them. They didn't even glance in my direction. This always happens: Every time I come with my mother to Bubby Shapiro, Anya cries and Bubby comforts her in Yiddish. But this time Bubby was crying as well.

I couldn't stand the sobbing so I announced that I was going to Néni[3] Basya Leah, Anya's sister who lives in the adjoining apartment, and ran out. It is always fun at Basya Leah's house; her home is full of children, and it is never boring there.

My aunt Basya Leah opened the door. She was holding the baby, Bruchi, and Yanky the toddler was pulling at her skirt. She hugged me with her available arm and called out, "Reizy, Suri, come quick — Leichu is here." Ruchele raced over and danced around me. She is about my age. Reizy and Suri also joined us.

I took a long, hard look at them all. All the children, as well as their mother (my aunt) have brown eyes just like Anya and Apa, just like the grandmothers and grandfathers. Even Moishy and Hershy have brown eyes; they weren't at home but I remembered. Only I had green eyes, the only one in the family! Even among the other aunts and uncles — from both sides — none had green eyes. I was also the only one with light-colored, curly hair; the rest had dark hair, mainly straight.

I went into the children's room where we jumped and played and acted a little wild. Basya Leah let us. She never got angry at our behavior; she just asked that we put everything back in its place after we finished. That wasn't hard at all — there were so many helpers.

I hugged Reizy, the eldest daughter, looked into her brown eyes and asked her, "Reizy, what is 'hereditary'?" Reizy explained to me what everyone else had told me: that it refers

---

3. Néni is Hungarian for "aunt", and is often used when referring to close friends and older relatives, such as cousins, as well.

to the things we get from our parents — such as our eye color, hair, features, and height.

"So why am I different?" I asked. "I don't look anything like Anya and Apa, or the grandparents or aunts and uncles. Why, I don't resemble even one of my cousins from both sides!"

Reizy looked at me carefully from all angles. "You are right," she concluded. "You don't look like us at all!" She pulled me into the kitchen where her mother was cutting vegetables. "Anya," announced Reizy, "look how Leichu is so different from us — she does not resemble anyone in the family. How can that be?"

My aunt glanced at me and answered immediately, "What are you saying, Reizy—don't you see that her nose and ears are exactly like her father's?"

Reizy burst into laughter. "Leibu Baści has a fat nose and Leichu has a small nose. But why are her eyes and hair so light-colored?"

Basya Leah said that her Bubby was fair like me; she said that hereditary things often skip two generations. Reizy was happy and said that from now on, she'll call me "Little Bubby."

I wasn't sure about that at all.

When I asked Bezhee at home about "hereditary" she just answered that I should become a lawyer. "All day long you ask questions — there is no end to your questions!" That's what she always answers, she never gives proper answers.

Zaidy Feldman also disappointed me. When we came this week to visit him in the store, he asked Bezhee if she couldn't find another place for children to play. A store is not a playground, he said, and did not so much as glance at me.

On Shabbos, Apa and Anya went to Zaidy and Bubby Feldman. I told them that my stomach hurt and stayed at home with Bezhee; I wanted Zaidy to know that my feelings were hurt. But when my parents came home, it turned out that Bubby and Zaidy hadn't even asked about me and didn't even notice that I was not there. I was very insulted.

Bubby Feldman came to visit. I got into bed and didn't want to come out. I heard Bubby talking to Anya very quickly. She talked a lot, but Anya didn't say anything. I didn't hear Anya's voice at all. After Bubby left, my mother came into my room, lay down with me in bed, hugged me tight and burst into tears. Bezhee went into the kitchen to make something to eat. At night, Bezhee whispered to me that this house has a secret, but she doesn't know — or care — what it is.

Bezhee is happy that she can live with us. She comes from a small town near the Romanian border and does not want to return there. She says that she hates the place, but she always described her parents' house to me, and the little town and the people who lived there. She told me so many stories and in such great detail that I could close my eyes and see the place with its people, houses and streets.

Bezhee said that she came to the big city in order to marry a "good Jewish city fellow" and not, *chas v'shalom*, "a fellow from a tiny village." Meanwhile, until she found him, she worked in our house to earn a little money.

Anya used to laugh that no "good Jewish city fellow" is good enough for her; she just liked living with us, that's all. Bezhee said that she was happy with us except for the big cleaning days and the two of them burst out laughing.

❧ 10 ❧
Among Devoted Neighbors
[SEVLUS]

SHEINA RUCHEL FRUCHTER returned to Sevlus a broken woman, both physically and emotionally. She returned empty-handed: The child whom she had promised would never leave her side, was in Budapest with distant relatives. Mama's physical condition was grim. Inexperienced medical students had performed the operation — she could not afford the small fortune that skilled surgeons charged. Even the minimum sum that the students charged was a great deal of money for her. But the students' treatment was grossly unprofessional, and as a result, Mama suffered excessive deformation and pain. The train journey was difficult as the amputated stump did not stop bleeding, and every bump of the train sent waves of pain searing through her. And if that wasn't painful enough, the only scene she saw through the train window was the mental picture of the baby she had left in Budapest.

The coach was full of non-Jewish villagers who were returning from the big city after selling their produce, and many of them were drunk. Mama was afraid that they would notice her — a lone Jewish woman with an amputated arm, crying and in pain, and single her out as an easy victim. Who knew what a group of drunken *goyim* might do? So she tried with all her strength to restrain herself, not to shout from the pain or cry out in her misery. It is no wonder that the entire journey was to remain etched in her memory as one long nightmare.

Once Mama arrived back in Sevlus, she breathed a great sigh of relief. She took her bag to her home and then headed straight for Dr. Lezman's clinic. As soon as she entered the front door, she felt true Jewish concern emanate from the very walls. The women who were waiting in the kitchen surrounded her excitedly. One woman brought her a chair, another served her a cup of hot tea, yet another supported her while she drank, and a fourth woman went into the doctor's examination room to tell him that Mama had returned from Budapest in very bad shape and needed his immediate attention.

Dr. Lezman finished treating the patient in his room and then received Mama. As soon as he saw the amputated stump, he started to shout, "Butchers! Barbarians! Is this how one amputates a limb?!" However, when he saw that he was frightening Mama, he made a visible effort to change his tone. "Mrs. Fruchter," he said quietly, "please don't worry, I will take care of you. Even though you are now in terrible pain, be assured that your condition will improve eventually."

When the doctor heard the price that Mama had paid for the operation, he lost his composure again. "Butchers! Highway robbery!" It was hard to calm him down.

He leaned backwards in his chair, closed his eyes for a minute and then leaned forward and propped himself on the table with the palms of both hands. Gently, he said, "Mrs. Fruchter, I am truly sorry. The only way I can heal your arm is by giving you very painful treatments, though the Budapest doctors did not specify this in the release forms they gave you in the hospital. If I only administer the injections they specified, it will take a very long time and your arm might not recover at all."

Then the good doctor got up and went out to the waiting room, to look for someone to help him. He brought back Mrs. Bella Neuman, a tall, robust woman with a kindly face. He asked her to hold Mama during the treatment, so that she would not faint.

While the doctor treated Mama's arm, Mrs. Neuman held Mama, stroked her head and talked to her soothingly. Mama didn't remember a word of what she said, but she never forgot the stroking and the motherly compassion. Mainly, though, she would never forget the horrible pain the treatment caused. She didn't know if it was ten minutes or ten hours because it seemed like an eternity.

Reb Menachem Mendel and Bella Neuman, Hy"d, who helped Mama so much.

At the end of the treatment, the kindly Mrs. Neuman helped Mama put her sleeve over the stump and walked her into the kitchen. The women there led her to a bed where she rested, and they gave her hot tea to drink slowly. Only when she had recovered somewhat slightly did Mrs. Neuman escort Mama to her relatives, the Klar family.

As soon as Néni Rivka Klar saw Mama she ran to her, hugged her and burst into tears. "This is what a splinter can cause?" she cried. Mama started sobbing; Rivka thought it was because of the pain. Mama sighed and said, "True, the pains are almost unbearable, but the pain of parting from my baby was the worst of all. I just can't believe that I was forced to abandon my own child to strangers." Mama couldn't be comforted.

"Perhaps we should try to pay someone to travel to Budapest and bring the baby back home? I am sure we will be able to find someone," suggested Rivka. Mama, however, knew that she was in no position to take care of me and shook her head sadly. Rivka didn't give up, though, and said, "You're right. We can't bring back little Leichu now, when you are still in terrible pain. But as soon as you feel better and are able to rehabilitate yourself, as soon as you have a little more strength and can take care of the baby, then you will go to Budapest to bring the baby back home. We'll all help you; I promise you."

Those words gave Mama hope, but although she was comforted, she was still unsure. "I just don't know if I will ever be able to take care of my daughter," she admitted woefully. "I never knew that such excruciating pain existed; I don't know if I'll be able to withstand this terrible pain, day after day." She stopped for a moment and looked at Rivka intently. "Rivka, if I die, will you raise my daughter?" Mama knew that the Klar family was in difficult economic straits. Nachman Klar was not always able to find work, and there were times when Rivka only had bread and tea for the whole family to eat. But she also knew that there was no better, warmer Jewish home for her daughter than the Klar family, no matter how difficult their material lives were. And although Rivka was upset at Mama for speaking that way, she understood her concerns, and she promised.

Later that evening, after Mama had rested, the Klar's two oldest daughters walked Mama home.

Mama then began to go to Dr. Lezman every day. On her way, she would pick up Bella Neuman, the kindly woman who had held Mama the first time that the doctor treated her hand, and she had agreed to continue doing so. The good doctor would massage Mama's arm for a long time, rubbing special creams into her arm all the while. Only afterwards, he injected her with the shots that the physician from Budapest had prescribed.

This treatment was painful and exhausting. At first it seemed to Mama that her arm would never improve, that she would suffer her whole life. However, slowly but surely, the stump started to recover and the pains decreased in intensity. Bella Neuman was unwavering in her devotion: She assisted Mama every day by holding her during the treatments, encouraging her, speaking words of hope and comfort.

The wonderful, generous Bella Neuman and her husband Reb Menachem Mendel Neuman — who was a member of the Jewish Administration of Sevlus — were murdered by the Nazis in Kaufering near Landsberg. Four of their children were murdered in Auschwitz, together with almost all the Jews of Sevlus, Hy"d. Only the two eldest children, Sima Rachel and Avigdor, survived and settled in Eretz Yisrael after the war.

Mama used to tell me how every time she went to the doctor, she brought along a strong leather strap. While Mrs. Neuman held her and stroked her lovingly, she would bite on this strap with all her strength to keep herself from screaming. But sometimes, even the strap and Mrs. Neuman's encouraging support was not enough, and Mama's heartrending screams would escape from her throat, as if on their own accord. Mama was also full of praise for Dr. Lezman who treated her with great devotion. Whenever he saw that the pain had become too much for Mama to bear, he would leave the room and return with a hot glass of tea. Mama would sip the tea until she felt ready to continue. Dr. Lezman kept repeating to her that the pains would eventually cease and the stump would heal. At the time, this was a faraway dream to Mama, but she took comfort in his words.

There was a tremendous difference between the cold, indifferent treatment of the Budapest "experts" and the compassionate treatment of the local Sevlus family doctor. Dr. Lezman, unlike the Budapest physicians, treated Mama with fatherly kindheartedness; he tried to be as gentle as possible, he comforted her and told her stories about my father whom he had known from youth. Mrs. Neuman also constantly encouraged Mama, telling her that soon, soon she would be able to take care of Leichu all by herself. As soon as Mama heard my name, she would feel the return of her fighting spirit and hope for the future.

◇◇

During the Nazi occupation, Dr. Lezman treated a Russian paratrooper and member of the underground who was injured when he parachuted into town. The paratrooper subsequently recruited the good doctor into the underground resistance and hid a transmitter in his home. The Germans discovered this and hung Dr. Lezman, together with all the members of the underground — nine Jews and three non-Jews — in Sevlus, in the town square. After the war, the residents of Sevlus established a monument in Dr. Lezman's memory

on the very spot on which he was hung. May these words memorialize
the good Dr. Lezman who dedicated himself to his patients with all
his heart. Hy"d.

After each painful treatment Mama would go over to Néni
Rivka Klar, Tatte's cousin who lived close to the doctor's
house. All the members of the Klar family took care of Mama,
but Rivka, especially, was like a mother to her. She insisted
that Mama lie down to rest after her treatments. Rivka would
sit at Mama's bedside and talk to her until she was able to fall
asleep. The whole household would walk on their tiptoes in
the cramped apartment to allow Mama to rest undisturbed.
This was a family with small children living in a tiny apartment — which consisted of a kitchen, living room and one
bedroom — yet Rivka made sure that everyone remained
quiet.

When Mama would wake up, they would not let her return home until she had eaten with them. Mama knew that
their economic situation was difficult and she tried to refuse,
but they insisted. She actually had no choice; she had no income and nothing to eat, and Rivka Klar knew this.

This situation continued for three long, painful months.
Then the longed-for day arrived: The doctor told Mama that
the treatments had been concluded successfully. Now she
would need to plan for the future and learn to live with only
one hand.

For the first time, Mama began to consider her options.
During the months of treatment when the pains were still intense, Mama sustained herself with one thought: to hang on,
day by day by day, to hang on for the sake of her Leichu and
not give up. But those were short-term thoughts and she did
not, could not, think about the future.

But the day had indeed arrived, as Dr. Lezman had promised her, when the pain ceased. Now was the time to look ahead. The wonderful neighbors had supported her with tremendous devotion, but she was not one to rely on neighbors her entire life. She must move on, organize her life, and find means of support. Yes, she would have to learn how to do everything with one hand, so that she could bring me back to her as soon as possible.

❧ 11 ❧
The Grocery Store
[SEVLUS]

MY MOTHER'S LIFE was unquestionably very difficult, but with tremendous willpower and tenacity, she slowly taught herself how to do almost everything with one hand.

She learned how to launder her clothes by using her feet, after making sure that the door and window were well closed. But she realized that she couldn't do laundry for other people this way in order to make a living. In those days before washing machines, washing clothing was hard work for everyone, but for Mama it was back- breaking. She used to joke that she was lucky she did not have many clothes.

Mama learned how to draw water from the communal well. She would situate the pail in its place and use her good hand to push down on the handle of the pump. But since she didn't have a second hand to direct the pail to the exact spot, much of the water spilled on her and it took a long time until the wooden pail filled up. In the summer it wasn't so terrible, but in winter, by the time she got back home, she was freezing and trembling from the cold. The heavy pail seemed even heavier on her one good hand. She would walk a few paces, and then would have to put down the pail and rest, before she could go back to dragging the pail; all this in the snow and frost, with soaking, freezing clothing.

Cleaning the house was hard. Mama taught herself all kinds of shortcuts and maneuvers in order to accomplish everything with one hand. But she realized that she could not support herself by cleaning other people's homes, even though that's what other indigent woman often did.

It was important to Mama to have a sparkling clean house. She had worked hard at it when she'd had two hands and, with only one hand at her disposal, it was even more difficult. But she refused to compromise her standards — she did not want to be labeled as someone who neglected her home because she was disabled.

It took Mama a while to learn how to iron without damaging the clothes. She had to fill the iron with coals from the oven, flatten the cloth on the ironing bench, and move the heavy iron over the clothes without allowing sparks to escape and burn holes in the clothes. As with all the other household tasks, Mama persisted, refusing to give in to despair, until she mastered this as well.

But the big question was that of supporting herself. Mama could no longer pick grapes, as she had once done. And she also could no longer sew and embroider, as she had enjoyed in the past. How, indeed, could she make a living?

In the end, it was the neighbors who came to her rescue again. Mama decided to open a grocery store and Nachman Klar built her a wooden partition along the length of the one room, dividing the room in two. The larger section became the store, and the smaller one became Mama's living quarters. In the large room, Nachman built shelves along two walls, and a shorter closet along the third wall, which was actually the partition. A thick, wide board that he attached to the top of the closet served as the store's checkout counter. The closet's doors opened toward the partition — only Mama had access to its contents. Behind the partition remained a tiny room with one bed, a box that served as a clothing closet, and a shelf with a water bucket and basin for *netilas yadayim* and washing. The stove and heater were in this small room but positioned in such a way that they heated up the store as well.

Nachman did not want to accept money for his work and even managed to acquire the building materials he needed for a pittance. But Mama had spent a lot of time in his house during her medical treatments and had seen, first hand, just how poor his family was. So she borrowed a small sum of money from Rav Yechezkel Weingarten and his wife Edith, a loan without a repayment date, and she insisted on giving this sum to Nachman as a first payment for his carpentry work.

Years later, the Weingartens were also murdered by the Germans. Hy"d.

Mama organized the store aesthetically. The grocery was always immaculate, all the foodstuffs on the shelves sparkled from cleanliness.

Where did Mama get the money to establish the store? She sold her beautiful table and chairs; there was no room for them anyway. She also sold the buffet and stylish wardrobe that Tatte had bought for their wedding, as well as the two beds. With the small amount of money she received for her furniture, she invested in buying foodstuffs for the store. She never regretted selling her possessions; she decided to be happy with her lot and hope for a better future.

✤ 12 ✤
Where Is My Daughter?

[SEVLUS]

INALLY, EVERYTHING was in place: The store was organized; the products were ready on the shelves. The small bedroom was also ready for me. Yes, the time had come: Mama took the small amount of money left and traveled to Budapest to bring me home.

Mama always told me how during this time period she was very busy at work during the day. She constantly told herself that she must learn how to do everything with one hand as quickly as possible, so that she could bring her daughter home again.

The nights were hard, full of tears and longing for the beautiful baby that she had left in Budapest. But the night before her trip, Mama didn't sleep; instead she danced. Yes, she was finally going to bring her beloved daughter home! A combination of love and joy filled her heart, and she danced and danced. She was ready to run to the train station in the middle of the night, but she managed to control herself until morning. The train ride the next day went by quickly as she silently sang from happiness.

Mama found herself in Budapest, in front of the door to

the Goldman house. She was sure that she wouldn't have to knock — her heart was beating so loudly they must hear it from inside the house! When she finally did knock on the door, her one good hand was trembling so hard that she could barely control it.

When the maid opened the door, Mama immediately began calling my name. "Leichu! Leichu!" The maid thought that she was some kind of crazy woman, perhaps someone who wanted charity, and she tried to block her entry. But Mama pushed her aside and ran into the house, crying, "Leichu, my darling Leichu; Mama is here!"

Mrs. Goldman, the relative who had promised Mama that she would take care of me until Mama could come for me, ran toward Mama and sat her down in a chair. But Mama continued to shout, "Leichu, Mama is here to take you home!"

"Leichu is not here, Leichu is not home," said Mrs. Goldman, over and over again. At first, Mama thought that someone had taken Leichu for a walk. It took her a long time to understand that her baby was no longer with the Goldmans.

Mama started screaming. "Tell me where she is! Give me the address, and tell me where she is!"

Mrs. Goldman talked and talked. She used long, complicated, confusing sentences. Mama had to listen carefully until she finally understood the bitter truth: Her baby had been given up for adoption. Mrs. Goldman had given me to a family who could not have children of their own. All this, without asking Mama, without speaking to her at all! The Goldmans had decided on their own that a poor widowed woman with only one hand could not possibly take care of a baby, and certainly not support her. They figured that Mama would live off charity, so they decided to give me up for adoption. They were sure that Mama would thank them.

It is hard to describe the depth of the calamity that landed on Mama when she learned that she had lost me. She told me the story of that day many times, and each time she burst into tears and relived that worst day of her life, over and over again.

Mama had nursed two husbands through protracted and painful illnesses until they died; she had been widowed twice. Her older children had left her, and only infrequently did they send her letters — very short ones. She had lost her hand in terrible agony; she had battled poverty much of her life. Yet all these were nothing compared to the ultimate blow of all: Her child was taken from her!

Mama's tormented cries echoed throughout the house and even outside it. "My daughter, my child, Leichu! Where is my Leichu? Tell me the truth: Has something happened to her? Is she alive? Does she need help? Can we save her?"

Mama shouted and screamed in agony, banging the walls in sorrow and torment. Mrs. Goldman hovered near and tried to calm her down, but to no avail. Finally, Mrs. Goldman shouted, "Leichu is alive and healthy! But she is not here!" Mama finally absorbed these words, and this is what she told me:

"I felt that my entire life collapsed. There was no longer anything to live for: all the torments I had undergone seemed in vain. My Leichu was gone. I felt like Rachel Imenu, who said (*Bereishis* 30:1): 'Give me children, for if not, I am as good as dead.'

"Then everything turned black. I didn't know where I was, I didn't recognize anyone, didn't hear anything. Only Mrs. Goldman's words rang in my ears: 'Leichu is not here! Leichu is gone.' They took her, they adopted her; a childless family adopted my baby. How could they put my Leichu for adoption when she has a mother; she is orphaned from her father, not her mother!

"The promise I made to your father that I would never be separated from you—I didn't listen to him, and my daughter was taken from me.

"I threw myself down, put my head on the floor and shouted: 'Leichu, my Leichu, come back to me! Dovid, my dear husband up in Heaven, I implore you: Help me to bring our daughter back, from the evil people who stole her from me, so that I can raise her as you begged me before you died."

Mama stopped for a minute to compose herself, then continued her story.

"Mrs. Goldman and her maid tried to raise me up from the floor. They kept telling me to calm down, but I only shouted louder and louder. 'I should calm down? First you steal my child, and now you want me to go away quietly? Yes, I'll quiet down — when you return my child to me!'

"I shouted so loudly that the neighbors came to see what was going on. Mrs. Goldman was embarrassed, so she told them that an unfortunate crazy woman had burst into her home, and she didn't know what to do.

"I heard her saying this and jumped up from the floor. 'Crazy? I'm crazy? That's what you call me?' I shrieked in my pain. I turned to the neighbors, pointed to Mrs. Goldman, and yelled, 'It's her, Mrs. Goldman, who stole my daughter from me with her soothing words and promises. She told me that she would take care of my daughter like a mother until my amputated stump would heal, and then she would return my Leichu to me. Meanwhile, behind my back, she stole my child and gave her up for adoption to a childless couple. If someone stole your child from you, wouldn't you cry and scream? Wouldn't you react like me, in your pain?'"

My mother wiped away her tears at the memory, and returned to the present. "If I had been a violent or hot-headed person," she often mused, "I might have even killed Mrs.

Goldman that day. But I just lifted my one hand to the Heavens, and cried: "*Ribbono shel Olam*, Father of orphans and Judge of widows, repay this woman for the evil she has done!" Every time she told me the story, Mama would raise her one hand to the Heavens and repeat, "*Ribbono shel Olam*, Father of orphans and Judge of widows, repay this woman for the years of pain and anguish she caused me."

Mama remained at the Goldmans for hours, demanding over and over again that Mrs. Goldman provide her with the names of the people who adopted me and their address. Mr. Goldman returned that evening from work and also tried to persuade Mama to stop crying and shouting, to no avail. It was then that Mama fainted. The Goldmans brought a doctor over and when even he could not revive Mama, they hospitalized her. She remained in the hospital for a week, alternating between consciousness and unconsciousness. She simply could not tolerate the emotional pain and the sense that she had nothing left to live for. The doctors there could not help her either.

After about a week, a rebbetzin came to visit Mama in the hospital; she told Mama that she must try to recover as soon as possible and strengthen herself so that she could fight to regain her daughter.

Those were the words that brought Mama back to life. She opened her eyes and said to the rebbetzin, whose face she remembered but not her name, "You are right: I must get well so that I can fight for my daughter. I will not give up."

These very words became Mama's slogan: I must fight, I must not surrender! Mama would later say, however, that if she had known that it would take so many years to bring me back to her, she might not have been able to hang on that long to her sanity or her life.

❧ 13 ❧
Feldman versus Shapiro

[BUDAPEST]

WHEN I WAS six-and-a-half years old, I started going to school. Everything was so interesting. To get to my classroom, I would go into a big lobby that led into several corridors, and the corridor leading to my class was right at the entrance of the lobby. The corridor was lined with hooks for coats and under the coats are low shelves for boots. Each child was assigned a hook and a shelf. My classroom was very large with four rows of desks and two chairs next to each desk.

I sat in the second row next to Perry. I had to sit all day with my hands clasped. You were not allowed to talk at all unless you raised your hand for permission. And there were even instructions for doing that. You had to place your elbow on the desk, lift your hand a little, and only keep your pointer finger straight up. At the beginning I kept getting confused. My teacher would ask a question and I would just say the answer without having asked permission. Then my teacher would scream at me. Even when I remembered to raise my hand, I didn't always remember the exact rules; either I raised my hand too high or I didn't do a good job curling up the three fingers that were supposed to be folded. At first my teacher explained the proper procedure over and over, but after a week she told me in a very strict voice that she wasn't going to correct me anymore. "I've explained to you too many times how to raise your hand. I am sure that if you take this more seriously, you will stop getting mixed up." And actually, after that, I did not make mistakes any more.

My teacher always asked questions. I knew almost all the answers so I usually raised my hand, but other girls also raised their hands, so she didn't always call on me.

Two blackboards hung on the wall: one big one that the teacher used for teaching and writing the homework, and a smaller one. Every Monday, my teacher would write the name of the outstanding pupil of the week on that blackboard. The name was not erased until the next test. My name was often on that blackboard, and my friend Fanny's name was too.

Bezhee was happy to hear that mine wasn't the only name that appeared on the board. She says that it would stick out too much and would make the others jealous of me. But even so, when she came to take me home from school she always peeked at the small blackboard to see if my name was there. And when she saw my name, she would take her time putting on my coat and boots, so that all the other nannies would see us.

It was Bezhee who pushed me to excel in my studies. "You must study as hard as you can," she always told me. "Jews have no choice; they always have to be the best. We live in a land of *goyim*, and Jews must excel in order to survive." Fanny told me that they tell her the exact same thing in her house.

I couldn't pretend that I didn't know the material we learned at school, because I always did know. The teacher would write math problems on the blackboard and as soon as she finished, I would finish writing the answers. The teacher tried giving me harder exercises; she'd call me next to her desk and I'd watch her write the problems in my notebook. As soon as she finished, I would tell her the answer by heart.

One day the teacher met my mother and told her that I solve third-grade math exercises quickly. Anya announced this at home with great pride, and suggested to Apa that he let me keep the accounts of the store. My father told me that if I continued to excel in my studies, he would take me to the store. He said I would stand near the cash register and be in charge of the accounts.

I was not happy with this idea because I know that Zaidy Feldman, Apa's father, also works in the store and he would not want to see me. Every time we visit them, Zaidy Feldman doesn't look at me and quietly says things against me. He talks quietly so I can't hear his actual words but I know that it's about me because Bubby Feldman tells him that he shouldn't talk that way in front of me.

I was careful not to show them that I understood, but when I tried to talk about this with Anya she only said, "That's the way it is with old people; try not to take offense." But Zaidy Feldman is not old, and he acts just like everyone else most of the time. In fact, my mother's father Zaidy Shapiro is much older yet he treats me very nicely. He always smiles at me, always has a candy for me and is happy to hear that I do well in school. Zaidy Feldman doesn't care that I am a good student. I tried to make him happy, but I didn't succeed. I sat quietly when we visited them, I didn't speak if they didn't speak to me first, and I didn't get up from my place. But all this did not help; both Bubby and Zaidy Feldman ignored me completely.

Apa and Anya visit the Feldmans a lot, but I prefer to stay home with Bezhee. Anya didn't even try to ask me to join them; she also gets insulted at the way they treat me. Bezhee told me that I shouldn't think badly of them. "You can't change older people," she said. But I would get very hurt. I didn't understand why they don't like me, no matter how hard I tried. I had no idea why they treated me this way, especially since they treat the other grandchildren so well. Zaidy Feldman holds them, gives them candies, asks about their schoolwork and is happy when they do well in school. Bubby Feldman bakes special cakes and buys all kinds of sweets for the other grandchildren. It's only me that they ignore!

Sometimes Anya tells them that I did well in class and received a prize. Then Zaidy and Bubby nod their heads and say, "Very nice," and quickly change the subject. It's clear that I don't interest them in the least.

Even though Anya tells me that I'm just imagining things, I've heard her say the same things about the Feldmans when she complains to her own mother, Bubby Shapiro. True, I know that I am very different from the other grandchildren. They are all good-looking children and I realize that I was not blessed with the same looks nor a thin, tall build. But I am certainly not to blame; this is the way Hashem created me, this is the way He wanted me to look. Is that a reason to ignore me, to act as if I didn't exist? At least they should have enough manners not to ignore me in front of the other grandchildren!

In my second year of school, the winter was particularly harsh so we tried not to leave the house too much. Bezhee spent the days with me, teaching me and telling me stories. We used to laugh together a lot. Meanwhile, Anya would sit in the armchair in her room and read. When I wanted to sit and talk to her, she refused. "Tell Bezhee," she would say. "I'm in the middle of a book, and you're mixing me up."

In honor of Chanukah, Bezhee went to visit her parents in

the shtetl. On Chanukah night, Apa lit Chanukah candles between the dining room and the guest room. Anya explained to me that when Apa sits this way near the Chanukah menorah and sings *mizmorim* for the holiday, he is surrounded by *mitzvos*: on one side—the menorah and its candles, and on the other side—the mezuzah.

I sat next to him without moving, looking into the siddur together with him, mesmerized by the soft tune that he sang. His face shone in the reflected light. "He looks just like the face of the *kohen* who lit the menorah in the Beis HaMikdash," I thought to myself.

Bezhee had told me the story of Chanukah before she left, and I often dreamed about the Beis HaMikdash in our own land, Eretz Yisrael, and about *Yerushalayim Ir HaKodesh*. But we lived in Hungary; Eretz Yisrael and Yerushalayim were far away and appeared only in my dreams. Apa was here, next to me, singing *mizmorim* and surrounded by *mitzvos*. I wanted to preserve that magical moment forever.

Anya said that most people fry potato latkes on Chanukah, but since we were only three people, and Apa doesn't like latkes, we would just eat regular food. But on one of the nights of Chanukah we went to Bubby Shapiro, and she was busy frying tons of latkes for all the visiting children and grandchildren. She said that latkes taste best when they are eaten warm, straight out of the frying pan.

We, the children, played dreidel and also played a game with special, hand-decorated cards that were called "*cartlach*" (cards). I heard the story of Chanukah and the *Maccabim* again, from Néni Basya Leah's daughters, but their version was so much more exciting than Bezhee's. Their description of the Beis HaMikdash was so alive — I felt like I could see it! And I told everyone about the golden table in the Beis HaMikdash on which the uncovered breads were placed for an entire week. They did not dry out, and when the *kohanim* ate them after a week, they were as fresh as if they were baked on that same day.

I loved being with Bubby Shapiro. Anya let me to sleep over and return only the following night, because I had winter vacation from school. I had a wonderful time there, it was not boring at all — like it is at home.

❦ 14 ❦
The Courtyard Children
[BUDAPEST]

AFTER CHANUKAH, Bezhee returned to us, but it was not the same Bezhee; she had definitely changed. She and Anya closeted themselves in the kitchen and told secrets without letting me join them.

Finally, they let me in on the big secret: Bezhee was a *kallah*! Yes, she became engaged to a fellow in her small town and planned to return and live there. Despite all her golden dreams of a "good Jewish city boy" she would be leaving the big city of Budapest for her *chasan* in the small town.

Bezhee went shopping with Anya. They originally planned to leave me home but I put up such a fuss that they let me accompany them, despite the freezing weather, to our family's store where people buy material for clothes. I was on my best behavior and didn't make a sound so that Apa wouldn't notice me. From there we continued to the seamstress, the hatmaker, and all the other places they went in order to prepare Bezhee's dowry.

Anya and I went to the wedding in Bezhee's town. The only thing I remember is the train ride, when I was so very

74

tired and I wished I could sleep in my own bed. When we returned to Budapest it turned out that I was sick. I spent a long time in bed, and Anya took care of me devotedly.

When I finally recuperated, Anya told me that I was a big girl and did not need a new nanny. "A girl your age can manage on her own," she said. I knew she was right — I was already a big girl at age eight, and it was time for me not to be dependent on a nanny.

The doorman's wife, Mrs. Kantzuk, replaced Bezhee in cleaning the house; now, she would come to us once a week to clean. She never paid attention to me except when she wanted me to leave the room that she was cleaning, and then she would call me "the young lady" in that sugary voice of hers. I did not like her at all!

I was alone all the time. While I sat in my room preparing my lessons, Anya would either be in her room or she would leave the house. I studied by myself and played with all my beautiful toys by myself, and I was terribly lonely.

Anya didn't like me to go outside to the courtyard to play with the other children from the apartment building. "Those children are common," she used to say. "They live in the apartments that face the yard, not the apartments that face the street, like ours." But when Anya would go out with her friends, I would sneak downstairs to play outside with the children from the building. Those were some of my best hours.

My room was full of games and toys. Anya — and even Apa — bought me anything that appealed to them. Every time that Anya left me alone, she would come back with a present in her hand.

My room was really magnificent. The furniture and rug were very expensive, as well as my clothing. But I didn't like being cooped up in my fancy room, or our luxurious house with its expensive furniture, its silver and crystal. I took advantage of every possible opportunity to escape to the courtyard.

What I enjoyed most was the time I spent with Anya's sister, Néni Basya Leah. She had a simple house with worn, plain furniture, but her home that was filled with love and laughter. There was always someone to play with and to have fun with there. But Anya didn't have time to take me there; only on Shabbos, when she would visit her parents, she agreed to take me. Also, occasionally when she knew that she'd be out of the house for a long time, she'd be willing to take me to Basya Leah. At night, Reizy and Suri, her older daughters, would take me home.

Once when Anya wasn't home, I actually invited the courtyard children, as we called them, up to the house. At first the children entered my room in awe and sat on the edges of the chairs and played politely with the game I took out. But I made the mistake of leaving for a moment to bring refreshments and when I returned, tray in hand, I was horrified to see what had happened. The children had emptied out all the games and toys from the toy chest, and started to pull out my clothes from the closet. One sharp scream escaped from my throat as I put the tray of cookies on the table. Two of the girls who were going through my clothes abandoned the closet and ran to the table. When I went to close the closet doors I saw one dirty, neglected girl standing next to the cabinet and trying to stuff my shiny new crayons into her pocket. She saw me looking at her, so she immediately threw all the crayons back into the drawer and slammed it shut. The rest of the children ran to the table with toys in their hands, and gobbled up the tray of cookies in a flash.

"How do you play with this?" they asked me about each and every toy. "How do you turn it on?" "Can we dress and undress the dolls?" "Can we cook in these little toy pots?" and many other silly questions. And they didn't listen to my answers either.

In was nothing short of a disaster. They acted disgracefully, scattered the toys and games, touched everything without my permission and even broke some things. Some tried to make holes in the eyes of my new ceramic doll, and all of them shouted and screamed and ran wild. They didn't pay attention to me at all, only fought over my things and shouted at the top of their lungs.

I tried to tell them to stop but no matter how much I begged, they ignored me. It was as if they didn't see or hear me at all. I was horrified.

Finally, I reluctantly called Mrs. Kantzuk to come to my aid. She helped chase the children out of our house, and told me that she would not tell Anya about the visit, in return for a promise that I would never do such a thing again. As if I would ever want to! I promised wholeheartedly. Then she helped me clean up and put the room in order.

Anya never noticed that anything was amiss in my room. She did not even detect the broken toys or the torn doll clothing. During the following week, I sat and fixed the torn clothing with tears in my eyes. Most distressing of all were the toys that couldn't be fixed at all, such as the game that Apa brought me as a prize for excelling in class.

I had received this prize after my name appeared at the top of the classroom list of outstanding students for a full month. The game was a miniature merry-go-round, the kind that one sees in amusement parks, made of wood and iron. White horses, decorated with red and gold, adorned a round, red and green wooden surface. When you wound the spring, the whole apparatus moved just like a real merry-go-round: The horses raised and lowered their heads and the floor moved round and round. As the merry-go-round turned, it played a familiar tune, and the horses' manes and tails (made from real horsehair) would rise and fall to the beat.

I really liked this toy and spent a lot of time winding it up. The horses were meticulously exact and majestic; they truly looked like real horses in miniature. The courtyard children, in their never-to-be-forgotten visit in my house, had pulled and turned the spring so roughly that it broke; the merry-go-round never rotated or played music again. Mrs. Kant-zuk pinned the horses' manes and tails back on with needles. I gently placed the toy back on the shelf, hoping that Apa wouldn't notice.

From then on, I never again went down to the yard to play. Instead, I spent time near the window and sadly watched the children playing outside. True, I was happy that I was not like them; I was not wild and never intentionally broke or ruined a toy, not my own nor my cousins'. Only then did I understand why Anya called them "common" and I certainly didn't want to become like them. But on the other hand, I was sad that I couldn't join them in running games or ball games. The fact that their ball was made from rags didn't bother them in the least, and their joyous cries rose all the way to my window. As I sat there, watching, I would pretend that I was playing, too. I imagined where I would hide during hide-and-seek, and when they played cat and mouse, sometimes I would "be" the mouse escaping the cat, and other times, the cat that managed to catch all the mice. But all this was only in my imagination. I remained all alone, looking down sadly from the window above.

A ray of light shined on me once every two weeks: when Chungarabi the gypsy used to come and wash our clothes. After Bezhee got married and moved out, Anya found laundry day to be very difficult. Chungarabi saw this and told her that she needn't tire herself out so much; she, the gypsy, would prepare the water herself and heat it, sort and wash the laundry, and thus relieve Anya's burden. But Anya was afraid to leave the gypsy alone in the house so she remained with her in the morning until I returned home from school. After I promised Anya over and over that I'd watch Chungarabi carefully so that she wouldn't steal anything, Anya left the house in the afternoon. She only returned at night with Apa, after Chungarabi had finished folding the dry laundry and had even done the ironing.

My hours alone with Chungarabi were the happiest hours of the week. If Anya knew what I really did then she never would have left me alone with the gypsy. But Anya hated laundry day, and was happy to leave the house as soon as she could.

During my time alone with Chungarabi, I would take my schoolbag into the kitchen, because that's where she washed the clothes. While I did all my homework, I explained to the gypsy exactly what we studied in class. After I finished, Chungarabi would tell me gypsy folk-tales. She taught me to speak Romany — the language of the Rom, as gypsies call themselves, which was a strange mixture of Hungarian words with some Czech and evidently other languages as well. Chungarabi was astonished at the speed with which I picked up the foreign language. She was very proud of her pupil and also taught me gypsy songs. In exchange I taught her something very important: I taught her how to read and write. This was difficult for me, as I was only a child, but Chungarabi was determined. She overcame the obstacles and actually did succeed in learning to read and write.

She told me about Eshto, her husband. Eshto played the cimbalom, a gypsy musical instrument, which is made of wood and strings and is played with mallets wrapped in cotton. Eshto had worked for a number of years in construction in Budapest and was very successful in his work; therefore, she explained, they remained in the city. Only occasionally, when Eshto and his group would finish one building and before they started a new project, then "wanderlust feet" would hit him. The desire to travel and see new places was an innate gypsy desire, I understood. So Eshto would take to his wanderings temporarily, but always returned after a short time until the next building was finished. Eshto never stayed away from his wife for more than a full month at a time, and Chungarabi was very proud of him, even though most gypsies did not behave this way.

Lula, Chungarabi's daughter, was a member of a joint Hungarian-Gypsy dance troupe at the time. But Chungarabi, for some reason, seemed reluctant to talk about her daughter, so I did not press her.

Chungarabi loved me, and not only because of the foodstuffs that I used to hide and save to give her each time she came. True, she was happy to get my little presents, but that's not the reason she treated me so well. She simply loved me for no reason. She used to hug and kiss me, happy to listen to my stories or whatever I wanted to tell her. She was natural and unaffected with me, not like Mrs. Kantzuk.

At night, when Anya came home, I would immerse myself in my notebooks, finish my homework, and pretend to ignore Chungarabi. Only at the very end of the day, Chungarabi would wink at me and smile. But she would hug me goodbye even before then, before Anya came home. It was due to that hug that I knew that Chungarabi was actually very thin even though she looked heavy. She wore many layers of clothes, one on top of the other, even in the summer. In the winter, she wore a kind of hand-woven cloak above it all, made out of a heavy woolen blanket. On her head she wore a large woolen kerchief instead of the summer silk kerchief.

I never told anyone in the world about my special relationship with Chungarabi. I knew that it was not considered respectable to get too close to gypsies, and if I let out the truth, I would most likely be ridiculed for it.

❧ 15 ❧
They Sold My Daughter
[SEVLUS]

MAMA RETURNED to Sevlus alone. The way home was difficult and interminably long. Each movement of the train caused the stump to hurt, each turn made her dizzy, and the trip seemed endless. Although Mama sat next to the window, she saw nothing. On the way to Budapest she had so admired the view from the train windows: mountains and forests, lush green fields and small villages, and countless little streams. But now, when Mama looked out the window, all she saw was the reflection of the darling baby who had been stolen from her.

When the train reached its destination, Mama dragged herself home. Her first visit was to the home of the Rav. She hoped that he — a God-fearing, wise Jew — would be able to advise her as to what to do to get her daughter back.

Mama, emotionally spent and physically drained from her journey, cried uncontrollably as she related her story. And even after she had finished speaking, her tears continued falling.

The kind Rebbetzin tried her best to give Mama support and convinced Mama to spend the night in their home. "It is already late and it's dark outside; in your state you should not be alone," she said.

Later that night, the Rav returned from the *beis midrash* together with several distinguished community members and they all sat with Mama to discuss a plan of action. To hire a lawyer, Mama would need money, and lots of it, and Mama had no money at all. She didn't even have anything left to sell, as she had sold her furniture for the store.

The Rav and the community leaders decided that Mama should do the following:

First of all, they told her to return to her work in the grocery store. It was important that "they" should know that Mama could support herself, and not rely on begging. In this way, she would invalidate "their" claim that she had no means of support.

They also decided to send letters to the rabbis they knew in Budapest, including the chief rabbi of the city. In the letters they would detail the whole sorry chain of events, and explain that Mama had a livelihood and there were no grounds for stealing her baby from her, as was the case.

They also suggested asking the chief rabbi's wife to give Mama advice.

"The important thing is, you must stay strong," they all said. "Gather your strength, and don't despair!"

Mama returned home with new hope in her heart, and opened the store on that very day. All the neighbors frequented her grocery store. Perhaps at the beginning they bought from her out of pity and desire to help her, but slowly, the store's reputation spread. Mama was fair and scrupulously honest, and when weighing foodstuffs, she would even add a bit without adding to the price. Her prices were reasonable, the service was excellent and the store always sparkled with cleanliness.

As time went on, Mama gained experience and learned how to work efficiently with one hand. She never allowed her disability to get in her way. She felt that she had to show a positive balance sheet as a woman with a proper livelihood who is capable of supporting her daughter and providing for all her needs.

Meanwhile, the Rav wrote the letters they had talked about and all the community dignitaries signed them.

After a long time, response letters began to arrive. Mama was very disappointed. She had hoped that the letters would bring good news. But the rabbis all had the same response: Although they were willing to help, regretfully, there was nothing they could do.

The Goldmans refused to divulge who had adopted the baby and were not willing to discuss the issue with anyone. One of the rabbis wrote Mama that he strongly suspected that the Goldmans received a significant sum of money to keep their silence.

Mama often cried, "They sold my daughter, they sold her like an animal or a piece of furniture!" This thought agitated her most of all. She claimed that they did not consider what was best for the child, but only money to line their pockets. How could she fight such corrupt people?

The hardest day for Mama was laundry day. Although she managed to do everything else by herself, doing laundry with one hand was impossible, and washing the clothing with one's feet, as Mama had learned to do, was cumbersome and strenuous. The results were also below Mama's expectations. Therefore she hired Ruzka, a non-Jewish neighbor, to do the wash once every two weeks.

Ruzka always told Mama hair-raising stories about kidnapping, especially by gypsies, and the way the stolen children were then enslaved. Mama knew that I was not stolen by gypsies; she knew that I was sold to a family who had no children of their own. But Ruzka made her life miserable with those horrific stories, and eventually worry and doubt crept into her thoughts: Perhaps I had been stolen, after all? Maybe I was suffering under some terrible master? Laundry nights became full of nightmares for Mama.

❧ 16 ❧
The Fortune-teller
[BUDAPEST]

ANYA ENJOYED CHATTING with Julia, a Jewish woman who lived in our neighborhood. True, Anya never invited her to our house and as far as I knew, Anya never visited Julia in her home either; the woman was poor and not part of the Orthodox community, so visits were out of the question. But they talked a lot on the street. Julia's two sons did not live with her, because she was a widow and did not have money to raise her children herself. One son lived with Julia's parents in their village, and the other lived with her husband's parents in their village. Julia cried a lot because she missed her sons very much. The letters that she received from them and that she wrote to them were inadequate, of course.

Meanwhile, Julia worked in her profession as a social worker in the Jewish community in Budapest. However, since she had only completed her studies through junior high school, she was not certified in her field, and as a result, received a very low salary. In order to supplement her earnings, she worked evenings for a fortune-teller.

Once I went out with Anya and we ran into Julia on the

street on her way back from work. I suspect that Anya would leave the house at a specific time so that she would meet her friend, because Anya knew what time Julia left work. Julia was always happy to see me — I was the same age as one of her sons, the younger son who lived with her parents in To-kai, the wine village.

Julia coaxed Anya to make an appointment with the for-tune-teller and hear what the future promised her. Eventually Anya listened to her friend and, in fact, the two of us went to the fortune-teller one day.

The visit was frightening. The waiting room was filled with women of all ages but mainly older ones who seemed to know each other, as they chatted freely as do acquaintances. It was a big room and the chairs were the only furniture. The chairs were old and shabby and came in all shapes and sizes. Evidently, they had been collected from all kinds of places. The women in the waiting room also differed from one an-other: There were fat ones and thin ones, elegantly dressed and shabbily dressed ones. Most were non-Jews, but there were also two Jewish women there. One was a very old Jew-ish lady who sat on an ancient armchair. I remember thinking that the armchair and the woman must be the same age! The old woman wore a very wide, dark green dress that looked like a tent, and on her head was a brightly colored kerchief knotted under her chin, in the way of the villagers. She spoke all the time, sipping a cup of tea as she talked. When she finished drinking she called to Julia to refill the cup. "Fill it to the brim!" she shouted. Julia went into the kitchen where there were additional tea-drinking women. The cups looked like they came from the same place as the chairs: There were no two cups alike.

The second Jewish woman was also an older woman, but she was thin, energetic and seemed to be in perpetual motion as she sat on the edge of her chair. She talked quietly with the woman next to her—also thin, tall and older—who did not say a word but kept nodding her head in agreement with her talkative neighbor.

Another woman sat in the center of the room on a chair that might have been very grand at one time but had since seen better days. She talked loudly and incessantly, telling the story of some girl. It seemed that all those present were well-familiar with the story, as occasionally they helped her remember details. They even corrected her version, mainly concerning the girl's clothes, and reminded her of various articles of clothing that she forgot — such as buttons or buckles.

To me it seemed that the only thing missing from the scene was a table with food: That would have made the party complete!

Julia scurried around, offering tea to all the women, but Anya politely refused. I am sure that the shabby room did not reach her standards of cleanliness.

As soon as we first entered, the old Jewish lady said something out loud in Yiddish. The thin Jewish lady laughed, as did Julia. Anya also smiled and later told me that the old woman had repeated a familiar Jewish proverb along the lines of, "Another fool falls into the trap." Evidently, this was in honor of Anya who had come to the fortune-teller for the first time.

Two women exited the fortune-teller's room: One was older and the second looked about Anya's age. They approached Julia and started to argue with her. Julia stopped them and directed them back into the fortune-teller's room.

Finally, it was our turn. Julia ushered us into the fortune-teller's room which was small and very dim. Dark curtains covered the windows and the only light was a tiny kerosene lamp that hung in the middle of the room. There was also a round table with a tablecloth pulled to one side.

Behind the table, on a giant chair, sat an older woman of ample proportions who did, indeed, seem to require such a large chair. She wore a very glittery dress made out of rustling taffeta, and a sparkling kerchief out of gold-colored transparent material was wrapped around her head.

The fortune-teller asked Anya to come and sit on the chair opposite her, and I stood behind Anya.

In the center of the table stood a large glass ball. Next to it was a large black box full of various cards. The fortune-teller moved the black box closer to us, looked inside and hummed quietly. Then she took the crystal ball and looked inside, and then shook it around, while continuing to hum throughout. She placed the ball down and picked it up, placed it down again and took the cards in her hand. Deftly, she spread the cards on the table. There were many cards and she organized them in three groups—ten cards in each group. The cards all had strange pictures on them — she studied them intently, humming all the while, drew a few cards from the three groups, and organized the rest in two new sets.

And then she started talking. She told Anya many things but I wasn't really listening because I was busy looking around at all the interesting things. The haziness in the room and the strange smells kept me more preoccupied than the talking. I took in everything around me: On a small table near the fortune-teller's right hand was a cup of tea and a plate with leftover food.

Suddenly the fortune-teller turned to me and said: "Little girl! You will live! You will reach some kind of mother, afterwards a forest. You will live in a sunlit land."

I burst out laughing, I couldn't stop. How will I reach a mother, when I already had one and lived with her all the time! And truly, our apartment was sunlit during the summers, and in the summer we always went to Margaret Island to make a picnic in the forest, like most residents of Budapest. The fortune-teller knows these things, I thought; that's why she can pretend to "see" the future!

Anya stood up, grabbed my arm with all her might, and rushed me out. Outside she began shouting at Julia, saying that it was a shame that she persuaded us to come to this horrible place. Julia answered her that evidently she heard what she would rather not have heard, or something she was afraid of, and that's why she was so upset.

Once we were outside, Anya told me not to pay attention to anything I had heard — it was clear that the fortune was just a lot of nonsense. But more importantly, she told me not to tell anyone, not even Apa!

ભ   ભ   ભ

The following day we visited Bubby and Zaidy Shapiro. Anya told Bubby about the fortune-teller and burst into tears. Basya Leah walked in and also heard the story. Both Bubby and Basya Leah tried as hard as they could to console Anya.

I didn't understand: If Anya really thought that it was all foolishness, that the fortune-teller's words were a pack of lies — then why should she cry about it? And why didn't Bubby and Basya Leah just remind Anya that the fortune-teller's words did not reflect reality? I saw that even Bubby wiped away tears, though she tried to hide it by turning her head. What did that crazy fortune-teller say that made them all so sad, anyway?

I approached Anya and reminded her that she herself called the whole episode "foolishness." Why, only the *Ribbono shel Olam* knows what will happen in the future, not mere human beings, and certainly not non-Jewish fortune-tellers.

She mustn't cry so over such foolishness! Anya hugged me tightly and kissed me and said that only I — out of all the people surrounding her — only I could comfort her, and it was lucky she had me.

It was fun in Basya Leah's home. I told everyone that I would live in a forest, and they reminded me that if I was going to live in a forest I had better find out which mushrooms were good and which were poisonous. Then they asked me if I knew how to climb trees, and whether I was afraid of the dark.

I was taken aback. How, indeed, would I know which mushrooms were poisonous? We all grew up on Bubby's stories about her friend the *kallah* who ate poisoned mushrooms and died from them. We all remembered Bubby's description of the *kallah's* jewelry and how it was returned to the *chasan*.

The children offered to teach me to climb the nut tree in the yard, but I was scared. I had never climbed anything before, not even a low gate, let alone a tree!

Basya Leah walked in and saw that I was anxious. She got angry at her children and said, "It's not enough that her mother is crying over this foolishness, do you want Leichu to cry too?"

When I heard that, I pulled myself together and stood up straight. "But it really is nonsense! Just idle talk. We should not pay attention to it at all," I announced and heaved a sigh of relief. Luckily, Anya also stopped talking about it, evidently because she decided not to take the whole affair seriously. And when she met Julia, Julia also told her not to take her "fortune" so seriously. To her, the fortune-teller was nothing more than an employer. Julia sorely wanted to save as much as she could, so that she could bring back her sons. Julia also admitted that her salary was dependent on the number of clients the fortune-teller had, so she tried to convince everyone she knew to go to her.

On the next laundry day when Chungarabi came to us, I told her about the frightening visit at the fortune-teller. Chungarabi took my hand, looked at it a long time and said that I have a long life line, though it was cut in the middle. That meant I would be in danger, maybe get sick, but I would survive to live a long life.

She also promised that one day she would teach me how to read palms. Palms don't lie, she insisted, they tell what will happen to a person. However, palms don't tell you whether someone will live in a city, village or forest. "That part of it is just foolishness," she said. "Don't think about it anymore."

❖ 17 ❖
Short and Sweet

[SEVLUS]

MAMA WROTE AN impressive number of letters. Rav Klein, the Rav of Sevlus, gave her the addresses of Budapest rabbis and she wrote to them. Every night, after she closed the store, she sat down with pen and paper. She wrote numerous drafts of every letter, until the final result was to her satisfaction. Then she would take the letter to Rivka so that she, too, could express her opinion. Only after Néni Rivka gave her seal of approval, would the letter be sent by mail. Mama prayed over every letter from the depths of her heart: that it would reach its destination and succeed in touching the heart of the addressee so that he would come to her aid.

Waiting for answers was agonizing. Mama sat near the window, watching and waiting for the mailman. The mailman, a kindly, husky gentile who delivered mail twice a week in Mama's neighborhood, would pass by Mama's house on his rounds and shake his head when no letter arrived. Mama's disappointment was crushing. When she did receive a letter, he would wave it in the direction of her window from a distance, as he knew that she always watched from that window.

Then he would rush to bring it to her and start his rounds from her house, even though it took him considerably longer that way. He would deliver the correspondence to her with great satisfaction — he knew how she waited for these letters.

When a letter would arrive, Mama would greet the mailman joyfully and bless him profusely, then put the letter in her pocket and go inside. Mama was very disciplined and never opened a letter outside. She forced herself to return to the store, and if there were customers waiting she served them with a smile though her heart beat like a hammer. Only when the store was empty did she sit, open the envelope, and begin to read.

Most of the letters began the same way. "Unfortunately, I do not bear good tidings today." It was as if they all learned the same style for bad news.

Most of the *rabbanim* and community leaders that Mama wrote to did answer her. Only a few ignored her letter. But all the people who did answer wrote that they were powerless to help. Mama suspected that they did not even make an effort, and Néni Rivka, Mama's close friend and privy to her secrets, admitted frankly, "Why should they knock themselves out? Why should they fight important, rich people of their community in Budapest, for the sake of a poor widow in a remote village in the Carpathian Mountains?"

Perhaps she was right. The important, rich people who were responsible for the disappearance of her daughter were local people: respectable, distinguished, the kind of people who donate money to Jewish causes. Why should the rabbis look too closely at these people and judge them? Mama didn't know the identity of the people who adopted me, but she did know that they were wealthy. Evidently, they paid her relatives, the Goldman family, a respectable sum of money.

The relatives emphatically denied receiving any money. They claimed that they did what they did for my sake: They considered my status in life as well as Mama's welfare, a poor widow with only one arm. At least she, the poor unfortunate soul, wouldn't have to support a child — that is what they said. But Mama did not believe them. If this is, indeed, what they thought, then after they saw all the efforts that Mama went to, all her tears, then they would surely have reconsidered. They would have realized that a poor disabled widow could raise her beloved child. Are only young, strong and rich people allowed to bring children into the world? Don't they understand that poor people also love their children deeply and raise them appropriately?

Mama suspected that the Goldmans were so adamant because they had received a large sum of money for me, and so would not or could not return the money.

One night, when Mama sat with Néni Rivka over another letter, Bácsi[4] Nachman came home and saw them both crying over yet another rejection. "I am going to write a letter to my brother-in-law," he decided. He had pushed off this step for many reasons but now he decided that he would no longer wait. He sat down to write to his brother-in-law, Shia (Yehoshua) Zinger who lived in Budapest. Shia was not a rabbi or an important person in the community; he was only a simple merchant. But he and his wife (Nachman's sister) were truly good people, and Nachman knew that if Shia would agree to help, he would move heaven and earth to find me.

The letter was sent, and then came the long wait for an answer. Mama always said that waiting was the worst. It is

---

4. Básci is Hungarian for "uncle", and like Néni, is often used when referring to close friends and older relatives, such as cousins, as well.

much easier to cope with a difficult situation when you can actually do something, she used to say, than when all you can do is wait and hope.

The answer finally arrived, and was shorter than all the letters Mama had received until then. Most of the letters were wordy and awkward, explaining why the author could not help. But this time the letter was short, barely half a page.

Shia Zinger wrote to the point: He would take upon himself to investigate what happened to Leichu Fruchter! He asked Mama not to expect miracles, but repeated that he was willing to take this mission upon himself.

Mama was barely able to contain herself until evening when she closed the store, and flew quickly to Rivka. "What a wonderful brother-in-law you have; he said that he would try!" All the others, the ones who sent long, flowery letters, did not even attempt to come to her aid. "A place in Gan Eden is already reserved for him, after a hundred and twenty years!" Mama gasped. "He is the only person who is willing to try!"

To Mama, this promise shone like a beam of light in the darkness of her life.

❧ 18 ❧
Aunt Eva
[BUDAPEST]

R OSH HASHANAH arrived. The big shul was full of
people. I stood between Anya and Bubby Feldman and
we all held *machzorim* in our hands. Anya and Bubby
were praying and crying. Many other women were crying,
and others davened quietly.

I know how to read Hebrew, but I barely understand anything. When I was little, my nanny Bezhee taught me the
aleph-beis and now, in the Jewish school we learned Hebrew.
Before Rosh Hashanah they taught us the translation of some
of the prayers and explained about *teki'as shofar*.

But we had been in shul for a very long time, and they
hadn't even blown the shofar yet. For a while, I was moving my lips, pretending to daven, but then I stopped that. I
wished I could go outside, but Néni Eva was sitting outside,
near the door. She came to Bubby Feldman for the whole
Yom Tov, and she was sitting outside the shul to keep an eye
on her children.

I don't like Eva even though she is Apa's younger sister.
And she certainly doesn't like me. At night, when we went to
Bubby for the *seudah*, right away she said something nasty

about me. I didn't hear what she said, but Bubby immediately shushed her and told her not to speak that way when I or Anya were around. That's how I knew that she must have said something mean.

Afterwards, when I wanted to play with her cute daughter Sherry, she pinched my arm and hissed at me not to get near her children and not to touch them. I told her that I just wanted to play with them because they were so cute, but she told me that she doesn't let me play with them. And when her eldest son Miklush, who is about my age, came to talk to me, she went over to him and pulled him over to the second room. I heard her angrily saying, "I told you not to speak to her!"

In school they told us about forgiveness. You have to ask forgiveness from everyone, and you also have to forgive everyone. The teacher told us that if we want Hashem to forgive us for all our sins, we must also forgive those who hurt us, because if we don't, then Hashem will say, "Since you don't forgive each other, then I will not forgive you either."

I thought about that a lot, and I don't remember anything that I could have done to hurt Aunt Eva and her family!

A long time ago they came here—I remember this clearly—and they stayed with Bubby Feldman for a few weeks. At that time, Anya told me that Bubby was very busy hosting her daughter and grandchildren, and I shouldn't impose. So I stayed home and didn't visit.

I know that they were in Budapest two more times, but I don't remember anything about those visits. I also don't remember much about the years that they lived near us until they moved to Berg, a few years ago.

Despite all this I went over to Eva and asked her for forgiveness; perhaps I did do something to hurt her though I don't remember what it could be. Eva looked at me and did not answer. I asked again for her forgiveness and said that if I ever did something to hurt her, it was not intentional. And then she said something very strange to me. "Because of you, we had to leave Budapest."

I was surprised. It was my fault that they had to leave Budapest?!

She saw my surprise and added, "Yes, because of you! I was involved in bringing you here and when they started investigating, I was afraid it would lead to me. So because of you, I left Budapest and moved to Berg."

I did not have the faintest idea what she was talking about. I looked at her, puzzled, but she completely ignored me. I understood that she was saying things that were not connected to me: I didn't do anything to her; they left five years earlier when I was only three-and-a-half years old. What in the world could I have done at that age to cause them to run away?

It seemed to me that she was making this up, just to get me to leave her alone. She simply could not stand me, for some reason, and was blaming me for things I knew nothing about. I asked her for forgiveness one last time and then went to sit far away from her, hiding behind Apa.

I never told anyone the strange things that Néni Eva told me, but I did try to avoid her and her children afterwards.

So if Eva was sitting in the entrance to shul, I just couldn't go outside to the yard to play. I was very bored, but I remained in my place—just to avoid passing her.

Our shul is very big and very grand. Downstairs is the men's section — it's huge and is full of large brown chairs and tables. There are four steps in the middle of the men's section leading up to a large wooden *bimah*. Four tall columns surround the *bimah* — one on each side. They are so tall, they almost reach the ceiling. In front of the *bimah* is a large table. A beautiful red velvet tablecloth embroidered with gold letters covers the table. The heavy *paroches* that covers the Aron HaKodesh is embroidered with gold letters too, but the *paroches* also has lions and a large golden crown embroidered on it. At the end of the *bimah* is a long bench that no one sits on.

Let me describe the women's section. It looks like a balcony that extends into the building and not outside it. All the benches have high backs and the top part turns into a little table for the people who sit behind us; that's where we place our *siddurim* when we daven. Then, under this little table is a compartment for storing *siddurim* and odds and ends that people like to leave in shul.

I was so bored — I had been there for hours already — so I started rummaging through the compartment in front of me. Someone who sat there before me had left a white handkerchief embroidered with blue thread, and a large, heavy siddur with a leather jacket that closes with a gold buckle.

Anya gave me a reproachful look, so I took my hand out of the compartment and closed it carefully.

I looked at the ceiling and examined all the decorations up there. There were paintings of the sun, the moon and stars, a lion crouching near young goats, and a dove with an olive branch in its mouth. I started yawning — one small yawn, then another and another. I felt my eyes starting to close, and then I noticed that everyone was standing. They were going to blow the shofar at last!

After the *teki'os*, many women left for home. Eva also left, taking her girls with her. Finally I could go outside, and I did! I met my school friends in the yard. They all wore new, fancy clothes with matching hair ribbons, and everyone's eyes sparkled happily. I was no longer tired and bored, and everything was lovely.

After shul we went to Bubby and Zaidy Feldman. The boulevard leading to their house was already full of Jews walking
home slowly, and as each shul finished, more and more Jews
joined the crowd. Everyone wished each other well in Yiddish
and Hebrew: "*A gut yahr! Besoros tovos,*" and other warm
blessings for a good year.

I was so happy! And it seemed like even the day was happy too! It was a cool day, but it was not raining, and white,
fluffy clouds floated in the sky. The leaves on the trees had
changed color from green to red and the whole boulevard
looked beautiful. Everyone's gardens were full of colorful
flowers, and the entire world seemed to be celebrating the
new year. The rain that had fallen over the last two days left
everything fresh.

I walked between Bubby and Anya while the men walked
in front of us: Zaidy, Apa, Bácsi Eizu — Eva's husband — and
Miklush, Eva's son.

I felt wonderful on that Rosh Hashanah! Everything was
just lovely. I felt very grown-up in my new dress with its
matching jacket. Anya and Bubby also wore new clothes, and
the entire universe could see that today was Rosh Hashanah.

I came home in such a good mood and then — it happened. Néni Eva was standing at the door, her lips pressed
together tightly and she was looking at me — very angrily.
When everyone passed she whispered a word after me, probably the same one she hissed the day before, but it was a word
that I didn't understand. Bubby and Anya seemed not to hear,
but I heard, and all at once the entire beautiful and renewed
world of Rosh Hashanah disappeared like a dream. The day
lost its brilliant glow, my dress did not seem so nice, and even
my new shoes started to pinch my feet.

You're not allowed to cry on Rosh Hashanah. If you cry
on Rosh Hashanah then you will cry all year long; that's

what they always told me. So I controlled myself with all my strength so I wouldn't cry. I went to Anya and, almost in a whisper, I said to her, "I want to go to Bubby Shapiro!"

Anya, of course, didn't know why I suddenly wanted to leave, and she absolutely refused. "We are invited to eat here, and we will stay here," she said.

"Just me," I begged. "I will go alone, you can stay here. I know the way to her house, and I can go by myself."

But Anya absolutely refused. "What happened to you all of a sudden? It's out of the question! There is nothing to talk about, don't even think of such a thing. You will stay here with us, together with our lovely guests who came from far away. Do you want to embarrass your Bubby? I don't want to hear this anymore. Go play with little Dutshka and Sherry, your adorable cousins."

But their mother did not let me play with my cousins. I didn't want to hurt Anya's feelings, so I didn't tell her anything. I went to the kitchen to help Bubby, but Bubby said she didn't want help and I should go to the living room.

Zaidy and Apa were talking with Uncle Eizu; Miklush was reading a book; Aunt Eva was busy with her girls, and Anya was in the kitchen with Bubby. Only I had no place to be; only I did not belong anywhere. I stood near the window and looked outside, watching the clouds, watching their changing shapes. When I was little, I really liked imagining that the clouds were all kinds of unrealistic creatures. Bezhee used to play this imagination game with me and we had such fun together. But meanwhile I've grown up, Bezhee left me, and for some reason, all the others have rejected me.

That Rosh Hashanah was very sad for me.

When we came home after the *seudah*, I understood from Anya that Néni Eva was staying with Bubby until after Sukkos. My heart sank, and I started to plan how I would convince Bubby Shapiro and Néni Basya Leah to persuade Anya to allow me to stay with them throughout the whole Yom Tov. The last thing I wanted was to be at Bubby Feldman's with Eva and her family.

Anya must have noticed how Néni Eva was behaving toward me. It was on Erev Yom Kippur when the three of us— Apa, Anya and myself—went to Bubby and Zaidy Feldman in order to bless them and be blessed by them for the new year.

As I went over to Aunt Eva to wish her a good year, Anya was watching. Néni Eva did not realize that she was looking, though. As was the custom, I said, "I kiss your hand" and curtsied, and then I extended my hand in order to wish her a *"gemar chasimah tovah."* At first she ignored me, as if I was invisible. I had to wait for a long time with my hand out to her, and only then did she reluctantly take it to accept my blessing. She did not bless me in return but instead, at the last minute before I had a chance to move away, she pinched my arm! I felt myself turn red, but then I got my nerve up and I said out loud, "Thank you very much, Néni Eva. I will return your 'blessing,' the way you blessed me, to sweet Dutshka!"

"Don't you dare touch my daughter!" shouted Néni Eva.

I just smiled sweetly and did not answer. I saw that she was really worried, because she got up to stand guard behind Dutshka's chair. Sherry was safely in Zaidy's arms, so Eva wasn't concerned about her.

I thought the entire thing was funny. What was she thinking? That I would pinch a little girl on Erev Yom Kippur? I felt that I was much more mature and respectable than my aunt. See, I can control myself and not cry. I can even smile and frighten her!

At night, after we returned from shul, Anya helped me undress and she stroked the blue spot where Eva had pinched me. Afterwards she stroked the other spots where Eva had pinched me on Rosh Hashanah; those had already changed color from blue to faint green. "I was very proud of your behavior," Anya said. "You acted like an adult, as befits a young lady on Erev Yom Kippur." I understood from this that Anya had seen what Eva had done to me. I wanted to ask her to explain my aunt's behavior, but I decided not to. I won't ask, I decided; it was Yom Kippur, I will act maturely and forgive.

On Sukkos we ate most of the meals with Zaidy and Bubby Shapiro — their house is a little farther away than Zaidy and Bubby Feldman's house. Anya promised me that I could sleep there throughout the entire week of Sukkos. Then I wouldn't have to go to Zaidy and Bubby Feldman with them, but I could stay with Zaidy and Bubby Shapiro. I never talked to Anya about Aunt Eva's behavior to me, and she never brought it up either.

After Sukkos was over, Chungarabi came to do the laundry. I couldn't wait to tell her everything and show her my arm. The blue and green marks had faded already but they still hurt, especially when I touched them.

Chungarabi told me that perhaps there was some kind of a fight between my parents and my aunt and uncle. Perhaps my aunt and uncle were forced to leave Budapest because of some disagreement, and Néni Eva took out all her anger on me—even though I am only a child and certainly couldn't have caused her to leave the city. Chungarabi also said that I'd best forget and forgive the whole incident because only I would suffer if I didn't. So I listened to her and tried to follow her advice. Chungarabi's advice was always helpful; even though she had never studied in school, she had a lot of wisdom and life experience. And I was the one who taught her reading and writing—she hadn't even known how to write her own name!

❧ 19 ❧
An Interesting Question
[SEVLUS]

VERY WEEK, Mama received a letter from Mr. Zinger. Even when he didn't have any news to tell, he would write — just to check in with her and ask her not to worry. What was important was that Mama should not give up hope, and that she should continue to daven to Hashem to give her wisdom and advice.

As if Mama needed to be prodded to pray! She didn't stop davening for a minute.

These letters encouraged Mama and she began to smile again. Whenever she received a new letter, she would take it to Néni Rivka to show her. Rivka was like a surrogate mother to her; she was always happy to see Mama and always had a good word for her. Sometimes when it was freezing outside, Rivka would tell Mama, "You are not going home on a night like this! You're staying right here tonight!" Their tiny home was always full of children and guests, but there was always room for Mama. "When there is room in the heart, there is room for a bed," Rivka used to say, when Mama tried to refuse by saying that she didn't want to impose. They would take out a bench from here and a mattress from there, and presto; there was room. The Klar home might have lacked luxuries, and even necessities—but it was full of happiness and love, and Mama enjoyed being there.

Shia Zinger made enormous efforts to find me, and despite the failures of his exhaustive searches he did not despair. He wrote to my Mama, Sheina Ruchel Fruchter, that even though there were more than two hundred thousand Jews in Budapest, he would leave no stone unturned until they found her daughter.

Two years passed. Then one day, Rivka's daughter Dori appeared at Mama's store. Dori told Mama that Mrs. Zinger had come all the way from Budapest to visit them, together with her daughter Edith. She said that Mrs. Zinger wanted to talk to Mama, and asked that Mama walk over to them after closing her store at night. Then Dori remained with Mama to help her organize the store so that she could walk over as soon as possible. It went a lot quicker with her two hands to help.

When everything was in its place, the two of them left the house. Dori and Mama walked together but Mama walked so quickly that Dori could barely keep up with her. Dori — and her whole family — had long legs and usually, people who joined the Klars had to hurry to keep up. But this time, it was Dori who ran after Mama!

They had a very touching meeting, as this was the first time that Chana Malka Zinger and Mama met face-to-face. "I am so happy to meet you," said Chana Malka, smiling warmly. "I have long wanted to meet the woman we have been corresponding with for almost two years, who has kept us busy with a lot of running around." Mama felt bad and started to apologize, but Chana Malka interrupted. "No, no. Please don't apologize! I didn't mean it in a bad way; we are happy to be busy 'running around.' This is our mitzvah; please don't try to take it away from us. Who knows—perhaps due to our efforts, we and our children are alive and will remain alive." She had no idea at the time that her words would, eventually, turn out to be true; she prophesied and did not know it.

The two women sat down to talk, and Chana Malka Zinger told Mama the latest development. "My husband spoke to a Rabbi Shlomowitz, one of the rabbis of Budapest, who had an interesting story to tell. He remembered that a few years ago, a young couple came to him with a *she'eilah*. They told him that a poor woman, who was widowed and sick, came to the city with a baby girl. The woman was hospitalized and her legs were amputated. Now the woman was disabled, in addition to her poverty and other troubles. She needed a wheelchair and couldn't care for her baby.

"This couple had acquaintances who were childless. The childless couple was willing to pay a large sum of money to the woman so that she could rehabilitate herself, and they would adopt the baby. They asked if it was permissible to do such a thing.

"The *rav* gave a *pesak* that not only was it permissible, it was recommended. If the mother could not take care of her baby, and the childless couple were willing to take care of her and bring her up, and even give the mother a sum of money for rehabilitation—then it was permissible and even desirable. And if this couple would act as intermediaries between the two, they would undoubtfully earn a big mitzvah. This is the story that the rabbi told my husband."

Mama burst into tears. "This could not have been about me," she said. "*Baruch Hashem*, I did not need a wheelchair; they 'only' amputated one arm — not two feet. And no one, no one in the world, paid me even one penny for my daughter. I would never have accepted such a thing, even if they had offered me a million dollars!"

"We should ask the *rav* how he gave a *pesak halachah* without hearing the other side, the mother's side of the story," said Nachman to his sister, Chana Malka. But she explained that the way Rabbi Shlomowitz told the story, there was no need for two sides. The people did not come to argue their case, but only to consult with the *rav* and get his stamp of approval.

Mama was very distressed after hearing the story, but Rivka was optimistic. She told Mama to see this as a lead. It was likely that the *rav* forgot the exact details of a story that took place years ago, and confused an amputated foot for an amputated arm. And as far as the money was concerned, that was suspicious and should be investigated. It was likely that the childless couple paid money, but the question is—where did the money go, as it certainly didn't go to Mama.

Edith, Mrs. Zinger's daughter, was older than me and Mama asked her if she knew of an adopted girl in her school. Edith didn't, but she said that she would try to inquire discreetly, without attracting attention, to find out if there was an adopted girl in any of the other classes.

"Perhaps Edith will turn up something," said Chana Malka Zinger as she encouraged Mama not to despair. Again, the light of hope burned brightly in Mama's life.

❦ 20 ❦
Anya Is Sick

[BUDAPEST]

WINTER HAS ARRIVED. It's been snowing non-stop for the past few days. I stood by the window and looked outside. I love watching the flakes of snow diving down and piling up; I think it's one of the loveliest sights that exist.

I looked up at the sky. It was completely dark, but countless white snowflakes were rapidly falling from the grey clouds and dancing in the wind until they dived down to earth. The trees and roofs are covered with white, pristine snow but on the road and sidewalks, the snow has already turned to muddied slush. I don't like looking down at the snow on the streets, I'd rather look upwards—to places where the snow is still pretty and pure, untouched by human hands.

Inside, the house was dark and sad. Anya was in bed, sick. The doctor came and prescribed medication for her; Apa went to the pharmacy and has not yet returned. It has been a long time, so I imagine that he went from there to work in his store and will come home with the medicines only after he closes up the store.

That made me angry. Anya was coughing a lot and groaning, and she seemed to be in a lot of pain; Apa should have come straight home to bring her the medicines.

I walked into Anya's room. She lay there with her eyes closed. A cup of tea that I had prepared for her a long time ago still rests on the cabinet, exactly as I left it there.

"Anya, please! Open your eyes!" I begged. She opened her eyes. "You must drink!" I said. I took the cup of tea and brought it to her mouth. Anya drank two sips and then signaled me with her hands that that was enough, and again sank back in the pillows and closed her eyes.

I stood next to her, at a loss for words, and then Anya was attacked by another severe coughing fit. I helped her pick up her head a bit and placed Apa's pillow behind her head, so that it would be easier for her when she coughed. Slowly the coughing fit subsided.

I went into my room and put on my boots and my warmest coat, covered my head and shoulders with Anya's scarf and went outside. I wanted to run to the store to take the medicines from Apa and bring them to Anya. But to my dismay, I could not run. The deep snow and slushy mush slowed me down considerably. I was also afraid of falling. So I stayed close to the walls of the houses.

"How silly of me!" I thought. "I thought it would take me five minutes to walk to the store and back and I didn't consider that on a snowy day, it would take a lot longer."

Finally, I reached the store. I pushed the door open and walked inside. Zaidy Feldman turned to me in confusion. "Where is Apa?" I asked quickly, without prefacing my words with all the polite introductions that the Feldmans like. Zaidy was taken aback and ignored my rudeness. "He didn't come to the store today," he whispered to me, like all the other adults have been doing lately.

"*Oy!*" I said. "He went to buy medicine for Anya and when

he didn't come back, I thought he came here to the store. So I came to take the medicines from him."

Zaidy walked over to me, patted me gently, and asked me to go home. "Be careful not to slip and fall in the snow, and go straight home," he said. "It's a long distance to the pharmacy and since he had to walk, it is probably taking him longer than usual." I hadn't thought of that.

I barely said "goodbye" to Zaidy as I rushed out of the store. The more quickly I tried to walk, the more I slipped and slid, so I forced myself to go slowly, though it was very frustrating.

When I got home, Apa was already there. I went into my room to peel off my wet socks. They were soaking wet, despite the overshoes that I had put over my regular shoes before I left home. Apa came into my room. He was very angry at me that I had left my mother alone, and even angrier when I told him why I went to the store. "Is that what you think of me?" he asked. "Do you think I'm such a bad person?" I explained to him that I was just scared. "Anya was coughing terribly and I didn't know what to do!"

Apa sighed deeply, left my room and went to Anya. He pulled a chair up next to her bed and sat there, learning Gemara at her bedside.

The next day when I returned from school, the doctor was in the house again. He stood and whispered with Apa and when he saw me, he told me to go and tell Anya what happened in school that day.

Anya looked dreadfully pale as she lay there; her eyes seemed to have grown in her face. I sat next to her and started to talk to her, and I saw that my story did not seem to interest her at all. But the doctor had told me to talk to her, so I continued, until I saw that she closed her eyes. I continued to sit next to her, but I stopped talking.

That evening Bubby Shapiro came and sat next to my mother. Afterwards she got up, went to the other room and whispered with Apa. It seemed to me that you were not supposed to talk out loud in a house with a sick person. Everyone whispered in our house; even the doctor whispered to Apa. Whoever walked into the house, or even people who met me on the street, whispered, instead of speaking in their normal voice. Even Zaidy Feldman spoke to me in a whisper. But I did hear, among the whispers, the word "pneumonia." I'm not sure, but I think that's the name of Anya's illness.

The next morning, no one woke me up so I got up late. Nothing was ready; Apa must have forgotten to warm up my cup of milk and slice me some bread. Just like yesterday, pale Anya lay motionless all day and occasionally had terrible coughing fits.

I just didn't feel like going to school. I went back into my room, and Apa didn't seem to notice that I was still home.

In the afternoon, Bubby Shapiro came and sat by Anya. She tried to talk to her, but Anya didn't answer. Then Bubby Shapiro went into the room where Apa sat on his armchair and napped. She woke him up, and then whispered to him.

Apa left again to get the doctor. Basya Leah also arrived, peeked into Anya's room, and then headed straight for the kitchen to start cooking. I went to help her. "Didn't you go to school today?" she asked in a normal voice, without whispering. I shook my head no, and Basya Leah didn't ask me any more questions. She worked so quickly! She cut up vegetables, cleaned a chicken that she had brought with her, placed it in a pot, and then added water and spices.

Then Bubby Shapiro came into the kitchen. Bubby said that she would finish the cooking, so that Basya Leah could go home and take care of her children. Basya Leah didn't argue. She put on her coat over her apron, wrapped the large scarf around her head and left.

Bubby Shapiro sat down next to Anya's bed and fed her chicken soup by spoonfuls, as slowly as one feeds a baby. With each spoonful Bubby cajoled her, "Eat, Mintzi, you must eat; it's chicken soup! A tablespoon of life. Eat, eat!" Anya ate so slowly that it took a long time until she finished the small amount of soup in the bowl. Bubby heaved a sigh of relief. "As if you crossed the Sambatyon river!" she declared. She smiled broadly and looking quite proud of herself, Bubby announced that she would come again in the evening to feed Anya another bowl of healthy soup.

The days passed, and there was no progress. Despite numerous doctor visits and the medicines he prescribed, despite the healthy chicken soup—everyone continued to whisper. Anya did not speak and spent most of the time lying in bed with her eyes closed. When I sat next to her and tearfully begged her to open her eyes and look at me, she did — but for a very short time. Bubby explained to me that Anya did not have strength to keep her eyes open.

Do you need strength to keep your eyes open?

When I lay in bed, I tried to see how much effort you need. I opened and closed my eyes slowly and quickly, and it did not take any effort at all! So why do they tell me that Anya doesn't have strength to open her eyes, if you don't need strength for this? I didn't understand. Everyone whispered ceaselessly, but no one let me in on their secrets.

In the evenings, I went with Bubby Shapiro to sleep at her house and I returned home in the morning. Sometimes I went to school, but I didn't feel like studying. No one paid attention to me or asked me anything. No one was interested in me.

Mrs. Kantzuk came upstairs to clean our apartment and succeeded in annoying Bubby. She was always loud and noisy when she cleaned, and this time was worse than usual. She had much advice about what to do for a sick person, how to take care of the patient, and mainly—what not to do. And everything that she said, she said very loudly.

Bubby Feldman sent us her maid one day so that she could clean and cook for us. But we can't expect this again from Bubby Feldman. At her age, it is hard for her to give up her maid.

Finally, the grown-ups decided to bring a young girl to live with us. She would take care of me and the light household duties — just as Bezhee used to do. The girl—her name is Briendy—came from one of the suburbs of Budapest and brought with her happiness and a smile to our sad family. Because of her, the entire household changed.

The morning after Briendy arrived, she went with me to school and explained the situation at home to the teacher. The teacher promised her she would help me make up my schoolwork, and gave Briendy all the homework that I'd missed. It's true that my friend Perry came over to visit me twice since Anya got sick but when she saw that I wasn't in the mood, she stopped coming. So I never got my homework.

Since Briendy couldn't help me make up my work, Basya Leah — who came every day to visit Anya — sent her daughter Reizy to study with me. After a few days with Reizy, I was caught up on my schoolwork and homework and was no longer afraid to go back to school. At first I skipped school because of Anya's illness, as I didn't want to leave her home alone. Then afterwards I was afraid to go because I had missed so much material, and I was worried that I wouldn't understand anything. Now I was up-to-date, I could return to school.

It was the first night of Chanukah.

Apa prepared the Chanukah menorah between the hall

and my parent's room. Every year, he set up menorah between the dining room and the guest room, but this time, because of Anya's illness, Apa changed its placement. He explained to me that it wasn't really important where the menorah was, as long as it stands opposite a mezuzah.

In honor of the candle-lighting, Anya sat up in bed and Briendy dressed her in her Shabbos dress and placed her white mesh scarf on her head. Since she got sick, I had never seen her dressed — she wore her nightgown all day. Even when she lit Shabbos candles during those weeks (with Apa's help) she did not put on a dress, she only changed her scarf.

Now, when I saw her dressed in her Shabbos dress, I had to contain myself from bursting into tears. She looked terrible! Anya had never been fat, but she was never thin either, and now the dress hung on her. For the first time, I noticed how much weight she had lost.

The winter was difficult and passed very slowly. Anya was sick in bed, Apa and Bubby took care of her, and the days just seemed to get longer and longer.

❦ 21 ❧
A Fertile Imagination
[BUDAPEST]

TIME PASSED, and Purim was around the corner. *Baruch Hashem*, Anya completely recovered and even decided that she was ready to bake the traditional apple and nut strudels she always made for Purim. Briendy worked with her — Briendy did most of the work. Anya made a lot of noise and tumult as she worked, while Briendy worked quietly, with a smile on her face. But all that wasn't important—the important thing was that Anya had gotten better! She was healthy, though still weak and very thin.

Bubby Shapiro assured me that Anya would regain all her strength by Pesach. Bubby always said that my mother got better because of the tearful *Avinu Malkeinu* that I davened in front of the *aron ha-kodesh* in the men's section, when Anya was very sick. It was Bubby who had thought of that idea and put me there. "Leichu's tears simply penetrated the gates of Heaven," Bubby used to say. She didn't mention how much she herself davened. She had said *Tehillim* all the time, tears running down her cheeks, and had also given a lot of *tzedakah*.

Apa also gave Rav Weissman a lot of money to distribute

to the needy—much more than he usually gave, and Apa was considered to be a *"ba'al tzedakah"* who always pitched in when there was a need. I even donated my savings so that he could give it to Rav Weissman to give to poor people.

Zaidy Shapiro traveled to Czechoslovakia to the city of Pressburg where he had learned, and also to the Vizhnitzer Rebbe. All the *tzaddikim* blessed Anya that she should get well.

I don't know how Bezhee found out about Anya's illness, but one day she came to visit Anya. Bezhee told her that she had gone to the cemetery of her town and prayed for Anya'a health at the graveside of a great *tzaddik*, and had lit a candle in Anya's merit.

They prayed for Anya in so many places! They davened in the yeshiva of Bácsi Aharon Dovid, Basya Leah's husband; in the shul of Bácsi Sholom Ber Shapiro; and in the shul of Bácsi Boruch Mordche Shapiro. Everyone prayed for her speedy recovery and after she did recover, they all came to tell us how they had prayed for her, given *tzedakah*, lit candles, gone to their Rebbes for a *berachah*, and everything else you are supposed to do under the circumstances. To me it seemed that all of Budapest prayed for her recovery and the prayers truly helped! The *Ribbono shel Olam* performed a miracle, and Anya is on her feet today making strudels.

Apa and I were happy when, before Pesach, Anya announced that she was completely well and even wanted to invite guests for Yom Tov. So she invited Apa's brother, Srul Ber, and his family for Pesach.

Immediately I announced that I would go with Briendy to her family, and would celebrate Pesach with them.

This announcement was not exactly well received by my parents. "Where did you ever get such an idea? To go away for Pesach? It's out of the question!"

No amount of tears or pleading could change their mind. My parents would not allow me to go with Briendy under any circumstances. So I raised an even more original idea: "I will go to Bezhee and help her." But Anya said that Bezhee was going to her parents and would remain with them until after giving birth, and I would only be in the way there.

Then Anya sat down next to me and tried to encourage me to open up. "Why do you want to leave home? Are you unhappy? What's wrong?"

I explained to her that I was happy at home, but I was worried about Bácsi Srul Ber and his family. Anya tried to calm me by saying that Srul Ber was like Apa in appearance as well as temperament, and since I wasn't afraid of my own father I had nothing to fear from his brother.

At this point I could not restrain myself any longer and I reminded her of Néni Eva, my father's sister, and how she had tormented me.

"Srul Ber is a good-hearted man, not like his sister Eva. He was never involved in the 'affair'!" Anya assured me. But no matter how I begged her, she refused to explain anything to me about the reference to the "affair" that had evidently slipped out of her mouth. She only promised me over and over that the visit would be peaceful and happy.

At night, I overheard her relating the whole conversation to Apa. In the middle she started to cry and shouted, "She will ruin everything, because of her they'll take the child away from me!" and she started to weep.

I didn't understand a thing. I would never let anyone take me away! And who would take me—Eva? Anya had no need to fear; I would never agree to go anywhere with that woman. Maybe Anya was just overly sensitive because of her illness. I guess I shouldn't have reminded her about Eva; but then again, she shouldn't have gotten so agitated. I promised myself that in the morning, I would talk it over with her and calm her down.

In the morning, when I went to talk to my mother, she looked at me strangely. "Me, crying? You are mistaken, Leichu. You must have had a bad dream."

I was sure that I hadn't dreamed it. I had been completely awake and heard the cries and shouts. I heard how Apa calmed her down; though I couldn't hear his words, since he spoke quietly, I heard his soothing voice clearly.

This was a real mystery. Why did Anya cry that she would not give me up? And why did she deny ever saying that? Who could help me decipher the riddle?

Immediately I thought of Reizy and Suri, Basya Leah's daughters. They are older and wiser; they would help me. I memorized the details so that I would not forget what had happened until my next visit with them.

Erev Pesach was a very busy time with a lot of work. A day before *bedikas chametz*, Briendy went to her parents. I was terribly sad to see her go. But that evening, I helped Apa check for *chametz*. He let me hold the candle and I hinted to him where each newspaper-wrapped breadcrumb was hidden.

The guests arrived in the morning: Bácsi Srul Bar, Néni Gitu and their adorable children: Luli and Leibele. I was delighted to have younger children around to play with.

Néni Gitu even brought me a gift—a wonderful set of colored pencils, the very same set that I had seen in the Kohinoor shop in the center of Budapest. Every time we passed that store, I would gaze longingly at that fancy set in the store window front. But since I had so many sets of crayons and coloring supplies, I never dared ask Anya for these, yet here was Aunt Gitu who bought me this magnificent set, as if she had read my mind.

She brought a large shawl for Anya — it covered her whole back. She had knitted a very complicated pattern, and it looked like she had spent many hours making it. When Anya told her that she needn't have worked so hard and brought such expensive gifts, Néni Gitu said that after such a difficult illness, she absolutely had to wear the shawl so that she shouldn't catch cold, *chas v'shalom*. And Anya told her that she shouldn't have spent so much money on such fancy colored pencils, since I have plenty of others, but Gitu only laughed.

She said that she remembered standing in front of the window of the stationery store when she was my age, gazing longingly at the exact same set, even though she, too, had a box full of coloring supplies. Then she turned to me and asked me whether I had ever pressed my nose against the glass admiring those colored pencils. I admitted that I had done this many times, and then she turned to Anya jubilantly and said, "You see? I knew it! Children are the same in every generation!" and we all laughed.

Gitu spoke in a loud, jolly tone of voice, trumpeting her words to everyone. This was the way she always spoke. She was so kind that everyone loved her, despite her boisterousness. Even Bubby Feldman, who was super-meticulous about "minding our manners," forgave Gitu and accepted her as she was.

For the first Seder, Bubby and Zaidy Feldman came to us and for the second Seder, we all went to them. And both Seders went as smoothly as possible.

It was during Chol HaMoed, when we were with Bubby and Zaidy Shapiro, that I decided to talk to Suri and Reizy. I took them out to the small porch that was far away from the guest room, and told them about Anya's tearful shouts.

I watched them carefully as I spoke and noticed that they

were flashing each other messages with their eyes. Then they both quickly said that I must have dreamed it, the same as my mother had told me. I was sure that they were hiding something, and I wouldn't let up. "I know there's something you're not telling me. Everyone is always keeping secrets from me!" I implored.

But they brushed me off. "Secrets? Is that one of your ideas?" they joked. "Maybe you should write a book about your secret!" They both laughed and I felt humiliated. I had trusted them so much, I had been so sure that they would explain everything to me, but they had disappointed me. Now I was sure there was a secret and even Suri and Reizy knew about it. I was the only one left out.

I started torturing myself with questions again: Was it possible to take me away from Anya? What were her screams about? Why does everyone tell me that my questions are silly?

Even jolly Néni Gitu looked at me strangely — when I asked her about the secret —and said that I was talking nonsense. If I continue to fill my head with imaginary stories, she said, I would have no room for anything else and I might even fail in my studies.

So who is right? My inner feelings, or all the others who tell me that I have an overactive imagination?

After Pesach, Briendy came back full of wonderful news from her town. When I told her about the secret that no one was willing to share with me, she looked at me and burst into laughter. "Leichu, you're amazing. This would make a great mystery story; let's write a book together!" She tried to stifle her giggle and said, "What an imagination you have! It's a thousand times better than all the books in the world!"

Briendy's sincere laughter was what ultimately consoled me, as I realized that I really did sound silly. Everyone was probably laughing at me. At least Briendy was genuine and laughed in front of me, and not behind my back.

❧ 22 ❧
Don't Give Up!
[SEVLUS]

DESPITE THE ZINGERS' immeasurable good will and despite the countless letters that went back and forth, there was no progress at all.

Slowly but surely, the light at the end of the tunnel began to dim for Mama until it became a tiny, flickering and remote spot. Night after night, Mama would sit opposite the window and fix her gaze on the heavens. When she could see stars, she would wonder: Was her Leichu also gazing at those same stars? Was she, too, hoping to find her own bright star, shining a light of hope just for her? She would try to imagine what I looked like, how I was dressed. Hardest of all were the worrisome thoughts: Was I being treated properly, or had I possibly been turned into a servant in some terrible, violent family?

If the night was cloudy and rainy, Mama would compete with the clouds: her tears versus rain from the clouds. Yes, every night Mama sat opposite the window with a broken heart. And every night she went to sleep with the words of her prayers emanating from the depths of her heart, the loving and sorrowful heart of a mother. And always, always she was comforted by her davening.

She was sure that her Father in Heaven, her Father as well as the Father of her orphaned daughter, listened to her prayers. Everything He did, was for the best. It would turn out to be for the best; some day, some day, she would be consoled.

The neighbors did their best to encourage Mama. Whenever they visited her store, they always spoke encouraging words to her, hopeful words — telling her not to despair of finding her lost daughter, and they always expressed their admiration of her — a woman who managed to maintain a clean, orderly home and store with only one hand.

Mama had, indeed, acquired all kinds of short-cuts and solutions in carrying out her various tasks with one hand and the use of her feet. No one saw how she worked, as she always locked the door of the store first, for reasons of modesty. The people who entered her store always saw a woman standing erect with her head held high and a gracious smile on her lips. Every single customer had a good word for Mama; those who didn't know her and her tragic story thought she was a happy woman. They barely noticed the empty sleeve that was neatly pinned to her blouse, because she served her customers quickly and energetically. It is no wonder that all her neighbors and acquaintances liked her so much.

Mama only allowed herself to speak freely with Néni Rivka Klar. Only Rivka heard about the letters, the disappointments and the nights laden with longing and tears. Rivka was a wise woman and never told Sheina Ruchel not to cry; she knew that she was Mama's truest and closest friend. Where else could Mama let her guard down and vent her troubles, if not in Néni Rivka's house? Rivka strengthened Mama by telling her, "Continue to daven; *HaKadosh Baruch Hu* hears your prayers and sees your tears."

One day, Mama decided she would travel to Budapest herself. This was a difficult decision because she was afraid to close the store. In her absence, her customers were liable to take their business elsewhere, and then when she came back she would have lost her livelihood.

Mama did not have to worry, though. Her devoted neighbors devised a plan to help her: They would take turns running the store! Each day, another neighbor would open the store. Mama never forgot the *chesed* of those devoted women, women whose lives were not easy either.

Housework in that time and place was very difficult. The rural women in those days had to draw water from a well, and the people who had wells in their backyards were considered lucky. The less fortunate ones were forced to wait on line at the central well in their neighborhood, and then carry heavy buckets of water home.

The women did their laundry by hand: They vigorously rubbed and wrung out each article of clothing. They baked their own bread and cooked their own jam. They even prepared their own noodles. Summertime was especially busy because that was when they prepared sauerkraut (pickled cabbage) and many other vegetables for the long winter, and packed the goods carefully in their cellars.

If you wanted to drink milk, you had to travel out of town to the local cowshed and supervise the milking in the early morning hours; otherwise the milk was *chalav akum* and forbidden to drink. Then you had to carry the milk home. Many housewives would prepare cheeses and butter from their *chalav yisrael* milk, all by hand with only simple kitchen utensils and no electrical appliances at all.

The wooden floors in the houses needed to be polished regularly. Aside from all that, most of the women sewed their children's clothes at home, and some of them sewed clothes for the adults as well. Some were fortunate to have sewing machines—the kinds that were powered by a foot pedal, not electricity—while the others patiently sewed tiny, dainty stitches by hand.

Despite all the hard work that these women had to do at home, they gladly volunteered to help Mama keep her store open when she went to Budapest.

ᘓ   ᘓ   ᘓ

Mama went straight to the Zinger family in Budapest. Reb Shia Zinger brought Mama to visit Rav Shlomowitz — who was happy to see Mama looking so well, walking on her own two feet and not sitting in a wheelchair. Again, the Rav told his story. He couldn't remember exactly whether he had been told about a hand or foot that was amputated, but he did remember that he had ruled that it was great mitzvah to give up the baby for adoption, because he did not imagine that this was being done without the mother's agreement. "On the contrary," he said apologetically, "I thought that the child's mother was the one who had sent them for a *berachah*, to verify that adoption was the right thing to do." Mama could not contain herself any longer and burst into tears. The Rebbetzin quickly brought her a cup of tea and begged her to drink.

The Rav and Reb Shia Zinger spent many months searching for the young couple who had served as intermediaries in the adoption. Through their inquiries, they found out that the couple had left Budapest; rumor had it that they left for a nearby country, perhaps Czechoslovakia or Rumania, and some even said that they emigrated to the United States. Rav Shlomowitz believed that the couple probably received some of the money, while Tatte's relatives, the Goldmans, took the rest. The Rav described his efforts to talk with them, and how they denied everything.

Mama wanted to visit the Goldmans again, but she didn't want to go alone. She remembered her last visit to them, when they called her "crazy" and "insane" and refused to tell her anything. She asked the Rav to set up a meeting with the Goldmans, hoping his presence would change their attitude. Rav Shlomowitz, however, told Mama that they would only repeat that they don't know anything and there was no point in "reopening old wounds."

Mama also went to Rav Weissman together with Chana Malka Zinger. He, too, could not help; he claimed that he knew nothing.

Mama went to my school that week and scrutinized all the girls as they walked out of the building. Mama felt certain that she would recognize me—that's what she said—even though she had last seen me when I was only six months old. And she was sure that she did not see me because I was not there.

After a week, Mama realized that she was not accomplishing anything in Budapest, despite the comforting words of the Zinger family and even the encouragement of Rav Shlomowitz and his Rebbetzin. No, Mama said, she was not giving up; she would just change her tactics.

She told Chana Malka Zinger that she would return to Budapest in a few months, but she would do so secretly, without telling anyone or speaking with a rabbi. She would try to change her appearance, perhaps wear a wig, and then go to the schools again and look for her daughter among the girls. The family that was holding her daughter would not know of her arrival and so would not keep her home from school. Thus she had a better chance, *be'ezras Hashem*, of tracking me down.

With an aching heart, Mama sadly returned to Sevlus, but

when she saw the devotion of her neighbors who had taken her place in the store, she was encouraged.

Her Father in Heaven would help her find her daughter. She was certain of that.

❧ 23 ❧
The Circus

ONE COLD WINTER day I stood near the window, looking outside and letting my thoughts wander. Soon Apa will come home and take me, together with Briendy, to Bubby Shapiro. My parents are going to Carlsbad where there are medicinal sulfur springs.

It's been a year already since Anya got sick and she is still very weak, pale and thin. She always says that something good came out of her illness — she is finally thin and doesn't need to worry about her weight. I think that she just says that to make us feel better. She is really weak, and the doctor suggested that she go to the special springs in the Carlsbad Spa (also known as Karlovy Vary) despite the cold.

I didn't want to show Anya how thrilled I was to go to Bubby because I was afraid I would hurt her feelings, but I was truly happy. Our house was much too quiet. I was not allowed to bring friends over because the noise bothered Anya, and she didn't allow me to go to my friends' houses either because she worried about me. She had gotten even more overprotective since her illness, and I felt hemmed in on all sides. I spent most of my time at home, and once in a

129

while my mother would call me to her room to see me. We would just exchange a few words, then she would send me back to my room. She only wanted to see me, she didn't want to speak to me or hear about my life or activities in school.

The house was hot, even overheated, and quiet—quiet and sad, and lonely.

But I was always happy at Bubby's home! The best part was that I could always run over to Basya Leah and play with her children. I was also sure that Bubby would let me go outside to play and run around. I was a quiet child, neither mischievous nor noisy, but the terrible stillness and loneliness at home made me yearn for some tumult and laughter.

I think that Anya sensed my excitement though, because she asked me if I was happy to leave her. I had to lie to her over and over that of course I wanted to be with her. I told her that I would miss her terribly, but I promised not to cry and to behave like a big girl. But inside in my heart of hearts, I was happy that they weren't taking me to some faraway place where they send weak people who are recuperating from difficult diseases and need the hot springs. I imagined that it would be deathly quiet so as not to bother the patients.

But Anya had gotten so terribly sensitive. I didn't want to hurt her, so I never told her what I was really thinking.

૭ﻭ   ૭ﻭ   ૭ﻭ

When I stayed with Bubby, Briendy accompanied me on the long walk to school every day and came to pick me up at the end of the school day. Since I was only staying at Bubby's temporarily, I didn't transfer to my cousins' school, even though it was much closer. Bubby waited for me by the window and waved to me happily when she saw me approaching.

After having lunch and doing my homework I was free as a bird: I could go outside to play with the neighbors' children or go visit Basya Leah and her children. And every few days, Briendy took me to the frozen river to go ice-skating. I loved ice-skating, but I hadn't gone skating since Anya's illness. She had become so overprotective and wouldn't permit me to skate anymore. Briendy was a great skater, much better than I, because her village on the outskirts of Budapest was on the very bank of the river. All the children in her town skated on the frozen river at every possible opportunity in the winter: even on their way to school, to the store, to the cowshed. So everyone in her town learned to skate from an early age.

When you skate, each foot creates a groove in the ice. The grooves I made never came out perfectly straight. No matter how hard I tried, they always were wavy, curving this way and that. But Briendy made straight, neat furrows or alternately, perfectly round ones. Even her figure-eights came out perfectly! I tried so hard to imitate her, but without success. Every time I told Bubby about this, she would laugh and promise me that if I persevered, I would eventually succeed. Finally, Basya Leah told me that when Bubby was my age, she won the ice-skating competitions every single year!

Sunday. Zaidy and Bubby went for two or three days to visit Néni Freidy, Bubby's sister who lives on the other side of Budapest in the distant suburbs. Néni Freidy is much older than Bubby, and weak and old. It was a long trip and my grandparents found it too hard to travel both ways in one day, so they went for two or even three days at a time. I went to stay at Néni Basya Leah's house.

In the morning, I said goodbye to Zaidy and Bubby. On our way to school, Briendy confided in me that she was very happy that Zaidy and Bubby were going away for a few days so that she and Basya Leah could surprise them afterwards. They had decided to clean Zaidy and Bubby's house from top to bottom, just like we do for Pesach! Briendy loved Bubby so much that she called her "Bubby," and not "Mrs. Shapiro" or even "Néni Shapiro" as was expected. She simply decided that Bubby could be her grandmother as well, and Bubby was happy to have another granddaughter and treated her accordingly.

I promised Briendy that I knew the way from school to Basya Leah's house. I could walk by myself, carefully of course, so that she wouldn't have to leave her work in the middle to pick me up. Briendy promised me that if she and Basya Leah managed to finish their cleaning project in two days, then she would take me on the afternoon of the third day to the Gypsy Circus that had come to town. The Gypsy Circus! I didn't want to miss this treat! I immediately offered my help. When I came home, ready to work, Briendy and Basya Leah told me that I would be in charge of watching the little kids, while Suri or Reizy would give them a hand in the cleaning. And the truth is, I don't know how to clean at all; I've been so spoiled at home that I've never had to lift a finger. Once or twice I washed the *milchig* dishes, and Anya made such a big deal about it, you would have thought I'd built a skyscraper!

On Tuesday afternoon, Briendy finished the cleaning project and we were off to the circus. Néni Basya Leah would not send her daughters with us, and I thought it was because the circus was too expensive. I told her that Anya had given Briendy money for the tickets — including tickets for her daughters — but Basya Leah said that this was just one of the differences of opinion she had with my mother. She felt that Jewish girls had no place in a circus.

So Briendy and I went alone. We wore pretty outfits and skipped happily to the city park where the colorful circus was located. When we were finally inside, we saw Rav Weissman's daughters among the stands. "You see," said Briendy, "even

Rav Weissman lets his daughters go to the circus."

The three girls sat behind us. I turned around and saw them, and suddenly one of them, Miri, looked straight at me and stuck her tongue out.

I turned forward again and resolved to ignore them. It was then that I heard her whispering to her sisters in a hushed yet clear voice:

"That's Leichu, the Feldmans' adopted daughter."

I froze. Then I heard her sister answer, "She and the Feldmans act as if she is really their daughter, as if they didn't buy her when she was a baby."

Those were the exact words. Those words echo in my ears to this very day. The scene is etched in my mind: the exact words, the sisters' tone of voice, even the older sister telling the other two to be quiet and stop talking about such things — I remember it all exactly!

I hastily turned to Briendy but she was busy arranging our coats on the seats. She did not show any reaction as she sat down. I wanted to ask her if she had heard what they said, but I could not utter a sound. I felt the blood rise to my head and my face turn red. Then there was a muscle spasm in my throat, and it became hard to breathe.

The lights in the big circus tent dimmed, but I was oblivious to my surroundings.

"That's Leichu, the Feldman's adopted daughter"— those words floated before my eyes and echoed in my ears incessantly.

Briendy enjoyed the performance; she laughed out loud and paid no attention to me. At first I tried to say something to her and attract her attention, but without success. Afterwards I was happy that she didn't notice me.

The tears welled up in my eyes but I remained firm. I

would not cry! I won't let them know that I heard!

There was so much noise in the circus tent that no one heard the pounding of my heart in my chest. No one saw how I pinched my hand until it bled, to keep from crying, or how I bit my lips until they turned blue. I wanted it all to be over, I wanted to get out of that horrible place. On the other hand, I knew I wouldn't have the strength to stand up — I needed time to calm my turbulent emotions.

It was only when the performance was over, when the lights went back on, that Briendy turned to look at me. She gasped, seeing how terrible I looked. "Leichu, what's the matter? Did the lions frighten you?" she asked. I just nodded my head. I still could not speak.

Briendy stood up and started giving me a speech, telling me why there was no need to be frightened. I didn't answer her, I just tugged on her hand. I wanted to leave that dreadful place as quickly as possible.

I ran the whole way home. Briendy did not stop trying to explain to me why there was no reason to panic, no point in running, the lions were not chasing us. She did not at all understand why I pulled her hand and forced her to run with me.

When we arrived, Zaidy and Bubby were home already. I fell into Bubby's arms and burst out in tears. Briendy told her that I was scared of the lions and I didn't bother to correct her. Bubby hugged me tightly and said, "Basya Leah is right; a circus is appropriate for coarse *goyish* girls, but not delicate Jewish ones."

I could not fall asleep that night. I heard those painful words reverberating in my head over and over again: "The Feldmans' adopted daughter... she's adopted, adopted, adopted."

When I got up the next morning, my eyes were red and

my head hurt. Bubby thought I was sick and wanted to keep me at home, but I insisted on going to school.

In class I asked Perry, "How do people adopt children?" Perry had no idea, though. She said she didn't know any adopted children.

I wanted to shout at her: Look at me, I'm adopted! But just then the teacher looked at us reprovingly and said, "No talking in class."

What a miracle that I didn't spill my secret! It's forbidden to tell her; people don't talk about such things. If Perry says that she doesn't know any adopted children, that means that she doesn't know that I'm adopted. Better that she shouldn't know; perhaps she won't want to have anything to do with me if she should find out.

❀ 24 ❀
The Thorny Garden
[BUDAPEST]

N O ONE UNDERSTOOD what had happened to me. I
had suddenly turned into a quiet, introverted girl
who no longer wanted to run around or play games
or even go skating. I just sat and waited for the day to pass.

Bubby thought that I was lonesome for Anya and I didn't
confirm or deny her theory. I didn't want to talk or even
to study. I didn't listen in class or prepare my homework.
Briendy couldn't interest me in her stories and even Suri and
Reizy, who tried to help me with my studies, did not succeed.
I didn't want to think, to listen, or to speak.

Anya returned. She raced into the house with a cheerful shout, ran to me, enveloped me in a big hug and started
to kiss me. "Leichu, my darling Leichu!" she cried between
kisses. "How I've missed you! I've waited so long for this moment, to hug you in my arms."

And I, embraced in her arms, clung to her and cried.

Anya looked wonderful. The color had returned to her
cheeks, the sparkle to her eyes, and she was no longer so terribly thin. Two months of vacation with Apa in the springs
and she had recovered; she looked even better than before

her illness. Even Apa glowed. The vacation had done both of them good. I was the one who had lost weight and become pale. Everyone thought that it was just homesickness and now that my parents had returned, I would become the old Leichu again.

Every time that Apa and Anya called me "my daughter," or "my child," I thought to myself: Am I really their daughter? Your daughter—that you bore or that you bought?

I knew that they both loved me, but I was tortured by the following thought: If adoptive parents love so much, then how much do real parents love?

I thought about my real parents through long sleepless nights. What happened to them? Why did they sell me? Did they really sell me? Did they really get money for me? I once read that slaves were sold in the slave market. But I am not a slave, I grew up like a princess! It makes no sense that Apa and Anya paid money for me, that they bought me. I don't even do any housework; on the contrary, they are always doing things for me. Maybe they were wrong, the rabbi's daughters, about the money. But they were right on the mark about the adoption. For some reason, I am sure about that. It is true: I am, indeed, adopted.

But the idea of the money issue tortured me, as did thinking about my real parents, and the reasons that they gave me up for adoption. I became very serious and very sad. Anya pleaded with me constantly to cheer up, to become the Leichu I once was, but to no avail.

Anya took me to a doctor; perhaps I had some kind of hidden illness. The doctor checked me out thoroughly but didn't find a thing. When Anya left the room to talk to the nurse about some tests that the doctor suggested, the doctor sat down to talk to me. He crossed his arms and looked into my eyes. "What is bothering you, Leichu? Has something terrible happened to you?"

I told him that I had simply grown up, but that didn't satisfy him.

"I've discovered that the world is not the lush, flowering garden I thought it was," I told him. "The world is full of thorns and thistles, and if there are some flowers, they are hidden and surrounded by lots of thorns."

The doctor looked at me and said, "You're right, the world is not full of flowers exclusively; there are many thorns. For this reason, I advise you to study and learn as much as you can. Studies create a path in the thorns, and the paths will help you to navigate your way through the garden of life without getting pricked too much."

I took the doctor's words at face value and threw myself into my schoolwork. I quickly made up the work I had missed and began studying seriously. At home, I asked for extra lessons. In addition to studying Chumash and *tefillos* at school, I wanted to learn the modern Hebrew language — as it was spoken in Eretz Yisrael. Sarah, a young lady who had lived in Palestine for a number of years and had returned to Hungary to care for her ailing parents, came to teach me how to speak and write Hebrew. I enjoyed Sarah's company and the studies — even though learning Hebrew came along with a lot of hard work.

Anya suggested that I study Romanian or Czech, but I wanted to study Yiddish. After days of begging, Anya finally agreed to hire an additional private teacher to teach me Yiddish. But when Briendy heard about this, she said that she could teach me Yiddish! She started with teaching me nouns, then slowly progressed to sentences and finally, entire conversations. I was a good student and after I learned to speak, she taught me how to read and write a little.

I became an outstanding student in class as well as in my

private lessons. I threw myself completely into my studies and blocked everything else out of my head. Meanwhile, Briendy sat and studied with me. Ostensibly, she was supposed to be helping me, but in fact she was also learning. She spoke fluent Yiddish, but she learned writing, grammar and literature with me and we would do our homework exercises together. In exchange, I asked her to teach me to bake cakes and eventually, to cook. I need to learn how to do everything! To pave roads in the thorny garden! Who knows who my real parents are? I want them to like me, if and when we ever meet.

I could not change my external appearance, and perhaps that was for the best. Perhaps I resemble my parents, or brothers and sisters. But I must do my best to study and excel, to run a household, to be confident in myself. I want my family to like me, to want me.

Perhaps it's better that I am not with them? I have no peace from this nagging thought. Why did they give me up for adoption? Did they really get money in exchange? Perhaps they were so poor that they had no food and almost died of hunger, and decided that it was better for me to live so they sold me? And if so, then the money they received in exchange helped them to remain alive.

Every day—the same thoughts; every night—the same worries. I did not stop thinking about my plight. Whose daughter am I? What does my real family look like? Do my parents have any other daughters or sons? Were there other children who were given up for adoption?

At school, I closely scrutinized all the older girls; was there someone who resembled me? I also checked the younger girls as well.

On the street I looked at the peddlers and the beggars. Were these my parents? Maybe the beggar who came to my parents' house was really my father, and came to see me and not really to beg?

When I visited my friends I looked at their maids; the Mermelsteins' elderly maid looks a bit like me. Her eyes are green, just like mine! And what about the nanny in my friend Mari's house? Maybe she is really my sister? Her hair is the exact same color and texture as mine.

I even noticed a maid with an artificial hand standing at the front door of my school, evidently waiting for one of the girls. I scrutinized her, as well. Perhaps she was the one? She was very thin, but maybe I resembled her. I actually thought that I resembled her, and went past her three times. She did turn to look briefly at me, but she did not recognize me at all. If she were my mother, she would certainly look closely at me and recognize me.

Wouldn't she?

One day Apa came home in the middle of the day when I was studying with Sarah, my Hebrew teacher. He stood by the door and when the class was over, he took out his wallet, paid Sarah and said to her, "This is your last class, Leichu knows enough Hebrew. Please don't come anymore." And I really only knew a little because although Sarah told me about Eretz Yisrael, the kibbutz and all kinds of strange things, she taught me very little Hebrew itself.

After she left, Apa exploded in anger — which was very uncharacteristic of him. "This *chalutzka* worked in our house?" he yelled at me and at Anya. "Should I support a heretic non-believer? Someone like her was teaching Leichu — in our very house!?"

His anger was real, and Anya did not dare say a word. Sarah did not dress like a *bas Yisrael* should, and she raised all sorts of new ideas in her lessons, things I had never heard before. All that, however, was just chatter — she did not try to influence me toward her "enlightened" lifestyle. I was prepared to learn the language from her and nothing else. My head was filled with thoughts of the adoption and had no room for anything but that and my studies. So I didn't really understand Apa's anger. I didn't understand why he couldn't have simply asked her to come dressed modestly. But Briendy justified Apa, so I kept quiet.

Apa suggested to me that instead of Hebrew I should learn how to sew. He would bring the choicest material from his store and would use his connections with seamstresses to find the best seamstress to teach me.

This made me very happy.

ℭ   ℭ   ℭ

On Chol HaMoed Pesach I was sitting with Bubby Shapiro in her house. Everyone else had gone — it was just the two of us together. Bubby was telling me hair-raising stories about blood libels.

"Bubby, why?" I asked, horrified. "Why do the *goyim* do such terrible things to us, why do they want to kill us?"

Bubby explained that the *goyim* are jealous of the Jews.

That made me laugh. "Most Jews are poor and miserable, why would anyone be jealous of them?" I asked.

Bubby said that their jealousy is not about material things, but about ethics and morals. All Jews do *chesed* with one another, and the ones who benefit from this are the ones who do *chesed*, not the ones who receive. Every act of giving and of *chesed* causes a Jew to become a better person, she said.

"So how can we do good deeds and *chesed*?" I asked. Bubby patiently explained that, for example, everyone is required to give charity — even the poor person who lives on charity must give to someone even poorer than him.

"And if a person has no money," I continued, "how can

he do *chesed*? It's not every day that you meet an old woman who needs help carrying her baskets."

"You can help a lost child find his way home," said Bubby. "You can return a lost object. Why, there are so many good deeds you can do; for example, raising an orphaned child— that's a big mitzvah."

Boom! I had heard it with my own ears. An orphaned child!

"Bubby, someone who raises an orphan adopts him?" I asked, trembling.

Bubby nodded her head. "Yes, people who raise an orphaned child — in effect they adopt him, and they become his parents."

I got up from my chair and approached the window. Outside, children were playing tag and several adults stood near the fence of the apartment buildings, talking among themselves. I called Bubby to come see who these people were, and asked whether she recognized them, or if she thought they might be coming to visit. As soon as she walked over to the window, I escaped to the big room.

So I am an orphan. My parents are not alive. They did not sell me, they simply died. That means that my parents were not bad people who sold their child for money; they simply do not exist. They're dead. Not among the living.

I was given up for adoption because I am an orphan. This news comforted me a great deal.

All the tension of the past few months dissipated, and I felt myself relaxing. No longer would I check all the poor people and beggars on the street. I simply did not have parents.

I went back into the room, and stood next to Bubby near the window. Suddenly I noticed that Bubby's garden was full of blossoming flowers. Small yellow flowers dotted the bushes that grew near the stone fence around the house. I knew those flowers let off a lovely aroma, and even though I could not possibly smell anything through a closed window, it seemed to me that the whisper of a pleasant evening scent did penetrate the room.

I hugged Bubby and burst out in laughter, freeing my pent-up emotions. My transition was very sudden. One minute I felt terrible, and the next moment I laughed. I was so happy that I was an orphan, strange as it sounds. Joy had replaced my depression, and I was suddenly aware of all the beauty and bounty around me. I had to give expression to my new-found happiness, and I turned to Bubby. "Bubby," I said, "the flowers are so lovely and they have such a sweet fragrance."

Bubby smiled and stroked me lovingly. After months of seeing me withdrawn and serious, she saw me smiling and happy. She couldn't have known that her very words had made me so happy, and not the spring in its flowering.

❧ 25 ❧
A Confidante
[BUDAPEST]

IT IS HOT OUTSIDE. I am sitting next to the sewing machine and nothing is coming out right. The thread keeps escaping from the eye of the needle; the elastic band that connects the wheels keeps shifting out of its course. I am so frustrated! I had to unstitch so many crooked seams that the material is stained with my tears.

Perry told me today that Serin, the most beautiful girl in our class, has a stepfather. She is orphaned from her real father — he died when Serin was a little girl, and her mother remarried. The man whom Serin calls "Apa" is not her real father, he "just" adopted her. Perry was aghast. "Can you imagine," she said, "an orphan! Adopted!"

"So what?" I said. "If she was a little girl then she doesn't even remember her real father, so her mother's husband is her father and that's all there is to it."

Perry looked at me in astonishment. "What are you talking about? Do you honestly think that it's so simple? Why, it's just awful!"

"Awful," I thought to myself. "Awful?"

"Listen, Leichu," explained Perry. "She doesn't even know

about all this. She thinks that he really is her father, the poor soul. She thinks that her two 'brothers' are really her brothers. And she is so pretty!"

"Perry, what do her looks have to do with all this?" I asked.

She didn't even bother to answer that one, she only repeated, "Can you imagine how awful? Just terrible!"

"You don't want to have anything to do with her because of this?" I asked, trying not to let her hear the fear in my voice.

"Well, it's not really that important, I suppose," Perry tossed her head. "After all, she's not my best friend anyway— you are, of course."

"And if she were a best friend," I persisted, "would it make a difference to you?" I tried to sound offhand, and not reveal my gnawing fear.

Perry simply answered that she had no idea, and changed the topic. And I was left with my worries. Would Perry, my closest friend, abandon me if she knew that I was an adopted orphan? Would she not want to be best friends with me anymore?

I had considered sharing my story with Perry, and only after much soul-searching had I decided that it would be best for me not to say those awful words, "orphan" and "adopted." It seemed to me that people just don't say those words out loud.

So, luckily, I hadn't shared my secret with Perry. When I saw how she reacted to Serin's family status, I realized that I couldn't tell her about myself. It seemed to scare her so; her words, "Just terrible!" reverberated in my mind. Why, she was liable to abandon me if she knew my secret, and I would be left without a best friend.

When Briendy came into my room later that day, she

found me crying over the sewing machine. I showed her my crooked seam and the way that the thread kept escaping the needle. She took my head in her hands and made me look straight at her. "Tell me, Leichu," she said gently, "what's wrong? What is the real reason for these tears?"

I told her about Serin, our classmate who was an adopted orphan.

Briendy didn't understand what the fuss was about. She explained to me that there are many cases in families where one parent dies and the spouse remarries; the second husband or wife adopts the children from the first marriage. Why, in some families there are even three types of children: the mother's children from her first marriage; the father's children from his first marriage; and the children from the second marriage. If the parents are wise and loving, then all the children love both parents and are secure in their new family.

"It is natural, and in fact a big mitzvah to raise an orphan as one's own," she explained. "It is not a shameful thing, and it is a pity that some insensitive people treat it like it is."

I yearned to tell her my secret; I wanted to talk to her about myself, but I simply could not utter a word. I wondered if Briendy knew about me; it appeared that she didn't. She was such an honest, straightforward person that if she knew, she would talk to me about it, now that I brought up the subject myself. But I, myself, just couldn't bring it up. I truly wanted to, but could not.

I was encouraged by Briendy's words, but it seemed to me that most people didn't share her honest, sensitive perspective. To most people, it seemed, "orphan" and "adopted" were shameful words. Every time I saw one of the Weissman girls, I avoided them. What if they were to tell other girls in my class? What would happen if my classmates found out that I was adopted? I saw how Perry, my best friend, had reacted. If one girl knew, she would tell the others and I would be left without friends. They would all talk about me and look at me. Every word I'd say, every movement of mine would go under their microscope of criticism.

But I felt that I absolutely had to tell someone. I didn't succeed with Briendy, and I knew that it was out of the question to bring it up to Anya and Apa. But I knew that before I exploded, I absolutely had to talk to someone who would truly understand me and not make fun of me.

I was to get my wish. The next morning, I complained about terrible stomach pains. Anya gave me some kind of bitter tea to drink and suggested that I stay home from school. Before I knew I was adopted, I had jumped at any chance to stay home from school. But after my personal earthquake — that was my private term for the big revelation — I did not particularly enjoy vacation days. School had become my life — I threw myself into my studies to forget everything else. This time, however, I was ready for a break and happy to remain at home.

I went back to sleep for a few hours. When I woke up, who did I see but Chungarabi washing clothes in the kitchen! I realized immediately that she was exactly the person I could confide in. I was so very happy to see her. And luckily, Anya wasn't home.

I sat next to Chungarabi and talked and talked, and as I talked I started to cry. At first the tears were silent, but then my sobbing became louder and louder. Chungarabi did not attempt to calm me down. She listened to me closely, and occasionally made sympathetic noises to show me that she was listening. Only after I finished speaking, and slowly stopped sobbing, Chungarabi got up from the low chair on which she sat and walked over to me. She raised my head and looked directly into my eyes. I stood up, and Chungarabi hugged me warmly. She did not say a word but as she hugged me, she swayed back and forth, as people do during davening. And thus, without uttering a sound, she comforted me as a mother would comfort her anguished child.

She opened her arms after some time had passed; the two of us stood facing one another. Chungarabi's clothes were wet from the laundry and my clothes were now wet as well. We stood there, looking at one another. Then Chungarabi raised her hands, stroked my head and said, "Leichu, it does not matter to me at all. I love you, and have always loved you and I continue to love you as you are, just as you are. Your status does not matter to me at all."

Those words were the very cure for my heartbroken soul, the words I had thirsted to hear. Chungarabi went back to sit on her low chair and continued to wash the clothes. She told me to please change my clothes and bring them to her to wash as well. "You shouldn't wear a wet dress," she said. When I asked why she could remain in wet clothes all day, she told me that she was used to it, but I wasn't and could catch a cold.

After I changed my clothes I returned to my place next to her, and then came the big surprise. "I am not surprised to hear that you are adopted," said Chungarabi slowly and quietly. "I think I always suspected something of the sort, because you are so different from the rest of the Feldmans, and even the Shapiros." Then she added, "I am happy that even though you know the truth now, you still continue to study so diligently."

I explained to her that once I saw how important it was to excel in my studies, and how much respect I receive from others as a result, I realized how important it was to continue. Chungarabi encouraged me. "You must continue to make an effort in your studies, as well as your sewing," she said. "You have good hands, your sewing is improving, and it's a shame to stop. And who knows when it will be useful to you—who knows what the future will bring!"

Yes, the best thing that has happened to me lately was that conversation with Chungarabi. It was exactly what I needed.

❧ 26 ☙
Flowering Bushes
and Flowing Tears
[Budapest]

THE SUMMER WAS especially hot. We were happy that vacation finally arrived. We had a full month of freedom from school, in addition to the three weeks of Pesach vacation.

But my parents didn't take me on vacation because the summer was peak season in Zaidy and Apa's store. Large numbers of tourists would come to Budapest from all the surrounding towns, and from outside Hungary as well, crowding the stores and making lots of purchases. Entire families used to come to Zaidy and Apa's clothing store and buy fabric and material for the whole year. Even Anya would help out in the store, and I stayed with Bubby Shapiro.

When Chungarabi came I stayed at home with her rather than going to Bubby. Of course, no one guessed the real reason that I stayed at home with her; they thought I stayed home to make sure she didn't steal anything.

That summer was when Chungarabi gave me the sad news. She told me that she and her husband were leaving Budapest.

"Until now, Eshto had work in the city," she explained. "In general, we are both unusual for gypsies; most gypsies like to wander — they don't stay in one place for long. We have been living here in Budapest for twelve years already, and we even live in a regular apartment — not a tent or caravan." Chungarabi stopped sadly. "Eshto is an expert builder and has been employed all these years by an important contractor who has been good to him, and paid him well. But now he's grown old and has given over the business to his son, who is the opposite of his father. Eshto can't work for him, and we must move."

I tried to catch my breath as sadness filled my heart. "I am so sorry to leave you!" she cried. "I love you and I will miss you, Leichu. But we have no choice. I promise that when we get settled—assuming we don't wander, but actually live in a set place—then I will be in touch with you to tell you where we are."

And that was the last time I saw Chungarabi for a long time. I missed her terribly.

ভ্ন   ভ্ন   ভ্ন

We had an interesting outing this week. Basya Leah's husband, Bácsi Aharon Dovid took his family and me to Margaret Island (Margitsziget). Bubby and Zaidy Shapiro also came along. We drove in a great big car until we reached the Danube River, and on the banks of the Danube, Bácsi Aharon Dovid hired a large motorboat. We cheered and giggled as we scampered into the boat. We had never done this before! The boat sailed slowly and peacefully, as we viewed the city of Budapest from the river.

We had walked on the bridges many times, and had always seen the river and its banks from above. Sitting in a boat in the midst of the river gave us a completely new perspective.

It was beautiful; both banks, Buda as well as Pest, were green and blooming. Within the green we could see large and small houses, magnificent gardens and castles.

We circled the river, reveling in the wonders of Creation, and reached the other side of Margaret Island. The driver docked the boat and agreed to pick us up in another four-and-a-half hours to take us home. We walked through the beautiful landscape of flowering shrubs and trees, entered a dense, impenetrable thicket of bushes and walked together until we reached a lovely green meadow that was surrounded on all sides by trees.

The trees around us had been artfully cut down to serve as tables and chairs. We all helped Bácsi Aharon Dovid collect branches for a campfire. Basya Leah had carried a pot of goulash with her the entire way, and Bácsi Aharon Dovid put it on the lit fire. Bubby set up the meal on one of the felled trees that served as a lovely picnic table. She spread out a red and white checked tablecloth and set the "table" with white enamel plates. I went to pick flowers to decorate the table.

We had a wonderful time eating the picnic meal. Afterwards the young children ran around and played games while the adults sat and chatted. At first I played with Ruchele and Shifra, the younger children, but after a while I tired of it.

I saw Reizy and Suri sitting on the side, on a high grassy platform, and I joined them. At first they stopped talking, as if they didn't want to include me in their conversation, but when they saw that I wasn't moving, they continued talking. They talked about weddings and wedding dresses and everything connected. Reizy told me that when she gets married, she wants me to hold her flowers and be one of the bridesmaids, together with her sisters. "I don't think I will ever get married," I told them. The two of them smiled and asked me why.

"Who will want to marry a foundling, an adopted child?" I said slowly, enunciating each syllable.

As soon as I said that, the two girls became quiet and looked at me in wide-eyed amazement.

"What are you talking about, Leichu?" asked Reizy, almost in a whisper.

I answered her just as quietly. "I know that you know. Can we stop pretending, finally?"

Suri exhaled loudly. "How do you know?" both girls asked me together.

I shrugged my shoulders and did not answer.

Reizy came over and hugged me. "You know, Leichu, we love you just as you are," she said, stroking my hair.

"But anyway, who will want to marry a foundling who doesn't even know who her real parents are?" I persisted.

"Why do you think that no one knows who your parents are?" asked Suri.

"Do you know who they are?" I retorted. She shook her head. I looked pointedly at Reizy, and she shook her head as well. "If they knew, then you would know as well," I told them.

Reizy, the understanding and compassionate of the two, said to me, "Leichu, we love you and you are wonderful. Anyone who knows you, loves you. Please don't worry."

I looked into her eyes and whispered the things that burned inside me. "Do you think that I am worried about my wedding prospects now? No, I have many years until I will have to worry about that. There are other reasons why I don't sleep at night. Do you have any idea what it feels like to be a girl without a name, without parents, a foundling who bears a name that is not hers, who lives a life that is not hers?

"Can you possibly understand what I am going through? How do you think I feel when Anya hugs and kisses me and calls me 'my darling daughter'? I know that it is not the truth, I am not her daughter, and she says it because she thinks that I don't know the truth. I am living a lie. No, you are not capable of understanding. You will never understand me."

Suri also drew closer and both of them hugged me. They both tried to comfort me — telling me that it is not important who were the parents who brought me into the world, but instead, the ones who raised me and love me.

"You see," I said to them as my eyes filled with tears, "you just don't understand." The two of them looked at me and started to cry together with me. We sat, the three of us, hugging each other and crying.

We could see the rest of the family from far away. Some sat and talked pleasantly, others played and ran around. But in one corner of Margaret Island, concealed by blossoming bushes, the three of us sat and cried.

❦ 27 ❦
A Laundress with Recommendations

I**T WAS ON** one of Mama's busy laundry days that Ruzka, Mama's laundress, told her that this was her last day of work. She explained that she would be leaving Sevlus soon and moving to Posen (or Pressburg, as the Jews called it) to live near her son. She was old and did not have strength to work anymore, and her son would support her from now on.

Mama was disappointed, though not because she would miss Ruzka. They got along well, but were not exactly friends: Ruzka was a non-Jew and Mama was Jewish. Mama could never forget Ruzka's horror stories about adopted children and was not sad to say goodbye. But she did need a laundress; where would she find one now?

Mama worked very hard and tried as much as humanly possible not to take advantage of her kind neighbors, though they helped her willingly and lovingly. She did not want to have to ask them to help her do her laundry. Mama used to say that if *HaKadosh Baruch Hu* tested her with the trial of having only one hand, that meant that she could prevail despite it. Perhaps she would have to try harder than everyone else, but there was no such thing as "impossible" or "I can't do it"—those words did not exist for her.

Still, what was to be done about the laundry?

It was as if Ruzka read her mind, for she promised Mama that she would look for another laundress for her. After a number of days, Ruzka came by to tell Mama that she had, indeed, found someone. "She is a wonderful woman who is quick, hard-working and faithful," promised Ruzka. Mama was happy, but when Ruzka admitted that her candidate was a gypsy, Mama was horrified. "A gypsy? Should I bring a gypsy into my own house and store?" she exclaimed.

No one in her community ever brought a gypsy into their home. The gypsies were known as professional thieves and were able to steal things under your very nose. When gypsies came into her store to buy things, Mama kept a careful eye on them. Yet no matter how she tried, something was always missing when they left.

As soon as a group of gypsies would reach their neighborhood, all the neighbors would rush to rip the clothes off the clotheslines and bring them inside, even if they were still wet. They would also bring in any containers and sundries that usually remained outside, and whenever someone forgot something outside, even if it was just a simple bowl or a can, it would disappear along with the gypsies.

And then there were the rumors that gypsies abducted children. This rumor really had never been proven as far as Mama remembered, but no one took any chances. All the mothers told their children over and over, "If you see gypsies—run home and lock the door!"

And here, Mama's faithful laundress Ruzka was suggesting that she employ a gypsy woman. Not only that, but Ruzka stepped aside to show Mama that the gypsy woman was actually standing right there, next to her.

Mama scrutinized the woman carefully. She was dark, not tall, thin but dressed in layers of clothing topped with a long black skirt, red blouse, and a black vest embroidered with colored ribbons. The strange gypsy wore no proper jewelry; not a necklace, bracelet or even a ring. This was unusual as the gypsies always wore an abundance of cheap ornaments.

A colorful kerchief covered her head and two long black braids plaited with colored ribbons peeked out from beneath it. She only had one piece of jewelry: a long chain around her forehead, in which was threaded a solitary coin.

The woman stood with folded hands in front of her prospective mistress. She did not move her body as Mama examined her from head to toe, yet her eyes followed Mama closely. Mama checked her hands; they were thin, very wrinkled but clean. In general, this gypsy was unusually clean and did not have the kind of strange smell of the gypsies. Afterwards, Mama looked straight into the woman's eyes, and surprisingly, the gypsy met her gaze directly. In fact, there was something else in the woman's eyes: a hint of surprise and curiosity, as if Mama looked familiar to her or she recognized her from somewhere. Perhaps, Mama thought, the gypsy had once bought something from my store?

Mama was satisfied with this little test. The fact that the gypsy was willing to look directly into her eyes, thought Mama, meant she had nothing to hide.

Still, this was an uncomfortable situation. Mama decided to be frank and tell the woman about her reservations.

"I am disabled, as you can see," said Mama. "I have only one hand and I am barely able to eke out a living from my small grocery store. Since I cannot carry the merchandise myself I have to pay other merchants to do so, and this cuts down my profit margin considerably. In addition, I can't do my own laundry and I have to pay someone." Mama paused. "I believe my friend Ruzka who warmly recommends you, but I must tell you honestly: Gypsies have earned a reputation as thieves. This is not idle slander; we have seen case after case ourselves.

"So tell me, please; what should I do? Should I bring you into my house and store, under these circumstances?"

The gypsy woman answered Mama just as honestly. "Yes, it is true that there are many gypsies who have nimble fingers and steal. I won't deny that," said the woman calmly. "But please understand, Mrs. Fruchter, that although my husband and I are both gypsies from a long gypsy line, we are different from the others. We lived until now in Budapest where I worked for many people, among them Jews. I will give you their addresses, and you can write and find out for yourself. I will also give you the name of the contractor who employed my husband for many years, and you can find out about him as well." She stopped for breath.

"I have never stolen anything in my life," said the woman slowly and clearly. "I know that if I swear this to you, you won't believe me. But here is the list; ask about Chungarabi the gypsy and you can judge for yourself."

At this point the woman took out a list of names of people and their addresses. She asked Mama to compose a letter right then and there, asking for the truth, and then she, the gypsy, would pay for the stamp and mail it.

Mama perused the list and noticed that one of the families were neighbors of the Zingers! It was a small world indeed, and that convinced Mama to go ahead and write a letter on the spot asking about Chungarabi the gypsy. She addressed the letter to the Zingers, although their name wasn't on the list. Then Mama gave the letter to the woman, who looked at the name on the envelope. "This is addressed to Zinger," she said. "I'm sorry, but I've never worked for people of this name."

This was a surprise: Mama had never heard of a gypsy who knew how to read. She explained that she was close to the Zinger family and they were neighbors of one of her former employers, as she could see by the address.

And, in fact, after just a few days, Mama received an answer from the Zingers. They had looked into Chungarabi's credentials and indeed, she had a reputation as an upright and faithful worker. Despite the fact that she was a gypsy, she never stole, and she was industrious and quick.

They added that they were sorry they had no news about her lost daughter.

❦ 28 ❦
The Revelation
[SEVLUS]

THAT WAS HOW Mama hired Chungarabi. On the appointed day, Chungarabi arrived and found everything waiting for her: hot and cold water, bowls with soap, and the dirty laundry. It was all neatly placed on the long porch at the entrance to the house. There was also a chair for the laundress and a stool for the washing bowl. A can full of water was heating up on the stove.

It had taken her hours to get it all ready.

Chungarabi politely knocked on the door to notify Mama that she had arrived. Then she took the can off the fire and sat down quietly to launder. She finished the laundry, hung up the garments on the clothesline, and went inside the house.

At that moment there were no customers in the store, and Mama was in the middle of davening. She wanted to signal to Chungarabi to wait until she finished her prayers, and then she would pay her. Suddenly, though, she saw the gypsy get down on her knees to scrub the wooden floor, using the special scrubbing brush she had found. Mama tried to signal to her that was not part of her job, but Chungarabi told her laconically, "Mrs. Fruchter, cleaning the house is included in the laundry price. I don't bother you in your prayers, and you—don't bother me while I work."

Later on when Mama told me the story, she laughed and laughed. I said that it was typical of Chungarabi to say such a thing, and hide her innate kindness under a gruff exterior.

Mama finished her prayers, and Chungarabi finished scrubbing the floor.

"I don't like it when you prepare the water for me," said Chungarabi to Mama. "Next time, I'll take care of the water myself, thank you. And I want to clean the windows now."

Mama tried to stop Chungarabi; after all, she only had enough money to pay the gypsy for doing the laundry. But Chungarabi gave the same answer: "Mrs. Fruchter, windows are included in the price as well. Anyway I have to wait until the clean clothing dries before I can iron it, so I'll use that time to clean the windows." Apparently, Chungarabi had decided that ironing was also "included in the price," because when Mama had hired her, she had only hired her to launder the clothing. Chungarabi realized how hard it must be for Mama to prepare buckets of water, scrub the floor, and clean the windows with only one hand. She wanted to help Mama, but she knew that Mama could not afford to pay anything extra, and she didn't want to embarrass her either. So whenever Mama protested, Chungarabi would answer with that one laconic phrase:

"Mrs. Fruchter, it's included in the price."

Thus Chungarabi became Mama's right hand: In addition to the laundry, she ironed and cleaned the house. She was truly honest, dedicated and faithful.

ॐ   ॐ   ॐ

One day when Chungarabi was working for Mama, Rivka Klar dropped by. The two women sat and talked, and Mama told Rivka that there was nothing new in Budapest. She began to sob.

Rivka spoke to her encouragingly, as usual. But Mama had reached the end of her rope. "For years I've been waiting, hoping for the best, and I have no more strength left," she said. "All I want is my daughter, the daughter they stole from me." Mama cried, and Rivka joined her.

Soon after, Rivka left. Chungarabi left her laundry buckets and approached Mama. "Mrs. Fruchter," she said slowly, "Mrs. Fruchter, I couldn't help but overhear you talking to your friend about some kind of 'stolen daughter.' I beg you, please tell me the whole story."

This was a most irregular request from a gypsy laundress. Ruzka, her former laundress, would never have pried into Mama's personal affairs. But this woman seemed very sincere, and was looking intently at her again. What did it all mean?

Mama decided that she would, indeed, confide in Chungarabi. It was obvious that she wasn't just any ordinary gypsy; after all, she prepared the water for the laundry herself and cleaned the house without taking extra money. There was something special about this woman. So Mama sat and told Chungarabi everything; from her late husband's exemption from the army, the birth of their dear daughter Leichu, her husband's illness and untimely death, the splinter that infected her entire hand, and the subsequent amputation. And worst of all, the family relative who had given her daughter to a childless family. "I don't cry over my disability," Mama said. "I accept that as a decree from the Creator of the world. But the evil that human beings inflict upon each other—that is the hardest suffering of all to bear."

Chungarabi forced herself to wait until Mama completed her story. Only then did Chungarabi wipe her hands, sit down next to Mama and hold her hand. "Mrs. Fruchter," she said slowly. "I will help you; yes, I — a gypsy — know where your lost daughter is!

"In Budapest, I worked for the Feldman family. They have a daughter and I became very close to her over the years. She would share all her secrets with me, and when she discovered that she had been adopted, she confided in me then, too. I was the one to console her then — we loved each other very much. Mrs. Fruchter, you have a wonderful child, and she yearns to know who her natural parents are, and why they gave her away."

Mama closed her eyes and started to tremble. Could this be real? Could the gypsy be telling the truth, after so many years, so many disappointments? She could not bear it if she were to get her hopes up, only to have them dashed once again.

"Please tell me," she whispered, "why you think this girl is my child? Could it not be a coincidence?"

"Because she resembles you," answered Chungarabi. "From the first time I met you, I have been amazed at the resemblance. Each time I come here, I say to myself: Mrs. Fruchter looks so much like my Leichu!"

"Leichu, Leichu! That's my daughter's name!" Mama cried. "My Leah, my very own Leichu!"

∽   ∽   ∽

Truth be told, Mama wanted to get up right then and there and travel to Budapest. She simply had to see me, she felt. But she was so excited that she couldn't think straight. "Please come with me to my friend Rivka Klar," Mama said. "Then tell her everything you told me. She will know what to do."

So Mama and Chungarabi set out together to the Klars on the other side of town. It was an unusual sight to see a Jewish woman walking with a gypsy. Mama was uncomfortable going to Rivka with a gypsy; what if Rivka wouldn't allow a gypsy into her house?

They reached the Klar household. Rivka was astonished to see the strange pair, but she did not say a thing. She ushered them both inside, and they all sat down at the table.

The children surrounded their mother, taken aback. A gypsy in their home? But Rivka did not pay attention to them and instead, asked Mama to speak. She realized that something very unusual, and very important, was afoot.

"It is the gypsy who has something to tell you," Mama said and pointed to Chungarabi.

So Chungarabi told the whole story again. She gave them the Feldmans' name and address, and told them that the missing child is still called Leichu. Mama kept whispering, "Leichu, Leichu," her eyes filling with tears. "I must get on the next train to Budapest," she cried. "I absolutely must see my beloved daughter; I can't bear to be parted from her for one more day!"

But Rivka stopped her forcefully. With iron determination, she explained over and over: "If you go there, they will see you and hide your daughter. They will smuggle her out, don't you see? We have to plan this very, very carefully — we cannot let our emotions control us."

Mama then had an idea. She turned to Chungarabi and begged, "Would you steal my daughter and bring her back to me?"

But Chungarabi refused to do such a thing under any circumstances. "The Feldmans know where I live now, and if Leichu disappears, they will send the police to track me down. They will arrest me and take your daughter back," she said. And she was right.

Finally it was decided to send a telegram to Reb Shia

Zinger with the new information. "Let's hear what he sug-
gests," said Rivka.

Mama ran immediately with Chungarabi to the post office
and sent a telegram. Chungarabi then wanted to go home,
but Mama begged her not to leave. "Please come and tell me
about my Leichu," she said. "It is so important to me to hear
all about her, to hear about all the years that I've missed!"

Chungarabi acceded to Mama's request, and they walked
back together to Mama's home. This time they sat in the little
bedroom and talked. Chungarabi told her stories about me:
how I looked, how I excelled in school, my friends, everything. But the most important thing to Mama was my religious background. Was my adoptive family Orthodox, or
chas v'shalom, Neologist (similar to Reform)?

Mama was relieved to hear through Chungarabi's stories
that my adoptive family was strictly Orthodox and meticulous in their mitzvah observance. I went to a proper Jewish
school and observed the holidays with my adoptive family.
Mama never forgot her three older children who had left her
and her observant way of life many years ago. She was happy
to hear that her youngest was, at least, growing up in an observant home.

Chungarabi sat until the late hours of the night talking
non-stop about me: She told Mama about my curly hair that
no brush could tame; my awards for scholastic excellence
in school; my facility for languages; my new hobby of sewing. Mama drunk up every word with a terrible thirst for
more and more information. She embraced me in her heart
through Chungarabi's descriptions.

From that day on, every time Chungarabi came to do
laundry, she would spend time answering Mama's questions
about me. She understood Mama's need for this, so she never
turned her down.

And in truth, there was probably no one else in Budapest who knew me as well as Chungarabi. She was the one who had really listened to me; she was the only one in whom I had confided freely, and she truly loved me.

❦ 29 ❦
A Letter from Mama
[SEVLUS]

IT WAS HARD for Mama to refrain from coming to see me after so many years of uncertainty, even though she finally knew where I lived. So one night, she sat down to write me a letter. She knew she could not mail the letter, but she wrote it, nonetheless, to express her longings and her love. It was a letter of great hope and anticipation of the day she could finally give it to me personally.

My Leichu,

My daughter, my dear and infinitely beloved daughter.

It is you, Leichu, whom I think about during the day, and it is you I dream about at night. You are the joy of my life and the purpose of my existence; it is because of you, and for you, that I carry on in life despite all my difficulties.

It is because of you that I have taught myself how to do everything on my own, despite my disability, so that you would not be ashamed of me, chas v'shalom. That is my biggest fear: that you won't accept or want me, a mother with a deformity. That you would be embarrassed by me.

And I miss you so much! I yearn to hold you in my arms and hug you, stroke your face, look into your eyes, comb your hair, and hold your hand.

But when I extend my one hand to you, there is nothing—emptiness. It is only in my imagination that I can see you — the picture I have created of you is stored there, in my mind.

I truly believe that we will meet, one day. And I ask myself: How will we be able to bridge the gap of our long separation, of all the years that have passed since we've been together?

I am the mother who did not raise you, did not watch you develop over the years, or share in your joys and sorrows. Will you believe me when I tell you that I loved you so very much despite the distance that separated us, despite the fact that I did not merit seeing all your "firsts"? I was not privileged to rub your swollen gums and see your brand-new baby teeth when they erupted. It was not to me that you ran when you took your first step, that most important step for any baby-turned-toddler. I was not the one to pick you up with a hug and a kiss when you fell and hurt yourself; I was not the one to encourage you to try again, take one step after another until you learned to walk confidently, then to run and jump. I was not the one you turned to when you first learned to say "Mama"; I was not the one to hear your first words, or smile when you stumbled over long words when you first started to talk.

My Leichu! I, the mother who gave birth to you, was also not the one to teach you the very fundamental Jewish pasuk that every Jewish mother teaches her children, "Torah tzivah lanu Moshe; morashah kehillas Yaakov." I was not able to teach you that we always say a berachah before putting anything to eat in our mouths. And that always—but always!—we must give thanks to HaKadosh Baruch Hu for everything that we have. I was not the one to tell you that the most important words for the Jewish nation are "Shema Yisrael." Everything is from Hashem; the good as well as what appears to be the bad. In fact, the "bad" is really the ultimate good, given to us by our Father in Heaven, only we, with our limited intellect and vision, fail to recognize this.

And you know, my Leichu, that I did not have the privilege to escort you to your first day of school, to prepare your school supplies, to check your homework and encourage you in your schoolwork. How I would have loved to see your first report card, and the ones afterwards; how I would have loved to teach you to say "thank you," "I'm sorry" and "please."

I don't even know what you like to eat, what

your favorite color is and what games you like to play. Tell me, dear Leichu, are you good in math? I myself have difficulties in this subject. It's very interesting — I am able to do most of the housework alone, without help; but math and bookkeeping work give me difficulty. But I am not embarrassed to ask for help, since people help me with arithmetic without feeling sorry for me. And I do not want people to pity me.

My Leichu, I have created a picture of you in my imagination, but I don't know what you really look like. You were taken from me at six months old, and that was too soon to know how you would look when you were older. True, Chungarabi the gypsy tells me that you resemble me, but it is still hard for me to picture you.

Do you know that the people who raised you from infancy are not your birth parents? Did you ever imagine that somewhere, someplace, is a loving mother who yearns for you, who thinks about you endlessly, day and night? Can you imagine the torment of a loving mother who was not able to raise the child she loves so much?

My Leichu, I raised three children in poverty and need. Without a penny to my name, I raised my beloved children. But when they grew up they turned their backs on our deprivation and on everything else we had, too. They left me for a place where they became wealthier and learned to live like "important" people. They come to visit only very infrequently and occasionally write short letters. But as sad as this makes me, I know that they are adults and responsible for their own lives. You, on the other hand, were stolen from my arms by a malicious hand. Thus it was not I who raised and nurtured you, and I was not the one to watch you grow and mature.

The sad, amazing thing is that you were stolen from me by Jews; not only Jews, but relatives of your father, z"l. And if I ever merit seeing you again in this world, it will be because of a gypsy. Gypsies are often accused of stealing children, but you were stolen by religious Jews who claimed they did it for my benefit, for my own good. But what did all their good intentions do? They inflicted on me the worst possible suffering a mother can bear—to lose her child.

My daughter, my beloved child; if I will have the privilege to win you back, as I pray for every day, as I have been blessed by many great rabbanim—will we be able to bridge the gap of the many years of our separation?

I believe, my daughter, that if we devote our hearts and souls, our desires and thoughts, then be'ezras Hashem Yisbarach, we will succeed. And then, once we meet, we will never be separated again.

We will remain reunited all our lives.
We will learn to get to know one another and love
one another. If we truly want, we will succeed, my
dear daughter.

I loved this letter from Mama and re-read it countless times until the papers wore thin. This letter remained in my mother's house, and was destroyed with her and the entire village.

The next evening, Mama received the following telegram: "We have seen her. She looks wonderful. Legally adopted in court. We need a lawyer."

Mama always told me how impressed she was by the Zingers. What wonderful people they were, and how sensitive! Every word in a telegram is expensive, and they could have written only about the court and lawyer. Yet they added that they had seen me, and that I looked wonderful—because they knew how important that was to her. They knew that those very words would lift up her heart to the very heavens.

Nachman Klar made a special trip to the Vizhnitzer Rebbe to consult with him. He took the telegram with him and all of Mama's hopes. When Nachman returned to town, he went straight to Mama's store before even returning to his home. "The Rebbe gave me the name of a lawyer in Budapest," he said to her excitedly. "He will take care of it all. However, we will have to pay him handsomely, even if we need to take up a tzedakah collection to obtain the money. And we have to be patient; it will take a long time, but we will succeed in the end." From there, Nachman ran to the post office. He had to send a telegram to the lawyer stating that the Vizhnitzer Rebbe personally requests that he take upon himself the mission of returning Leichu to her mother.

Reb Nachman and Rivka Klar. They were like parents to Mama. I lived with them in Eretz Yisrael, and they were the ones to lead me to my chuppah.

Almost every day, Néni Rivka sent one of her two older daughters to keep Mama company and remind her that the matter required that she be very, very patient. But Mama was exuberant. She had no idea what "a long time" meant; she thought of perhaps two or three months.

Had she known it would take more than a year, she would have given up in despair. It was just as well that she did not know.

ຕະ   ຕະ   ຕະ

All the Jews of Sevlus mobilized themselves to help pay for Mama's lawyer.

The lawyer from Pressburg recommended by the Rebbe of Vizhnitz was called Dr. Bulgar. The amazing coincidence was that after Shia Zinger hired him, Dr. Bulgar wrote a letter to Mama in which he told her that he had learned with a Dovid Fruchter many years ago in *yeshivah ketanah*, and they had been good friends. He, Bulgar, had not been born in Sevlus but in one of the villages in the area and had been sent to Sevlus for school; and had changed his name from Brown to Bulgar when he went to university. Evidently, that was why no one in Sevlus identified him. His pressing question was: Was the Dovid Fruchter he had known, connected to her, Sheina Ruchel Fruchter?

Mama wrote back and said that her husband, Dovid Fruchter, had passed away many years ago, and that the child is indeed, Dovid Fruchter's daughter.

Dr. Bulgar was very moved by this coincidence, and wanted to take on the case for free. But Mama did not agree; the Rebbe had said to pay him properly, and so it would be.

I remember the packet of letters we had in the house from Dr. Bulgar. He corresponded with Mama throughout the court case which lasted a few years. I loved reading his letters — Dr. Bulgar had the writer's touch and they read like installments of a story. The last letter he wrote was after winning the court case and it was a lovely poem. This pack of letters is one of the things that I am sorry to have lost.

◇◇

Dr. Bulgar himself died in Auschwitz, and the letters he wrote to Mama disappeared in Sevlus.

◇◇

❦ 30 ❦
A Forbidden Topic

O NE DAY A fancy bolt of fabric arrived in Apa's store, and Anya got very excited about it. She took enough of the deep blue fabric for a suit, and Bubby did the same. The two of them rushed to the new seamstress, the one that Bubby Feldman had discovered, and ordered elegant suits.

As soon as the suit was ready, Anya took me out with her on errands and she proudly wore her new blue suit. I wore my brown pleated skirt with the cream-colored silk blouse that I had received from Néni Loni. She often sent me clothes when her daughter Annie outgrew them.

After we walked around and Anya finished all her errands, we went into the Ruzke Café. As we walked in I saw Molly and Lottie, two sisters, who always went everywhere together. They were sitting at a table for three, and it seemed to me that they were waiting for someone. After we greeted them properly, we sat down at a table not far from them.

Anya ordered coffee. I knew that she was in a good mood because she had been successful in her errands, and felt great in her new suit. So I decided to try to order ice cream, even

175

though it was usually only for special occasions. How I loved ice cream!

I sat with my back to the door, and Anya sat opposite me. She was the one who saw everyone who entered.

We chatted as we enjoyed our treats; I felt like a grown-up, sitting with my mother in a regular coffee shop. Suddenly, Anya stiffened up. She turned white as a sheet, and didn't move a muscle. I turned to the door to see what terrible thing could make my mother react like that. And then I saw: It was a rather heavy woman who was wearing a suit almost identical to Anya's!

The woman was very elegant. Pink flowers trimmed her blue hat, which was a bit darker than the suit. Her bag and shoes were also the same dark shade of blue. I found this very amusing, but I tried not to smile so as not to offend Anya.

The woman sat down next to Molly and Lottie — she was the one they'd been waiting for. As soon as she sat down, Anya whispered to me, "We are going, right now!" I didn't want to leave, and I said, "I haven't even finished my ice cream! Oh, Anya, your suit won't change colors even if we leave now. And anyway, Anya, that suit really looks better on you."

So Anya agreed and we sat quietly while I continued to eat my ice cream. Suddenly, I heard a loud stage-whisper. It was one of the sisters. "That's Mrs. Feldman, from the material store," she whispered. "She's sitting with that adopted daughter of hers."

Anya, who had become pale, now turned very red. She glanced at me to see if I had heard the offensive statement.

I continued eating peacefully, and out of the corner of my eye, I saw how Anya breathed a sigh of relief. She was sure I hadn't heard. Suddenly I realized that this was the time to show her that, in fact, I knew the truth. I was sick and tired of this charade in which I had to feign ignorance. So I turned to

Anya with a smile and said, "Interesting, there are still well-dressed ladies in Budapest who don't know that I'm adopted." And I kept on eating my ice cream with artificial complacency.

Anya grabbed her lace gloves and tried to put them on. But her hands trembled so much that she could not. I didn't look at her; I just continued eating my ice cream and looking down on my plate, though I glanced at her occasionally out of the corner of my eye.

Surely Anya wanted to scream right there in the middle of the coffee shop. But she was too well-bred for that. As soon as I finished the last spoonful, we got up to go. I realized that Anya was about to go around the back to avoid the table with the three gossips, but I made believe I hadn't noticed. I deliberately walked right past them with my back straight and my head held high, a big smile on my face. Anya saw this, and followed suit.

As soon as we arrived home, Anya started to grumble, "I'll never wear this outfit again, it's awful!" She vented all her anger on that silly blue suit.

I was in seventh heaven. Finally, I would be allowed to talk about the big secret! I went over to Anya, hugged her and said, "Oh, Anya, please don't get rid of that lovely outfit. The suit is so beautiful, and it looks great on you. That woman is not important, and I love you."

Anya hugged me and burst into tears. "My child, my dear child," she cried. And I told her that what was important was that we loved one another and nothing else mattered.

The next day we went to Bubby Shapiro. Bubby hugged and kissed Anya and myself as usual, and before we had a chance to say hello, Anya started talking to her mother in Yiddish. I knew that she was telling her that I knew about the adoption. I didn't want to remain for the fireworks so I waved goodbye to them and walked over to Néni Basya Leah. When I got there, I said to Basya Leah, "I think you may want to walk over to Bubby and cry there together with Anya; I'll stay here and play with the children." Basya Leah was bewildered by this strange request. "Why should we cry?" she asked. "Because that's probably what Anya is doing at Bubby's right now," I answered, "and I'm sure that Bubby will cry together with her when she hears what her daughter tells her. If you want to know why—go there yourself to find out." As I finished my sentence, I turned into the children's room.

I saw Basya Leah walking quickly out the door. As I had guessed, her curiosity had gotten the better of her.

It was only after dinner that Anya came to call for me to go home. I went to Bubby to say goodbye and saw that, indeed, her eyes were red and puffy from crying. But she didn't say a word to me.

Anya and I did not exchange one word on our way home. I wanted Anya to be the first to talk to me, to explain, to tell me something—but she didn't say a word.

When we got home I decided to give up this silly game, and brought up the subject myself. Finally, finally, I asked Anya about the adoption. To my horror, she ignored my question. I couldn't believe that she simply became deaf, dumb, and blind every time I brought up the topic. This situation went on for days.

All my hopes were dashed. I had hoped that the tension and strain behind the "big secret" would disappear from our home at last, once it was no longer a secret and we could talk about it. But now it seems that I was wrong: It was still taboo.

A few days later, after Apa came home from work one evening, he came to my room. I was already in bed. Apa looked at me and told me that I was causing Anya a lot of grief with my questions. He said that I was a bad girl who didn't know how to keep her tongue and talked about things that shouldn't be talked about, and that he expected me to stop distressing my mother. I sat up in bed and asked sharply, "And what about me? What about the questions that have been disturbing me for years? Why is it forbidden for me to know anything about myself?"

Apa said to me, "You already know too much. There is no need to know more, and we will never talk about this again!" He left the room angrily.

I had rejoiced too soon. Nothing had changed. I had hoped that the mystery would be resolved and my torment would come to an end, but the opposite had happened: It only increased. If they refused to talk to me, then the secret must be a terrible one. Were my origins so terrible that they had to be covered over and hushed up? Were my real parents terrible, shameful people?

I confided in Briendy the next day, but she disappointed me. She tried to tell me that I was making things up and blowing them out of proportion. So what if some silly woman said silly things about me? And just because Anya didn't deny them—that doesn't mean anything. And how do I know that's what she talked about with Bubby Shapiro?

I went to Bubby Shapiro and tried to talk to her as well. She gave me a big hug and lots of kisses and said with a big smile, "You are my beloved granddaughter, that's all. No more and no less!" When she saw that I didn't smile back or respond to the hugs and kisses, she just called me a silly fool, and would not talk to me any more about the adoption.

When I asked Basya Leah about it, she answered me, "What are you talking about, Leichu? Who put such ideas into your head?"

The one person I really yearned to speak to, the one person who would understand and not judge me—was Chungarabi. And she no longer worked for us, she did not live in Budapest anymore, and I had no way to contact her. I missed her terribly.

I fell so behind in my studies that the teacher asked Anya to come and talk to her; when Apa heard about this, he punished me. He forbade me to leave the house at all except to go to school, and let me leave my room only for meals and washing. The rest of the time, I was locked in my room. Anya wouldn't even let Briendy go to the library to take out books for me. So I sat in my room in front of my notebooks, but I just didn't feel like doing my homework. Eventually I did do my work, but only the very minimum. The answers were superficial and inadequate.

My consolation was the sewing machine. I spent entire days practicing on remnants of material from the store until my stitches became long and straight. I knew how to sew by hand as well — tiny, neat stitches — but I concentrated on sewing by machine. I was very proud of my progress.

Every day when I came home from school, I went into my room and opened the machine. I oiled it expertly and knew how to sprinkle each drop exactly where it was needed, without soiling the whole area with oil. Every day I cleaned the machine from top to bottom, the wooden parts as well as the metal ones, until they all shined.

After I practiced sewing long, neat stitches on all the material remnants, even without marking it first with pencil and ruler, I then progressed to diagonal stitches. When I mastered these, I practiced other stitch styles that I had learned during sewing lessons.

My sewing made me happy. I'll learn how to sew circles, I thought, exact circles, and no one will outdo me! How many ten-year-old girls know how to sew as nicely as me?

Anya once told me that after I turned twelve, I would learn how to sew real clothes. And if I'd continue to practice for hours a day, in the end I'd become a great seamstress!

I tried to sew clothes, at least aprons. But I didn't know what I was doing and the aprons came out lopsided. I realized that I'd need to learn how to do this. And Briendy told me that Anya wouldn't allow me to learn how to sew clothes if I didn't improve my schoolwork. So that's what I did. My grades improved again, but I didn't even ask to leave my room. I stayed there for hours on end and only left to eat. I sat politely at the table at mealtimes, but I didn't volunteer a word. When Apa or Anya asked me a question I answered courteously, but that was all. I didn't share any news with them — I didn't tell them about school, my friends or my sewing. I knew that this distressed Anya very much, and I did not care.

After a few weeks, Anya looked like she couldn't take it any more. I looked happy despite my punishment, Apa was out of the house most of the time, and only Anya was irritable and nervous. She was the one who was punished!

One day, Anya came into my room and asked me if I wasn't bored in there all the time; didn't I want to leave my room? I curtly told her that I was fine. "Why don't you ask Apa for permission to leave the room? You've already made up your schoolwork and you are a good girl," she told me. I shrugged my shoulders and said, "What right do I have to ask anything of adoptive parents? Thank you for taking care of me and giving me everything I need. I will try to be good and not bother you. But that won't turn you into real parents."

Anya became white as a sheet, grabbed me and hugged and kissed me. "What do you mean, my Leichu? Why do you say such terrible things when you know that we love you so much?"

"If I tell you, you will say I'm being insolent," I answered quietly. "But I'll tell you anyway: If you were real parents, you would find out why I started failing in school. You know I've always been a good student, so there must have been a reason for the change. But you are not real parents, and that's why you don't really care. The only thing that is important to you is that I should excel in my studies and bring respect and honor to the family."

"I know what caused you to neglect your studies," said Anya. "It was Molly and Lottie's silly words."

"I've known about the adoption for almost a year," I corrected her.

Anya was amazed.

"Anyhow," I added, "I've gained a lot by staying in my room; I'm practicing my sewing. Eventually I'll learn to sew real clothing and become really good at it, and then I'll make money to earn my keep. I'll finally be able to repay you for all the money you've spent on me," I said to Anya with inner glee—I saw that she almost fainted.

"Pay us back? What are you talking about?" she started to shout. "You are my daughter! Even if I didn't give birth to you, you are my daughter!"

I didn't answer. I took out my notebooks from my schoolbag and involved myself busily in my homework.

Anya ran out of the room quickly so that I wouldn't see her crying. But I did see her and I was alarmed. I ran after her, hugged her and asked her forgiveness. She hugged me and we stood there in the hall, hugging each other and crying.

Later on, when I went over the whole scene in my mind and reconstructed what happened that day, I realized that I do love Anya a great deal. Despite my anger at her, and despite my complaints, she is the only mother I have ever known.

I decided to stop torturing myself about my origins, my

real parents. Apa and Anya are my parents; I love them and am attached to them, and must treat them so. Perhaps I shouldn't have troubled them with all my questions at a time when I saw that they were wrapped up with something else on their minds, something that they brought up over and over with Zaidy and Bubby Feldman and Zaidy and Bubby Shapiro: a trial. I had overhead all kinds of things about lawyers and lawyer's fees and other things connected to some kind of court case.

The trial didn't interest me; it evidently had something to do with the store, and I am not involved in the business and know nothing about it. But my parents are very worried, and I really should avoid upsetting them at such a delicate time.

❦ 31 ❧
A New Friend
[SEVLUS/BUDAPEST]

MAMA BOUGHT ALL the foodstuffs for her store from wholesalers called the Guttman Brothers. Once a month, she would place her order with them and at the same time, she would bring her accounts of the previous month's sales to them. One of the brothers would sit with Mama and check the accounts; everything always tallied properly. The Guttmans always praised Mama for her organized and accurate bookkeeping. The truth was that Mama was not good in math and it was the Klars who helped her with her ledgers. All the Klars were math whizzes and one of them would sit down with Mama and her paperwork to make the calculations and neatly write out the sums.

One of the reasons that Mama liked working with the Guttmans was their accuracy and meticulousness. They were known for their honesty; everything was on record without payments off the books. Perhaps they earned less money as they paid all their taxes, but they always said that money is transitory while honesty is inscribed in the Heavenly bookkeeping ledgers—and what is more important than that?

One day, Mama went to the Guttmans as usual to order

merchandise for the following month. After they finished their regular bookkeeping, Mr. Guttman called his brother in. Mama was puzzled, but not for long. The two brothers sat down, and one of them asked her, "Mrs. Fruchter, how much money will you need for the lawyer?"

Mama glumly cited the large sum that the Vizhnitzer Rebbe had said they must pay.

The Guttmans nodded their heads and recorded the sum on paper; they always recorded each sum immediately. "This sum must be doubled, at least, in order to cover all the other incidental costs and arrangements," the brothers told her. "And we might have to add even more in the future, if it becomes necessary."

"Mrs. Fruchter," they concluded, "from today, you won't have to worry about the financial side of this court case at all; you will be in charge of all the arrangements, excluding the money. From today, the money issue is our headache, not yours."

Mama was dumbfounded. They were talking about a very large sum of money! True, the Guttmans did well in their business, but they were not rich. They explained to Mama that they would not be paying the whole sum, but that all the Jews in Sevlus were contributing toward this; they were only acting as the organizers. "We'll collect and keep a record of the money. But of course, you must keep an accurate record of all your expenses connected to the court case," they said.

Mama was so touched that she burst into tears. "What a wonderful community I live in, what wonderful people!" she cried. "A holy city of *tzaddikim!*"

Meanwhile the attorney filed a suit against the Feldman family for holding a child illegally and without knowledge or agreement of the girl's mother, with a demand that the child be returned to her birth mother. Since he had the name of the adoptive family and their exact address, he could get to business immediately.

The court accepted the charges and set the date for the case to begin in another five months.

Mama almost went crazy. Five months! She never considered that it would take so long; she assumed that the court case would be held within a few days, and after two weeks at the most, her daughter would be returned to her.

The lawyer wrote Mama and explained that she must be patient. Although the hearing would start in another five months, the verdict itself would take even more time. He hoped that it would all be over within a year. No amount of crying or letter-writing on Mama's part could change things, he wrote. Alas, the wheels of justice turn slowly indeed.

Mama wanted to find out as much as she could about me, and flooded the Zingers with letters and questions. Néni Zinger decided that it was time to devise a plan to "spy" on me and then transmit the information to Mama. So she sat down one day to brainstorm with her daughter Edith.

There were no secrets in the Zinger family. Chana Malka Zinger always involved her children in family matters, so Edith was already familiar with the story of the missing Fruchter girl and was happy to help. The objective was that Edith would become friendly with me, tell her mother whatever she found out, and Chana Malka would then write Mama with the news.

After much detective work, Edith was sent to become friendly with a classmate of mine called Oniko Pfeffer, who was also the daughter of an old childhood friend of Edith's mother, Chana Malka. Edith was a very friendly, personable girl with a lot of friends but she was also knew how to be shrewd, and she encouraged Oniko to talk to her about her classmates. Oniko told Edith all about the social scene in her class — who was friends with whom, which girls had best friends, and which girls were considered popular. That's how she found out that I was best friends with Perry Edosh.

The Zingers dropped some nonchalant questions here, chatted a little there, until they found out that the Edosh family had a small cosmetics store. So Chana Malka developed a sudden need for cosmetics, despite the fact that the store was at a considerable distance from her house and that she had never used lipstick or face powder in her life. She became friendly with the Mrs. Edosh who worked in the store, and complimented her about her fine taste in makeup and esthetics. Not only that, she bought herself cosmetics that she didn't even know how to use! They became good friends and one day, Chana Malka invited Mrs. Edosh and her daughters to join her for coffee in a coffee shop. They set up a date for the afternoon, when the cosmetics store was closed.

Chana Malka and her daughter Edith planned carefully for this important meeting, and even held rehearsals. The problem was that Edith was older than Perry, my best friend. She was actually the same age as Shiri, the Edosh's older daughter. The challenge was for Edith to become friendly with the younger sister Perry without arousing suspicion.

The meeting in the coffee shop went very well. Luckily, it turned out that rehearsals were unnecessary; the two Edosh girls were both happy to have found a new friend. Both girls begged Mrs. Zinger to let Edith come visit them. Chana Malka used her acting skills to put on a show of hesitation: How could she let her daughter take such a long walk alone? Shiri and Perry promised to wait for her on Wednesday at four o'clock at the streetcar stop near their house. On the way back, they'd escort her to the stop and make sure that she would get on the right trolley. Perry explained that Wednesday was the best day, because that was the day her friend Leichu Feldman always came to play with her. She wanted her old friend to meet her new friend.

Neni Zinger "grudgingly" agreed to let Edith visit the Edoshes on the following Wednesday, and then the two went home. The unexpected turn of events — Edith would actually meet Leichu — that is, me, seemed too good to be true.

That Wednesday, when I went to Perry's house, she introduced me to her new friend, who was really Shiri's friend. I was not at all pleased. The two sisters had eyes only for Edith, and ignored me; and Edith herself seemed not to notice me at all. I didn't say a thing, but I hoped that she wouldn't show up the week after. However, she did—in fact, every time I went to visit Perry, the new girl was there. It didn't matter what day of the week it was, Edith was there.

Yet slowly but surely, I became friendly with Edith despite my initial misgivings. It was a feather in my cap that an older girl like Edith would want to be my friend. Shiri also became friendly with me, and that was good. Before Edith showed up, Shiri always turned her nose up at playing with Perry and me, the younger ones. It was so much better when the four of us were together.

Eventually Edith and I became very close friends. The only funny thing was that she never invited me to her house, and did not agree to come to my house. I thought it was because she was embarrassed that people would know that she was friends with a younger girl like me. I found out much later that the lawyer had told Chana Malka Zinger to make sure that my parents never met Edith, and that I never met the Zinger family. This way, Anya and Apa Feldman would never know that someone was spying on me and would never be able to trace anything to their neighbors, the Zingers. Later on, it proved to be very valuable advice.

Edith would tell her mother everything she found out

about me, and her mother would write to Mama. That's how Mama found out that I was a bright student and liked school; that I was a loyal friend and, most important, that I was happy, healthy, well-dressed, and lacked for nothing.

This information comforted Mama, on the one hand—but also pained her, on the other. It was clear that my adoptive parents were able to provide for me in a way that she could not.

Mama was an open, aboveboard person who was happy to involve the neighbors and friends in all the news she received from Chana Malka Zinger. In fact, they were all involved in the story of my life. They knew when Mama had heard good news about me, and they also knew when she had received bad news from the lawyer.

Mama received countless pieces of advice over the years. Luckily, she didn't rush out to do everything that she was told; she always consulted with Néni Rivka Klar first. If she had listened to everyone, she would have run herself ragged running in circles. Rivka suggested to Mama, though, that since all the advice-givers had good intentions, she should be polite and not reject them out of hand. "Because of that," said Mama, "I always thanked people sincerely for their advice, and then did what I felt was right. People saw that I listened to them, but followed my own instincts.

"This was the best advice I received in my entire life!" she would conclude.

❧ 32 ❧
The Trial
[SEVLUS/BUDAPEST]

T
HE ENTIRE SEVLUS Jewish community contributed to
Mama's "lawsuit fund" under the aegis of the Guttman
brothers, and they all felt part of the general efforts
on Mama's behalf. So everyone knew that the hearing would
be held in only five months, and that the case was expected to
take a long time.

The *rabbanim* of the town blessed Mama that she should
not worry or suffer; "It will end well," they assured her every time they saw her. Men of the town who traveled to their
Rebbes for advice or a *berachah* would mention Mama as
well. When they returned, they would send their wives to
Mama to tell her what the Rebbe had said. Mama was happy
with each and every *berachah*. Still, time passed slowly for
her as she waited for the trial to begin.

Finally, three days before the date, Mama went to Budapest. The townspeople decided that it was best she not go by
herself: Aidah Weingarten was the one who escorted her.

Aidah was a very special woman who masterminded most
of the *chesed* enterprises in Sevlus. She took care of these
projects wholeheartedly and was always there when some-

one needed help.

The train left Sevlus for Budapest in the mid-morning hours. Mama was at the platform a full hour in advance. She restlessly walked up and down in the square while waiting for the hands of the big clock to move.

Aidah Weingarten arrived shortly before the train arrived. She never imagined that Mama would come so early! But as soon as Aidah made her appearance, Mama felt that a weight was lifted from her shoulders. She was glad that she didn't have to make the trip all alone.

Mama was torn by conflicting emotions: On the one hand she wanted the train to speed up and go faster. On the other hand, she wanted it to stop moving altogether. Moments of optimism alternated in dizzying sped with pessimism. When she was hopeful, the train seemed to crawl, but when she was attacked by despair that she would lose the court case and her daughter forever, the train seemed to be moving dangerously fast.

Finally the long trip was over and they reached the city of Budapest. It was there at the station that Mama was attacked by fright and fear, and she fell down and couldn't move. Aidah, a small and dainty woman, could not lift Mama — but she managed to pull Mama into a sitting position. Finally, after sitting on the platform floor for a long time, Mama was able to stand up. She shakily walked to a nearby bench, and sat there for a while, too. Aidah held Mama's hand and spoke encouragingly, trying to assuage her fears. She reminded Mama that the Father of orphans and Judge of widows was helping her, and with His help, it would all turn out fine. Then she brought Mama a glass of water to drink, and Mama felt strong enough to continue. The two of them got up and headed to the trolley car.

Meanwhile, Chana Malka was very worried; she knew

that the train had arrived hours before, and she couldn't understand why Mama still hadn't knocked on her door. She began to fear that perhaps Mama had ignored the lawyer's instructions not to go near the Feldmans' house, and was indeed there, hoping to catch a glimpse of me. When nightfall came and Mama still hadn't arrived, Chana Malka sent her sons, Ari and Mickey, to the Feldmans' street. They had strict instructions not to let Mama get close to the Feldman home.

The two boys returned to tell their mother that they had checked thoroughly and could not find Mrs. Fruchter anywhere. Perhaps Mama decided not to come to Budapest for the trial, and forgot to tell Chana Malka? The only thing she never considered was the possibility that Mama would feel ill, and remain in the train station for a long time.

Finally the two women appeared at the Zinger home and made their explanations. When Chana Malka served them soup, Mama politely refused. She said she simply couldn't eat. But Chana Malka wouldn't let that go by and said to her, "If you won't eat my soup on your own, I will sit and feed it to you like a baby!" The three Zinger children came to see how their mother would force-feed a grown woman like one does to a recalcitrant baby. The whole idea was so funny that everyone, including Mama, burst into laughter, and the tension dissipated. Mama felt a lot better, and to the disappointment of the children, she ate the entire bowl of soup by herself, including a second helping!

The next day, Mama and Aidah went to Dr. Bulgar the lawyer in order to coordinate some final details. His office was in one of the rooms of his private home.

The lawyer sat behind an impressive mahogany table, and he rose when they entered the room. Dr. Bulgar made his way around the table to welcome them happily. He recognized Mama immediately (probably because of her one hand) and said to her, "If you only knew how much I loved my friend Dovid Fruchter, and how happy I am for the opportunity to help you, his widow, and Leah, his daughter." He asked them to sit, and he also sat down again.

Then he bent down and pulled something out of a drawer. It was a picture of Dr. Bulgar, Tatte, and two other men. Mama excitedly studied the picture, and Dr. Bulgar said, "Mrs. Fruchter, don't think that I brought this picture to work only in your honor. This picture has been here ever since I began to work as a lawyer. The four of us were close friends, and I am the only one of this group who is still alive. That's why I leave the picture here, to remind me that I owe a great debt to the families of the other three.

"I feel that if *HaKadosh Baruch Hu* has let me live, then it must be to help the families of my three deceased friends. Why, I've already conducted a court case for my friend Yitzchak Weiss's parents," he pointed to one of the faces in the picture. "Now it is your turn, Dovid Fruchter's wife, and I will do my best."

With that, he got down to business. He took out a cardboard file folder and showed Mama the statement of claim. He asked Mama a few more questions and added those details. Then he turned to Mama and said gently, "Perhaps, Mrs. Fruchter, it would be best if you didn't come to the courthouse. Please understand, I don't mean to insult you, but if you lose control over something said at the trial and you shout or say unpleasant things, it could make a very bad impression on the judges."

Mama was shocked to the core. "You think I should stay outside the courtroom when the fate of my own daughter is on trial? How can I possibly do that? On the contrary: I will compose myself within the courtroom and act politely. But if you think I should stay outside, I don't know if I would be able to control myself there. "

Dr. Bulgar knew that he couldn't force her, so he explained to Mama how a trial is conducted, and how one must act within a courtroom.

He also told Mama that I would not be present in the courtroom. Mama understood this. She wanted to see my adoptive parents, she was very curious to see what they looked like. But she promised over and over that she would not say a word to them; she would only speak when spoken to. She would act with extreme dignity and proper restraint.

❧ 33 ❧
The Feldmans Visit

[Budapest]

Zaidy and Bubby Feldman arrived just as we were eating supper. That was unusual, as they hardly ever came to our home at all. In fact, I don't remember the last time they visited us, certainly not together. When Anya was sick, Bubby Feldman came a few times and once, I think, Zaidy came for a few minutes to wish her *refuah sheleimah*, and then he left immediately. From then on—I don't remember them in our house.

Apa and Anya were so excited to see them that they both got up from their seats at the same time. I also rose.

My parents respectfully escorted Zaidy and Bubby to the guest room. Briendy ran into the kitchen quickly, to prepare refreshments. I tried to help her, but when I picked up a delicate crystal dish to fill it with cookies, the dish slipped from my hands. Luckily it fell on Apa's cushioned chair and didn't break. But that was enough for Briendy. She guided me to my chair and told me to finish eating and not bother her.

"I didn't mean to bother you, I only wanted to help," I told her quietly, "but every time I try to help, I just ruin things!" I burst into tears.

195

Meanwhile Briendy finished setting up the refreshments on the tray and brought it into the guest room. When she opened the door, I heard Zaidy say angrily, "Enough already! Don't go to court, why should you? You are sinking too much money into this!"

Then Briendy left the room and closed the door behind her, so I didn't hear the rest. She came into the kitchen and sat down next to me. Briendy thought that I would still be crying because of the plate, but I had already forgotten about that. Now I was very curious about what Zaidy said. In fact, he didn't say it, he shouted it.

The entire visit was very unusual. Zaidy comes to us unannounced, and shouts, or at least talks in a loud, angry voice—not like his regular self. It was all very strange.

I left Briendy in the kitchen and went to the back porch. The guest room's windows opened to that porch. As I had hoped, the windows were opened a crack. Anya liked to keep the windows slightly open in order to ventilate the room.

I sat on a stool near the window and listened to the conversation. I knew that what I was doing was wrong, but my curiosity was so strong that I forgot the rules. I sat down to concentrate.

Apa spoke, as usual, in a quiet, level tone of voice, so I couldn't hear what he was saying. Then Zaidy spoke again. He said something about money that the parents had sacrificed. Anya answered him, and that was unusual too. Since when does Anya speak around Zaidy Feldman? Strange things were certainly happening.

Suddenly I heard Anya burst into tears.

Zaidy's tone of voice became progressively angry. "You will not invest any more money in this! Give up, give in. Stop sinking so much money into this; she is simply not worth it!"

Were my ears playing tricks on me? Did he say, "It is not

worth it," or did he say, "She is not worth it"?

Could they be speaking about me? No, that was ridiculous. What did I have to do with any of this?

I didn't hear Apa's answer, only the echo of his voice. Then Zaidy shouted, but literally shouted, "If you don't stop this trial and don't give up, I will erase your name from my will. I will leave my money to families of Feldmans, and only Feldmans!"

I heaved a sigh of relief. No, they couldn't be talking about me. This was about that court case that our lives seemed to revolve around lately!

I had been curious for no good reason. Anya always told me that people who poke their noses into other people's business risk having their long noses snipped off. And she was right! Here I had been so convinced that they were talking about me, that I had already built entire plans, and now—my nose was cut off. The court case was simply money — lots of it, but nothing more.

So why didn't Zaidy want them to continue the trial? Was the other side right? Was Zaidy afraid that a court case would reveal something that should not be revealed? Did my honest, straightforward parents do something bad?

I had a lot more faith in my parents than in Zaidy. I did not have a good relationship with Zaidy and Bubby Feldman. They didn't love me and made that clear to everyone. When I was much younger, I had tried to be on my best behavior, polite, obedient and successful in my studies—I tried so hard to find favor in their eyes. When I got a little older I realized that all their grandchildren were tall and handsome while only I was short and skinny, with curly hair that was impossible to subdue. I thought that was the reason they didn't love me.

After I discovered the secret of my adoption I knew that

was the reason that they ignored me. I am not one of them, I don't belong, and I knew it wouldn't help in the least if I am on my best behavior or excel in my studies. So I stopped trying to get them to like me, and it became much less important to me over time.

I didn't ask anyone to adopt me. I was happy that Zaidy and Bubby Shapiro loved me despite the fact I was adopted, and that was the end of that.

But it seems that my feelings toward Zaidy and Bubby Feldman remained so strong that I thought they made this surprise visit because of me, and that it was because of something to do with me, that Zaidy — cultured and dignified Zaidy — actually raised his voice.

After I heard that the trial was to blame, I breathed a sigh of relief and went to my room without listening in on the rest of the visit.

Even when I heard the door opening and the guests leaving, I didn't go out of my room to say goodbye. I tried not to see them if I didn't have to, and I don't think anyone noticed.

Every day, there was more and more talk about the mysterious trial. People came over at night and sat with Apa in the guest room. Anya tried to stay out of the house; she didn't seem to want to be part of the discussions.

At night I heard Apa trying to convince her, over and over, but Anya just repeated the same sentence. "I don't care, I will fight." The words "will" and "inheritance" were repeated over and over again. Anya said she didn't care about an inheritance, but Apa begged her to reconsider — an inheritance is a very important thing, he said.

Anya just kept repeating that they had no need for an inheritance, they'd live until a hundred and twenty—and by that time, Mashiach would come.

Finally it was the day before the trial. The tension in the

house was enormous. You couldn't talk to Anya at all. Shortly after I came home from school, Anya packed a few things for me in a knapsack and sent me with Briendy to Bubby Shapiro's house. She told Briendy that for three days, I should not go to school and in fact, not show my face anywhere. I must stay in Bubby's house or in Basya Leah's house.

This order was odd, but frankly, I was overjoyed to leave my house with its unbearable tension. "I'm better off staying with Bubby during these difficult days," I thought, and went off happily with Briendy.

❦ 34 ❧
Red Days
[BUDAPEST/SEVLUS]

THE DAY OF the trial arrived. It was very important to Mama that she should look her best so she wore her Shabbos dress and shoes, and walked to the courthouse together with Aidah Weingarten. The two women took seats on the last bench in a corner of the public spectator's gallery. Mama wanted to blend in with the crowd and not stand out in any way.

Mama wanted to see my adoptive parents. She wanted to look into the eyes of the woman who had bought her child. Later on, Mama explained to me that she figured that a woman who had paid such a large sum of money for a baby would take care of the child's physical needs. But did she love me? When a child is brought up without love, his or her soul can be damaged irreparably. A child can receive everything he physically needs, but will grow up in a barren emotional wilderness without love. Just as children cannot flourish without basic food, clothing and shelter, so they cannot thrive without love. And indeed, children who grow up under abusive, loveless conditions often become cruel, problematic adults.

As Mama waited, she reminded herself of the promises

she had made to the attorney: She must not say a word, even if she would hear falsehoods about herself or anyone else. This was the condition for allowing her to come to court and she promised to guard her tongue, come what may. She must make a good impression. It must be clear that she is a respectable woman who, despite her disability and widowhood, earns her own livelihood and can take care of her daughter's needs. That's why she listened to Chana Malka Zinger and borrowed her friend's beautiful necklace — a diamond-studded gold necklace — to wear in court.

The benches for the public were full. Most of the spectators were male gentiles, evidently unemployed, who had come to the warm courthouse to pass time.

Mama searched throughout the entire hall, and did not see people who looked like the adoptive parents. They simply did not come. Two people sitting on Mama's bench played cards, and they weren't the only ones. In fact, many people were either playing cards or napping on the warm benches, and some were even snoring. Then there were the others who came to enjoy a free show; people who took joy in other people's misfortunes.

The exceptions were two women sitting in the front row. They followed the trial carefully, occasionally exchanging a few words between each other, and often looked around to examine all the attendants. They especially kept their eyes on Mama and Aidah Weingarten. Mama told me that she heard one woman refer to the other as "Julia," and then I knew for sure: Anya must have sent them to report back to her, and they wanted to have a good look at my birth mother.

The audience benches were located behind a wooden partition, reminding Mama of the women's section in shul. But at least in the courtroom there was no curtain, so the spectators had a clear view of what was going on.

There were two doors in the courtroom in addition to the door of the spectator's gallery. One door was on the long side of the wall and Mama's attorney entered through it, dressed in a long black robe. Another man entered as well, dressed in the same manner.

The second door was on the short wall opposite the gallery — the judge would enter through that door. There was a long desk near the judge's door, and a large, impressive chair. Next to the large table was a smaller table with a court clerk who took minutes of the proceedings.

There was a tumult of noise in the courtroom. Mama's lawyer spoke to the other lawyer, and then they took their places behind tables facing one another in the space between the judge's table and the spectator's gallery.

Then a very old man, dressed in black, entered the court-room. He cried loudly, "Honor in the court!" Everyone be-came quiet, and then he announced, "All rise: His Honor the judge is entering." The entire audience stood up and then the old man approached the judge's door, opened it and waited respectfully on the side. He stood there, at the side, until the end of the proceedings.

The judge entered. He was an older man with a respect-able, distinguished appearance.

Mama was happy to see this. She was afraid of a young, impatient justice who wouldn't have time to hear what her lawyer had to say. But she felt reassured that an older, expe-rienced justice would listen carefully and patiently and not render hasty judgments.

The judge sat down and talked quietly to the two attor-neys, who answered him just as quietly. They seemed to be chatting politely. Mama was taken aback: Did they think they were in a coffee shop? Perhaps someone should offer them some cake and coffee while they chatted about the weather?

This was a most serious occasion; the trial was a matter of life and death, Mama thought, having difficulty understanding how they could waste time on pleasantries. Aidah Weingarten felt the same way, so she asked the man sitting next to her if he could explain what was happening. It turned out that he was a regular spectator at these trials. He very quietly told them that the two lawyers discuss all sorts of procedural issues before the actual beginning of the trial. "Don't worry," he whispered, "this is only the pre-trial section. The interesting part will come later, and it will be conducted in regular voices — you'll be able to hear everything." Yes, court trials were simply entertainment for these people.

Mama described the trial to me many times. She described the Budapest courtroom, the large brass chandelier that hung decorously in the middle of the ceiling, as well as the smaller chandeliers that lined the walls of the hall. She described the picture of "Justice" hanging behind the judge's chair: a woman with blindfolded eyes holding a book in one hand and scales in the other. Mama also described the people in the courtroom; how they were dressed, how they behaved, what they said.

But Mama would not, could not, tell me anything about the trial itself. Every time she tried, she burst into tears. The only thing I gleaned from her was that the trial went on for many days and that they discussed all kinds of details that did not seem at all important to Mama.

One day, Mama was called upon to testify. She walked up to the witness stand, but when she started to talk, she fainted. She did not give in, though, and when they revived her, she continued to testify. Every time she told me this part, she would turn pale and look ready to faint again. So that's why I don't know a thing about what was said at the trial, though I could give a precise description of what the courtroom looked like and could tell you how many people played cards in the audience.

After many days of proceedings, the trial was concluded. The judge announced that he would deliver his verdict in about a month.

A month! An entire month to wait for the verdict! Could there be greater torture than that? A month contains four weeks; each week contains seven days; and each day — twenty-four hours. It seemed like an eternity.

Mama called this waiting period the "red days." I never understood why "red days" and not "black days," but Mama said that's all she saw during the waiting period —red.

Aidah Weingarten accompanied Mama back to Sevlus.

Mama didn't remember a thing about their trip home; she simply woke up to find herself in the store. She couldn't even remember how she functioned that month, or whether she worked in the store, whether she even ate. The month passed by like a nightmare, and she couldn't talk about it.

The only thing she would say was that those days of waiting were "red days."

❧ 35 ❧
Thirteen Months
[BUDAPEST]

A MONTH LATER, Mama went back to Budapest to hear the verdict. Aidah Weingarten could not accompany her this time, so another kindly woman, Mrs. Weinberg, took her place. She, too, was one of Sevlus's "women of valor" who involved themselves in *chesed* activities.

Mrs. Weinberg and her entire family were killed in the Holocaust. Hy"d.

Mama told me about the verdict innumerable times. She didn't even go to the courtroom; instead, she and Mrs. Weinberg waited for her lawyer in Liberty Hilltop near the Parliament building. They sat on a bench quietly and davened for good news, *besoros tovos*.

Finally, Dr. Bulgar arrived. He sat down on the bench and said, "Hello." Instead of returning his greeting, Mama burst into tears. The lawyer tried to calm Mama down. "Mrs. Fruchter," he said, "everything is fine, *Baruch Hashem*! I hope you'll invite me to a *kiddush* in celebration."

Mama immediately understood his cryptic statement and

drew in her breath sharply.

Mrs. Weinberg started to shout, "*Nu*, tell us already; don't keep us in suspense any longer."

Dr. Bulgar responded slowly, "I have good news, but there is a down side to the good news."

"Never mind!" shouted Mrs. Weinberg. "Just tell us already!"

He turned to Mama and said, "Mrs. Fruchter, you will get your daughter, but not immediately."

Mama rose from her seat and whispered, "What do you mean—not immediately?"

Dr. Bulgar explained, "This is the verdict: The court feels that the Feldmans adopted the baby in good faith, irregardless of the money they paid — which evidently, the middlemen pocketed. On the other hand, Mrs. Fruchter never gave up her daughter for adoption. In light of all this, the court decided that when Leah turns twelve years old, she will return to her biological mother for six months. At the end of six months, she herself will decide where she belongs and with whom to remain."

Mama sank back heavily on the bench. She simply could not utter a word as she absorbed the import of the verdict. She realized immediately that she would have to wait more than a year until Leichu's twelfth birthday, and that seemed like an eternity.

But it was more than that. Much, much more than that.

Once Leichu reached her twelfth birthday, she, Sheina Ruchel Fruchter, would be forced to compete for her daughter's attentions with a wealthy Budapest family who could afford to give their daughter anything she wanted. She, Sheina Ruchel Fruchter, a widow with an artificial arm in a remote village, a woman who eked out a living in a grocery store, with only a tiny bedroom to live in—how was it possible that a girl who was raised in luxury for twelve years, would ever want to join such a life with her mother?

Other wrenching memories gripped her: Kreindy and her two brothers. They had left her and Sevlus as soon as they could, without a backwards look, and they weren't even "adopted" by anyone else.

Mama looked around her. Liberty Hilltop was beautiful, full of trees and flowers. The neo-Gothic Parliament Building towered in the background; tourists from all over the world come to see this magnificent building. Even the very bench on which she sat was beautifully crafted. All Hungarians say that Budapest is the most beautiful city in the world.

Buda, the ancient city with all its stylish buildings and its castle on the mountaintop looked straight out of a fairy-tale book. Next to it was the church though of course, Mama as a proper Jewish woman would not praise its beauty so as not to transgress *"lo sechanem."*

On one side was the Fishermen's Bastion, and the entire Gellért Hill. What an indescribable view! And the city itself: the Vàci utca, a pedestrian square with magnificent stores and special street lamps, and a promenade area on which noblemen walked in the eighteenth and nineteenth centuries.

On the other side of the Danube was Pest, a new, modern city that was just as beautiful as Buda. And the lovely bridges over the Danube that connected Pest and Buda—the Chain Bridge and many others.

And what did she have to offer in contrast to Budapest, one of the most beautiful cities in the world? Sevlus. True, Sevlus was not a tiny village — it was a district town with its own satellite villages. Sevlus's main streets were spacious and pleasant. The banks, businesses and many elegant stores lined the few main streets. There was a bustling industrial zone in Sevlus, too. And there were numerous shuls and *batei me-*

drash, as well as a large yeshivah and many *cheders*. But even with all these, could one compare Sevlus to Budapest?

Mama had never been in the Feldmans' apartment, but she had seen other beautiful homes in Budapest. And her daughter, her Leichu, would have to decide where to live when she turned twelve years old: in the Feldmans' luxury apartment, or in the tiny apartment/grocery store of her biological mother?

Had there ever been a more draconian verdict?

Mama sat, dumbfounded, unable to lift a finger. The lawyer immediately understood what was on her mind, and tried to encourage her.

"You are wrong, Mrs. Fruchter. Blood is thicker than water, and one can't switch the emotional and biological maternal bond for all the money in the world. I am sure it is all for the best, and you will see—your daughter will want to live with you, only with you." Dr. Bulgar kept repeating these words over and over, and Mrs. Weinberg reiterated them as well.

Finally, Mama went to the Zinger family. They had already heard the verdict, and they too encouraged Mama with words similar to Dr. Bulgar's. The next day Mama took the long train ride home with Mrs. Weinberg. Mama laughed bitterly: She had thought that a month was a long time to wait for the verdict, and now she was being forced to wait for more than a year to meet her daughter.

Mrs. Weinberg opened her bag and took out her *sefer Tehillim*. Placing it in Mama's hand, she said, "You will see that David HaMelech wrote *sefer Tehillim* specifically for you, Sheina Ruchel, to comfort you during your trials and tribulations. Promise me that you will complete the whole *sefer Tehillim* every week, and place your trust in our Father in Heaven. If this is what He decided, it must be for the best, though we do not understand why. Somehow, somewhere, there is a reason for all this. Place your heart and trust in Hashem; He hears your cries and will come to your rescue."

Thus Mrs. Weinberg's *sefer Tehillim* was placed in Mama's hands. And truly, the words of David HaMelech were to help her through the thirteen long months that awaited her.

❧ 36 ❧
To Live in the Present
[BUDAPEST]

I HAD BEEN at Bubby's house for the past few days, enjoying myself thoroughly. It was always a welcome change to visit Zaidy and Bubby Shapiro, but this time I welcomed the change three-fold. I was happy to have left the tense atmosphere at home and was reveling in the calmness of Bubby's home and the love and attention I was receiving. One afternoon, Anya appeared. Her eyes were red and swollen; it was clear that she had been crying. She sat down on the couch with Bubby immediately.

I walked over to the shelf in the corner to pick up the book I had left there, but Anya didn't even wait until I left to spill out her heart to Bubby. I guess she didn't realize how well I understood Yiddish, even though she knew that I was taking lessons in the language. But I have a knack for languages—I had even learned the gypsy language from Chungarabi, before she left us—and I was pretty fluent in Yiddish already.

Anya started talking to Bubby about the trial, as usual. I was ready to go back to my book and ignore their conversation, but then I heard my name. Was I connected to this court case, after all? This nuisance that put so much tension into our lives, that caused everyone to be so nervous? The court case that I had thought was related to the store and Apa's business?

I curled up with my book in a dark corner of the room and pretended to be reading. I heard Anya's voice clearly. She was very angry and was talking louder than she usually did.

"She took all the money for herself!" Anya said. "The poor mother did not receive a cent, it was Néni Eva who took it all! She gave some to the family who gave her the baby, and kept the rest herself! What kind of sister-in-law would do such a thing? To steal the money from a destitute woman, to lie to me, to steal money from me? You all chipped in to help me raise the sum of money she demanded: you, my dear parents, my brothers and sisters—and Heaven knows, none of you have money to spare. I took a big loan and I sold the diamond in my engagement ring and replaced it with a piece of glass so my husband wouldn't realize. All this so that a family member — not a stranger, but my husband's sister — could buy herself a mansion in Berg and live in the lap of luxury. You must have heard my mother-in-law talk about that mansion!"

Anya could not continue because she was crying so hard. Bubby brought her a glass of water, and after a few minutes Anya resumed her horrific tale.

Anya told Bubby about that horrible episode on Rosh Hashanah a few years before, when Néni Eva had told me that she was forced to leave Budapest because of me. I remember how cruel Eva had been to me, for no reason I could understand at the time. "Eva and her family left Budapest not because of Leichu at all," Anya sobbed, "but only because she couldn't buy a luxury house next to us here in the city. We would have been suspicious; we would have realized immediately where the money came from. She spun lies, lots of lies, telling us that she had found a real bargain, that she bought her mansion on some special deal, and it cost her very little. Now we understand where the money really came from!"

Anya got up and circled the room like a caged lion. I thought that she'd ask me to leave, book or no book, but she didn't even seem to notice me.

After a few minutes, Anya sat back down next to Bubby. "That poor woman never received a cent, and she never gave up her daughter for adoption. They stole the baby from her! Now I understand why she is fighting to get her back. I guess if I were in her shoes, I'd do the same thing. And you know something, she is not as poor and indigent as they described to me. My informant at the courtroom told me that she is dressed nicely, looks respectable and wears expensive jewelry. Not some kind of disabled wretch. Lies, lies, lies!

"Of course, I have no intentions of giving up my Leichu. But at least I understand that woman now. No wonder she is fighting so hard; after all, the baby was stolen from her. But I am also stubborn. I raised Leichu, I brought her up, I gave her everything a parent can give a child: clothes, special lessons, a nanny, everything she ever wanted. I won't give her up!"

Now I finally understood what the tension of the last few months was all about. It was all about me! The court case had nothing to do with the store — Apa and Anya were fighting for me!

And my biological mother, my birth mother—what do they call it?—she was still alive. They didn't mention a father; perhaps he was dead? I had been stolen from my mother, just like in those scary fairy tales. Two mothers were fighting over me, two mothers wanted me.

Where do I belong? Where is Shlomo HaMelech to command: Cut her in half![5]

I belong to two mothers. Both of them are in the right, both of them want me. And what about me? Where was I supposed to go, with whom was I supposed to live?

Anya got up and left. She didn't even look for me to say goodbye. Come to think of it, she had hardly paid attention to me at all since the trial started.

Only since the trial started? This was the time for me to face the truth. No more lies, no more lies!

It was painful for me to admit, even to myself, that Anya had always been so busy reading books or doing things outside the house to pay attention to me. It was Briendy I confided in, and Bubby Shapiro, and Basya Leah and her girls. And of course, Chungarabi. But Anya? "Don't confuse me, I'm reading." "Go tell Briendy." "We don't talk about those things."

Was I, Leichu Feldman, really important to Anya? Or was it only the fight over me that was important? If she was investing so much effort in fighting for me, why did she ignore me?

Was it the money that Néni Eva took that infuriated her? Or was it the money she had invested in me all these years — the clothes, the shoes, the toys?

Meanwhile, Bubby Shapiro had been escorting Anya out. When she returned she noticed me on the chair in the corner, and came over to me. I immediately started talking to her in Yiddish because I wanted her to know that I understood her conversation with Anya. No more secrets, no more lies.

---

5. Leichu remembered *Shlomo HaMelech's* famous ruling when two women came to him, each claiming that the same infant was hers. See *Melachim* I 3:25.

"What will be with me, Bubby?" I asked, and burst into tears.

Bubby hugged me and did not answer. She just held me close and stroked my head.

"Where do I belong, Bubby?" I asked through my tears. "Who is my real mother?"

But Bubby had no answers either. She had a difficult role to play: to comfort her daughter, and then me, her granddaughter.

Her granddaughter? Am I really her granddaughter? She isn't really my grandmother; she is the mother of my adoptive mother. I am no blood relation of hers; we are connected only by love. I really love my relatives on Anya's side, and they love me as well. The relatives on Apa's side, on the other hand, don't love me; they never did. I couldn't imagine Bubby Feldman, Apa's mother, hugging me the way Bubby Shapiro did.

"It doesn't matter how our relationship is defined by the law," Bubby Shapiro kept saying, over and over. "There is only one thing that is clear: I love you dearly, and that is what is important. Nothing else matters; I love you as you are."

After a few days, Anya and Apa came to Bubby Shapiro's house to pick me up. The trial was over and they had come to take me home.

Both my parents looked terrible. You could see that Anya had cried for days on end; she was pale and had lost weight. Apa was also pale and he sighed a lot. They told Zaidy and Bubby that the judge would render his verdict in another month. An entire month to live in uncertainty!

"How can they do this to us?" asked Apa painfully. "If this isn't miscarriage of justice, then it is torture like in the Inquisition."

Zaidy and Bubby nodded their heads in agreement. This

was real emotional torture—waiting an entire month! Why were they doing this? Why didn't they deliver the verdict immediately? What was so complicated that the judge needed an entire month?

"What a cruel judge, a man who does not take the suffering of others into account. One whole month—how can we endure the uncertainty for so long? When you wait for only a half hour, it seems that time stands still. And a month, thirty days? It's impossible to wait so long!" said Anya passionately.

I looked alternately at Apa and Anya, and at Zaidy and Bubby, and thought: In another month, they'll return to the judge and he will say: Cut her in half! I must pray that one of the mothers will give in. The important thing is that they shouldn't cut me in half. I want to live, never mind with which mother!

And I—to whom do I really belong? To the one who would say: Cut her in half! or the one who will give in to spare my life?

But the judge is not Shlomo HaMelech and I am not an infant during the time of the Beis HaMikdash. The judge is a gentile, and I am not in Eretz Yisrael or in Yerushalayim. I am just Leichu, almost eleven years old, in the city of Budapest in Hungary.

I finally went back to school. All my classmates said that they could see that I had been sick. They even asked if I was sure that I was well enough to resume my studies, as I was very pale and still looked ill.

Of course, I did not say a word about what had really taken place.

For Anya, those terrible days of the court case had been more stressful than any other ordeal she had experienced. I only found out after the trial was completed that the entire fuss was about me — that it was not connected to the store after all. At that point, I was still unaware of the far-reaching change it would have on my life. Even so, with the newfound knowledge, I felt like a displaced person, my identity uncertain, and the nights that followed were full of heartache and despair. But for Apa and Anya, it was a hundred times worse. They had known everything in full from the very start of the trial, and had been plagued by the fear of the unknown and the pressures of the trial for months already. The tension at home was so thick, you could cut it with a knife.

On my first day back in school, I went home to find that Anya was not there. Briendy told me that Anya had cried a lot before she left. I figured that she probably went to Bubby.

Then Briendy announced that she wanted to go back home. I guess that the tension at our house was too much for her. I realized that she had no clue as to what was going on, so I told her everything that I knew about the court case and my birth mother. I convinced her not to leave just yet; I didn't want to be alone without her, and I didn't want anything to cause Anya more heartache on top of everything else.

Briendy thanked me for sharing the news with her. She told me that the past few months in our tense house had been unbearable for her, but now that she knew what our family was going through, she would have an easier time dealing with the unpleasant environment.

The two of us tried to figure out what the judge would decide. The truth is that I really wanted to meet my birth mother. On the other hand I was also afraid that the judge would decide that I had to live with her, and I didn't know her at all. I had no idea what kind of person she was. But here in Budapest, with Apa and Anya, I was comfortable. I knew exactly what my place was; I was content with my parents, my cousins and relatives, my friends, my school. Even if there had been difficult periods and bumps in the road with my parents because of the adoption and everything connected to it—still, this was my familiar world.

I must say that I still thank Briendy with my whole heart for helping me survive that tense month.

On the day of the verdict, I went to school. At first Anya wanted me to go to Bubby Shapiro, but I thought it would be better if I acted like it was a regular school day. I hoped that before I returned, Anya would have the judge's answer.

Briendy was wonderful! She promised to pick me up in school and walk me home. She understood how difficult it was for me.

When Briendy left home to pick me up at school, Anya still had not returned. Briendy didn't even know where she had gone. Anya said that she would not go to the courtroom; she had never been there and was afraid to go. But this time, Apa went—for the first time. During the trial he had gone to the store every day.

That had seemed queer to me. How could there be a trial if my parents never went to court? Did their lawyer manage it all by himself? Didn't he need their help at all? I didn't understand it.

When we came home from school, Apa and Anya were sitting with the lawyer. I had seen this man in our house many times, but only now did I realize that he was my parents' lawyer. He was the one they had paid handsomely, as I had overheard them saying in the past.

Anya hugged me tightly, twisting me until it hurt, and she burst into tears. "Leichu, my Leichu! You are mine, you will always be mine! Six months is nothing, it will pass quickly. You will remain mine, only mine!"

Of course I didn't understand her words; the lawyer explained them to me. "You will remain here, with your parents, until your twelfth birthday," he said. "Then you will go to your birth mother for six months. After that, you—and only you—will decide where you belong, and where you want to be."

"Of course," he added confidently, "you will want to remain here with the Feldmans, with the wonderful parents who raised you so well and did so much for you."

Afterwards Briendy and I had a long talk. "You have a long time until your twelfth birthday," she said. "It's over a year away. Meanwhile you have to live your regular life and try to forget the future." She told me that if I always thought about "what would be," I wouldn't be able to live normally.

"Just live in the present," she would say to me, over and over, when she saw me start to daydream, or when I became irritable and snappish. "Don't think about the future, Leichu. You will cross that bridge when you come to it."

And that's exactly what I tried to do. Once in a while I'd start to wonder what it would be like to move far away from Anya and everything familiar to me, but I stopped myself. I tried to be happy and get the most out of the situation. And, truth be told, it was quite a pleasant time indeed.

During that time period, Anya bought me tons of things: clothes, shoes, boots and toys. Almost every day, a gift waited for me in my room; from small simple gifts like a new pencil or small mirror, to expensive jewelry.

Briendy told me that Anya was trying to buy my love. "I'm sure she's worried that you'll like it better with your birth mother and not return to her, so she's getting you all this stuff." Briendy stopped to think for a minute. "You know what?" she said thoughtfully. "Your birth mother probably does not have a lot of money, maybe she's even poor and can't buy you these things. So this way, Anya emphasizes the difference between herself and your birth mother."

To be honest, I admit that I enjoyed the presents even

though some were really superfluous. I gave away a lot of things to Briendy and my cousins. Anya told me that the gifts were mine and I could do with them as I pleased. I even gave away some of the more simple pieces of jewelry to Briendy. At first she didn't want to take them, but I convinced her.

Briendy and I both knew that she would leave when I went to my biological mother at my twelfth birthday. So whenever I gave her something, I told her it was a goodbye present. When I gave her jewelry, I told her it was for her dowry. Briendy laughed and said, "Maybe your presents will enable me to stand on my own two feet."

Meanwhile, I got whatever I wanted. My parents never got angry at me or asked me to do anything. I did whatever I felt like. I felt that I was living on borrowed time. I could have taken advantage of the situation, but I did not want to. My parents wanted me to be happy with them so that I would not even consider not returning to them after the six months. But I didn't want to think about it at all.

After all, I was certain that I would return to them and not exchange them for some strange woman I had never met. Here I grew up, here I was loved, and here was my life. Why would I exchange these familiar, comfortable surroundings for a strange woman in a foreign, distant, poor village?

In the past whenever I had asked Anya for something, she'd laugh and say: When we get to that bridge, we'll cross it. So now I decided the same thing: Today I am living in the present, and I don't have to cross that bridge as yet. I won't think about what will be and how, since I have no idea what will be. Why make plans out of the blue? No, I hadn't reached the bridge yet and had no need to cross it.

I took lots of walks in those days. Briendy and I investigated a different section or neighborhood of lovely Budapest every week. There is a lot to see in that city, and I enjoyed touring each place anew. I also went to visit extended family whom I had not seen in a long time. Anya also thought this was a good idea and took me to anyone I suggested.

That's how I found myself walking every day, either with Briendy or Anya. When I went with Anya, we found ourselves concluding our excursions in Bubby Shapiro's house. I also frequently went to visit Néni Basya Leah's family, and then Anya would sit and chat with Bubby.

Anya told me every day, "We have X days left." But I closed my ears; I didn't want to participate in this frightening countdown. I was determined to live the present and not the future.

But at night, at night I could not control my dreams. I had nightmares every night, nightmares about my birth mother and her home, nightmares from which I awoke with a pounding heart and tears. I dreamed of grinding poverty; a dark, filthy hut, and a life of begging for alms.

The year passed like a dream. Only one month remained until my twelfth birthday, until I would be responsible for the *mitzvos*. Apa sat and taught me many *halachos*. "You must know all this," he repeated. "Once you are twelve, you will be responsible for your own actions. If you do an *aveirah*, you will be held accountable by Hashem."

❧ 37 ❧
The Approaching Change
[BUDAPEST]

RIENDY DECIDED to leave before I did; she said that she didn't have the emotional stamina to see me off first. I helped her pack her things, and one entire box contained only things I had given her! She arranged that her brother would come to pick her up and take her home.

This was the first time I ever met one of her family members. I was familiar with Briendy's family only from her stories about them. She came from a family of five children, and she was the oldest. Her brother Hershi, the next in line, was two years younger, and they were very close. Briendy once told me that she was much closer to him than to her three younger sisters.

Though I had heard so much about Hershi, I was still amazed to meet him. He looked remarkably like a male version of Briendy. He had the same features, the same bright eyes, even the same walk and voice as his sister. When he came into his sister's room and saw two boxes and a suitcase, he was shocked. "Is all this yours?" he asked. "How on earth were you able to accumulate so many possessions?" he kept repeating over and over in amazement. After all, Briendy had

221

arrived with only one small suitcase.

True, I had given Briendy many presents to take home, but so had Anya! She had supplied her generously with linens and towels that she had decided she no longer needed. And as she folded and packed them up, she said, "This is for your dowry." So Anya filled one box with her presents, and I filled the second with mine — though not in front of Anya. Hershi joked that he needed to hire a carriage, otherwise how would he manage to carry it all to the train station?!

When Hershi left the house with the first round of luggage, I rushed to push some more things into Briendy's luggage. But suddenly she objected, and she didn't even want to take the box that I had already packed for her. The truth is, every time I gave her something, I had to persuade her to take it, so why should this time be different? I just repeated what I told her all the other times — that I wouldn't be taking any of these things with me when I go to my birth mother, and that the Feldmans don't have any other children to enjoy them. "Briendy, you just have to take them," I said resolutely.

Hershi came upstairs for the next box and found the two of us crying and hugging one another. He was totally confused; just a few minutes ago we were laughing, and now this? He complained about how heavy the box was ("What do you have in here, rocks?!") and this made us laugh, but suddenly we found ourselves sobbing and wailing at the top of our lungs. When would we see each other again, if ever? Neither of us said this out loud, but that was what we were thinking. Briendy had been wonderful to me; she had brought happiness and optimism into our sad household and I would never forget that.

Hershi tried to stop us from crying and when he was not successful, he gave up and took down the second box. When he came up again to take the suitcase as well as a few additional bags and — of course! — his sister, he found us in the same exact position as he had left us, crying hysterically. "The Danube is already dangerously full to the brim with water," he proclaimed. "This year was even more rainy and snowy than usual, and there is fear of flooding. You are crying so much that you will cause the villages on the riverbanks to be flooded. Enough of this already!"

His words didn't exactly calm us down; instead, we cried even more. Finally, Hershi took Briendy's hand and started to pull her away. It was only at that point that we got up and said our proper goodbyes to one another.

Luckily, Anya wasn't home. She said she had something to take care of and wished Briendy well before she left the house. Anya had lived through the past year in the shadow of parting from me, and probably couldn't bear another parting from Briendy. But in any case I was glad that she wasn't home to see the box that I had packed up for Briendy, full of all the presents Anya had given me. True, she had told me that the gifts were mine to do with as I pleased, yet who knows how she would have reacted. I would tell her later, when it would be too late for her to stop me.

Briendy went down the stairs and I followed her. We hugged again next to the carriage for the very last time. As she entered the carriage she called to me, "Don't forget to stay in touch and write me those letters you promised!"

A cloud of dust rose as the carriage rolled away, and I was barely able to see Briendy as she waved her last goodbyes.

I walked back into the house, my head bent in sorrow. Mrs. Kantzuk, the doorman's wife, welcomed me at the door. "Miss Feldman, I see that you have parted from your nanny," she said snobbily. "Young lady, you are much too old to cry over something like that; you should be happy that you are a young woman who no longer needs a nanny. You must cease your crying at once, you look absolutely horrible." As she spoke, she clapped her hands for emphasis. At first, I was shocked at her words and stopped in my tracks to listen, but then I immediately ran up the stairs. I could still hear her below, clapping her hands and talking, on and on.

Mrs. Kantzuk used to clean our house once a week until Briendy arrived and took over that function. Briendy cleaned quickly and tastefully; under her care, the house was neater and cleaner than it had ever been. Of course, Mrs. Kantzuk did not like Briendy very much. I imagine that she was happy to see Briendy leave because she probably counted on being able to clean the house again and earn more money.

I didn't like Mrs. Kantzuk at all, and not only because of this incident. I had often found her pocketing objects in our home when she thought that no one was watching, and there were times that I forced her to return items from her pockets. I remembered how Chungarabi had kept her eyes on Mrs. Kantzuk, in that wonderful time when Chungarabi had been part of my life. Chungarabi always said that the woman felt free to steal because she could blame it on Chungarabi the gypsy.

Yet I had never told Anya about this. Somehow I was afraid of Mrs. Kantzuk, the doorman's wife; there was something about her sly, cruel eyes that made me uneasy. But this time, I promised myself, I would tell Anya. It was time that Anya hired a nice Jewish cleaning woman. I would see to it that Mrs. Kantzuk would never step foot in our house again.

I went right to my room. Even though I had just parted from Briendy, I sat down to write her a letter. It was the first of a long series of letters that I wrote to her over the years.

◇◇

I did meet Briendy again, many years later in Eretz Yisrael. Briendy told me that with all the jewelry and valuables I had given her, she

bribed a non-Jewish neighbor to hide her family during the war. The
entire family — except Hershi — hid in the woman's attic throughout
the war. Briendy promised the gentile that the jewelry was only an
advance payment, and that after the war she would travel to Budapest
and bring her much more jewelry. And truly, after the war, the entire
family went to Budapest—and from there they left for Eretz Yisrael.
So my gifts had, indeed, helped Briendy — and her entire family —
stand on her "own two feet."

Hershi — the only one whom they were not able to hide in the attic
— was murdered al Kiddush HaShem. Hy"d.

The day finally arrived: the day of my twelfth birthday. They
did not make a party for me; only little kids get birthday par-
ties, I guess. And they didn't even buy me a present. Nothing.

On the night preceding my birthday I couldn't sleep. I was
facing two major events in my life: One—just like any girl
my age, I was about to celebrate my *bas mitzvah*, the day I
became obligated to carry out the *mitzvos*. Apa had taught
me well. Of course, I had carried out the *mitzvos* and scrupulously avoided *aveiros* for many years, but that was only
because of *chinuch*, of education. However, from the day of
my twelfth birthday, I was obliged to follow the Torah as a
bona-fide adult. If I sinned, it would be written against me
in the Heavenly books. I must be extra careful about every
word and every action, and that seemed like a formidable
task. How would I be able to plan every little action or conversation in advance, to think it through first so that I would
not do the wrong thing? My life would not be so simple and
serene as before. Yes indeed, life was certainly getting complicated!

And truly, my life was about to be transformed for another reason, and that was my second major life change: I was

leaving my home, the father and mother who raised me with devotion, to meet my birth mother. I was leaving Budapest, the large, beautiful and modern city for a small, backwards town. I was leaving an elegantly appointed home with my own private bedroom, a home where I received every object I ever desired, and moving to a poor woman's home. And finally: I was leaving a family with a father and mother to join a lone, disabled widow.

When I stood on the balcony of our apartment, I looked into the distance at the city. I could see up until the place where the heavens touched the hills behind the last houses; this was the horizon. This is what they call, "looking into the future, looking ahead." But I thought to myself — as I was trying to envision my future lifestyle — it's as if a thick, heavy curtain is hanging in front of the porch, completely obstructing my view. I simply have no way of knowing what the morrow may bring.

From my bed in my room I heard Apa and Anya talking. It was very late and they, too, could not fall asleep. I knew that they were afraid of this farewell, especially Anya.

I, on the other hand, was not overly concerned about this temporary separation. I knew it was only for half a year and it was clear to me that after the six months were up, I would return to my comfortable and secure life in Budapest. But I was curious about my trip and eager to meet the woman who gave birth to me. I wanted to become acquainted with my birthplace and with the lifestyle of the small town. I hoped I would make friends there as well. Would my friends there be different from my friends in the big city?

In fact, I was so curious and excited that I was not sorry to leave the place in which I had grown up. Six months was not a long time until my return. No matter what I found in the village, I would certainly return to my familiar life. These thoughts calmed me down.

The preceding day had been an emotional one — on that day I parted from my extended family. First I went to Zaidy and Bubby Feldman and parted from them decorously and respectably, as was appropriate. Then I went to Zaidy and Bubby Shapiro. There I found my uncles and aunts and cousins who had come to see me off. My farewell from them was not at all "decorous and respectable" — it was noisy and sad, full of tears and weeping.

When I returned home, I realized how the farewells from the two families attested to the very nature of my relationships with the respective family members. On Apa's side—everything was cold, proper and restrained. True, they kissed me as was customary; first on the right cheek, then the left. There were handshakes and then my rehearsed curtsy. But it was all mechanical and unemotional, without tears or requests for letters, and no one called after me from the balcony down to the street. Bubby Feldman had always said, "The Feldmans are not common people; we are a respectable family and must act accordingly." She had always admonished me when she even suspected that I wanted to run, jump, speak out loud or do some other unseemly act. As if I would even consider doing anything not "respectable" around the greater Feldman family!

But it was in the Shapiro family—a family without any pretensions — that there was warmth and love, and we said our goodbyes accordingly. It was very hard for me to say farewell, and I clung to Bubby as we hugged for a long time by the door. And when I went outside to the street, the whole family stood on the porch, waving.

I waved and waved, and was not at all embarrassed at the tears that flowed freely down my face.

❧ 38 ❧
Farewell
[BUDAPEST]

I DON'T KNOW when I fell asleep, but when Anya came to
wake me up in the morning I was already awake. She saw
that I wasn't sleeping so she prodded me, "Get up, Apa
will be home soon from davening and then he has to go to
work. Get dressed quickly so that he can give you a *berachah*
before you leave."

I was a bit taken aback. "What? Apa isn't even coming
with us to the train station?" I asked Anya. Anya bit her lip
and didn't answer. Later on I realized that for Apa, saying
goodbye to me must have been so painful that he preferred
to make his farewells as quickly as possible, and not prolong
the pain. But at the time, I was hurt.

Apa was waiting for me, and the three of us sat down to
eat breakfast. Truth be told, none of us actually ate anything,
though I played with my cheese with a fork. "At least finish your bread so that you can *bentch*," Apa requested. With
great difficulty, I managed to finish that piece of bread: I had
to force myself to chew every single bite.

After the meal, Apa approached me and gave me the traditional Friday night *berachah*. He placed his white hand-

kerchief on my head and his voice broke when he said, "Lei-chu, I will miss you. I won't have anyone to bless on Friday nights when you're not here." I cried silently as he continued, "Please, Leichu, return to us the same wonderful daughter we are sending off now." He looked at me intently for a long moment, then turned around and left the house.

I ran to the big window, hoping he would say something else or at least wave to me—but he didn't even turn around. I did see him dab his eyes with the handkerchief he was still holding.

I turned around to face Anya. She, too, was crying quietly. When she saw that I was approaching her, she recovered her composure and launched into her "etiquette lecture." "Please remember, Leichu, you must speak respectfully to 'her.' *Chas v'shalom*, don't be rude! Remember to sit straight, the way I've taught you; no slouching and for heaven's sake, don't stick your feet out in front of you!" The list went on and on: how to laugh and how to speak; how to address adults and a million other instructions. I knew this lecture by heart. From the time I was a young child, Anya would give me this speech every time we went to visit Zaidy and Bubby Feldman. I pretended to listen, and nodded my head in agreement. I didn't want anyone to think of me as rude; after all, I was already a *bas mitzvah* girl!

We went into my room, and Anya started to pack a very small suitcase for me. She took a few pairs of underwear out of my dresser, one weekday dress and one that was a little nicer. I was surprised. "What about all my lovely Shabbos dresses?" I asked. "They cost me a lot of money," Anya replied. "It's best that they remain here. After all, you'll be back in six months; there's no need for you to take so much stuff." She wouldn't even pack my new Shabbos shoes, and only let me take my weekday shoes and weekday winter boots.

My room was lined with all the presents I had received during the previous year: an impressive mélange of expensive coats, sweaters, shoes and boots, as well as toys, games and expensive stationery. Anya didn't allow me to pack any of these, either. "It will all remain here until your return," she said. "This way, all your belongings will wait for you and you'll be happy to come home."

Without a word, I removed my jewelry. If my Shabbos clothes were too fancy to take along, I didn't want to bring my jewelry either. I only kept the ring that Bubby Shapiro had given me.

I gave my siddur, my *machzorim* and *Tehillim* to Anya to pack. I saw her hesitate. "I need to take my *sefarim kedoishim* with me," I announced firmly. Reluctantly, she placed them in the suitcase, and then closed the top. That was it.

We left the room together and Anya went into the kitchen. I didn't follow her — instead, I tiptoed quietly back into my room and took my diary and my ceramic piggy bank with my savings. I went to the balcony, broke the piggy bank, put the money into a sock and threw the broken ceramic pieces into the yard below. I crept back into my room, opened the suitcase and inserted the sock and diary between the underwear. I closed the suitcase again and left the room.

I went into the dining room where I sat on a chair and tried to understand why I felt guilty, like a thief. It was, after all, my own money; money that I'd saved up over the years from presents, not only from Anya and Apa. But I felt sneaky. I even considered telling Anya, but I didn't move.

The clock struck ten, and someone knocked at the door. Anya rushed to open it, and to my amazement Edith Zinger was standing there. What was going on? No one in school knew that I was leaving; I hadn't said goodbye to anyone or told my friends. I had studied as usual until the day before.

So what was Edith doing there? She was, after all, a friend of Perry's sister, not even my own age.

Edith strode into the house and did not give me time to think. "Come, Leichu, I've come to take you," she said. Anya wouldn't be accompanying me to the train station either, I realized.

Anya started to cry, and she came to hug me. We went to my room, and I picked up the suitcase. I scrutinized every corner of my room. "Please leave everything the way it is," I asked Anya. "When I come back in six months, I want everything to be just as I remember it." Anya nodded her head, and could not say a word. When we reached the door, she kissed me on both cheeks, smiled and said, "See you soon!"

I left the house and Anya remained in the doorway. This was a respectable parting, proper and decorous, the way civilized, well-bred people say goodbye. Not like the backward Shapiro clan at all!

Edith took the suitcase from me and we went down the steps. "Why, this suitcase is so tiny and light; you hardly have anything here!" she exclaimed. I shrugged my shoulders but didn't say a word. At the bottom, a very nice woman was waiting for us. "Leichu, meet my mother," said Edith. I curtsied politely, like a young lady. If she was watching me, Anya would be proud of my manners.

We took a trolley to a neighborhood that I had never set foot into before. It was very pleasant, full of gardens and greenery, though the houses were older than the ones in my neighborhood. I learned that we were going to the Zingers' house. We rode in silence, so I had time to think and plan.

I wondered if my birth mother would be waiting for me there, but I didn't voice my thoughts. When we entered the Zingers' house, no one was there.

I was disappointed. "I had hoped that she would be here,

waiting for me," I told Edith. Edith and her mother exchanged looks, and Mrs. Zinger sat down to talk to me. "Leichu, let me explain. I will be taking you to Sevlus. The lawyer asked that your birth mother remain there. He doesn't want anyone to spy on you when you finally meet each other. You see, the lawyer does not want any kind of meeting between your birth mother and the Feldmans.

"And I think that it's probably just as well," she continued. "The past and the future will remain forever separate. You will remain with us today, and we will go to Sevlus tomorrow."

Then Néni Zinger started to tell me all about Sevlus, my mother's town. "Although it is much smaller than Budapest, Sevlus is not a tiny village either," explained Néni Zinger. "In fact it is a municipal center for all the villages in the district; it contains all the district offices such as a post office and a health clinic. It is at the foot of the Carpathian Mountains, near the Tisza River not far from the Czechoslovakian and Rumanian borders.

"Sevlus is part of the Carpo-Russian territory that had been part of Hungary for many, many years. But after the first Word War, that whole territory was taken from Hungary and divided up into many different countries. Sevlus itself was annexed to Czechoslovakia together with other sections.

"The inhabitants remained Hungarian in language as well as culture; you don't have to worry about that as you know Hungarian from Budapest. But they did have to learn Czech because that is the official language in the schools, the municipality and the government. They don't have problems at all with the tolerant Czechoslovakian government, though, and they do get along well with the authorities. Oh, I should tell you that most of the Jews speak Yiddish among themselves."

The truth was that I was bursting with curiosity about my birth mother, and didn't have much patience to hear about Sevlus, its languages and history though the information would turn out to be very helpful in the future. But Néni Zinger was a wise woman; she waited until I was comfortable sitting with her and listening to stories about my new town. Only then, did she feel that I was ready to hear more personal information about my birth mother and the story of my birth and kidnapping.

It was quite some story that Néni Zinger told me. She told me how I was taken from my mother when I was half a year old, when she had come to Budapest for some medical treatment. She described my mother's intense pain and sorrow when she was told that I had been given up for adoption "for her own good." Néni Zinger told the story dramatically, empathically. "Your mother never gave up on you through all those long years," she kept repeating. "She made tremendous efforts to find you, to track you down, and then restore you to her. She was assisted by the entire town of Sevlus: The neighbors ran her grocery store for her when she stayed in Budapest for the trial; they all went to their Rebbes for blessings and advice; they contributed money for the court fees."

Neni Zinger told me how she had become involved in the search for me. She told me about her brother and sister-in-law, Nachman and Rivka Klar, who were dear friends of my mother. Rivka was actually related to my father — she was his cousin. After years of searching bore no results, Nachman suggested that my mother ask the Zingers to help. Neni Zinger smiled as she described the "detective work" she had done to find out about my well-being.

I was astounded. This was not at all what I had thought. I had felt so sorry for myself over being adopted, over being different from my adopted parents and extended family. I had suffered with the tormenting secret of being abandoned by my birth parents, of being given up for adoption by parents who evidently didn't want me. I had even comforted myself with thoughts that both of my parents were dead, and that was the reason that I was given away. None of that was true, none of it! And while I was feeling sorry for myself, my birth mother was making superhuman efforts to track me down. For almost my entire life since I had been taken from her, she had worked tirelessly to find me; she and her relatives and friends, even the faraway Zingers in Budapest. I was full of admiration for my Mama.

"And what about Anya and Apa?" I asked Néni Zinger. "Did they know that I had been kidnapped? After all, they paid a large sum of money for me."

Néni Zinger looked at me intently. "Leichu," she said, "the Feldmans did pay lots of money for you, but your mother did not receive a penny of that money and did not know a thing about any such transaction! Leichu, your mother would not have given you up for all the money in the world."

I closed my eyes and remembered the conversations I had overheard between Anya and Bubby Shapiro, the conversations I had understood because I learned Yiddish. "That poor woman never received a cent, and she never gave up her daughter for adoption. They stole the baby from her!" And what had Anya said about Néni Eva, Apa's sister? "She took all the money for herself! The poor mother did not receive a cent... She gave some to the family who gave her the baby and kept the rest herself!"

At night, Néni Zinger opened the suitcase to take out my nightgown. She, too, was taken aback to see how little was inside. "Are these all the clothes you have?" she asked in amazement.

"Anya says that it's enough because the other clothing cost

her a lot of money," I repeated Anya's words to her. Then Néni Zinger saw the sock—the sock with all my savings. "That's my savings from over the years," I explained. "I felt uncomfortable taking it without telling Anya about it, but..." My voice trailed off uncertainly.

"No, no it's your money," said Néni Zinger thoughtfully. "You did the right thing."

She put aside my sock with the money, my diary and my *sefarim*, and returned the rest to the suitcase. "I'll return this to the Feldmans tomorrow," she said. "These things cost money too, as well as the dress you're wearing now." She gave me one of Edith's nightgowns, which was big on me, and returned my clothes to the suitcase.

"Don't worry," she said, smiling reassuringly. "You'll go to your mother tomorrow with plenty of nice clothing."

I was so tired that as soon as I got into bed together with Edith, I fell asleep. I didn't have time to think about the clothing issue — I was completely drained. I had barely slept the night before, and had spent the preceding day saying good-byes to the family. The profusion of tears and farewells had been emotionally and physically exhausting. And then that day's emotional revelation about my mother and my kidnapping had sapped me of my last ounce of strength. I slept soundly and didn't even dream — even though I had been sure that I would dream about my kidnapping.

In the morning when I awoke, there was a large suitcase filled with clothing on a table in the room: sweaters, coats and shoes, dresses, skirts and blouses—everything I'd need for the next six months, at least. A lovely dress was laid out on a chair next to the bed. Everything was second-hand but clean and respectable. I realized that Néni Zinger had worked hard to get it all ready for me while I was slept peacefully. The clothes were obviously not from Edith; she must have asked her friends for them. Yet somehow I sensed that they were given to me joyfully and wholeheartedly, not as a grudging favor or a calculating bribe — like all the expensive clothing I had received in the past year. My heart warmed to all the anonymous givers, and of course to Néni Zinger for orchestrating it all.

I thanked Néni Zinger in the morning, and we talked about the whole issue. Why did Anya send me off with almost no clothing, I wondered out loud.

"I suspect that she knew that your birth mother could not afford to buy you much, and she wanted to demonstrate the difference between what she could give you, and what your birth mother couldn't," she said sadly.

I thought about all the expensive gifts I had received this last year and how Anya wouldn't let me take anything. Now I understood that she wanted me to see that my birth mother could not buy these things for me, and I'd lack so many things I'd gotten used to, so that I'd want to return to her in Budapest.

I knew that I'd return to Anya and Apa in Budapest after the six months, but Anya shouldn't have done this. Didn't she understand how humiliating it would be for me to go to my birth mother like some kind of beggar, without even proper clothing? I didn't want my birth mother to have criticisms against Anya. And I didn't like being the position of being Anya's defender, either.

I think that Néni Zinger must have read my thoughts, because she said to me, "Leichu, you don't have to tell your mother that I prepared this suitcase for you. It's best that you let her think that these are your clothes, your clothing that you brought from home."

I was so touched that I went over and kissed her. I couldn't utter a sound as I was overwhelmed with happiness. She had understood me, and had solved the problem with her wisdom and tact. She promised to send the small suitcase back to the Feldmans.

"At first I wanted to include a letter, but I decided there was no need," said Néni Zinger. "The suitcase speaks for itself."

∽ ∽ ∽

The next morning, Néni Zinger, Edith and Ari Zinger accompanied me to the train station; Ari carried my big suitcase. Néni Zinger gave Ari money for train tickets and when he came back, I saw that he was holding three tickets. He gave them to his mother and said goodbye.

So the three of us got on the train together, much to my satisfaction: Néni Zinger, Edith and I. As soon as the train started to move, I breathed a sigh of relief. I had been worried about traveling to Sevlus and meeting Mama by myself, and until the Zingers actually boarded the train, I was still apprehensive.

At first the three of us sat together, but then Edith got up to look at the view from the large train windows. Her mother started to talk to me, and continued the narrative that she had begun the previous day. "As I mentioned yesterday, my sister-in-law Rivka Klar is your father's cousin, *alav ha-shalom*," said Néni Zinger.

"When did my father pass away?" I asked quietly. "What was he like?"

That was when I found out that my father's name was Dovid Fruchter, and my mother's name was Sheina Ruchel. Néni Zinger told me the story of my father's stint in the army, the large sum of money they paid to secure his release, and his subsequent illness. This was the first I had ever heard about my father, and I hung on to every word. She told me about my birth and the joy I brought with me into my parents' lives. She told me about my father's untimely death and about the splinter in my mother's hand. She did not stop speaking the entire trip, telling me about my mother's life for the past twelve years — how everything had revolved around finding me — her stolen, beloved daughter.

I listened transfixed and hardly uttered a word during the entire journey. I only wanted to hear more and more.

Edith was wonderful. She must have been very curious to hear the whole story herself, but she pretended to be engrossed in the scenery so that I could have some privacy with her mother. "What a lovely landscape our country has," she'd say from time to time. "I simply can't tear myself away from these windows!"

Chana Malka Zinger and her children: Edith, Ari, and Mickey.

Three hours passed quickly, and then Néni Zinger told me that the next stop was Sevlus. She stopped talking, and we sat in silent anticipation of the upcoming meeting.

I returned to my dream; the dream of our meeting.

❧ 39 ❧
A Joyful Reunion
[SEVLUS]

T HE TRAIN SLOWED as we approached the station. I saw the sign from afar: Sevlus, in large, ornate letters. My heart beat like a hammer, and my hands and legs trembled uncontrollably. Néni Zinger and Edith stood opposite me, expectantly, but I simply could not get up from the bench.

Néni Zinger put her arms around me and lifted me up, helping me walk to the door of the coach. Then she went

The train station

back to the bench and pulled out the suitcase from underneath. The three of us stood next to the door, waiting for the train to come to a full stop and the doors to open.

It seemed to me that I had waited and looked forward to this moment for many, many years. I was breathless and excited, but also fearful. I thought that as soon as the doors would open, a shadowy and frightening image of my mother from my nightmares would fall upon me, crying and screaming.

I remembered hearing Anya talk about women beggars all the time. Of course she never said anything to me directly but I knew that she talked about it in a loud voice when I was nearby on purpose, so that I should hear. "Those poor, disfigured women like to take children with them when they beg passersby for charity; they know that people will pity them and give them more money if they are accompanied by children," she'd say. It was no wonder that I developed such a frightening image of my mother.

The door opened, and we got off the train. But no one approached us. Néni Zinger put down the suitcase on the platform, looked around for a moment and then said to me, "There she is—your mother is standing next to the station building."

I looked in the direction she pointed. A slim, poised woman stood there on her own two feet without a wheelchair. The figure had two arms, two legs, and a head and was not wearing thick glasses like blind people wear. I'd had no idea what to expect because I only knew that my mother was "a poor, disabled widow"; even Néni Zinger had not explained to me exactly what her disability was. That's why I had always imagined a frightening figure.

Yet here, opposite me, was an attractive, slim woman. She did not run to me and fall upon me with shouts and tears as

I had feared but approached me slowly, with measured gait. We, too, approached her slowly, with tiny steps.

Néni Zinger walked ahead of me, approached my mother, and shook her hand joyfully. Then it was my turn.

I stood opposite her, silently. She looked at me and smiled; I smiled in return. Then she said to me in a lovely, clear voice, "Leichu, my Leichu." But she did not fall upon me or make a move.

I approached her and held out my hand. "Hello, Mama; I have returned to you."

Mama used her left hand to shake mine. Only then did I notice that her right arm was an artificial one, but this did not detract at all from her stately and dignified appearance.

Edith, who had been standing quietly observing, suddenly cried out, "I can't believe how much you two resemble one another!"

The three of us burst out laughing, and the tension between us dissipated. Mama hugged me with her one arm and tenderly held me close.

I lifted my head and looked into her eyes. They were, indeed, just like mine—light green! We looked into each other's eyes, smiling, and only then did I stand on my tiptoes and kiss my mother on both cheeks. I smiled when she kissed me back.

This was a gentle, serene and happy reunion and not the meeting I had imagined to myself during sleepless nights: frightening, tense, full of sobbing and recriminations.

Edith ran back to the platform to take my suitcase and together we left the station. Outside, a horse-drawn carriage waited for us. The wagon driver carried the suitcase for us and then we all entered the coach and started to move.

I was so busy examining my mother that I paid no attention to the road. My mother sat opposite me next to Néni

Zinger, who was telling her something. I did not listen to their conversation; I sat transfixed, looking at my mother. What a lovely woman! Why had I imagined her as frightening and repugnant?

Mama sat erect, wearing a black and white checked dress with a large white collar. She wore a tasteful kerchief on her head. It was black with a floral design — pink flowers and green leaves. She wore stylish black patent-leather shoes with three side buttons.

I took in every detail. I had expected a poor woman in rags with an emaciated body. And now, even the artificial arm did not frighten me. It was slightly bent at the elbow, and the palm looked like a regular palm.

Just as I examined my mother, she examined me. I was happy to be wearing the dress that Néni Zinger had brought me, and not the one that Anya had given me. I felt better this way — without having Anya, or anything connected to her — "taking part" in this meeting.

We reached a long, low building with many doorways, evidently belonging to many tenants. Mama pointed to the second door and said that was our home.

The wagon driver stopped and carried down my suitcase. Meanwhile, Mama took out money and paid him. Secretly, I was happy that she paid and not Néni Zinger because this proved that my mother was not the destitute pauper I had been led to believe.

Mama opened the door and we all went inside. I was surprised to see a large store with groceries lined up neatly on shelves around a wall. The place looked extremely clean and organized and a faint scent of cinnamon was in the air.

Mama turned to me and said in her clear, musical voice, "Welcome home, Leichu!" and I immediately answered, "I am happy to be home at last." Then I looked around again.

Yes, it was a respectable grocery shop, but I had to ask the obvious question. "Mama, do we live in a store?" I asked.

Everyone burst out laughing, and I joined in though I didn't understand the joke. Mama led me around behind the check-out counter and showed me a door that I hadn't noticed. She opened the door to reveal a small bedroom. It contained a combination cooking-heating stove, whose chimney was part of the wall of the store so that it heated both the living quarters and the store. The only other furniture was a simple bed, a small table and two chairs. The furniture was extremely plain and spartan.

The door also served as a small closet — Mama hung her clothes there, covered with a curtain. There were curtains on the two store windows and on the bedroom window, all from the same material. A large crate also stood in the small room, evidently for clothing, and above it were shelves.

It was a simple cubicle, furnished only with the bare essentials, but everything was extremely organized and clean.

Then I looked at the lone bed; there didn't seem to be room for a second bed in the tiny room. Mama saw my glance and said quietly, "Yes, there is only one bed. We will have to share it."

I held my breath. To share a bed, how wonderful! I had always envied Basya Leah's children; they slept two to a bed and I was always alone in my cold, silent room. Alone in the room, alone in the house.

Mama misinterpreted my reaction and quickly added, "We can get you your own bed, but not today; it will take a few days. Then you can sleep in a private bed in the store."

I went over and hugged my mother quickly. "No, of course not!" I exclaimed. "You don't understand; I want to share the bed with you. Why, I can't wait until nighttime!" And we laughed again. There were no tears at all in this meeting, only happiness and joy.

Then Néni Zinger and Edith walked over to the Klars, and we were alone. Mama suggested that we unpack my suitcase, but even before we could start, the store filled with people. Slowly, one after another, the neighbors stopped by, ostensibly to make their purchases, but mainly to welcome me. Everyone brought a small gift in my honor, generally some kind of food or special delicacy. I was touched. How different this small town was from Budapest! In the big, bustling city, we had little contact with neighbors and here, it was clear that the neighbors truly cared about Mama and me. Each customer entered with a plate, saying, "Just something small to welcome our very special guest!" And everyone commented on how strongly I resembled Mama.

As night approached, the procession of neighbors slowly dwindled, and once night fell, Mama and I sat down to eat our wonderful dinner on the small table in our room. It was a meal made up of the many small delicacies and gifts of food the neighbors had brought. That was when Mama told me that the procession of well-wishers would probably continue on the following day as well. "Today, the women who live nearby stopped over," she explained. "Tomorrow, the ones who live further away will come." Then Mama did something interesting; she placed the leftovers on special shelves between the glass windowpanes. "This way, everything will remain cold and fresh until tomorrow," she remarked. I had never seen anything like that before, and suddenly it dawned on me: Mama had no refrigerator — her apartment did not have electricity!

I opened my suitcase, but it was late and I was yawning. Mama suggested, "Let's wait until tomorrow. We have had a long, full day. It's time to go to sleep."

❧ 40 ❧
Mother and Daughter
[SEVLUS]

WE BOTH GOT into bed. It was a simple bed with a straw-filled mattress — not at all like my fashionable bed in Budapest. But I was so overjoyed to be sharing a bed with my mother that I did not feel any discomfort. "I'll leave the lamp on if you prefer," suggested Mama. Now I noticed that the only light in the apartment came from a kerosene lamp and I realized that Mama probably put out the light at night, to save on fuel. In Budapest we had electric lights, and a light always remained on in the kitchen throughout the night. But here I didn't mind the darkness; here I wasn't alone in my room, I was with my mother. "No, you can put out the lamp, Mama, that's fine," I said proudly.

Mama moved over against the wall, trying to make more room for me in the narrow bed, but I hugged her and pulled her closer to me. "Don't stay so far away now that we are finally together." I wanted very much to talk to her, but I was so tired that as soon as I felt her arm around me, I placed my head on her shoulder and fell asleep immediately.

The next morning, we woke up together. "I wanted to talk

245

to you last night and hear from you as well, but I was so tired that I fell asleep just as soon as you did!" Mama exclaimed. "The truth is, I hadn't slept well for a number of nights before you came because of excitement and anxiety. I guess it all caught up with me last night."

I, too, had suffered a number of sleepless nights. True, I had slept well at the Zingers, but the excitement and tension of the last day had totally exhausted me.

There were so many things I wanted to tell Mama about the years that had passed—and she, in turn, wanted to tell me what had happened to her throughout those long years as well. But every time I started to talk, she also started, and we burst into laughter. After our laughter subsided, we both tried again — at the same time, and the laughter began once more. This cycle kept repeating itself, so that we couldn't tell each other anything; we just laughed and laughed.

In our small room, a large, white enamel pail with a matching cover stood on a small stool. Next to it was a large blue enamel pitcher, and near that was a wooden plank on the floor. A large bowl rested on the plank.

I watched Mama curiously. She took a ladle with her one hand to transfer water from the pail to the pitcher, and standing near the bowl, she artfully spilled water from the pitcher to wash her face, her eyes, and brush her teeth. All the dirty water landed directly in the bowl on the floor. Then she took the *negel vasser* bowl that was near the bed, and poured the water into the other bowl as well. I did exactly as Mama did.

After we had washed and dressed, Mama bent down, steadied the bowl with her one hand, and used her feet to push the plank into the store, then to the front door. I was amazed to see how she pushed that bowl full of water all the way out of the house to a field, where she emptied out the dirty water. And she did not spill a single drop on the way!

"How do you do that?" I asked in amazement. "Why, even with my two hands I wouldn't be able to do that without spilling half of the water on my way!"

"It wasn't easy to learn," Mama laughed. "At the beginning the bucket would spill and the floor would get all wet. It took lots of practice and many years, but with patience and determination, I got it just right." And that's how Mama taught herself how to do almost everything with her one hand. "The only thing I don't do by myself is the laundry," admitted Mama. "Laundry is simply too difficult to do with one hand."

I hadn't even paid attention to see how Mama washed the supper dishes last night. I decided not to ask about it; I'd just pay attention the next time.

"Speaking of laundry," Mama remarked, "the laundress will be here soon, and you'll get to meet her." Mama's eyes sparkled at the mention of the laundress, and I wondered why she seemed so excited.

There was a knock at the door. Mama went to open it, and... in walked Chungarabi! She ran straight to me, calling, "Leichu! Leichu!" and I ran into her warm, welcoming arms. How happy we both were to see each other again.

When Chungarabi left Budapest, she had promised me that we would see each other again. But I didn't hear from her afterwards and we lost all contact. As time went on, I sadly became resigned to the fact that I would never see her again. I had missed her very much, and seeing her now, my joy was complete.

When we calmed down, I tried to understand how Chungarabi had shown up in my mother's village. The "coincidence" of it just took my breath away—Chungarabi had moved from Budapest to Sevlus, from work at my adoptive mother's house to work at my Mama's house! "It was because of Chungarabi that I was able to track you down, after years and years of unsuccessful attempts," exclaimed my mother. "She noticed the resemblance between us, Leichu, and when she heard me talk about my 'stolen daughter,' she connected it to your story of being adopted. Once I found out that you lived with the Feldmans, then we were able to bring the case to court."

Yes, it was a true miracle and I thanked Hashem from the depths of my heart.

Mama realized that Chungarabi and I would want to talk, so she suggested that Chungarabi do the laundry in the small room where we could have privacy.

Mama began sorting the laundry — generally she did it before Chungarabi came, but yesterday was no ordinary day. Chungarabi, always efficient, hurried to bring water and fill up the brasswashing bowl. She turned up the gas flame, placed the bowl of water on the stove, and then inserted some of the dirty laundry. By that time, Mama finished sorting the clothing. Throughout the entire morning, Mama remained in the store to serve the customers while I sat next to Chungarabi. Occasionally Mama would call me to meet people whom I hadn't met the day before. And again, just like the previous day, everyone was truly happy to see me. All of them greeted me warmly, and commented on my resemblance to my mother.

I brought Chungarabi the dress I had worn the day before because it was full of soot and dust from the train ride. That's when I noticed her staring at the dress in my hand, as well as the one I was wearing, and suddenly I understood. Neither dress was one that Anya would have ever bought for me. "Did Anya send you off in these dresses?" Chungarabi asked in a whisper.

So I told her the story of the suitcase.

Chungarabi understood immediately, and she shook her

head in amazement. "I think that you're old enough to know the truth, Leichu. The truth is that Anya loved you, but she also needed you to prove to everyone that she wasn't childless. She needed you for her pride, so that she wouldn't feel humiliated without children. But your birth mother is the one who loves you truly, love that is unconditional and real. She suffered terribly when you were stolen from her and she moved heaven and earth to find you. That, alone, shows that she is the real mother."

And I knew that she was right. From the moment I saw my mother standing in the train station I had felt great waves of love emanate from her, though she restrained herself from running to me. She had remained in her place and greeted me from afar so as not to frighten me with the intensity of her emotions. But I especially felt her love that surrounded me at night, when we shared the same bed.

Chungarabi finished her work by the afternoon. I was delighted that, for the first time, I did not have to conceal my connection with the gypsy. Mama knew all about us, as Chungarabi had told her about our relationship. It made Mama laugh to hear us chattering away in Romany, the gypsy language, mixed with Hungarian. "I am good with languages," I admitted. "I also learned Yiddish from Briendy, my nanny; otherwise, most of the Jews in Budapest don't seem to speak Yiddish."

Anya knew Yiddish and spoke to her parents, Zaidy and Bubby Shapiro, in that language; in fact, she spoke to her sister Basya Leah and her other siblings in Yiddish as well. The Feldman clan, on the other hand, spoke only Hungarian, and as far as I knew, they didn't know Yiddish at all.

Mama explained to me that the school system taught all the classes in Czech, and repeated the information that Néni Zinger had told me on the train about Sevlus being ruled by the tolerant Czechoslovakian government. "You will also learn some Russian and German," she told me. I was happy to hear that I would acquire additional languages. In Budapest I had learned a bit of German and knew how to read and write, but I had not mastered the difficult German accent.

"You will have your first week to rest up and spend time with me at home," explained Mama. "But then you'll have to go back to school. In order to make the transition to a new school easier, Gizzie, our neighbor, will stop by this afternoon after school to meet you. She is your age and lives nearby, so that is convenient. She promised to show you the schoolwork and help you, especially regarding subjects that are new to you or different from what you studied in Budapest—for example, the new languages. I hope that you two will get along."

Later in the afternoon, Gizzie did come by with her mother. The two of us sat on the bench in front of the house. I noticed that many of the houses had benches in front of them, and these were the places where the women sat, relaxed and talked to one another, particularly on Shabbos afternoons. These benches were not made out of wood, though; they were formed out of large stones.

Both Gizzie and I were too shy to be the first to talk, so we shared an uncomfortable silence. I was tempted to get up and go back into the house, but I didn't want to insult Gizzie. Finally, two little girls came and joined us. They were Gizzie's sisters, and their names were Lonie and Mattie. The two of them chattered away and asked us questions, so we answered them and that broke the ice. We didn't become friends immediately, but at least we weren't embarrassed to talk to each other.

∾   ∾   ∾

In the late afternoon hours, the guests started to arrive from more distant neighborhoods. I said goodbye to Gizzie and went into the house, and immediately saw two distinguished-looking businessmen. I curtsied and greeted them as a well-behaved young lady, but I felt anxious. Who were they, why were they here? Such well-dressed gentlemen were not a common sight in Sevlus, and I was pretty sure they weren't just some more well-wishers coming to welcome me. True, Mama was smiling but I didn't know her well enough yet to know if she was really happy, or just pretending.

I couldn't even imagine that these two distinguished men had come to see me, to share in Mama's happiness at her daughter's homecoming. These men were the wholesalers, the Guttmann brothers who had helped Mama in raising the funds needed for the court case, and they had contributed a great deal themselves. They usually never came together to Mama, only one at a time, but now they both came to welcome me. But I didn't know that at the time.

Before the men had come, I felt like I was in a summer camp; and everything in camp is always fun and pleasant. But important men like these don't pay visits in camp!

I stood on the side, staring at the merchandise on the shelves, lost in my world of worries and fears. I didn't even hear what they were saying. Finally, I saw them move toward the door and heard Mama saying goodbye, so I approached my mother, stood behind her and politely wished them goodbye.

After they left, I burst into tears. "Mama, who are these men? Why did they come and what do they want from me?"

Mama was taken aback. She looked at me, hugged me and told me that these were the Guttmann brothers. "The Guttmanns have your best interests at heart, Leichu. They have helped me greatly over the years, and they were especially involved in raising money to bring you back to me," she explained. "Today they also came to accept my order for new merchandise for the store."

I breathed a sigh of relief, and sat down next to Mama. She had sat down to do some bookkeeping. Since she used her one hand for writing, she would put a small red brick on the paper to keep it from moving. She wrote smoothly and quickly.

"Mama, from now on I'll write everything for you!" I announced my new idea happily. I sorely wanted to help my mother, but I didn't know what I could possibly do, as I had never done housework in my life. But I was good at writing, and was happy to find one thing that I could contribute and help my mother.

"I don't mind doing it myself," she said, "but I am happy that you want to be involved and a full partner in what needs to be done here."

"I can also fix clothing, I learned how to sew," I continued. True, Mama didn't have a sewing machine, but I could sew by hand. "I love to sew," I told Mama. "I know how to sew all kinds of stitches: straight ones and curved ones in all kinds of shapes. But I haven't learned to sew clothing yet."

"Why, once you have mastered the stitches, I believe that learning to sew clothing won't give you any difficulty," said Mama. "Perhaps you'll study sewing and learn how to sew clothes professionally... though not in the near future when you have to go to school. Afterwards, when you finish your compulsory education you'll be able to study anything that you please."

At that moment, both of us were struck by the same awkward thought: After my six months of school, where would I be—in Sevlus with Mama, or in Budapest with my adoptive parents? But neither of us said a word.

That night, more people came to see me. I never imagined that I was so famous! One of the well-wishers was Aidah Weingarten. "This is the wonderful woman who accompanied me to the trial in Budapest," whispered Mama.

Afterwards, Fanny and Dori Klar came, the daughters of Nachman and Rivka Klar. I discovered very quickly that of all the well-wishers and neighbors, Mama was closest to the Klars. Nachman and Rivka — my father Dovid Fruchter's cousins — treated Mama like a sister and had been her mainstay of support all the years that I was gone. We often referred to them as Bácsi and Néni Klar— uncle and aunt — though they were actually Mama's contemporaries in age.

Fanny and Dori invited us to them for the Shabbos meals. I was very happy about that, because despite the differences in age—they were years older than I—I felt comfortable with them from the very beginning. The two of them told jokes and laughed, and I joined in naturally.

I noticed that as we spoke, Dori casually picked up the pail that was on the floor. She poured the water that was left in the bottom of the pail into the blue jug, then ran out and returned a few minutes later with a pail full of water. She put it back in its place and continued telling jokes as if she had been there the whole time. Quietly, I asked Dori about her actions and she said, "I imagine that it's hard for Néni Sheina Ruchel to draw water with one hand, so I try to fill her pails with water whenever I come by." That gave me an idea.

"Can you show me how to fill the pail, so that I can do it tomorrow?" I asked.

Dori looked at me and asked, "You've never drawn water by yourself?"

"No," I admitted. "In Budapest we had water faucets with running water in the houses."

"It's a skill that needs to be learned," explained Dori, "because it's hard to draw water and the pail is very heavy, but I promise to teach you next time I come to visit."

It was late, and the two Klar girls said goodbye. All the other guests and customers made their farewells as well, and Mama and I were alone again together. I helped her clean up the store and rearrange the products on the shelves, and then we went into the bedroom.

Mama went over to the pail to fill it up, and noticed with surprise that it was full. "It must have been Dori who filled it," she said, and I nodded my head. "Every member of the Klar family is a true person of *chesed*, of charity and good deeds," said Mama. "But in addition they are all modest; they don't draw attention to their good deeds. They just seem to do the right thing naturally; it's a way of life for them. They are truly wonderful people who have been supportive of me all these long years."

The two of us got into bed and hugged each other. This time we weren't so tired, and could chat. That night, I did most of the talking. I told Mama about my life, my family and the house. I told her about my school, the city and my friends. I had many stories to tell, until tiredness overcame me and I fell asleep in the middle of a story. That night started a pattern; the two of us would get into bed and talk and talk until one of us fell asleep. There were hardly any nights that we didn't chat.

I told Mama everything, everything I had experienced from my earliest memories. From my ninth birthday and on I had a diary in which I wrote faithfully over the years, though not necessarily in formal diary style; for example I usually didn't remember to write the date. But when I read what I had written in my diary, this jogged my memory to tell my mother the events of my life.

And Mama, on the other hand, told me about her life.

Thus it transpired that the two of us told each other our life story several times, and over time, my mother's life story became intertwined with mine so that I could hardly separate them. Until this very day, I remember everything—everything that she told me and repeated over and over until it became engraved in my heart.

❦ 41 ❧
Shabbos with Mama
[SEVLUS]

EIL SHABBOS arrived, and the entire house was transformed into something else.

In Budapest we had a *Shabbos tzimmer*, a "Shabbos room." We ate our Shabbos meals in that room, which also served as a space for entertaining important guests. It was the loveliest room in the house, with an oval table surrounded by magnificent heavy wooden chairs, a luxurious breakfront that contained expensive china dishes, dainty paper-thin glass cups, and a glass silver closet full of intricate silver pieces and crystal works of art.

Special lights surrounded splendid pictures on the wall, casting a royal glow on the artwork, and the crystal candelabra that hung from the center of the ceiling illuminated the room with dozens of candles. When the candles were lit, the crystal pieces hanging on the candelabra sparkled and reflected all the colors of the rainbow. We did have electricity — the candles were not our only source of light — but the light they gave off was extraordinary indeed.

The shining parquet floor boasted a large green rug with a pink and red rose pattern. On one side of the room stood an overstuffed couch, three armchairs and dainty coffee tables. Everything was magnificent and grand.

And here with Mama in Sevlus we only had a tiny room that was part of a grocery store. Yet remarkably, when Shabbos arrived the shabby room was transformed. Mama spread starched and ironed white tablecloths all over the room, and covered the small table with a lovely embroidered tablecloth. A brass tray with a nine-branched brass candelabrum stood on the table. I remembered Anya's silver candlesticks and I was amazed that Mama's inexpensive brass ones shined a thousand times brighter — they looked like they were made of pure gold and they illuminated the entire table.

"Mama, why do you light so many candles?" I asked.

It was then that Mama told me about my half-siblings; two brothers and a sister. Though we shared a mother, they had a different father than I. They had left Mama long ago, but they were still her children, nonetheless. She had given birth to them and raised them, and still continued to light candles for them. She also lit a candle for me throughout the long years that we had been separated. She lit one light for my father, one for her first husband, one for herself, and another two candles for those who had no one to light candles for them. All in all, she lit nine candles every week in honor of the holy Shabbos.

"Until now, even though I lit all these candles, my inner world remained dark," Mama told me. "But now that you have finally come back to me, my world is illuminated with a million beams of light. This Shabbos is the most glowing and radiant."

"Then why do you sigh, Mama?" I asked.

"I am sighing out of happiness," Mama laughed. "My cup is not yet full and probably never will be, as my three oldest children are gone; but they are adults and are responsible for their own decisions. I accept that." Mama sighed again. "They were not taken from me deceitfully or by force, they left of their own free will and their actions are beyond my control. I have made my peace with that. But on this Shabbos, I am the happiest of mothers." Then she hugged me gently and lovingly, and her eyes were wet with tears.

"It is forbidden to cry on Shabbos," I reminded her, but Mama laughed and said that tears of happiness are permissible.

I was sorry that we were going to eat the Shabbos meals at other people's homes, as I wanted to be alone with Mama, but she explained that we must show our appreciation for all the people who helped her throughout the long, dark years. Many people had begged Mama to join them for the Shabbos meals to get to know me a little better, and she felt that it would be wrong to refuse. "We will have many more Shabbos meals together," she promised.

Mama davened *Kabbalas Shabbos* with a lovely tune. I sat next to her and thought how holiness seemed to surround her. Her white kerchief shined brightly and even the small lace apron tied around her waist sparkled radiantly. She looked like one of the four holy *Imahos*. I was so happy that this was my mother, that this was how she looked, and that the sparse room had become a palace in honor of Shabbos. "Maybe it's better to be poor than rich," I thought to myself. "This way we are closer to Hashem and can become truly holy."

We went to the Weingarten family for the Friday night meal. On the way, Mama told me that when Mrs. Weingarten—or as everyone called her, Néni Aidah—had accompanied Mama on her first trip to the court case in Budapest, Mama had promised her that when I would be restored to her, we would eat the very first Shabbos meal with the Weingartens.

The Weingarten family lived not far from us, on Kings Street (Király utca). The name made me laugh because my school in Budapest had been located on a street of the same name, Kings Street, but the street in Budapest had been far grander and larger than its counterpart in Sevlus. That was the difference between Budapest and Sevlus: size and magnificence.

We reached the Weingarten home even before the men returned home from shul. Néni Aidah greeted me warmly and with great joy, even though she had already met me in the store on the day after I arrived in Sevlus. In fact, she actually ran toward me, grabbed me and examined me from head to toe. Then she cried out, "Oh, Néni Fruchter, all your efforts were worth it. She looks wonderful, what a lovely young lady! How marvelous you are!" while she hugged me tightly and called her daughters to come see me.

I was very embarrassed and found it hard to talk to them. I sat next to Mama and only answered direct questions as quietly as I could. Mama seemed to understand my discomfort; she put her one hand on my shoulder and answered for me. I felt tremendous relief; if this had happened in Budapest, Anya would have gotten angry at me and would have forced me to talk. Then when we came home, she would have told me that I had embarrassed her in public. But Mama understood, and I was amazed at how relaxed I was in her presence as if I had lived with her for years and years, and not only for a few days.

The men returned from shul. Mr. Weingarten immediately sang *Shalom Aleichem* with his sons and two other guests who had accompanied him, and immediately afterwards he made Kiddush. After *netilas yadayim* and *lechem mishneh*, Mr. Weingarten talked about the *parashah*, presenting his *divrei Torah* in a very interesting manner until the fish was served, and then he invited everyone to eat. After the fish course, it was the children's turn to tell everyone about what they had learned in school. The rest of the meal was conducted quickly because Mr. Weingarten wanted to go to the Spinka Rebbe's *tish*. Mama and I were happy to get home early, and as we walked home we met many other people on their way to their Rebbes' *tishes*. And once at home, of course, we talked and went to sleep very late. We were in no rush to get up on Shabbos morning, the only day of the week we could indulge ourselves and sleep later. Laughing and happy, we left the house at mid-morning to join the Klars for the Shabbos day meal. The world was so beautiful! When you are happy, the world smiles back at you. You realize that gold and silver and wealth are not the key to happiness at all.

And so we strolled along the streets of Sevlus. We passed Király utca (Kings Street) and reached Sevlus's main street Vasút utca (Train Street), and from there, we continued to Magyarsor utca (Hungarian Street) and then to the *Scheilhoiv* (the courtyard of the shul and *beis medrash*) where the Klar family lived. On the way we met a number of women, as well as entire families who had gone out for a Shabbos walk. Most everyone greeted us warmly and wished Mama *mazel tov*. Mama laughed and said, "It's true I deserve a *mazel tov*; even though I gave birth twelve years ago, my Leichu has just been reborn to me!"

Mama had warned me that it was a long walk to the Klars, but it seemed to me that we arrived in a flash because we enjoyed the stroll so much.

I had already met the Klar girls so I was not as shy there as I had been at the Weingartens. I thought that I was ready to answer their questions because I felt comfortable with them, but they didn't even ask me anything! Instead, the women sat and talked while Fanny set the table and Dori watched the little ones. They involved me in the discussion in a casual, non-threatening manner so I didn't feel that I had to prove myself. I felt at home and relaxed.

Then they introduced me to a little boy who was named after my father. Little Dovid was an angelic little boy with blond curly *payos* and lovely blue eyes, a quiet and sweet child. His younger brother, on the other hand, ran around incessantly and wouldn't sit still even for a minute. He had brown *payos* and hazel eyes, and looked like a perpetual motion machine: His legs jumped, his hands turned and his *payos* hopped; even the clothes he wore seemed to shake! His shirt crept out of his pants and his socks dropped over his shoes. In short, everything about him was in continual unrest.

Néni Rivka Klar used to say that if the two children had been combined they would be normal children, but since the division was unequal, one child was the mischievous one while the other was so quiet that they called him "the *shtiller*,"

Néni Rivka Klar and her children. Below, second from the right—Dovid, named for Dovid Fruchter, and above — Fanny and Dori.

the quiet one. But Fanny warned me that the "*shtiller*" also had his pranks, only he performed them quietly without attracting attention to himself so no one knew that he was the perpetrator. It often happened that the more active brother was punished for the deeds of the "*shtiller*." When Fanny told me this, the prankster burst into laughter and the quiet one smiled. I guessed that they cooperated with one another and got along well, despite their differences.

Meanwhile the men returned home, and I saw that Dovid'l resembled his father very much.

Bácsi Nachman Klar was very happy to see us and couldn't stop blessing me. I already knew from Mama's stories how much effort he had expended all these years in the search for me and I was happy to see that he was a smiling, joyful man. Cheerful people like him feel that helping another Jew only contributes to their joy, thus they help others with real sincerity — and not out of a grim sense of religious obligation to help another Jew.

After the meal we went into the yard. The children played while the women and girls sat on the stone bench in front of the house. Women and children streamed out of the nearby houses and everyone chatted amiably. The festive Shabbos atmosphere could be felt in the very air.

On our way home, Mama pointed out all kinds of interesting things. For example, most of the stores on the main street (Train Street) were closed up with heavy metal shutters. Mama told me that only some of the stores were owned by Jews, but even the non-Jews didn't work on Shabbos. Since the Jewish merchants don't do business on Shabbos, the villagers don't bother coming into town to shop since so many stores are closed. Since there are no buyers anyway, it is not worthwhile for the non-Jews to open their stores on Shabbos. Then, they have two days off — Shabbos and Sunday.

However, Mama told me, their womenfolk were not happy with this state of affairs. "That's because the *goyim* spend their days of rest by drinking in the town pub," she said. "This gives the *goyim* of Sevlus two days to drink, and the women don't like that at all!"

We continued to walk until we came home. My first Shabbos with Mama had been wonderful and happy.

❧ 42 ❧
Comparisons
[SEVLUS]

MAMA AND I became very close in the short but intensive initial time period. Perhaps it was because we both craved closeness, perhaps because we really did belong together though we had lived apart for almost twelve years. Mama exuded love and warmth and as I got to know her better, I grew to love her even more.

With Anya and Apa I had enjoyed an abundance of material wealth. I received everything in the way of material goods from them: an elegant room full of luxuries, closets full of clothes and games, and an entire house that was elegantly appointed. And here, with Mama, I didn't even have my own bed. I had to learn to sleep so as not to bother my mother who slept next to me.

The food was simple, out of the most basic inexpensive ingredients, while I had been accustomed to high-quality foods that were served on elegant dishes, on starched, ironed linen tablecloths. Mama and I ate lots of noodles all week long; she made the noodles herself. We ate a favorite Hungarian dish of wide noodles and cabbage, as well as noodles with sugar and cinnamon. Mama made all kinds of dishes out of peas, beans and lentils, especially soups. In Sevlus we had meat only on Shabbos, while in Budapest we ate meat frequently in the middle of the week too.

Here, even the food on Shabbos was simple. For the morning Shabbos meal in Budapest, we ate a special dish of egg with goose liver, in addition to fish and meat of course; in Sevlus, on the other hand, it was usually bean-filled cholent that we ate with the Klar family. On Friday night when Mama and I ate alone, we usually had some chicken or other fowl, though it was often the legs and other leftover pieces from the butcher.

In short, there was simply no comparison between the two homes.

I loved my mother and warmed to her love. But I also loved Anya and Apa, and I liked my lovely room and my house in Budapest. I could not help but compare.

Of course I never told Mama what I was thinking or about my opulent lifestyle in Budapest because I didn't want to hurt her. I tried to act as if drawing water in buckets and using gas lamps was normal, even though I had been used to electricity and modern plumbing in Budapest. Mama tried her best to give me what I needed. But her best efforts—the shoes and clothes I needed as I grew taller, for example—were shabby and cheap, in contrast to what I had received from Anya and Apa. Of course I was careful not to breathe a word of this to anyone.

Everyone around me was pleasant and friendly. Everyone told me about my mother's difficult life and her efforts to find me. Thus I couldn't discuss my inner conflict with anyone from Sevlus or with Mama, though I felt that I just had to talk about it with someone. No one from Sevlus would understand the kind of life I had lived before I came to Sevlus or how different those two worlds really are.

No one? There actually was someone who did know— someone who had shared my life and my confidences in Budapest, and now lived in Sevlus. Suddenly I realized what I had to do.

In the middle of the week, Chungarabi came to do the laundry. Although I didn't fall on her like the first time, I was very happy to see her again. I knew that I could tell her what I was feeling, and she would understand me. She was the only one familiar with the world I had come from, and with the world I lived in now.

The only difficulty would be finding the opportunity to talk privately to Chungarabi — she usually did her washing on the balcony at the entrance to the apartment. That was a public area, and I knew that it was not accepted for a Jewish girl to be seen chatting with a gypsy woman. Nor could I suggest that she do the laundry inside the store, where people would also see us talking. But mainly, I wanted to talk to her privately out of Mama's earshot. I didn't want to hurt my mother's feelings.

Chungarabi sensed that I wanted to talk to her privately, and she whispered to me that she'd figure something out. I felt a weight lifted off my shoulders.

After Chungarabi finished the laundry, she went inside to mop the floor. Mama had learned to do that job by herself, but once Chungarabi arrived, she took it over by saying, "It's included in the price." At this point Mama, who understood that I wanted to talk privately with Chungarabi, went outside to sit on the bench on our porch. I stayed inside to wash the dishes and Chungarabi got down on her hands and knees to scrub the wooden floor. This was my opportunity!

The words tumbled out of my mouth. "I love Mama," I said simply, "and it is wonderful here with her. Yet I also miss Anya, and I miss the life I had in Budapest. On the other hand, I don't feel that I'm lacking anything here in Sevlus with Mama, though truthfully I have very little here. Yes, I realize that I'm contradicting myself every other sentence! Still, I can't say that I don't miss the wealth I left behind.

"Chungarabi, I am so confused. What should I do? You know that I will have to come to a decision after half a year and decide with whom I should remain."

Chungarabi had never gone to school and gypsies in general were considered to be primitive, but Chungarabi was special: She had a wealth of life experience and inner wisdom. "Leichu," she sighed. "There is nothing much you can do because you do, indeed, live in two worlds. This new life is interesting and even exciting, but of course you can't just erase the first twelve years of your existence. We may live in the present, but the present is based on our past, on our previous life experience. You must accept this duality: that you enjoy your present life, yet miss your past life at one and the same time. That's the way it should be, that's exactly how you should feel, and you may well feel that way for a long time." Chungarabi stopped to think. "I want to tell you that you can, and should, talk about this with your mother. She will understand, Leichu."

I finished washing the dishes and went outside to sit with Mama on the stone bench in front of the house. We didn't talk at all, we just sat close together, happy to be near each other.

I knew that the time would come when I would bring up the issue with her. But not just yet.

      ∾   ∾   ∾

The week was over, and the time had come for me to go back to school. Mama told me that before I arrived, she had deliberated long and hard about which school would be best for me. In Sevlus there was a Jewish school called "Tarbut" (which means "culture") where they taught reading and writing Hebrew. This school was closed on Shabbos and Yom Tov. There was also a non-Jewish school, but it, of course, was open on Shabbos and Yom Tov.

Yet Mama was not eager to enroll me in the Jewish school, because she was afraid that it wasn't religious enough. She knew that the classes were co-ed, boys and girls learned in one class together. Actually, the non-Jewish school was also co-ed but the boys and girls didn't sit together — there were two rows of benches for the boys and then two rows for the girls. In a non-Jewish school, Mama noted, it is easier to tell the children to ignore the *goyim*; this would be harder in relation to non-observant Jewish children in the Jewish school.

On the other hand, of course, there was the pressing problem of the Jewish holidays.

"I received all kinds of conflicting advice about this," Mama told me. "I kept changing my mind. Finally I decided to go to the two schools myself and see what I could find out.

"I arrived at the Jewish school just in time for recess. The boys ran after the girls, trying to catch them, and the girls then reciprocated by running after the boys. I didn't like that at all! Some of the children sat on the side and played games, but they also sat in mixed groups. A teacher stood outside, supposedly to keep an eye on the children, but he stood with a cigarette in his mouth reading a book, completely ignoring his charges. The bell rang and the children went back inside the building, pushing each other — boys and girls together.

"Then I went to talk to the principal. He was very respectful and explained the syllabus to me — they teach secular studies in Czech, according to the requirements of the authorities, and they also teach some Russian. And they teach *limudei Kodesh* in Ivrit. During the course of our discussion, I discovered that the teacher who had been standing outside was the Hebrew teacher. Yet the man didn't even wear a yarmulke! The principal explained that this teacher had arrived from Eretz Yisrael and taught the Hebrew language, while an Orthodox rabbi taught *limudei kodesh.*"

It turned out that the school was run by Neologist Jews, who were similar to Reform Jews in other parts of Europe. The school was nothing at all like the Orthodox Jewish girls' school I had attended in Budapest.

Afterwards, Mama paid a visit to the non-Jewish school. She also arrived during recess and saw the boys playing ball on one side and the girls playing on the other; there was no contact between them. There was a teacher who actively supervised them and when the children went over to talk to her, she answered and smiled. Mama liked that. Then Mama went to speak to the gentile principal. He, too, explained that the studies were in Czech and that Russian was also taught, as was German. Instead of joining in the theology lesson, all the Jewish children gathered in one classroom and a rabbi came to teach them *dinim.* Those who wanted to learn more religious studies, said the principal, went to a Jewish *cheder* in the afternoons.

After all these deliberations, however, Mama still had not decided and wanted to know my opinion. That was easy: "I want to go to the *goyish* school because that is where Gizzie studies," I said simply. We had become friends and I wanted to go to school with her. So that's how the decision was made.

The big day came, and on Monday morning Mrs. Weingarten came to take me to school. I was ushered into the principal's room. While the principal spoke to Mrs. Weingarten, a teacher tested me in all the subjects.

"You are quite a good student," the teacher said with great satisfaction. "You can join my class."

She brought me into her class. Just like in Budapest, the teacher sat on a kind of podium. The pupils all stood up when the teacher entered and after they sat down, the teacher explained that I am a new pupil and they should accept me graciously. The departmental teacher who was teaching the class at the time showed me where to sit and the other teacher who had introduced me left the classroom. Everyone rose and sat down again when she left. I sat next to a non-Jewish girl who smiled at me but did not speak.

All the pupils sat straight, their hands clasped behind their backs. It was a math class, and I realized that I knew all the exercises on the blackboard; they were easy exercises that I had mastered in Budapest a year earlier! I was astounded. I had been assigned to a class of children older than myself, yet the material was what I had learned over a year ago.

It was forbidden to remain in the classrooms during recess, and we all went outside when the bell rang. The girls exited first according to the same order in which we sat, two by two, then the boys followed.

Outside, some of the girls stood in a circle around me. Although the teacher had introduced me by name, they asked me again.

"My name is Leichu Fruchter," I said. "I lived with my grandmother in Budapest for many years after my father passed away, but now I have returned to my mother in Sevlus."

That was what I had decided to tell my classmates; I felt that there was no need for them to know the complicated details of my life. Luckily, everyone accepted the story and did not make a big deal out of it.

I was sorry that I had been skipped to a higher class and

wasn't in Gizzie's class. "If I had known in advance, I might have pretended not to be so smart during the test," I complained to Mama. "Then they would have put me into Gizzie's class."

"I don't think that would have helped, dear," said Mama. "How long can you pretend to be ignorant? You would have been very bored, and eventually the truth would have come out anyway and they would have skipped you to the higher class. I'm sure it's all for the best."

I did have one big problem: I needed to learn a new language, the Czech language, because in Budapest we had studied in Hungarian. So it turned out to be a blessing in disguise that the classwork was easy for me and that I had learned much of the material before, because I was able to concentrate on acquiring the new language. Also, every teacher has his or her own method of teaching the subject matter, so even though I was learning the same thing for a second time, it was still interesting.

During recess everyone spoke Hungarian, including the teachers. That was fortunate because I was able to make friends with my new classmates even before I was fluent in Czech. And since I wasn't in Gizzie's class she couldn't sit next to me and help me, but the girl who sat next to me was given permission to translate for me, and I started to pick up the language. When I went home with Gizzie from school, I told her how sorry I was that I wasn't in her class, but she comforted me and promised to tutor me in Czech anyway. Gizzie sat with me every day in the afternoon to teach me; Mama helped as well — we started to speak Czech at home. I learned the language and quickly became integrated in the class, as I had been in Budapest.

The truth was that while recess in the Sevlus school was just like recess in my old Budapest school, the studies were on a lower level. The teacher had to repeat the material many times until the pupils understood.

My class in Sevlus. I am in the second row from the top, fourth from the left. It is a gentile school, the principal and teacher are gentiles though most of the pupils are Jews. The only non-Jewish boy in this picture is the fellow in the top row with a striped shirt. The Jewish boys have payos, but are bareheaded because it was forbidden to wear a yarmulke or hat in school. The poverty is evident in the shabby clothing and barefoot feet. (This was photographed during the summer season.)

The Jewish children understood the classwork much faster than the non-Jewish students. I don't know how to explain this, but I noticed this phenomenon many times over the years: Jews learned a lot more quickly and easily than *goyim*. Perhaps it's because it was more important to the Jewish parents that their children succeed in school, so they helped them at home and made it a priority. In general, Jewish parents believed in *chinuch*, in educating their children from a young age to study. All Jewish children start learning the *aleph-beis* at the age of three, and parents teach their children from a very young age to make the appropriate *berachah* before putting anything in their mouths and after they finish eating. The parents explain to their children that everything a Jew does is accompanied by a blessing, when appropriate, and a prayer for success. Perhaps this process of *chinuch,* of Jewish education in the home, served to sharpen the minds of Jewish children so that they found their secular studies to be easier as well.

I decided that I wanted to help my mother with the chores around the house. I saw how Gizzie and the other girls in the neighborhood helped their mothers with housework, and I was embarrassed that I did not know how to help. At first Mama refused because she knew how I had been pampered in Budapest, and she said she only wanted me to be happy. But when I told her that I'd only be happy as a true partner to her, she reluctantly acceded to my request to teach me.

Luckily Mama was a very patient woman, because it probably was harder for her to teach me at the beginning than to do it herself. I had never filled a bucket or washed a floor in my life, and in Budapest we had running water. It was also harder for Mama to teach me because she worked with one hand and had developed all kinds of shortcuts and techniques to do everything with one hand. Now she had to try to demonstrate how to do the same things with two hands. It was a little complicated, but I did learn.

My first job was drawing water in the early morning hours before school and carrying the big heavy pail home. At first this was very hard indeed, but slowly I got accustomed to it and was able to fill the pail higher and higher each time. Finally I was able to carry a pail full of water without spilling a drop. When I came home from school, I would do all the dishwashing, make the bed and organize the store. The work became easier and faster from day to day, and I was content.

Then in the evening, after the customers left and the store was closed, I washed the floor, dusted the shelves and polished the furniture. Every Friday afternoon, I would wax the wooden floors until they shined. I was very proud of myself for learning how to do housework. In Budapest I hadn't lifted a finger while here, with Mama, I was a real partner.

Mama promised that she'd teach me how to cook, but not quite yet. "It's enough that you have to focus on your school-work and homework, and carry out all the other household chores that you've taken upon yourself," she said proudly. "You don't have to learn everything in a day. And I do want you to have time to play with your friends."

I think that one of the reasons she said this was because I had told her that in Budapest, I was never allowed to play with the children in the yard. "Anya always said that those children were not cultured enough for me," I had said. "I was only allowed to visit my classmates after Anya had checked out the family. And even then, Briendy had to walk me."

In Sevlus I could go outside to play whenever I wanted. There were always girls in the adjacent yards and they invited me to join them. *Baruch Hashem*, the girls accepted me very quickly, and if there was a game I was unfamiliar with, the other girls taught me the rules and helped me until I caught on. This was wonderful, because one of my biggest worries before arriving in Sevlus was not being accepted there. I was afraid that people would talk behind my back and make fun of me: After all, I was a stranger from the big city. I spent sleepless nights in Budapest seeing myself standing alone in the corner, rejected by all the children and teachers who made fun of me and sang mocking songs. Instead, I was im-mediately accepted. The local girls were happy to include a newcomer in their group, someone else to join their games, and even their comments about my strange Yiddish were friendly and inoffensive. In fact, it was amazing that my fears of the new group were proved false, just as my worries and fears about my mother had been completely unfounded.

We, the children, spoke Hungarian mixed with Yiddish. How fortunate it was that I had insisted on learning Yiddish in Budapest! Here in Sevlus they could hardly believe that Jews in Budapest spoke only Hungarian and not Yiddish. True, it turned out that the Yiddish I had learned was a different dialect than the one spoken here; they told me it was "Germanized Yiddish." However, it was not long before I quickly acquired the local dialect.

℘   ℘   ℘

I often thought to myself how fortunate I was that Mama had won the court case, thus granting me the opportunity and privilege to live with her and get to know her as I did. My beloved mother, who received me with a heart full of love! My beloved mother, who taught me how to live a life of honor and principle despite an amputated arm and very little money. She was the one who taught me that it is not wealth that makes a man honorable or noble, but integrity, virtue and respect for everything created in the image of God. Mama demonstrated to me that the honor accorded to a wealthy person only because of his wealth is a mockery. Honor and respect that are dependent on material objects is transitory; when the wealth is gone, so is the respect. I learned from Mama's stories to despise flattery. One who flatters another only thinks about himself and despises the other in his heart.

My dear mother was the one who opened my eyes to see the world as it is, without the glitter of gold and material possessions. It was her teachings, her nobility, and her personal example that taught me the absolute truth — and showed me the true Torah path to follow for the rest of my life.

It was by virtue of my mother's teachings and Hashem's mercy that I was able to rehabilitate myself after the terrible Holocaust that was visited upon the Jewish nation.

❧ 43 ❧
Where Are They Headed?
[SEVLUS]

WE SPENT ALMOST every Shabbos in the same fashion. On Friday night, *Leil Shabbos*, Mama davened and I sat next to her quietly. The flickering candles and gas lamp that hung from the ceiling lit up Mama's face. The room was suffused with tranquility.

Mama's Shabbos dress was dark blue with a white lace collar; Fanny Klar had crocheted the collar for her. Mama wore a spotless white kerchief on her head, and around her waist, a starched white apron with a lace trimming identical to the lace on her collar. She held her large *"Korban Minchah"* siddur, and her lips moved in silent prayer. To me, Mama looked like the Shabbos Queen herself, or at least one of her princesses. I couldn't help but be reminded of Anya who, at that exact moment, was most probably closeted in her room, reading one of her books as she usually did on Friday nights. I also thought about my beautiful room, which stood empty and dark, but I didn't miss it or any of the expensive objects in it. I liked being with Mama; I felt loved, but I also thought about Anya and missed her. I could imagine how lonely Anya must be, and I felt sorry for her. Sometimes I missed Anya and Apa very much, as well as Zaidy and Bubby Shapiro, Basya Leah and her family. When my yearnings got the better of me, I wrote them letters; in fact, I wrote them all letters very frequently. Even though I didn't receive as many letters from them as I wrote, I didn't give up. I knew that Anya couldn't write to me when she pleased; she was only allowed to write once a month. The others had their own lives, and I guess they didn't miss me as much as I missed them.

But despite all my homesickness—I wouldn't exchange *Leil Shabbos* with Mama in Sevlus for *Leil Shabbos* in Budapest for anything! The majestic tranquility and serenity in that small, sparsely furnished room in Sevlus far surpassed all the pleasures of Budapest.

After Mama finished her davening we would go outside and sit on the stone bench in front of the house, where many of the neighborhood women congregated. At first I'd sit with Mama, listening to the conversation, but inevitably I would end up joining my friends in their games. We played until the fathers and brothers came home from shul, and everyone went into their houses. Mama and I also went into our room, where Mama made Kiddush and we sat down to eat the Shabbos *seudah* together.

Mama knew lots of stories from Tanach and *aggados* of *Chazal*, and she told them to me during the *seudah*. I also told Mama stories about what I had learned in Budapest. Those were wonderful hours, and even after we had finished our meal we'd continue to sit and talk.

Mama loved to tell me about the Beis HaMikdash. She was a gifted storyteller and I could really visualize the *leviyim* playing their musical instruments, the *kohanim* in their white garments, quietly walking shoeless on the shining marble floors. I could almost smell the *ketores* and see Bnei Yisrael thronging to the Beis HaMikdash on the *Shalosh Regalim*.

We would sit until very late, telling each other all the stories we knew, basking in the Shabbos tranquility.

On Shabbos morning, after we straightened up our room, Mama sat down to daven and I sat watching her. Little by little, Mama taught me how to daven until I learned all the *tefillos.* I had never davened in Budapest.

We would join the Klars for the Shabbos day meal almost every week and then we would spend the rest of the day there. After the *seudah* we would go outside; the women would sit down on the bench in front of the house to chat, while the children would play.

Every Shabbos, guests would come to visit the Klars. Rivka Klar's sister-in-law, Chaya Sara, would come with her only son Azriel, who would play with his cousins. Zelda Shimonovitz also came with her children, as well as Rivka's other sister-in-law, Miriam, and her children.

Feivel Shraga and Miriam Klar and their children. The twins are in the top row.

Miriam Klar had twin girls my age named Dina and Leah, and although we played together a lot, I never was able to tell them apart. Even though they told me that Leah wore a green dress and Dina wore a blue one, I would still get confused: Was Dina in the green, or was Leah? But once I saw that everyone else mixed them up as well, I didn't feel bad that I couldn't tell them apart.

We all played together; that is, the boys played on one side of the large yard and the girls on the other. The Wurtzburger and Rosenthal girls, the Klar's neighbors, also played with us, as well as many other girls whose names I no longer remember.

Most of these childhood friends were murdered later on by the Nazis, yemach shemam. Their memories are preserved in my heart, among my lovely childhood memories. Hy"d.

When twilight fell, the men and boys went to shul, the guests all returned to their homes, and we went into Néni Klar's home with her family. There we sat while Néni Klar, who had a marvelous voice, sang songs in Yiddish and the rest of us accompanied her softly, so as not to drown out her beautiful voice.

One *motza'ei Shabbos*, after the men returned from shul and Bácsi Klar made Havdalah, we heard some shocking news—news that was forbidden to talk about on Shabbos.

The Klar family was planning to leave Sevlus!

Mama and I were astonished. Néni Klar had to put the children to sleep and couldn't talk at the time, and we promised to come over the next day in the afternoon to hear the details. Mama and I walked home in silence, and even at home we hardly said a word.

For me, the Klar family was a sort of substitute for Zaidy

and Bubby Shapiro and Basya Leah's family. I loved Mama very much, but I was an only child to a widow and I loved being with a family with lots of children. And here, again, I was about to lose my extended family—that's how I felt. My homesickness for Budapest returned more powerfully than ever.

The next day, we found out the details.

The Klars were, indeed, in very difficult economic straits. Although Bácsi Nachman Klar was an expert carpenter, he had little work as there was a surplus of carpenters in Sevlus. Nachman's brother, Feivel, was also a carpenter but unlike his brother, he was lucky enough to work for Berger and Sons as a hired laborer. Even though he received a meager salary, it was a fixed amount that arrived every month, giving him some peace of mind.

But Bácsi Klar was not a hired worker and didn't have a regular salary; he was only paid when he was lucky enough to get work. One of the prominent men of Sevlus had given Nachman the regular work of maintaining his wooden house and furniture; all the wooden houses in the village needed constant care. However, even though Nachman Klar's financial predicament was well-known, for personal reasons, the man suddenly transferred the renovation work to another carpenter. Evidently, Nachman took this news very badly.

At the same time this happened, Nachman received letters from his other brothers who had immigrated to Argentina. The brothers sent tempting offers to Nachman to join them in their new country, and offered to send travel tickets for the whole Klar family. Nachman, who was the oldest in his family, had raised and supported all his younger brothers and sisters when his father had died in his childhood, and now they wanted to pay him back by bringing him and his family to Argentina.

Néni Rivka Klar objected to traveling so far away to an unfamiliar place called Argentina, and even convinced her brother-in-law Feivel, not to go, either. But now, the economic situation in Sevlus was so dire for them, that they had to do something. They could not possibly feed their nine children under these circumstances.

And just on that day, another letter arrived from Argentina. The brothers wrote that the place that they lived in had a shul and a *cheder* as well as a *rav*, a *shochet*, and everything a Jew needs. The only thing lacking in their town was a *"Sefardishe shul"* (a shul in which the *tefillos* were in *nusach Sefard* — the *nusach* of the *chassidim*). Nachman understood this to mean that the people in their town in Argentina were a bit compromising in their Judaism and were not on the level of the truly zealous Jews in the *Sefardishe shul* in Sevlus.

Bácsi Klar arrived home just when Mama and I were there, and he read the letter. He immediately announced that he would not join his siblings in Argentina; he had children to raise and educate, and eventually to marry off. If there was no *Sefardishe shul*, perhaps other things were missing; how, then, could he raise his children to remain true and faithful Jews?

I was secretly very happy to hear this. As a young girl I did not understand their financial difficulties, but I was happy that they weren't leaving. *Baruch Hashem*, my new extended family was remaining near me in Sevlus.

On *Rosh Chodesh Tammuz*, when I came home from school, all the women were sitting in all the yards and chatting, just like on Shabbos. That was because they followed the custom that women should avoid working on Rosh Chodesh as much as possible, so they all finished the work that could be done on Rosh Chodesh in the morning and now they sat outside and relaxed with their friends.

I went home and "chased" Mama outside. "I'll take care of the customers," I told her eagerly. "Please go out and relax with the women."

Before I came to live with her, Mama couldn't leave the store to sit with her friends on Rosh Chodesh because she had to be there for the customers. Now she already trusted and relied on me to run the store in her absence. I had learned all the secrets of the small grocery store: the prices of the various items, how to use the scales, the proper method of inserting the groceries into the paper bags and, most important, service with a smile and a kind word.

These greetings and words of welcome were Mama's secret. Because of Mama's honesty and her caring words, her customers always returned. Mama knew each and every customer and their family members and knew what to say to each: "How is your Bubby Fayga feeling today?" she'd say, or "Mazel tov on your new grandson!" I, of course, didn't know the townspeople as well as Mama, but I followed her instructions to speak pleasantly and treat people graciously. Everyone used to say, "The daughter is like the mother; they look alike and sound alike too," and I was thrilled to hear this compliment.

And then Fanny and Dori Klar came over to talk to Mama. Fanny worked only half a day on Rosh Chodesh in her hat store and Dori didn't do housework, so the two of them were able to take a walk in the middle of the week. I started to go outside to greet them, and then I stopped. I noticed that they were explaining something to Mama, and Mama was not smiling. She didn't look happy at all — which was unusual; it must mean that they were telling her something serious. I didn't know if it would be proper for me to listen in on the conversation. But the two girls noticed me, and turned around to greet me so pleasantly that I did not hesitate any longer. I walked over to them and said hello.

The street leading to the train station. On the right— the Spinka Rebbe's house.

The girls told us that their father had gone to the Spinka Rebbe, who lived in Sevlus, the night before. Although Bácsi Klar was a Vizhnitzer *chassid*, he could not make the trip to his Rebbe in Rumania more than once a year, so in the middle of the year, he would consult with the Spinka Rebbe on various issues. Each Rebbe had his *derech*, his own methods for advising his *chassidim*. The Vizhnitzer Rebbe would tell his *chassidim* exactly what they should do, but the Spinka Rebbe would listen to his *chassid's* question and simply repeat certain words that the person had used. The *chassid* would have to use his own logic, coupled with the advice he deduced from the "repeated words," to make the proper decision on his own. The Rebbe would then bless the *chassid* and wish him *hatzlachah*.

But this time, unlike his usual manner, when Bácsi Klar

explained about his financial circumstances, the Rebbe told him in no uncertain terms that he must leave Sevlus and go to Eretz Yisrael.

◇◇

The Admor of Spinka, the tzaddik Rabbi Yitzchak Isaac Weiss, son of Rabbi Yosef Meir Weiss, was a well-known gaon in Halachah. The Spinka Rebbe was also famous for his tefillos and attracted thousands of chassidim to his court. He was taken to Auschwitz together with the rest of the townspeople and died on 13 Sivan, 5704 / June 4, 1944. Hy"d.

◇◇

Mama and I were dumbstruck. Eretz Yisrael? An entire family with little children? To leave everything and move so far away? This was extremely irregular!

A customer came into the store. I went to serve him, so I missed the rest of the conversation. But soon after, Mama joined me in the store, and after the customer left, she told me that we were closing the store and leaving.

The four of us— Mama, Fanny, Dori and I —walked together down Train Street toward the Klar home. We walked at an unhurried pace, stopping to look at all the lovely display windows of the stores on the street. There were shoe stores, clothing stores, jewelry stores and stores with expensive silver objects. Fanny showed us where she worked: Mrs. Landau's hat store for women. We all gazed at the lovely hats in the window; Dori proudly pointed out one of the hats that Fanny had designed.

As we walked along, we admired the jewelry in Williger's jewelry store, and then looked at the different paints and building materials in Mr. Klein's store. Afterwards we examined the shoes in Mr. Mitchell's window—one of the few stores on this street belonging to a gentile.

Dori told us that when the shoe store first opened, Mr.

Mitchell invited a band to play and invited all the townspeople to hear the band and, of course, see the new shoes.

We admired the dresses in the Kaufman family's store, the elegant shirts in Mr. Wasserman's store, and finally reached Weinberg's hat store for men. Fanny and Dori told us the famous story about that store.

"One day," they said, chortling at the recollection, "Mr. Weinberg received an entire shipment of white hats by mistake. He couldn't return the hats and didn't know what to do, so he hung up a large notice in his shop window, announcing that the latest fashion in Budapest was white hats for men. Only he, Weinberg, was offering these stylish new hats at a special price.

"All of us in Sevlus believed him, and many bought the new white hats which, of course, were not considered stylish at all. That's why the Jews in Hungary made fun of us, calling us *Di Seilush na'aroinim mit a veisse hiten* — 'the Sevlus fools with the white hats!'"

We reached Hungarian Street; there, opposite the *Scheilhoiv* was the Klar residence. Bácsi Nachman's two brothers and their families, and most of Nachman and Rivka Klar's family were all there — talking, arguing, very involved. The conversations were peppered with the words "Argentina," "Eretz Yisrael," "*chinuch,*" "tickets," "the Rebbe," "the *Sefardishe shul*" — over and over. Children shouted, babies cried, and there was great tumult.

The Spinka Rebbe

As soon as Mama saw what was going on, she took hold of my hand and steered me outside again. "This is a family meeting, we shouldn't interfere," she explained. We intertwined our hands and walked slowly to the big square at the edge of town. The square was empty; on either side was a church, one large and one small. The local market was held on this square twice a week, on Mondays and Thursdays. Then the square was filled with a multitude of farmers in the area who would come to sell their wares: crowing roosters and quacking ducks, bleating goats and sometimes even neighing horses. There were also fruit and vegetable stands, grocers selling various foodstuffs and much more. A large percentage of the stands were owned by Jews and one could get everything at the market, from hairpins to furniture. Each peddler would announce his wares in a loud voice, calling on the buyers to come to his booth. The cacophony of noises and hustle and bustle was a sight to be seen. But on a regular day, the square was quiet and empty. A few children played ball in the corner, but that was it.

We walked home slowly. "Why did we leave the Klars so quickly?" I asked Mama. "After all, the girls came all the way to invite us."

"Well," said Mama slowly, "it's true that Néni Klar and I are very close; she has been like a big sister to me." Actually, the two women were about the same age but this was how Mama felt because of Rivka's help to her throughout all the years of her widowhood. "Yet we must remember that we are not actually close family, and in critical time periods they must make their decision only with close family members."

I, too, faced a fateful decision. The clock was ticking: I had been sent to my Mama for six months, and then I would have to decide where I wanted to live: here in Sevlus, with Mama, or in Budapest with Anya and Apa. But I would have to make the decision on my own and could not involve anyone else. When I took Chungarabi's advice and spoke to Mama about my upcoming decision, she said firmly, "It is your decision, and only yours." Chungarabi had told me the same thing.

This was a critical juncture in my life with a decision that would determine my fate.

During the days I was happy and busy; it was only sometimes at night, after Mama and I stopped chatting and she fell asleep, that I would remain awake, tormented by my dilemma. Yes, I still had time; but the qualms, the uncertainty and worries!

44

Righteous Women

[SEVLUS]

EANWHILE, OUR lives continued as usual. Every
morning I woke up happily and did housework while
singing songs to myself. Sometimes I pondered the
irony of it all: In Budapest I woke up like a princess without
having to do a thing, yet I was never happy to get up in the
morning. I always tried to postpone the inevitable and remain
in bed another five minutes, then another two minutes. In
Sevlus, on the other hand, I awoke a lot earlier in order to
do my chores, chores that I would never have dreamed of
doing in Budapest. Yet here I never tried to remain in bed for
a single minute; I woke up quickly and happily.

Perhaps this was because I realized that my work was valued. I felt that I was needed, so the work didn't feel like a
burden. True, Mama had done everything alone before I had
arrived despite her one hand—but as soon as I took some
of the housework off her shoulders and she saw that I did it
happily, she was greatly relieved. Although she never admitted it, it was hard for Mama to do all the housework alone.

I was happy that I was really needed and not just doing
make-believe work. In Budapest, when I peeled one potato,

Anya and Bezhee had clapped their hands and praised me as if I were a prize-winning chef. Then they made fun of me and said that my peels were so thick that there was no potato left to eat. But here with Mama, in Sevlus, I peeled large quantities of vegetables each week. Mama had shown me how to hold the knife and vegetable to peel thin strips properly, without cutting myself.

I also learned how to knead dough, braid challah and bake bread. Mama taught me how to do a lot of things; she succeeded, with her one hand, to accomplish a great deal and also to teach me to work with my two hands. I never worried about cutting myself or getting burned, and she never made fun of me when I did not succeed right away. She simply explained to me how to accomplish the task so that I would succeed, and this spurred me to want to take on more and more responsibility.

In school I slowly became accustomed to the Czech language, with the help of Gizzie and the girls in my class. My studies were very easy and I didn't have to work hard, so that I could spend more time and effort on acquiring the new language. The games in the yard were almost the same as in Budapest. Although there were boys in the gentile school, there was no interaction between the boys and girls at all, not in the classroom, or during recess. We, the girls, played on one side of the yard near the school while the boys played on the other side. The truth is that my studies in the Sevlus school occupied a relatively small part of my life, unlike in Budapest where the Jewish Orthodox school had a much higher scholastic level and had been the focus of my daily schedule.

In Sevlus, like Budapest, laundry days were the best days of the week — laundry days brought with them my beloved Chungarabi. But in Sevlus, unlike Budapest, I did not have to hide my relationship with the gypsy from Mama. Chungarabi

and I found a way to talk so that outsiders would not easily notice: We sat not far from one another on the porch in
front of the store and I sewed — by hand, Mama didn't have
a sewing machine — while Chungarabi washed the laundry.
We talked quietly, and when people approached the store we
stopped talking so than no one would know of the connection between the Jewish girl and the gypsy.

Mama and I spent most of our evenings telling each other
stories. After we had finished catching up on our lives, Mama
told me stories of *Chazal* that she knew from the *Tzena
U'Rena* as well as other stories that she had heard over the
years, and I told her the stories I had heard in school in Budapest as well as those I had read in books there. Here in Sevlus I had no books, and truth be told—I had no time to read.
There were never enough hours in the day to do everything
I wanted, and at night I usually fell asleep quickly—except,
of course, when I was overcome with waves of homesickness
for Anya, Apa and everything I'd left behind in Budapest. It
was in those periods that I lay awake, wondering about my
future. But in general, I was very happy.

During my homesickness-attacks, Mama understood
what I was feeling and she lovingly left me alone. Only after a considerable time passed would she approach me, place
her one hand on my shoulder and hug me without saying a
word. Sometimes I just snuggled up next to her and thought
of my former life in Budapest, but after some time the waves
of longing would dissipate and I would relax. Sometimes at
night I would dream about Budapest, but even so, I never
woke up sad in the morning.

I was truly surrounded by happiness.

∽   ∽   ∽

The two Klar brothers, Bácsi Nachman and Feivel, left for

Eretz Yisrael by themselves on a tourist visa. Their families remained behind while the two men went to look for work and housing. The plan was that if they would succeed, they would send for their families and if not, they would return to Sevlus.

Néni Rivka Klar continued to manage the household in her husband's absence, and Mama and I continued to join the Klars for Shabbos meals. It was as if Bácsi Nachman Klar was on his yearly trip to visit the Rebbe. None of the family traditions changed, the absence of the head of the family was not felt, and the children behaved as they usually did: The mischievous ones continued their mischief and the quiet ones remained quiet. I felt a special affection for Dovid'l, who was named after my father. He was the quietest child in the house.

I was also especially fond of baby Ettu'ka, an adorable little girl with big blue eyes and blond curls. All the children loved her and fought over who would hold her. I also participated in the fray, I also wanted to hold her!

ов   ов   ов

The night of Tishah b'Av arrived.

I had never really felt the gravity of the day in Budapest. I knew, of course, that everyone fasted, and I also fasted on *Leil Tishah b'Av* as well as a few hours the following day—but nothing more than that. Anya always stayed in bed on Tishah b'Av because she had no strength, Briendy also didn't do anything all day, and I walked around aimlessly.

Anya said that it was forbidden to play games or sew, so I didn't play or sew all nine days, and we didn't sing or listen to music. We only waited for the monotonous days to pass, and that's all.

But in Sevlus, we felt the gravity of the Nine Days — from

the first day of the month of Av until the afternoon of the tenth day of Av. All the Jews in Sevlus were very serious for the duration of the Nine Days — they didn't laugh, sing or tell jokes.

On *Erev Tishah b'Av*, after the *seudah mafsekes* we went outside. All the men went to shul, and the women and children gathered in the Greenbaum family's yard where we sat on the ground. Mrs. Weingarten (Néni Aidah) sat on the ground as well, holding a candle in her hand. That was the only light in the vicinity, all the nearby houses were dark. Néni Aidah read the *kinos* of Tishah b'Av in a mournful, wailing voice and then translated them into Yiddish. The women cried; even some of the children cried, but all of them sat quietly and did not play. Néni Aidah and the other women told us heartrending stories of the destruction of the *Beis HaMikdash*. I had never dreamed that the *Churban* had been so terrible.

On the morning of Tishah b'Av we left the house and went to the *Scheilhoiv* where we sat in one of the corners of the giant yard. Almost all the Sevlus women were there. This time, another woman began reading *Megillas Eichah*, she translated and explained it, and after some time, another woman took over. All the women cried, and I did too. The stories were frightening and distressing, and the atmosphere was shrouded in deep sorrow. I never knew that Tishah b'Av epitomized such terrible destruction.

Bubby Shapiro had talked about the *Churban*, though she never went into detail. She only said that the *Churban* was the result of unfounded hatred, *sinas chinam*, a quarrel among brothers. She used to say that Mashiach doesn't come because of the quarrels and divisions among the Jews and that these bitter quarrels only increase as each community and group thinks that they are better than the others. That's why Mashiach doesn't come, because he doesn't know where to go! After all, *Mashiach* can't only go to part of the Jewish nation, he must come to everyone—but since the Jewish People are so divided, this is the reason that we remain with our disputes and dissension and without *Mashiach*. Yet, I had never heard from her or anyone else, how terrible and horrendous the *Churban* had been. In Budapest we had only waited until the end of the oppressive fast day without talking about it at all.

We remained in the *Scheilhoiv* until the afternoon, then we went home. On the way we saw the men walking slowly to shul with their tefillin bags in their hands. This was the first time I learned that on Tishah b'Av, the men don't put on tefillin in the morning. We all walked slowly, no one ran and everything was extremely quiet. Even the non-Jews looked different than usual. Although most of the stores were open, there were no customers on the streets and the stores were empty. It was not a regular work day at all.

When we got close to home, Mama said that many people would probably come to the store now, in the afternoon, because the women only started to cook in the late afternoon on Tishah b'Av. And, sure enough, there were many customers and both of us were very busy. Everyone who came in to shop spoke quietly. No one said "Good afternoon" or "Good evening," and Mama explained to me that people don't greet one another on Tishah b'Av. I tried to remember if we refrained from greeting one another in Budapest, but I guess I don't know since we never left our home or saw anyone on Tishah b'Av.

     ɷ   ɷ   ɷ

After Tishah b'Av, summer vacation started. Many people left Sevlus for the villages surrounding the Tisza River, where they could relax and swim in the river waters. Sevlus, meanwhile, became full of youths from all over Czechoslovakia and Hungary who came to work picking grapes in the Carpathian Mountains. As a result, sales in our grocery store declined precipitously; the Sevlus people who left for vacation stopped buying in our store for the duration and the grape-pickers didn't buy much either. The grape-pickers preferred to explore the large stores on Train Street, or frequent the market that was held on Mondays and Thursdays in the city square.

I was worried about the drop in our sales, but Mama remained unperturbed.

In Budapest, when there was a drop in sales from Apa's store, the whole family worried together and tried to think of ways to help the business. Mama, on the other hand, only said that *parnasah* is from Hashem. We do our *hishtadlus*, make our effort, of course; we order the supplies, clean and organize the store and mainly, we work honestly with exact weights and honest accounts. The rest is not in our hands, Mama reminded me, because *HaKadosh Baruch Hu* sends us exactly what we need, whether we embark on a publicity campaign with large-size advertisements (as I wanted) or continue our regular, quiet, honest work (as Mama insisted we should).

This was Mama's path in life: to trust in *HaKadosh Baruch Hu*, to do His will by relying only on Him and keeping honest accounts. Honesty and integrity were her watchwords; her scales were scales of justice and her accounts and bills were exact and reliable.

But I really didn't understand this. Since Mama's business practices reflected her scrupulous honesty, since she trusted faithfully in Hashem that He would provide for her needs, and since she carried out His will to the exact letter of the law, she should have been blessed with abundant wealth! But, as far as I could see, this was far from reality. My beloved Mama barely eked out a living for our most basic daily needs. And she always used to say, "*Baruch Hu u'baruch Shemo*" over the little she had.

She always would tell me, "We have, *Baruch Hashem*, what we need. And I am actually relieved that He does not give us the *nisayon* of wealth, because that is the hardest trial of all. Very few people remain uncorrupted by wealth and remain steadfast in their principles of righteousness."

It seemed to me that Apa had not been so successful with his "*nisayon* of wealth." I would never judge him, *chas v'shalom*; Apa worked very hard and gave generously to charity, he always davened in a *minyan* and learned Torah regularly. But it seemed to me that they were not scrupulous about exact measurements in the store and did not tell customers when the material was of inferior quality. They were not always as exact in their accounts and bills as was Mama. But perhaps I was mistaken? It was forbidden for me to think ill of Apa.

Apa was a good man, though very exacting and meticulous. Zaidy and Bubby Feldman were even more exacting, and Apa had been brought up in a home where great emphasis was placed on the proper behavior, good manners and propriety of each child. He, then, brought me up the same way as his parents because he felt that was the best way to bring up a daughter.

On the other hand, I had many doubts about the way I had been adopted and didn't know what to think. Was it really true that Apa and Anya didn't know that I had been stolen from my mother? Did they really think that they were doing a good deed in paying a large sum of money to a poor widowed woman, and selflessly raising an orphan in their home? I had heard Anya whispering as such to Bubby, and it seemed that the judge also believed that the Feldmans didn't know about my kidnapping. Yet if so, when Mama brought them to trial and the truth was known, why did they fight her so much? After the verdict was given, Anya had shouted that the trial had been another means for Mama to extort more money out of her, and she had even tried to bribe Mama with large sums of money for me. When she saw that Mama was not willing to touch even one cent of hers, did she still believe that the court case was just a way to extort money from her? There were so many contradictions that I thought my head would burst.

One night, I finally decided to talk to Mama about all these innermost thoughts. I was amazed at her response.

"I do think that Mina Feldman really believed that she was paying a large sum of money to a 'poor, disabled, widowed woman,'" Mama sighed. "Why would she imagine that her sister-in-law Eva would take the money for herself? After all, Eva was a family member who had shared their sorrow of being childless and seemed to care about them. It certainly is a lot easier to accuse a strange, unfamiliar woman of extorting money, than to accuse a family member. It must have been hard for them to accept that the 'poor, disabled, widowed woman' cared nothing for money, and only wanted her lost daughter!"

This must have been what Anya thought. True, she paid for me, but afterwards I became her daughter, she raised me as her daughter and she loved me. And if she loved me as a mother loves her daughter, why would she want to willingly give me over to someone else? Why would a strange woman coming from afar interest her?

Mama never said a word against Mina Feldman; to the contrary, she understood her. Even though Mina was her adversary and rival, Mama didn't hate her—even when I told her all the things that Anya had said about her when she knew that I'd overhear.

"If she felt that the mother sold her child and only wanted to extort an additional large sum, then it's understandable that Mina would be angry," Mama said. "And even if not— even if she knew the truth — when someone feels that the most precious thing in their life is being taken from them, they may say or do rash, unfortunate, untrue things. I won't judge her," said Mama slowly.

Yet Mama herself saw her precious daughter stolen from her deceitfully! She, too, had undergone the worst of all, yet she did not think of speaking ill of Anya nor of her own relatives.

"Even my relatives, who gave you away, felt that they were doing the right thing — they felt that a 'poor, disabled and widowed woman' simply couldn't bring up a child," sighed Mama.

"But what about the money that our relatives took? What about the money that Eva took?" I cried.

"They could not resist the temptation they faced; a large sum of money is a very difficult temptation indeed," said Mama sadly. "But it is not up to you or I to judge them."

∾   ∾   ∾

On Shabbos we went to the Klars as usual. I managed to take Néni Klar on the side to talk to her privately and told her everything that Mama had said about Anya. "My Mama is, truly, a *tzadekes*," I said. "She only looks at everyone's good side."

Néni Rivka Klar thought about it, then answered, "Your Mama is right. That is the correct way to look at this whole situation," she said. "I don't know if that makes her a *tzadekes*; she is simply acting as a person should, and as she always does, with honesty and uprightness."

I knew that Mama always related to Néni Klar as her big sister and mentor, so I was not surprised to hear her opinion. But I never knew how to decide which of them was a greater *tzadekes*.

❧ 45 ❧
Before the Verdict
[SEVLUS]

T HE DAYS OF Elul arrived.
All the vacationers returned and the spirit of Elul,
of *teshuvah*, was in the air. Everyone seemed more
serious and somber; my friends were more restrained, and
they even mentioned the word "Elul" occasionally. This, too,
was new to me. Most of the stores also opened later than
usual in the morning.

"Most of the shopkeepers try to daven all year in a faster
minyan," explained Mama, "but during Elul, all the *minyanim* daven more slowly, with exceptional *kavanah*, taking the
time to say each and every word faithfully. Even when the
tefillah is over, the storekeepers don't rush out of shul, but
leave slowly and seriously. That's why they open their stores
later. They also try to daven Minchah in a *minyan* in shul
during Elul. All year round they daven privately, in a corner
of their store. So most of the stores also close temporarily in
the afternoon hours during Minchah."

Mama also was careful to daven more slowly than usual
and say more *Tehillim* than she usually did every day. She
also gave more money to *tzedakah*.

Apa and Anya also gave a lot to *tzedakah*, I remember that. But they could easily allow themselves to do so while still maintaining their own high standard of living. Mama, on the other hand, had barely enough to live on, yet she always gave to those less fortunate than herself. In my heart of hearts, I felt that the pennies she gave had so much more significance than the larger sums the Feldmans gave. I knew that Mama's pennies were taken from her basic necessities, and I learned to appreciate this very much.

❧   ❧   ❧

It was Erev Rosh Hashanah. Mama sat and told me the story of Rebbi Amnon of Magentza, whose arms and legs were cut off because he refused to convert. "They laid him down in shul near the Aron HaKodesh on Rosh Hashanah," Mama said as the tears streamed down her cheeks. "There he davened the holy prayer of *U'Nesaneh Tokef*, and then he died." Mama wiped her tears. "Then afterwards, Rebbi Amnon came to Rav Kalonymus ben Meshulam in a dream, and taught him the words to this important prayer."

I knew why Mama cried to tell this story; she was reminded of the terrible pain she suffered after her arm was amputated when an infection developed in the stump. She remembered how she could not help screaming during Dr. Lezman's treatments, and how she had to bite down on a piece of leather with all her might to stifle her cries. Who can imagine the great suffering that Rebbe Amnon suffered, when both his arms and legs were amputated!

"I believe that one of these days, a medication will be found to cure infections," Mama used to tell me. And she was right — a few years later, antibiotics were invented that have done so much to prevent pain, deformity and death to all humanity.

Mama taught me every word in *U'Nesaneh Tokef* as well as explanations and interpretations of other Rosh Hashanah prayers. Thus this Rosh Hashanah was different than all the previous ones in my entire life, as I understood the words in the *tefillos* and uttered them with real *kavanah*. After the end of *tefillah* on both days, I felt great happiness. My *tefillos* were more real than ever, and I felt certain that they were accepted in the Heavens.

The days between Rosh Hashanah and Yom Kippur were truly *"Yamim Noraim,"* days of awe. Mama taught the *Viduy* to me and explained the significance of every confession. As she taught me she cried, and she also cried in shul afterwards on Yom Kippur itself.

Mama also told me about the *avodah* of the *kohen gadol* in the Beis HaMikdash. She described the magnificence of the Beis HaMikdash, the majestic clothing of the *kohanim* and explained the significance of the *korbanos* and of the *Ne'ilah* prayer that we say at the very end of holy day, just before the Heavenly verdict is sealed.

On Erev Yom Kippur, when Mama blessed me with the *Birkas HaBanim*, she told me about my father's last day on earth. She was reminded of that particularly on Yom Kippur because Tatte had said *Viduy* then and they both had said *Ne'ilah* together, before he died. I had been an infant in my mother's arms, taking it all in with wide-open eyes.

The story had a big impact on me. I, too, cried on Yom Kippur during the *Ne'ilah* prayer. But I was not only crying for the father I would never know; I cried because I, too, awaited a verdict that would determine my fate, a verdict that I would have to determine myself, and the gravity of it filled my heart.

✺　　✺　　✺

I knew that immediately after Sukkos I would have to travel to Budapest, to the courthouse, and announce my decision to the judge: whether I wanted to return to Apa, Anya and an easy life of the wealthy in Budapest, or remain with Mama and her grocery-store in Sevlus, despite her hard life.

Mama continued to refuse to advise me or express an opinion about my decision. "It is your decision, and only your decision," she would tell me firmly. "I don't want to carry the knowledge for the rest of my life that I told you what to do or affected your decision in any way," she would say. "You must think and decide, and know throughout your life that it was you who made your own decision."

I understood her, but now time was running out. There was one last thing I wanted to do, and that was to show Mama the diaries I had kept in Budapest. I had never shown them to anyone else before, of course, because my diaries were personal. I was also embarrassed because I had not written according to the rules. Briendy had told me that I ought to write every day and always include the date; if I skipped a day, I should fill it in the next day. But it bored me to do that. I wrote without dates and without order; I wrote when the urge struck and then I would write a lot. Afterwards, I would often leave the notebook in my drawer for weeks with no more entries until the next time I had something to say.

But now I took my diaries out of my bag to show Mama. I wanted her to really understand what I had experienced in the past, and not just from hearing me talk, but to read what I had written. Mama didn't want to infringe on my privacy, and I had to beg her stubbornly until she acceded to my request.

Finally, she took the diaries reluctantly from me. I didn't want to be present when she read them, so I went out to play with Gizzie in the yard. When I returned I saw the closed notebooks on the table.

"Did you read them?" I asked eagerly.

"Yes," she answered quietly.

"Please tell me what you think," I begged.

"You have a lovely handwriting," she smiled.

I looked at her in amazement. This was not the response I had expected.

"I read every word," she explained, "and I find no fault in the way you write; this was not a paper for a school assignment to be graded. These pages reflect your thoughts and feelings; things that you did, as well as things that happened to you. You wanted me to read them—so I did, and I can say that now I know your life history even better than before." She sighed. "But what right do I have to express an opinion about what happened to you?"

My dear mother, what an innocent and upright soul!

ল্ড   ল্ড   ল্ড

We spent most of Sukkos with the Klar family, as usual. We did not mention the verdict that awaited me; when I tried to ask the Klars for advice, they reminded me that we do not talk about such things on Yom Tov.

In honor of Yom Tov, the oldest Klar son, Chaim Michel, came home from Prague for Yom Tov. All his little brothers danced around him day and night. It seemed that he never stopped laughing, and he kept picking up his little sisters and carrying his brothers on his shoulders. All the children told me that it was their big brother who built the *sukkah* at the entrance to their house and created a special cover for the *sukkah* for rainy days. And in fact, we were able to eat in the *sukkah* only during the first two days. Afterwards it rained so hard that the men lowered the cover over the *s'chach* to protect the Sukkah decorations from the rain.

The fateful day arrived. Mama accompanied me to the train. I took only a small bag with a few things. We separated with many kisses, but no tears. Mama stood on the platform, smiling and waving to me with her kerchief as the train pulled out of the station. I stood near the window and stuck my head outside until I could no longer see her.

❧ 46 ❧
The Decision
[BUDAPEST]

I SAID TEHILLIM throughout the entire train ride. Again and again, I asked Hashem for His help in giving me the wisdom and insight to come to the right decision. The truth was that I had already decided in my heart, but had not expressed it verbally to anyone. I decided that if I would change my mind at the last minute, it would be a sign from the Heavens; if not—I would know that Hashem was guiding me, and He was the One Who gave me the wisdom to decide on my own.

When I got to the train station, Néni Zinger was waiting for me. She hugged and kissed me happily and kept exclaiming over how much I'd grown over the previous six months. She asked me about the news in Sevlus and especially about her brothers' families. I told her about the letters Nachman and Feivel had sent from Eretz Yisrael, that they were well and had found work in a city named Haifa.

After a while, though, I began to suspect that I wasn't telling her anything new. Her brothers and sisters-in-law had probably written to her as well; she was probably only asking me questions so that we wouldn't have to talk about the fateful decision I was about to make. Néni Zinger walked me to the corner of a street and showed me the way to the courthouse; for some reason she did not want to walk me to the courthouse door, but she would not say why.

I walked slowly, holding my bag firmly. It was just in front of the gate that I saw Anya and Apa.

I ran to them with all my might. I fell upon Anya with cries of happiness, kisses and hugs, and she also hugged and kissed me endlessly while she wiped away her tears. Even Apa wiped away a tear when he thought no one was looking, but I saw.

We walked over to a bench near the courthouse's entrance. Anya turned me round and round in all directions and exclaimed that I had not changed at all; I remained the same Leichu as I had been half a year ago. But I knew that was not the case; I had changed a great deal. Inside I was a completely different girl from the child I had been six months ago.

I took a small, embroidered napkin out of my bag and gave it to Anya. She looked at it, astounded.

"You did this by yourself?" she exclaimed. "How were you able to do this? The embroidery is so precise!" She examined my work and exclaimed over it again and again, until I took the napkin from her hands, folded it up and put it into her handbag.

Meanwhile, Apa's lawyer arrived and said that it was time to enter the judge's chambers. Anya and Apa rose from the bench and wanted to come in with us, but the lawyer said that they must stay outside. Only I was to enter.

Anya kissed me tenderly and Apa smiled at me, and I went to stand next to the lawyer and said, "Let's go." Together we strode through the large brown doors.

On the way the lawyer asked me, "Have you decided where you want to live?"

"I have made my decision as to where I belong," I answered cryptically, and did not tell him my decision.

We walked up two flights of wide stairs, then strode though a very spacious hallway. The walls were painted an oil-based paint the color of wood, and portraits of honorable-looking people covered the walls. We walked past a number of doors; on each door was a glass sign with a name. The lawyer knocked on the third door.

The door swung open and a young man ushered us in. A black-robed judge sat near an enormous writing table. He pointed to some seats, and we sat down.

The young man, who seemed to be the judge's assistant, gave him a cardboard file. My name was on that file folder. The judge opened the file and began to read. He turned a page and read some more, turned more pages and read again, until he reached the last page, which he studied at length. After he finished, he removed his small, round glasses, looked at me and asked:

"Are you Leah Feldman?"

I stood up and answered proudly, "I am Leah Fruchter, also known as Feldman."

The judge looked at me and smiled at the lawyer.

"And so, Leah Fruchter also known as Feldman, now you alone must decide where you want to continue your life—with your parents here in Budapest or with your mother in Sevlus. Have you reached a decision?" asked the judge soberly.

"Yes, I have, Your Honor," I answered. "I have decided."

"Has anyone instructed you how to decide? Has anyone tried to influence you or promised you payment or reward for your decision?" the judge asked.

"No, Your Honor," I answered carefully. "I came to this fateful decision all by myself and I did not reveal it to anyone: not to my mother in Sevlus nor to my parents who are waiting for me outside."

"Well then, you must now tell me your decision—as you called it, your fateful decision. I will write it in the file, and render it legally valid," said the judge in a stern tone.

I approached the table. I wanted to talk in the same stern tone as the judge but my hands and legs started to tremble, and it was in a choked voice that I said, "Your Honor, I belong with my birth mother from whom I was stolen. I want, and I see as my agreeable duty, to remain and live with her in Sevlus."

"Are you completely sure about your decision?" asked the judge.

This time my voice was a great deal more forceful when I answered, "Yes, Your Honor, I am sure. I want to live with my mother."

The judge mopped his brow with his handkerchief and asked again, "Is this your final decision?"

Again, I answered confidently, "Yes, this is my final decision. I know that I cannot change my mind."

Then the judge took a pen in his hand, dipped it in ink and wrote while reading aloud, "I asked the young lady, Leah Fruchter also known as Feldman, three times about her decision and each time she repeated and announced that she, Leah Fruchter also known as Feldman, chooses to live with her mother Sheina Ruchel Fruchter in the city of Sevlus. The young lady Leah Fruchter also known as Feldman is an intelligent young lady and it seems that she has weighed her words and understands the consequences of her decision."

The judge looked at me and I nodded my head in the affirmative. He continued writing while reading out loud: "Thus, I certify her decision, and from today the young lady Leah Fruchter will return to live with her mother in Sevlus. On that, I hereby sign—Justice Volnoi."

The judge picked up his seal and stamped the verdict, and asked his assistant and the lawyer to sign their names as witnesses.

I parted from the judge with a curtsy. The lawyer and I waited outside a few minutes, until the assistant prepared copies of the judge's decision. The assistant submitted the copies to the lawyer and then we went downstairs.

On the way out, the lawyer told me that he respected my decision very much. "I imagine it must have been a difficult choice for you," he said. "But you should know that this was the most correct decision that was possible under the circumstances." Inside I was surprised and impressed; he was, after all, Anya and Apa's lawyer. But I did not say a word.

When we reached the bottom of the staircase, I saw Anya and Apa waiting for me. I took a deep breath; this was not going to be easy. I had dreaded this moment for a long time.

I hugged and kissed Anya with all my strength while the lawyer gave Apa one of the copies. Apa read it and turned pale. Anya grabbed it out of his hands and read it herself. She looked at me and almost collapsed on the spot. I grabbed her and said, "Anya, I love you with all my heart. I can never repay you and Apa for what you have done for me, and can never finish thanking you for it. Yet I belong to my mother, from whom I was stolen."

A river of tears washed over my face. "My mother never received a penny for me," I said clearly. "The money that you paid, must have been taken by the relatives who stole me, and by the intermediary.

"I belong to the woman who gave birth to me," I declared. "Although I love you very much, by all standards of justice and honesty, I must return to my mother whom I also love very much."

Anya and Apa stood near me, helpless and dumbfounded.

I turned to the lawyer. "Please send a telegram to my mother," I said, "telling her of my decision. However, before I return to Sevlus, I would like to spend a few days with Apa and Anya."

The lawyer asked Apa and Anya if that was agreeable to them, and they said yes. Then he left us, and the three of us walked together to their house on Flower Street No. 36.

Nothing had changed; neither the street, the house nor the apartment. Everything remained as it had been, especially my old room. Anya hadn't touched a thing in my absence; the games and toys remained in their places on the shelves, and next to them were the books I had loved so much. The closet was stuffed with my dresses and the drawers were full of clothes.

Even the dress that Néni Zinger had taken from me and sent back to Anya was still hanging in the closet.

Everything looked so petty and trivial to me now. I didn't understand how only half a year ago, I enjoyed playing with such babyish games. The dolls sat neatly on their shelf, and all the doll accessories were on the second shelf. All the doll clothing was neatly placed in the lovely wooden box that Apa had bought me.

Why, to think that I had been so childish! I didn't even want to look at my beloved sewing machine. True, it was the only thing I really missed from Budapest, especially after sewing by hand all these months. But I knew that it was no longer mine, and as a result, I didn't want it at all.

I left my room and sat down next to Anya at the table. I didn't sit at my usual place at the table — I sat at the spot that was reserved for guests. "You are a guest," I said to myself. "You no longer belong to this family, so act accordingly."

With great politeness, I decorously asked all the accepted questions. Apa sat with us for a few minutes and then excused himself and returned to the store. I continued sitting with Anya. She asked me a lot of the usual, accepted questions, but finally she could bear it no longer. She cried, "Why did you choose your birth mother over me? What do you have in Sevlus that you didn't have in Budapest?"

How could I explain to her that I had nothing materialistic in Sevlus compared to the luxuries I received in Budapest—yet despite that, I wanted to remain in Sevlus with my birth mother. How could I hurt her that way?

I surveyed the beautiful room: the large table with the expensive damask tablecloth with its perfectly ironed diagonal folds; the matching chairs, the breakfront with its gleaming silver utensils, the expensive glass closet with all its crystalware—all the things that Anya was so proud of. I looked at the large, luxurious rug on the shining wood floor, at Apa's expensive leather armchair and Anya's rocking armchair.

But I looked at it all from afar. I was familiar with everything in that room, as I was with everything in the entire house. I even remembered the day when the furniture was switched, and how hard Briendy had to work at polishing it all so that everything would shine and glow the way that Anya liked.

But I did not feel a smidgen of regret or disappointment that I no longer lived within the walls of this beautiful home.

Mama's tiny room was far closer to my heart. With Mama, I did not have to watch every movement to make sure that nothing would spill or break. Even when a cup did break, it was no big tragedy because it was a simple glass cup, not an expensive part of a rare and priceless set. If something spilled on the floor, we simply mopped it up and nothing more was said.

But that was not the reason that I was happier in Mama's home. After all, in my twelve years with the Feldmans I had learned not to spill, not to break, and how to act in a home with such expensive trappings. I had learned how to curtsy, how to ask the right questions, how to act with proper manners as Anya had taught me, according to the rules that were so important to her.

Anya got up, walked over to the kitchen and returned after a few minutes. She was holding an expensive china plate heaped with cookies, which she placed on the table, along with matching china plates for the two of us. Then she returned to the kitchen and brought out the expensive tea set on a silver tray.

She sat opposite me, poured me a cup of tea and offered me the plate of cookies. With great propriety I put one cookie on my plate and started to drink the tea. I held the cup daintily by its handle and made sure my pinky was raised in a perfect arch, as Anya had taught me.

I looked at Anya; she, too, was holding her cup just as she had taught me. Suddenly our eyes met, then I placed the cup on the plate and both of us burst into jolly laughter. We laughed and laughed until my ribs ached. Anya came around the table to give me a hug, and the two of us continued laughing.

In the afternoon we went to Zaidy and Bubby Shapiro, who received us with exuberant joyfulness — with much oohing and aahing and hugs and kisses. After that joyful welcome I continued on to Néni Basya Leah's home, where everyone was also excited to see me.

In the evening, we passed by the store on our way home, and politely greeted Zaidy Feldman. I knew that I had to go to the Feldman home as well and say hello to Bubby Feldman, but I pushed that off until the following day. I was not looking forward to that visit.

At night I lay in my bed and had a hard time falling asleep. This was my bed, my room, my clothes—everything was top quality and expensive. But I, I was happier in the tiny room, sharing a bed with Mama, with all the chores and housework I had taken upon myself.

And suddenly I knew that I truly belonged there, with Mama. How strange it was: I had already made my decision, of course, yet it was at that moment that I knew, I knew in the depths of my heart that I had made the correct decision indeed. Here I was just a guest. For twelve years I had been a guest, and even now I did not belong here. On the other hand, from the moment I had entered Mama's tiny room, I had felt at home. The feeling of belonging was so strong, so deep and intense that I had decided to remain with Mama despite her poverty. The intensity of the feeling of belonging was much stronger than all the wealth and luxuries that the Feldmans could offer.

The next day I went out with Anya for a stroll on the streets of Budapest and we visited the loveliest places. During our walk we passed my old school; I was happy that the girls were in class and did not see me. Everyone now knew that I was adopted, and I remembered how my old classmates had turned up their noses at adoption.

We continued to a restaurant and had lunch there, then turned to relax in a park. I fulfilled my duty by stopping in at Bubby Feldman, and then Anya and I continued our walk together until evening. At night the two of us returned, tired and happy.

Anya wanted to give me many gifts, but I did not want to accept anything. Mama and I had no space in our tiny room for all these unnecessary things, and I had no need for them. I had the feeling that Anya wanted to give me things in order to bribe me, and I was not interested.

At night, the three of us—Apa, Anya and I—sat together and talked a lot. I didn't want to tell them about Mama so I

told Apa and Anya about school, my new friends, about Sevlus and the market days in the town square and all kinds of
general things like that. But I did not talk about Mama and
my life with her. I knew that Apa and Anya were very curious to know why I chose to remain with Mama, and what I
preferred in Sevlus over life with them. But how could I hurt
them by telling them the truth? They had, after all, brought
me up and treated me like a real daughter for so many years.
How could I explain that I now realized how shallow, superficial and materialistic the Feldmans' lives were, in comparison
with Mama's wisdom and depth? How could I tell them that
I learned true *yiras Shamayim* from Mama? Yes, it was from
Mama I had learned true righteousness, true *bitachon*, true
faith in *HaKadosh Baruch Hu*.

In the morning, I said goodbye happily to Apa before he
left for the store. Then Anya and I went to visit Zaidy and
Bubby Shapiro again to say goodbye, and together with them
we walked to the beautiful train station. Anya bought me a
train ticket, but I did not let her buy me anything else. I took
the bag of food Anya had given me for the trip and the small
overnight bag I had brought with me, and that's how I returned to Mama. Anya hadn't offered me any of the objects
in my room, so I was spared my internal conflicts on the issue.

The train arrived. I parted from Anya with tears, hugs and
kisses. But in my heart of hearts, I felt relieved.

I promised Anya that I would visit. I told her that if I
would decide not to remain with Mama, I would return to
her. Then the train started moving. I stuck my head out of the
window and Anya waved at me with her handkerchief until
we could no longer see one another.

❦ 47 ❀
A Mother Is Irreplaceable

[SEVLUS]

I RETURNED TO Sevlus. After beautiful Budapest, Sevlus seemed small and provincial; but to me it was beloved and precious. I had lived in Sevlus for only six months, compared to the twelve years I had spent in Budapest, but I loved the small town much more. During my six months I had become familiar with practically every nook and cranny of Sevlus, while there were large sections of Budapest that remained foreign to me. Budapest was so large and impersonal that although I was familiar with many of its neighborhoods, there were many sections I had never visited and places I had passed through but never gotten to know. Yes, it was true that the beautiful and modern capital city of Budapest always filled me with wonder: from the historic buildings in Buda to the modern new houses in Pest; the hundreds of bridges that connected the two cities — the ancient and modern — thus transforming them into one unified city; the lovely and numerous well-groomed parks; all the squares and plazas, the benches with lovely, intricate metalwork decorations; the street lamps that looked like columns from antique houses; and last but not least, the remarkable cleanliness that

315

prevailed throughout.

On the other hand, I loved every street and every site in Sevlus even though it didn't hold a candle to Budapest — not in size, beauty, or even cleanliness. But it was in Sevlus that I belonged, and Sevlus belonged to me — though I had lived there for only six months.

Mama was very, very happy. For the second time, I was her full-fledged daughter. She had borne me and cared for me lovingly for six months, and now, at age twelve and a half, I had returned to her loving embrace.

"I made up my mind not to tell you how afraid and worried I was during your six months with me," she told me. "I knew that I could never give you all the things that the Feldmans did; I can't even imagine the kind of wealth they enjoy. I would never even try to compete with them on that level. I knew that you would have to make your decision based on what I could give you, and not what I couldn't. And I knew that it must be your decision only.

"I felt that neither I, nor anyone else, had the right to interfere or try to influence your decision in any way. But I admit, my Leichu, that I had grave doubts about the wisdom of entrusting that kind of fateful decision to a twelve-and-a-half-year-old girl—a decision that requires decisive maturity. I didn't think that a girl at that age is mature enough. So I prayed to Hashem that He would grant you wisdom and insight, and that I would have the inner strength to accept your choice, whatever that would be. I also told myself that if the judges deemed it correct to entrust such a young girl with a decision of this sort, then *HaKadosh Baruch Hu* would guide you in your decision and place the right words in your mouth."

After I arrived home the neighbors all came over, shook Mama's hand and joyously wished her *mazel tov*. It turned out that they all had known that I myself would have to decide where I belonged, after a six month trial period with Mama. So they all had davened that Hashem would inculcate in me the desire to remain with my mother. Most of the town had been partner to Mama's pain all the long years she had searched for me. Throughout those times, they had tried to strengthen her flagging spirits and had prayed for my return. Dori told me that her mother Néni Rivka Klar had davened and cried so hard on the day that I went to the judge with my decision, that one would have thought she was davening for her own daughter.

When the telegram arrived with my decision—all the Sevlus townspeople rejoiced from the bottom of their hearts.

෴ ෴ ෴

Life went back to normal. I continued attending school, working at home and playing with my friends. As the winter approached the days got shorter and we had less time to play outside. Then it started to snow and the freezing temperatures outside chased us into our warm houses.

Diligently, I wrote letters to Apa and Anya as well as to Zaidy and Bubby Shapiro. I knew that Zaidy and Bubby would show my letters to Basya Leah and her family, so I directed my letters to them as well. I told them about my studies and my friends, the people in Sevlus and their good deeds. It was important to me that they wouldn't have a negative opinion of my townspeople. I was worried that the Shapiro clan in Budapest would be angry at the Sevlus people, with a certain amount of justification. After all, as they saw it, Mama and the Sevlus townspeople had "taken" me away from them.

The letters I received in return were not as lengthy as mine were. But in every letter, Apa and Anya reminded me that if I should change my mind, I could always return and they would accept me happily. Evidently they simply could not understand how I, of my own free will, was willing to relinquish a life of wealth in Budapest for a life of poverty in a remote village at the foot of the Carpathian Mountains.

On the other hand, all the Sevlus people that I met on the street told me that I had made the correct and just decision: A mother is irreplaceable. A life of wealth is a great temptation, but motherhood—the bonds of motherly love and mother-child affinity—prevails over wealth. And virtually everyone I spoke to complimented me on my insight and wisdom in making the correct decision.

For an entire week, I heard the story about Moshe Rabbeinu over and over. When Moshe Rabbeinu was a baby he sat on Pharaoh's lap and was offered two bowls to choose from: one with burning coals and one with gold. Little Moshe started to reach his hands toward the gold, because he was wise even as a child. But an angel pushed his arm so that Moshe would do as any ordinary child would, and he picked up a glittering coal — and burnt his hand. Moshe put his burnt hand in his mouth to relieve his pain, and burnt his tongue! This caused him to stammer and stutter when he learned to talk. Hashem wanted him to appear as a regular child and remain alive, in order to redeem Bnei Yisrael later on, because Pharaoh would have killed him if he had chosen the gold.

My strict upbringing helped me remain polite and attentive to the story over and over again, without even hinting that I had already heard it dozens of times. Thus I listened patiently each time until the end, and responded as I was expected. I said that evidently, an angel from the Heavens came to me to whisper the correct answer in my ear. Thus I made the correct decision, and for this we must thank Hashem.

The truth is that no angel whispered the answer in my ear at the last minute. I had wrestled with my decision over many sleepless nights. I knew all along that the right thing to do was remain with Mama, but I can't say that the easy life in Budapest didn't tempt me. And Mama won; my connection to her prevailed.

ה ה ה

That winter, Mama bought me large, heavy, black galoshes. I remembered all the galoshes I had owned in Budapest: red ones with gold buttons on the side; plain black ones for schooldays and fancy black ones with buckles for Shabbos. Those galoshes matched my shoes, and the shoes matched my coats. And here in Sevlus I had only one pair that Mama bought with great difficulty, a size larger than I needed so that they would fit me the following year as well. Yet I valued that pair more than all the galoshes and shoes that Anya had bought me. I always felt that Anya bought me expensive new clothes just as she bought herself jewelry: to flaunt her wealth and good taste, and show the world how well she dresses her only daughter.

On the way to school we would slide on the snow with our galoshes, creating a smooth line on the snow. Each one of us wanted to make the longest line, but I always "won." Since I had learned to ice skate on the Danube River that intersects Budapest, I was experienced. Of course, all the girls tried to imitate my long, straight marks.

ה ה ה

Chanukah arrived, and Mama lit the candles at the entrance to the store. On the second day of Chanukah Mama removed everything from our small room and kashered everything for Pesach, saying that it was time to make *shviskim* for Pesach. This was puzzling to me; Pesach was months away and I had never heard of such a thing in Budapest.

Mama explained to me that housewives in Sevlus cooked goosefat now for Pesach because geese developed the most fat in the winter season, so that was when they were sold and slaughtered. Housewives would melt the goose fat over the fire, then add onion. When this cooked goose fat solidified, it was known as a delicacy called *shviskim (or gribbenes)* that was preserved until Pesach in the special window shelves that remained freezing cold throughout the winter. Then, the *shviskim* were used on Pesach for cooking and also for spreading on matzah.

After everything was clean, tip-top and kashered, Mama melted the jellified goose fat over the fire, and our small apartment was redolent with the special fragrance of Pesach. Everyone who entered the store—there were only a brave few who dared the cold weather to do their shopping—immediately said, "Aha! You're frying *shviskim* for Pesach!"

After Mama finished her frying, she cleaned and polished the Pesach dishes and put everything back in its place. Then she showed me that she had left out a few *shviskim* to eat on bread, and some more of the fat for frying latkes for Chanukah.

On the last night of Chanukah the weather had warmed up to the extent that we could go outside and walk to the Klars. There was a lot of excitement and joy at the Klars. Nachman Klar's brother Feivel lived close by, and his wife, Miriam, and their children had also come to visit. All the children played dreidel and a special game with *aleph-beis* cards. The *lamed* letter card was the winning card.

"This year, we are not taking down the chess game from the closet," Fanny told me. She explained to me that this was a special game of chess that Bácsi Nachman Klar had laboriously carved when he was imprisoned in Siberia during the First World War, and the family took it down only on Chanukah. But this year, Nachman and Feivel Klar were in Eretz Yisrael. Perhaps they were playing chess in Eretz Yisrael, she said, if they had a chessboard and time available. Even though both fathers were not present, there was still great happiness and we did not feel deprived.

Néni Miriam Klar walked home with her children at night, despite the cold. The older girls carried the little ones in their arms, wrapped up like teddy-bears in many layers. Néni Rivka Klar wanted us to sleep over and not brave the cold, and Mama argued with her, "If Néni Miriam can walk home in the cold with her little ones, we can certainly do it!"

But Néni Rivka argued back, "How can you compare the two? She lives so close, and you have a very long walk."

Finally, after many entreaties, Mama agreed that we would stay and sleep over. I pulled Mama's hand and asked her quietly, "Where will we sleep?" The Klars had only one room and a kitchen. True, the two older boys were in yeshiva. Still, that left seven children and there were only two beds that I could see. Mama smiled and said, "Soon you'll see how they make room!"

Meanwhile the children had tidied up the small apartment, cleared and cleaned the kitchen table. To my surprise, the two older girls grabbed one side of the table, the three younger ones grabbed the other side and they turned it over and lowered it down to the floor, against the wall. I was amazed to see a mattress under the table board. "This is where the three boys sleep," explained Dori.

The children were obviously used to this nighttime ritual as they quickly set up two chairs facing another two chairs, and placed a small mattress between them. "This is where the two little girls sleep," they told me.

In the big room they set up two benches side by side, and another two benches next to them. They placed mattresses on them: one for Mama and me, and an additional mattress for Fanny and Dori.

The girls spread immaculate white ironed sheets over the mattresses, and placed soft, snug feather quilts on top. Then they took out lovely, hand-embroidered nightgowns for us. The transformation was complete.

And so they made room for everyone: on the table, on chairs and benches—and everyone slumbered restfully that night.

In the morning, Mama told Néni Rivka that we had to rush to return home because she had a commitment to open the store early for her regular customers. I was sorry to leave so soon because I enjoyed being with the Klar family.

"I don't want to burden the Klars more than is absolutely necessary," Mama told me on the way home. "They are wonderful hosts and wonderful people, but their financial situation is very grave and we already ate their latkes and doughnuts yesterday. I don't want them to feed us breakfast."

Mama's argument about having to rush to get back to her customers was really an excuse so as not to insult Néni Klar.

Mama also explained that in any case, no one had time for games in the morning. Fanny went to work and Dori helped her mother with the demanding housework. So it was good that we left early, after helping to return our "bed" to its "morning" position and not cause them additional bother.

It was only years later that I found out that when the Klars had guests for meals during difficult times, they would serve the guests steaming bowls of hot soup — while they themselves received steaming bowls of hot water. I never knew that.

❧ 48 ❧
Two "Bubbies"
[SEVLUS]

THE HEAVY SNOWFALL drew snow flowers on the panes of the double windows as it fell to the earth. I had never seen such heavy snow in Budapest and even when it did snow there, workers cleared the streets with special snowploughs and scattered salt and gravel on the roads to melt the ice. The workers also pushed the snow off the sidewalks making tall, frozen, black piles. But in Sevlus, there were few cars and the municipality did not provide these services. Instead, the snow was kneaded by the feet of the horses and the people on the sidewalks.

All of us school children had to contend with the "bundling up for the snow" ceremony every morning before we left for school. It took a while to wrap ourselves up in layers of gloves, scarves, heavy coats and overshoes. Once we were outside, though, we enjoyed the snow and preferred to bypass the clear streets in favor of the pristine snow wherever we could find it, such as on the sides of the fences that surrounded the homes. Then once we got to school, we helped each other unpeel all the layers. The teachers of the younger grades helped the younger children, but we older kids helped one another. The whole routine was rather tiring, but there was no choice; it was so cold that you didn't dare venture outside without wrapping yourself carefully in layers.

ɔↄ   ɔↄ   ɔↄ

Purim was approaching.

Mama decided to make a big *seudah* on Purim for all the townspeople. "When I looked for you, Leichu, throughout all those years," she said, "I told all the neighbors that when you'd come back to me, I would make a big, lavish *seudah* for them and all the people who helped me in my difficult hours. And now, the time has come to fulfill my promise."

Mama invited practically all the Jews in Sevlus. Most people expressed their thanks at the invitation together with their regrets that they could not come and take part in the *seudah*. In my heart of hearts, I was relieved; where would we seat all the townspeople in our little store-apartment? As it was, many people had responded in the affirmative — the joint *seudas Purim* and *seudas hodayah* would be well-attended.

Mama started her preparations way in advance. Due to the cold weather before Purim, most people did their shopping only in the afternoon hours when it warmed up a little, and avoided the morning and evening hours. This left Mama many available hours to cook, though I couldn't help in the morning when I was in school. It took Mama a long time to cook because she had only one hand, and every simple action necessitated sophisticated maneuvering to compensate for her missing limb. I was very proud of my Mama who succeeded in overcoming her disability time and again.

Purim day was very special. Many guests brought us *mishloach manos* and visited briefly. I ran around all morning delivering *mishloach manos* to the neighbors, while Mama made the final preparations for the festive *seudas Purim*.

I helped Mama set up the large table in the store and covered it with a large white tablecloth. Mama arranged the food, buffet-style, on this serving table, and borrowed numerous chairs to seat the people around the large room of the store. I saw how people came, ate, blessed Mama and myself and then *bentched*, before leaving quietly to make room for others who waited their turn outside. I had wondered how Mama would fit everyone in the store!

The guests and neighbors could not stop singing Mama's praises, for the splendid meal as well as the *mishloach manos* that was arranged so artistically on the plate.

I also received *"mishloach manos"* from Mama: a large, heavy notebook. "I want to encourage you to write again," she told me. She had suggested this to me earlier, but she dropped the issue for a while when she saw that I was not interested. Now she brought it up again.

"I re-read your diary when you went to Budapest," Mama explained. "Leichu, you have real talent. I decided that if you would come back to live with me, I would buy you a notebook and try to encourage you to write again. You write well, but of course you need practice. I hope that, eventually, you will write real stories and books."

After Purim the weather warmed up a bit. The snow started to melt slowly and the icicles that hung from the drainpipes and slanted roofs started to thaw. Large chunks of snow started to drop from the roofs and people walked in the middle of the street to avoid being struck by the falling clumps of snow or getting wet from the melting icicles.

Occasionally, horse-drawn carriages, and very rarely, an automobile, would drive by in the street. The drivers would shout at the pedestrians, who would then jump aside quickly to clear the road for the wagons and cars. But I knew that the shouts were not ones of real anger; everyone was happy that the worst of the winter had passed.

       ∾   ∾   ∾

We celebrated Pesach happily as well. We went to the Weinbergs for the first Seder and were invited to the Klars for the second. Mama at first declined the Klar invitation because Nachman Klar was still in Eretz Yisrael, but Néni Klar would not take no for an answer. When we went to their house, we were surprised to see Dr. Lezman, the physician who had ministered to Mama after her arm was amputated, together with his daughter. We also met the third Klar family that resided in Sevlus—Aharon Klar and his wife and only son. It was Aharon Klar who led the Seder, together with Néni Rivka's two older sons, who were also home.

The spring bloomed in full glory. The grapes in the vineyards started to sprout their green leaves, and the forests of tall oak trees were at the height of their splendor. The entire landscape erupted with the bright green of the leaves and the vibrant colors of the lovely flowers. Even the flowers that I had planted at the entrance to our house, now sprouted gloriously—even though I did not get up before sunrise every morning to water and weed them, as did Fanny and Dori. Despite my laziness, my flowers were no less lovely than theirs. The world around me bloomed, and I blossomed as well.

Then the hot summer was upon us.

Gizzie introduced a new friend to me, Rochel Filman, with whom I became very close. Rochel lived with her grandmother and I went to visit them almost every day. I loved visiting them — they were a cheerful pair, always smiling and laughing. Rochel and her grandmother earned their meager living by embroidery. (In those days, it was accepted that Jewish parents supplied their daughters with a *nedunyah*, or dowry, when they got married. This dowry included linens and quilts for the young couple, but these items were not bought in shopping centers, but laboriously sewed. The final, finishing stage of embroidering the linens was considered most important.) The women and girls of Sevlus brought their linens to the Filmans, and their home was always lively and bustling from all the guests. The grandmother hardly got up from her place, and it was Rochel who greeted all the customers, taking new merchandise or returning the completed embroidery jobs.

Most people did not call Rochel and her grandmother by their names, however. The townspeople called them "*de groiseh Bubbe*" and "*de kleineh Bubbe*"— "the big grandmother" and "the little grandmother". After some time, I asked my new friend the source of these strange nicknames. "My mother died giving birth to me, so I was given her name, Rochel," my new friend explained. "But my grandmother, who brought me up, is my mother's mother. She couldn't bear calling me by the name of her daughter who had died so tragically and unexpectedly at such a young age. So instead she gave me the nickname of '*Bubbe*'—grandmother. As time went on, slowly but surely all the Sevlus women started calling us the big *Bubbe* and the little *Bubbe*, to distinguish between us."

One day when I was alone with Rochel and her grandmother, I asked to use their sewing machine to sew their linens after they finished the embroidery. The truth is, I missed sewing ever since I had left Budapest and my sewing machine behind, and I had eyed their machine longingly for quite some time. At first Mrs. Filman didn't want to hear of it, but I worked hard to prove her fears wrong. I took a leftover piece of material and sewed long, straight stitches on the machine. After I showed Mrs. Filman my handiwork, I took another piece and this time, I sewed symmetrical squares. Then I sewed diagonal stitches that created an exact diamond shape. Secretly I was pleased that I had not forgotten my skill, and I enjoyed the work.

When Rochel's grandmother saw that I did good work and that I really liked sewing, she told me that she would let me sew — but only if I would allow her to pay me for my work. Of course I didn't agree to that. Finally, we decided that I would sew and as "payment" they would teach me how to embroider, True, I had already learned to embroider simple stitches in school and I had embroidered something small for Anya, but this was special, artistic embroidery—something unique.

I immediately sat down at the machine and got to work. As I worked, I sang. I was in seventh heaven!

"Thank you so much," I announced to Rochel and her grandmother. "This is my payment—letting me use your machine to do what I like so much!"

The two of them laughed. In a few days, I had sewed a considerable amount of linens. This arrangement worked out well, because while Rochel and her grandmother liked to embroider and did so quickly, neither of them liked to sew. This meant that the sewing part of their work was often delayed for a long time. Now that I was in the loop, I finished all the sewing that had accumulated, and worked quickly and happily.

Then Rochel's grandmother turned to me and told me that she wanted to fulfill her part of the bargain by teaching me the special embroidery tricks, and I began to re-think the deal we had made.

"Embroidery is your *parnasah*," I wondered out loud. "If you teach me your skill, wouldn't it be unfair for me to compete with you?"

The jolly pair burst out laughing, but the grandmother

became serious quickly. "This is only a small payment to your mother, out of the great debt that we owe her," she said.

This was something new. Until now I had only heard from Mama how the Sevlus people had helped, supported and encouraged her during her difficult times, and suddenly I found people who felt beholden to my mother. I was unprepared for this.

"For a long time, we had no livelihood and only very few women came to us asking for embroidery," Rochel told me. "During that difficult time period, when we would go to your mother's grocery store she gave us twice the amount of what we asked, and then charged us only for the amount we had requested. When we tried to argue with her, your mother would innocently insist that she gave us what we had ordered and charged us the regular price. Of course, we knew the truth.

"Then when we tried to stop buying, your mother noticed. She would bring all the food staples to our house, and would even apologize for 'bothering' us at home! She said that she figured that it was probably hard for my elderly *Bubbe* to venture out to the store in the cold—or the heat, depending on the season—and also probably difficult for me, the little granddaughter. She would say something like, 'I just decided to pop over to visit a friend in your neighborhood, so I may as well bring you what you need; please don't be angry at me!' This was your mother's way of putting food in our mouths so that we could survive the difficult times.

"When business picked up and we had enough work to support ourselves, we tried to pay your mother back for the foodstuffs she had given us in the past. But she was not willing to accept even that. 'But you paid me already!' she would say."

When Rochel told this story to me, she had tears in her

eyes. They, of course, knew my mother's difficult financial situation, and that she did *chesed* notwithstanding.

Now they were delighted to be able to return the favor to my mother, by teaching me how to embroider.

❧ 49 ❧
The Scent of Eretz Yisrael
[SEVLUS]

ROCHEL HAD REVEALED to me a facet of Mama's personality that I had not known. True, I saw that she always had a coin in her pocket and a smile on her face for charity collectors. I had heard the good word and seen the cup of hot tea that always accompanied the coin. And I admired my mother all the more for the fact that she gave even though she herself was not exactly a woman of means. Still, the story of the *kleineh Bubbe* (Rochel) was totally new to me, and I decided to surreptitiously keep my eyes open and see if Mama still gave certain people more foodstuffs than they asked for without taking any more money. In any case, my admiration for Mama only grew from day to day.

Apa and Anya always gave money to *tzedakah*. But they were wealthy people and did not take from themselves in order to give to others. In addition, they made sure to talk about their good deeds and let other people know. Mama, on the other hand, never spoke about her *chesed*. It was only after I asked her that she admitted the story of the "two *Bubbes*" was true.

"I was brought up to believe that it is a Jew's obligation

331

to give to those who are in need, even if he can only give a small sum," Mama told me. "Also, he should not talk about it afterwards."

I spent many hours with Rochel Filman and her grandmother and practiced their special embroidery techniques on small scraps of material. Finally, the *groiseh Bubbe* declared that I was ready to embroider a whole tablecloth.

On that very day, I took some money from my savings that I had brought from Budapest—I had not touched it before—and ran to buy material and thread. Rochel joined me on my shopping trip to the material store and helped me make my selection.

Now my visits to the Filmans were even lengthier. Aside from the sewing I did for them, I spent time embroidering at their house. I left the embroidery at the Filmans, though, and kept it a secret from Mama. Mama, on her part, was happy that I had found such a good friend and was spending time with her; Mama liked Rochel and was glad that I had become close with her. When she heard that I was doing sewing for them, she was even happier — she knew how much I liked sewing on a machine. She even dreamed of buying me a sewing machine some day when she would have enough money.

"It is wonderful that you are sewing for them," she said to me. "You are able to do a mitzvah by helping two wonderful women and — at the same time you get to practice your sewing."

I didn't breathe a word about the tablecloth I was embroidering.

One day, Fanny and Dori knocked on our door. Both of them were so excited that their words tumbled out quickly, almost incoherently. After a while, we finally understood what they were saying: Their father had finally returned from his long voyage to Eretz Yisrael, and he would be taking the whole family back with him. And, said Fanny, as she opened her bag and pulled out a round, luscious orange, they had brought us an orange — an orange from Eretz Yisrael!

Mama carefully placed the orange in the porcelain bowl in the middle of the table. Occasionally she would sniff its lovely fragrance, and pass it to me to do the same.

Its fragrance was wonderful: the scent of Eretz Yisrael, *Eretz HaKodesh*, the holy land. The lone orange transformed our little house, as a festive atmosphere enveloped the room.

"Can we give a section to Rochel and her grandmother?" I asked. Mama agreed enthusiastically, and thought of other people with whom she would like to share the orange.

I looked at her. "Mama," I said anxiously, "do you really think there are enough sections in this orange for everyone?!"

She laughed. "Don't worry, Leichu," she promised. "First I'll put aside one section for the two of us, then we'll offer the rest to other people. As long as there are more slices, we'll continue to share. That's the best we can do."

Then I had a great idea. "Can I go visit the Klars and see if they have another orange for the rest of the people?" I asked pleadingly. The truth was that I wanted to hear stories of Eretz Yisrael from Bácsi Klar.

"You can go," Mama said. "I'll come later — after I close the store. Then we'll walk home together."

I ran most of the way to the Klar home, and arrived there out of breath. The small apartment was full of guests and Bácsi Klar was telling everyone stories of Eretz Yisrael.

"The skies there are so blue," he was saying, "that it's as if you can look deep into the heavens. There is no other place in the world where the skies are such a deep blue!" Nachman went on to tell us about Haifa, the city where he and his brother Feivel had found work.

I was surprised. I had always thought that the only city in Eretz Yisrael was Yerushalayim, and here I discovered that there were all kinds of cities and places there. We always spoke of "Eretz Yisrael and Yerushalayim" in one breath, and I had thought that it was one and the same place. And now, Bácsi Klar was telling everyone about the road from Haifa to Yerushalayim — how he and his brother had taken the train to an Arab city called Lod, and from there they switched to another train that took them to Yerushalayim. The trip took them an entire day, and the trains were dilapidated and old — much older than the trains in Czechoslovakia and Hungary. That made sense to me. After all, Eretz Yisrael is a very ancient land from the past, from the period of the Beis HaMikdash, so of course everything there would be ancient and antique.

I recalled my old Hebrew tutor in Budapest whose name was Sarah; she had also told me stories about a place in Eretz Yisrael called "Kibbutz" and many other things. The truth is that I didn't really remember her stories, since I had only listened with half an ear and didn't really believe them. Apa had called her a "*chalutzka*," and even though I didn't know what that meant, Apa made it clear that it was not a good thing to be.

Meanwhile, Bácsi Klar was continuing. "As you approach the holy city of Yerushalayim on the train," he told us, "the train travels so close to the mountains that you can actually touch the boulders without even extending your arms! And once you reach *Yerushalayim Ir HaKodesh*, you can feel the very holiness in the air."

Bácsi Klar told us that he had spent a Shabbos in Yerushalayim with a family who had lived in Sevlus many years ago, and now lived in a neighborhood called Beis Yisrael. "Throughout the entire time I spent in Yerushalayim," he related, "I felt how each and every step I took there elevated me; this was where David HaMelech and Shlomo HaMelech walked, this was where the *nevi'im* and the *melachim* strode!" As Bácsi Klar spoke, tears welled up in his eyes from emotion.

There was absolute silence in the room as we all sat there — spellbound and teary-eyed. Then, when Bácsi Klar got up and said that it was time for Minchah and Maariv, the men stirred themselves as from a dream. They all left together to go to shul, but the women and girls didn't move. We remained transfixed.

Suddenly Dori got up and came back with a white cloth bag. The bag contained soil and small stones. "This is from Yerushalayim, from Har HaZeisim," she explained in a hushed voice.

We trembled as we reverently touched the soil and stones that Bácsi Klar had brought from such a holy place. Fanny brought some pieces of paper, prepared small cones and inserted a bit of the soil in each. Then she distributed them to us.

When we left to go home, we tightly clasped our paper cones containing soil of Eretz Yisrael and walked in small, measured steps, full of fear and awe.

Just a short time after the Klar brothers had returned to Sevlus, we went to say goodbye to Feivel Klar's family. In those days the British held a mandate over Palestine, and Jews who wanted to settle in Eretz Yisrael had to receive "certificates" (entry visas) from them. The Klar brothers were fortunate enough to receive certificates, and Feivel's family wanted to use their precious certificates and leave for Eretz Yisrael as soon as possible.

On our way over to Feivel and Miriam Klar's home, I asked Mama why Nachman and Rivka Klar's family were not hurrying to leave the country together with Feivel's family.

"Nachman and Rivka Klar's two older daughters—Fanny and Dori—are over the age of eighteen," Mama explained. "That's why they cannot be included in the family certificate. They need their own certificates, and the British authorities are not willing to give it to them. But their parents will not leave them behind, and are trying to find a way out of the problem.

"Meanwhile, Feivel's family does not want to wait. They are afraid of pushing off the trip in case the authorities will find an excuse to invalidate the certificates. So they rushed to sell and pack what they could, and are leaving Czechoslovakia tomorrow."

When we reached the Klar household, we saw how everything was already in boxes. Even Mama was amazed at how quickly they had packed. Only the heavy furniture remained—the beds and closets that had not yet been packed. The apartment was so crammed full of people that it seemed as if all of Sevlus had turned out to see them off and say goodbye.

There were many words of farewell and kisses; there were tears and even requests. Some people asked to send regards to their relatives or friends who lived in Eretz Yisrael; others came to ask the Klars to pray for them in the holy country. Many others just came to say goodbye.

I stood on the side and watched the tumult. My friend Gizzie had come along, even though she didn't know the Klars. She stood next to me and made non-stop comments. She only knew the Klar families from my stories so she had no emotional connection to them and the farewell was one big show for her. I, on the other hand, stood on the sidelines not because I was emotionally distant from the Klars but because of the exact opposite reason: I didn't want people to see just how excited and overwrought I was to say goodbye.

True, our connection with the Feivel and Miriam Klar family was an indirect one; they were related to "our" Klar family. Miriam Klar was Néni Rivka Klar's sister-in-law, and it was Néni Rivka who had adopted Mama and myself as if she was Mama's big sister. Yet I still felt this departure keenly, and I wondered: If I feel this way when Miriam's family is leaving, I will be ten times more overwrought when "our" Klar family leaves!

I asked Mama that troubling question on our way home. How will we manage with the separation from our beloved Néni Rivka and her family?

"I am happy that the two families are going to Eretz Yisrael," said Mama. "It is the right thing for them. But I have to admit that I dread the separation from our only family in Sevlus. Of course, I will make every attempt to restrain myself and not show how worried I am about the parting. I don't want them to feel bad."

The next day I went to Rochel and found her grandmother crying bitterly.

"I wish I was doing my embroidery in Eretz Yisrael, and not here in *galus*," she said to me. "The limited livelihood we have here, we could have in Eretz Yisrael!"

It turned out that she had submitted numerous applications for a certificate to go to Eretz Yisrael, on behalf of herself and her granddaughter Rochel.

"But all my applications were turned down, one after the other," she cried.

Everyone knew that the British preferred to issue certificates to families and not singles, and only to families whose fathers had work.

"Listen to me, Leichu, and remember what I'm telling you!" said the *groiseh Bubbe*. "If we remain here, my granddaughter and I, we will die an unnatural death and our bodies will be scattered — like dung — on the face of the earth. Remember this! Only if we are worthy to go to Eretz Yisrael, will we have a Jewish burial and funeral."

◇◇◇

And how right she was. She, the groiseh Bubbe, didn't ignore the rumors that were floating around. She realized bad times were upon us and prophesied the truth: that the bodies of Jewish men, women and children would be burned, their ashes to be scattered — like dung — on the face of the earth. And that was the fate of the grandmother and her granddaughter, who were taken to Auschwitz on the day after Shavuos on 8 Sivan, 5704 / May 30, 1944. On that day, their souls, together with the souls of many other Sevlus townspeople, rose through the chimneys of the crematorium — up to the Heavens. Hy"d.

◇◇◇

❧ 50 ❧
Two Tablecloths
[SEVLUS]

IT WAS Erev Rosh Hashanah, my second Rosh Hashanah with Mama, and I had a surprise for her. I had finished embroidering the tablecloth and had washed, starched and ironed it at my friend Rochel's house. Today I had finally brought it home, to surprise my mother.

Mama went out to wish all the neighbors *"a gut yahr"* — a good year, and I spread out my new tablecloth and set the table. I placed the brass tray on the table, and on it, the large, gleaming brass candlesticks. I also prepared the glass holders, filled them with oil and placed wicks inside. I put the challah tray on the other side of the table and carefully set down the *challos* that I had baked that very morning, under Mama's supervision. I placed a saucer of honey on a ceramic plate and artfully arranged apple slices around the honey bowl. That went in the center of the table.

It was only then, when everything was clean, arranged and organized, that I went outside to wish my friends *"a gut yahr."* I didn't want to be home when Mama would see my tablecloth, even though I was curious to see her reaction.

When I came back, I was astonished to see my mother

sitting by the table and crying, holding a corner of the table-cloth in her hand. I was taken aback; I never imagined that this would be her reaction. I approached her cautiously.

"Mama, what happened? What's the matter?"

Mama released the tablecloth to hug me with her one hand, and asked quietly, "Was it you, Leichu, who embroidered the tablecloth? Where did you get this pattern?"

That's when I finally told Mama the secret I had been keeping until that moment: Rochel and her grandmother had taught me the secrets of embroidery and I had worked on my project at their house, so that I could surprise Mama on Rosh Hashanah with an embroidered tablecloth.

"Rochel Filman gave me the pattern," I explained. "She bought the fabric with me and printed the pattern on it, and I did the embroidery, of course. But Mama—why are you crying?"

Mama wiped her eyes and lifted her head to answer me. "Leichu, I embroidered a tablecloth very similar to this one many years ago, when I still had two hands. It was exactly the same pattern and had similar colors!"

She got up, went over to the clothing chest, and out of its depths, she extracted a tablecloth. I could see how it was, indeed, the same pattern as mine. It was worn out and frayed from use, but the embroidery on it was still impressive and vivid; only the surrounding fabric was threadbare.

I drew in my breath as I examined Mama's handiwork. "Mama, how can you even compare? True, it's the same pattern and similar colors, but the embroidery, Mama! Why, your embroidery is magnificent! Look at those precise and beautiful stitches!"

Mama smiled. "You'll see, my Leichu. If you continue to embroider you will get better and better until you surpass me."

From then on, I spread my tablecloth on the table every Friday afternoon, in honor of *Shabbos Kodesh*.

Mama's words encouraged me and I continued to embroider energetically. Rochel taught me how to embroider perfect stitches and the secrets of excellent handiwork. "Even if you place the tablecloth upside down," she explained, "no one should notice. If the left side is good, then the right side will be beautiful indeed!" She taught me all the tricks of professional embroiderers and I tried very hard to do my best.

But I still preferred to sew on the sewing machine, and I was always happy to see the sewing work that greeted me at the Filman house. I sewed hems on the sheets, joined together the sections of quilt covers and pillowcases, and more. I sat by the machine, my foot dancing on the pedal while I quickly and efficiently pulled the material through the machine and sang happily out loud.

My greatest dream was to buy myself a sewing machine, though of course I did not dare tell Mama about this. I knew she did not have the means to buy me something so expensive, and I didn't want to make her feel bad. Out of all the things I had left behind in Budapest, the sewing machine was the one thing I missed. I knew that my entire room waited for me, that Anya still hoped that one day I would return to them and that all my possessions remained as I had left them, but I knew that I would never go back. The truth is, I thought about that machine far more than Anya and Apa and the family in Budapest.

I still occasionally dreamed at night about Budapest. I dreamed about Zaidy and Bubby Shapiro, even Zaidy and Bubby Feldman, about Basya Leah and her family and Anya and Apa, the house and my room. But my main dream was that I was sitting next to my sewing machine and sewing long stitches that extended from Budapest to Sevlus.

I once told Chungarabi about my dream. She told me that from her own experience, when a person really and truly wants something they will eventually achieve it. She said that if I really wanted a sewing machine, I would, somehow, get one.

She was right about this, as she was about many other things. I eventually received a sewing machine from Eshto, Chungarabi's husband. He also brought material and work that supported all of us.

But I am running ahead of myself. That happened much later.

◇◇◇

Until this very day, I love my sewing machine. Of course today I have an electric sewing machine that far surpasses the foot-pedal kind I used in my youth. But when I work, my feet dance on the ground instead of the missing pedal and I still sing the old, lovely songs of my childhood.

◇◇◇

❧ 51 ❧
"Our" Klar Family Departs

[SEVLUS]

THE IMPENDING DEPARTURE of the Klar family really pained me. In my heart, I prayed that it would not happen. I could not reconcile myself to the thought that our only "family" would leave us. But it did happen, and even faster than I had anticipated.

One day, when I returned from school, I met Fanny in the store. As soon as I saw her, I knew that something had happened; why else would Fanny come to our store in the middle of a work day?

I went into our small room to put down my school bag— the blue bag that my friend Rochel had sewed and embroidered for me. I stood there, confused, still holding the bag in my hand, rubbing my hand absently over the embroidery. I didn't want to leave the room; I didn't want to hear what Fanny came to tell us. In my heart, I already knew why she had come. I knew—they were moving to Eretz Yisrael. So why should I go out to hear about it? I thought to myself that if I wouldn't let myself hear about it, then I wouldn't know, and then maybe it just wouldn't happen, after all.

I had had enough of goodbyes. My life was full of them.

But of course, it didn't help that I tried to hide. Mama called me to help her in the store and I rushed to do as she asked.

Fanny, who looked as if she'd been crying, was standing on the side with Mama. Mama's eyes also glistened with a hint of tears.

I quickly and efficiently took care of the customers in the store, so that Mama could talk to Fanny.

Fanny was different than the other Klar children. The others were all tall and robust, only she was short and thin. Now Fanny stood next to Mama, leaning on the bean shelf while nervously folding and re-folding a piece of paper, fixing her blue eyes on Mama in total silence.

Mama spoke and Fanny just nodded her head. I wanted to walk over to them, but at that moment, new customers walked into the store. Mama and I served them.

After they left I walked over to Fanny but I couldn't say a single word; she hugged me and cried.

"Fanny, are you really and truly leaving?" I whispered, and she nodded her head yes. She hugged me again and the tears poured from her eyes.

"Are you upset about it? Are you sorry that you are leaving and moving to Eretz Yisrael?" I asked.

"No, I am not sorry that we are moving to Eretz Yisrael, but we are very sorry that we must leave you, all our close friends and acquaintances; to leave the place where we were born and grew up. But despite it all, I am very happy that we are going to our country. Just imagine, to go to Eretz Yisrael!" Fanny barely whispered these words through her sobbing.

I brought her a cup of water. She made the *berachah* silently, drank and calmed down. Afterwards she said goodbye and left the store. As she left, she told us that she was going to say goodbye to her friends.

The Klar's journey had been delayed until now because

the municipal clerk who prepared the registration for the certificate was not willing to include Fanny and Dori, the oldest girls, on the family certificate since they were over eighteen. In fact, he had gone to school with Fanny and knew exactly how old she was. So there was no getting around him. Their parents, Nachman and Rivka, did not want to leave them behind and the issue had reached a stalemate. But, as with everything in this world, an Upper hand was directing the matter. The clerk went away for vacation, and he was replaced by a substitute clerk who was not really familiar with the registration process nor with the people whose applications were being registered. As soon as the Klar family discovered this, they immediately went to the municipality to sign up with the substitute clerk.

Thus the substitute clerk, who did not know anything about the Klar family, accepted their account that Fanny and Dori were seventeen-year-old twins. He prepared the registration for the certificate, and now all the paperwork was completed.

The Klars were afraid, however, that when the regular clerk would return from vacation, he might reveal the small deception and cancel the certificate. Therefore, they felt they had to leave the country as quickly as possible.

In short, the Klars would be leaving Sevlus in a week. They were planning on traveling to Rumania to visit Nachman Klar's mother, and wait there for a ship to take them to Eretz Yisrael.

After we closed the store, we walked over to the Klars to help them pack up their belongings. On the way, Mama told me what Fanny had told her about the urgent registration of the "twins" at the municipality.

When we arrived at the Klar household we were greeted by great pandemonium. Many people wandered around the kitchen. Everyone was talking excitedly and loudly — giving advice, making announcements, and creating a lot of noise. After all, it's not every day that a Jew from Sevlus goes to Eretz Yisrael, let alone an entire family!

Mama hugged Néni Klar and burst out in heartrending sobs, and I "helped" her weep even more. Even Néni Klar cried; the parting from everything familiar was very difficult for her. She knew that it was all for the good, but it was hard for her. In Sevlus everything was familiar, well-known and beloved. True, they were going to Eretz Yisrael, the Holy Land, and there it would be good, very good—she was sure of that. This belief lightened her load and the pain of parting, but the pain was still there.

Mama decided that she had cried enough and it was time to get to work. She took my hand and the two of us went into the inner room where Fanny and Dori stood helpless near the crates. A number of women who stood there spoke in loud voices and gave each other orders and advice, but nothing was getting accomplished.

Mama took one crate, set it up near the closet, and with her one hand she took out clothes from the closet and packed them neatly into the crate.

One of the women, a neighbor of the Klars, approached Mama and started to explain to her how to pack. Mama nodded her head and continued her systematic packing. When the woman realized that Mama was not listening to her advice, she grabbed Mama's one hand and started shouting at her. Mama looked into the woman's eyes, and when she stopped shouting to take a breath, Mama said to her quietly, "This room is reserved for people who came to work. Advice-givers are invited to the kitchen." The neighbor let go of Mama's hand and looked dumbstruck.

Mama continued to pack quietly but when she saw that

the woman was still staring at her, she said, "Advice is a useful thing, but real help is much more practical and constructive."

The woman blushed and finally pitched in to help; she took a crate and started to pack up the linens and feather quilts. With both hands, she pressed each feather quilt with all her strength to expel air until it shrank in size, and then Dori helped her to stuff the quilt into a pillowcase. This is how they managed to insert one feather quilt and three pillows into one quilt cover.

Afterwards, the neighbor suggested to Dori to pack up the glass dishes in the same crate. "They will be protected by the quilts, and on top we can place another quilt," she said.

Dori and I went to the kitchen and brought back the glassware. Another neighbor wrapped up each and every dish in clothing and placed them on top of the quilts, and on top of that, the ladies placed an additional quilt. We also inserted glass dishes in Mama's clothing box by distributing them among the clothes, so that the clothes and bed linens would protect the glassware from breakage during the long journey by ship.

All the women and girls in the room slowly packed up different belongings. Néni Klar managed to extricate herself from all the people who surrounded her in the kitchen, and she entered the room. When she saw that we were busy working, she was overjoyed. Finally, things were getting done; people were actually working and not only dispensing advice!

We worked until very late that night and promised to return the next day. And that's what we did for three days: Every night we came and helped to pack, organize and to prepare provisions for the journey itself. We prepared a bag for each family member with the necessary articles for the journey itself. The packing was also an opportunity for us to spend as much time as possible with "our" beloved Klar family before their departure for Eretz Yisrael.

Most of the time we worked according to Mama's instructions, while tears streamed from my eyes. At night I dreamed about Anya, Basya Leah and my life in Budapest. I guess that the separation from the Klar family brought me back in my nighttime dreams to my departure from my family in Budapest.

On Wednesday night, after we finished the packing work, Mama and I did not return home. Everything was finally packed up in crates, organized and ready for the trip. The Klars wanted to sell those items that they could not pack or take with them, but there was no time left. Aharon Klar promised his brother that he would sell what he could of their possessions and send the money to them in Eretz Yisrael.

Aharon Klar and his wife Chaya Sara were good-hearted people who did much chesed for others. They were not zocheh to reach Eretz Yisrael. They were murdered in Auschwitz on the same day as most of the Sevlus townspeople—8 Sivan 5704 / May 30, 1944. Yehei zichram baruch. Their only son Azriel survived and later immigrated to the United States.

All night long, Mama and I sat with Néni Klar and their daughters, Fanny and Dori. The men of the family also sat with friends who came to say goodbye, and the conversations went on all night. We didn't want that night to end. We had so much to talk about and tell one another. But time did not stand still, even though that was our hearts' desire.

Toward morning, Bácsi Nachman Klar told me the following: "Leichu, the day will come when you, too, will join us in Eretz Yisrael. Remember: We will always save you a place in our home, a bed to sleep in at night and a chair by our table."

Those words remained engraved in my heart and I never forgot them. And one day, many years later, I did, indeed, arrive in Eretz Yisrael, in Yerushalayim. When I found the Klar family in Meah Shearim, these words were repeated again to me.

In the morning, after all the younger children woke up and the men returned from shul, a large wagon pulled up in front of the Klar's house. Everyone helped load all the suitcases and crates in the wagon, and Fanny and the little children climbed in as well. All the others walked by foot to the train station.

The distance to the train station was short, but everyone walked very slowly. The laden wagon was followed by the Klar family members and townspeople, and the spontaneous "parade" grew in number from minute to minute. Everyone came to wish a farewell to the dear family going to Eretz Yisrael.

Many additional people were waiting in the train station to see the family off and say goodbye. All of them helped unload the packages from the wagon and carry the little children.

I went over to Dovid'l and he promised me that he would never forget me—and would always remember that he was named after my father, z"l.

The tears we had shed over the last three days were nothing at all compared to the tears I shed in the train station that morning. I hugged Néni Klar and the older girls over and over, I kissed the two little girls again and again while I barely was able to see them through tear-filled eyes.

The train sprang to life with a loud, noisy whistle. The luggage was already on the train and the family members now climbed aboard. They stood crowded by the windows, waving at us while we waved back at them, calling out our last goodbyes.

The train whistled again, and this time, it started to move. Slowly it gained steam and disappeared from view.

Mama and I were decisively, crushingly alone, without family. Mama rested her arm on my shoulder and together we walked home, bowed and crying.

In those days, there were no airplanes for transcontinental visits or long-distance telephone calls. None of us knew when, or if, we would ever see the Klars again. Until the beginning of the war, Mama and I were able to correspond with the Klars; but when the war broke out, their letters did not reach us. Much to our sorrow, we were cut off and lost contact with them.

After the war, many years later, I was *zocheh* to reach Eretz Yisrael and join the Klar family. But I was alone; my dear Mama never saw the Klars again.

❦ 52 ❦
Caroli's Wedding
[SEVLUS]

ONE DAY, Mama received a long letter from her older daughter Caroli, or Kreindy as Mama preferred to call her. It had been quite a long time since she had received a letter from any of her children—whether Kreindy, Izzy and Ari.

The main mode of transport in Sevlus.

When she finished reading the letter, Mama burst into tears and it was a long time until she calmed down. Kreindy had written that both boys, who were both completely secular, lived somewhere near Budapest. They had become Zionists and were undergoing training and waiting for a group certificate in order to go on aliya with their group to Eretz Yisrael.

Caroli expressed her disapproval of this step in no uncertain terms. She, Caroli, was much more enlightened; redemption would come to the world only through equality of all its citizens, she claimed. She had become a zealous communist, and believed that only communism could save the world.

Caroli saved the most important announcement for the end of the letter: She was getting married! The young man was Jewish, *Baruch Hashem*, and his name was Yoshke Zicherman—his Jewish name was Yosef. In fact, he came from a small village in our own area, a village near Sevlus called Anik.

Mama was not personally acquainted with the boy's family, the Zicherman family, but she was happy that they were from the same vicinity as us. A neighbor of ours, Helen Kramer, knew the Zicherman family and told Mama that all the families in that village were God-fearing, upright Jewish families who worked the land. In the large farm they owned, they grew a variety of vegetables and cultivated a large grape vineyard.

Before long, Mama contacted the Zicherman family and a week later, a wagon pulled up in front of our house. Yoshke's parents had come to pay us a visit! The wagon was heaped with agricultural produce as a present to Mama. Though Mama did not want to accept such a valuable present, she yielded when they insisted that they would not return to their village with the produce. So Mama, in turn, gave them a present as well: the new set of silverware she had bought in honor of Pesach.

(Mama had bought the silverware from Mrs. Neufeld, who had returned from Budapest after a five-year sojourn in the capital city. Mrs. Neufeld didn't stop talking about how beautiful the capital city was —and about the many Jews who lived there who did not act as Jews are supposed to act.

There were many Neologist Jews in Budapest. Those were Jews who could not decide if they really wanted to observe the *mitzvos* as Jews or follow the behavior of the *goyim*. As a result, they stopped midway between the two: They observed only some of the *mitzvos,* prayed "selected prayers" while skipping mainly those connected to Zion, the building of Jerusalem and *korbanos.* Many *rabbanim* spoke out against them and in Sevlus they were mocked. They were nicknamed, "People who claim that the sun does not shine properly, and prefer to use the light of a candle instead." These were the Jews whom Mrs. Neufeld referred to.

Mrs. Neufeld brought many belongings with her from Budapest, and she sold them at very low prices. Mama finally had a chance to buy elegant, affordable silverware. She was so excited that she would have a lovely and respectable set of silverware for Pesach! If guests would come, she could set the table with the new set.

When Mama talked about guests on Pesach, she was referring to Caroli, Izzy and Ari—as they were like strangers who may come for a visit on Pesach. But the minute she gave away the cutlery set, she abandoned the comforting thought that one day, her children would return to stay with her on Pesach.)

Avraham and Rivka Zicherman, Yoshke's parents, were very happy to meet Mama. They were very respectable people and sat with Mama to write a request to Yoshke and Caroli to come to Sevlus for their wedding so that the families could also take part in the *simchah*.

Mama did not receive a reply from Caroli, but Yoshke's parents did receive a letter from their son, and they forwarded the letter to us in Sevlus. Yoshke wrote that he and Caroli had no intentions of holding their wedding in Sevlus, and the parents should be happy that they were willing to marry according to Halachah. Yoshke wrote the date of the wedding and location. The Zichermans told Mama that they planned on traveling to Prague with the grandfather of the family, to participate in the wedding. They invited Mama to travel with them.

It was hard for Mama to make up her mind to attend the wedding, though I begged her to go. Néni Weinberg promised her that she, or one of her older daughters, would sleep with me at night so that I would not be alone. After interminable vacillation Mama finally decided to make the trip, but not before she made sure that I would sleep at my friend Rochel's house, and that the Neufelds would help me run the store in her absence.

I accompanied Mama to the train station where we met the Zicherman family; they were waiting there for Mama together with the grandfather of the family. The grandfather was a very unique person. Though his hair and beard were white as snow and his wrinkled face testified to the fact that he was old, his body was that of a younger man: tall, erect, with tall leather boots on his feet and his pants tucked into the boots. His blue eyes sparkled and his gaze was direct and penetrating.

He greeted Mama cheerfully, and then turned to me and said, "Young lady, do not worry about your Mama. From now on I will take care of her, so that there is no need for you to worry as well."

I burst into loud laughter. Would I worry about my mother? The situation was exactly opposite; Mama was the one to worry about me. The Zaidy did not understand why I laughed, and he said again, "Young lady, I can take care of her. Do not look at me like an old man because despite my age I still have strength to plough and sow, to reap and to pick grapes. I can still stop a running horse. So please, don't worry!"

I looked at him and realized that he was right. Despite his age, he looked stronger and more powerful than many younger men.

◇◇

And, in fact, I eventually found out that he, the old man, survived the Holocaust. His children and grandchildren all died in Auschwitz, and he was the one to escape to the fields and remain alive. But when he discovered that he was the only one to survive, that all his progeny had been murdered and even his farm and everything in it had been stolen from him — then he lost the will to live. True, he was zocheh to go to Eretz Yisrael, but he came as a broken person. He lived only one year in Eretz Yisrael before he died: frail, sick and very depressed.

◇◇

When I returned from the train station I opened the store. Many buyers came to the store on that day in the afternoon, but I managed fine even though I was alone. In the evening I went to Rochel and her grandmother and they set up a mattress on a bench for me. I went to sleep alone, without Mama's shoulder to lean on.

The house was very quiet, but I could not fall asleep. All night long, I tossed and turned from side to side. I missed Mama's soft breathing near my ear. I tried to remember my lovely room in Budapest; a large room with expensive furniture. Even there, in that lovely room, I had slept by myself and had not felt lonesome. And here I slept in the same room as the grandmother and Rochel; Rochel slept on a bench right next to me. Still, I couldn't fall asleep. I felt all alone.

Mama returned after two weeks and told me that she had been hosted by relatives of Yoshke's family, who treated her like a queen and gave her her own room with a special, large bed. The top and bottom of the bed was artistically decorated with white nickel latticework, adorned with balls of bright silver nickel. Best of all, the bed boasted a real mattress, not a sack full of straw as everyone had in Sevlus. Her bedroom was large and beautiful — actually, the entire apartment was spacious and elegant. It was clear that her hosts were wealthy people and Mama told me that their apartment was probably similar to Apa and Anya's in Budapest. But despite all this, every night Mama tossed and turned from side to side because she missed me. She missed leaning her head on my shoulder and she missed listening to my breathing at night. And I was doubly amazed: This was exactly how I had felt in a small, narrow room on a straw mattress on a bench in my friend Rochel's house!

Mama talked a great deal about Prague, a beautiful city with unique houses. On Shabbos she davened in the Maharal's shul — the Maharal was one of the great *tzaddikim* in the world, she told me. The Maharal created a *golem* from clay and I had heard stories about him from the time I was a little girl.

There was only one thing that Mama did not want to tell me about — that was the wedding. The only thing she was willing to say, after much pleading on my part, was that she was happy that she was *zocheh* to see her daughter marry according to Jewish law. Presumably it was due to the merit of Reb Elya *z"l*, Caroli's father, who must have beseeched Hashem that his daughter marry a Jew.

❧ 53 ❧
Hard Times
[SEVLUS]

THE YEARS PASSED contently in much the same way. Mama and I corresponded frequently with the Klars in Eretz Yisrael; we were happy to hear that both Fanny and Dori married there. I also corresponded with Anya and Apa and Zaidy and Bubby Shapiro, and even traveled to Budapest occasionally to see them.

Alarming, foreboding news reached us from Germany.

People talked incessantly about what was going on there, and every one of our customers at the store considered themselves "experts" on the news that arrived from there. But none of the Jewish speculations helped at all and indeed, the war broke out just as all the "fainthearted" among us had feared. Now the discussions started as to whether the war would be connected to the Jews or not; would we be harmed, or just frightened. This was the only subject wherever we went; everyone talked only about the war.

That war, later to be known as World War II, officially broke out on September 1, 1939, when Nazi Germany invaded Poland. It turned out to be the largest and deadliest war in history for all of mankind; and for the Jews of Europe, of course, the Holocaust proved to be the most terrifying of all. We would not know all of that for quite some time, of course, though the very word—"war"—struck fear in all of us.

Those Jews in Sevlus who had endured the preceding world war, and even those who had not been affected directly by the war itself, did not stop telling us frightening stories about it. What a frightening word was "war"! Sometimes it seemed that people competed among themselves to narrate the worst possible stories. Everyone remembered terrible things about those times, memories that had remained buried until now.

ॐ   ॐ   ॐ

The truth was that we had been buffeted by the winds of war even before it officially broke out. One day in 1938, we heard news of a meeting called the Munich Convention between Neville Chamberlain, England's Prime Minister; Edouard Daladier, France's Prime Minister; Benito Mussolini, Italy's Prime Minister; and Hitler, *yimach shemo*. Those men thought that they were great and important enough to manage the entire world, and they decided that Czechoslovakia must cede the Sudetenland, the border region of Czechoslovakia, as a present to the German Reich. A lovely present, indeed—at the expense of the Czechs, of course, but mainly at the expense of the Jews. The many ethnic Germans who lived in the Sudeten region were very happy. They greeted their fellow Germans with flowers and candies, to the resentment of the Czechs and the fears of the Jews.

The annexation of the Sudetes affected us as well in Sevlus. True, the Carpathian area was far from Sevlus but it had still been part of the same country that was now ripped apart—part to Germany and the remaining section to the Czechs.

The Sudeten region contained many factories — mainly metal and iron ones — that had marketed their products throughout all of the Czech Republic. The products of the factories no longer reached the rest of the Czechoslovakian regions, and this caused shortages. It did not take long until prices began to rise on various metal commodities and the prices continued to spiral out of control until there seemed to be no limit.

One day, Mr. Neufeld showed up at our store and brought Mama a large crate full of metal pots and frying pans — which were now extremely expensive. Mama was taken aback; she had no money to pay for such costly merchandise. But Mr. Neufeld begged Mama to take the crate off his hands.

"I have a large warehouse full of crates such as these," he whispered to her. "If the authorities should ever reveal that I have accumulated this merchandise they will most certainly confiscate it. It won't help me to explain that this stuff has been lying around uselessly in my warehouse for years, with no buyers at all. Only now, has it become so rare and expensive."

Mr. Neufeld continued his tale to Mama: One of his clients had gone bankrupt several years ago and had given him these crates of merchandise as part of the enormous debt that was owed him. He had been able to sell only a few of the crates and thus he, Mr. Neufeld, had been forced to absorb the lion's share of the monetary loss caused by the merchant's bankruptcy over a period of three years.

"Now, finally, my financial situation has stabilized, *Baruch Hashem*; but here I am, stuck with merchandise that I am afraid could bring me lots of trouble." Mr. Neufeld sighed again.

"One or two crates won't do me any harm, I reckon," he explained to Mama. "But the quantity I have at present is enough cause for the authorities to bring me to trial for hoarding. In these crazy days, the penalty for defrauding the government is death — and we know that no one these days hesitates to kill a Jew."

After Mama heard Mr. Neufeld's tale, she agreed to accept a crate of pots and another crate of enamel plates and cups. However, she stipulated that Mr. Neufeld sign a document that she, Mama, had received merchandise from him and would pay for it only after the merchandise was sold. Of course, the agreement did not mention the nature of the merchandise that Mama received.

Mama was wary of letting on to her customers that she carried such expensive items. However, I recklessly removed a single pot, plate and cup from the crate and placed them on one of the shelves for sale.

And that was that: Within one week, we had sold all the merchandise! People snapped up the items gratefully, as we did not raise the prices to the present inflated rates. Mr. Neufeld was very happy, and brought over two more crates late one night. Mama agreed to accept only two crates at a time.

And that's how we managed to sell all of Mr. Neufeld's merchandise in one year. After Mama paid him what she owed him, we saw that we had turned a tidy profit. "In war time, you don't keep money at home," Mama told me. Instead, she asked Mr. Neufeld to buy two diamonds for her with the money. She sewed a tiny cloth pouch for each diamond, attached a long ribbon to each bag, and the two of us wore the pouches under our clothing.

I was a teenager, and did not like this idea at all. With the money we had earned from our sale we could have bought so many things we really needed, but Mama would not hear of it.

"We can still wear our old clothes," she insisted. "During difficult times such as these, Leichu, it is unwise to spend money on clothes and coats. This is the time to save our money for the uncertain future."

I was disturbed by Mama's idea of hiding the diamonds. Why, it would be much nicer to insert them in jewelry—a ring or earrings, for example—and wear them openly! But Mama was adamant. She even insisted that I also hide the gold chain and gold ring that I had received from Apa and Anya and Zaidy and Bubby Shapiro during my visits to them in Budapest. I had worn my new gifts on Shabbosos and Ya-mim Tovim, but now I had to hide them together with the diamond in the special pouch I wore under my clothes. I was only to appreciate my mother's wisdom years later, when I arrived in Eretz Yisrael and still had the diamonds. Those diamonds were my *"nedunyah"* — I used the money I secured from their sale to set up my new home.

"Gold and diamonds are not only jewelry," Mama explained. "They can be a true salvation in times of troubles and scarcity. War-time is not the time to adorn ourselves with expensive jewelry." The situation around us was difficult indeed and the war was felt everywhere, even though it had not officially been declared in our region.

Mama hurried to buy a lot of foodstuffs for the grocery store, in addition to the pots and dishes. She stored the sacks of beans and legumes in the cellar and filled the crates that Bácsi Nachman Klar had given us with flour. These wooden crates were lined with tin so that hungry mice could not gnaw their way into the foodstuffs. She filled the cabbage barrel until the brim and made sure that even the vat of jam, which Mama mixed with her one hand, was full.

When customers tried to buy food staples in large quantities, Mama refused; she apologized profusely and explained that if she gave a large quantity to one family, nothing would be left for others.

I did not understand Mama's behavior. In fact, I was shocked. Mama had always loomed in my mind as the epitome of integrity, even to the point of being extreme in her honesty.

"If, *chas v'shalom*, the war reaches our own area, I may not be able to buy more food items for our store, Leichu," Mama explained. "I am trying to preserve as much as I can for the benefit of my customers so that my supply will last as long as possible. I can't allow one person to hoard food at home at the expense of the others." In fact, it was Mama's integrity that governed her actions for the sake of her customers.

And, indeed, the times of real scarcity did arrive. Later on, we could only buy foodstuffs with special tickets and there was hardly any food that one could actually get with those tickets. But my wise Mama still had some groceries in her store and she sold them at the regular, pre-war prices, though she was careful to sell only to her regular customers. Thus, those who had frequented Mama's store during the good times were fortunate to continue to receive foodstuffs even during the bad times at the same price. This was unique among all the grocery stores, since all the storekeepers including Mama could not purchase new goods at the old price. Yet, Mama continued to sell whatever she had without buying new foodstuffs and, indeed, most of the items ran out toward the "end."

When I escaped, Mama gave me almost all of the foodstuffs that had remained in the store; there was virtually nothing left for the non-Jews who took over our house when Mama left. But I am getting ahead of myself again.

ം   ം   ം

It was Wednesday, 8 Marcheshvan 5699/November 2, 1938, an utterly bitter day when the governments of Hungary, Russia and Germany carved up the Czech Republic. Sevlus, together with a few other cities in the area, was turned into a new autonomous state ostensibly under German patronage, *yimach shemam*. We even had a new name: The state was called Transcarpathian Ukraine, or Kárpátalja.

Most of the Sevlus townspeople were frightened. They had been sure that we would remain part of Hungary, as Sevlus had been part of the Hungarian Empire for a long time before it was given to the Czech Republic together with the Carpathian areas. After all, Sevlus was Hungarian in mentality; Hungarian was the mother tongue spoken by the inhabitants and reflected the sentiments of most of the people. Only a few considered themselves real Czechs. As for ourselves, we called ourselves Hungarians and that's how we had felt even under the Czech government. Suddenly now we found ourselves annexed to the Ukraine, even under the dreaded German rule!

It was true that there were a few who said it was better to be part of Germany than Hungary, as the Hungarians were known for their anti-Semitism. As if the Germans or Ukrainians were not anti-Semitic! The Czechs themselves did not excel in love for the Jews, and the pogroms in Czech cities are also written in blood in the annals of the Jewish nation.

During that time period, we could not imagine what lie in wait for the Jews under German rule. These events I describe in 1938 took place almost a year before the war broke out, so that when the war actually did break out—in September 1939—we were already under German rule.

On March 15, 1939, after a few months that were marked by difficulties and suffering—particularly for the Jewish residents—the Hungarians entered and conquered the new state.

The ephemeral state ceased to exist.

Now that we lived under Hungarian rule and returned to being part of Hungary, I was happy to discover that Apa and Anya's letters started to arrive again, and at an accelerated pace. It was as if they were trying to make up for lost time when the Germans had received the Sudetenes as a present and the mail connection to Budapest had stopped.

That was the only benefit, though. The authorities began to issue decrees against the Jews, to the glee of the neighboring gentiles. Anti-Semitism again raised its ugly head, and every day brought with it terrible news. Many Jewish families from villages in the area were dispossessed of their lands— lands that had belonged to their parents and grandparents before them — and these families were deported to Sevlus, the district town.

The financial state of the Jews in Sevlus deteriorated with each passing day. The streets became filled with people who had no work and looked desperately for some means to earn a few pennies for food. The beggars multiplied; even regular middle-class people who had supported their families comfortably in the past, were left penniless and deprived of all. They had no choice but to beg. A group of philanthropic people established a charitable enterprise to help the poor and offered basic foodstuffs and money to the unfortunate.

We hoped that when the summer passed, the situation would improve; and then, when the winter passed, things would get even better. But instead of improving, the situation only became worse as hordes of refugees from all kinds of places proceeded to flood Sevlus. Among the newcomers were many Polish Jews who brought horrific tales to our ears. Our neighbors did not believe these stories and told Mama and myself that these people probably fabricated horror stories so that we would take pity on them and offer them help.

After all, they had been deported from Poland, leaving their homes and property behind.

It was understandable that Mama and I preferred to believe our neighbors whom we had known for a long time, over the tales of these foreign Jews who spoke a strange Yiddish, wore different clothing than us and even davened with a different *nusach* than ours. So how could we believe them? But they were truly unfortunate, they had lost everything, and we sincerely pitied them. Mama gave them more and more foodstuffs from the store, far more than she could really spare. She even gave away the little clothing she and I still had, even though we had nothing extra; after all, they had nothing at all.

Yes, anti-Semites again raised their ugly heads in earnest. If a Jew was caught on any minor infraction, or even if a non-Jew thought that the Jew intended to commit an offense—they would take the Jew to the police station and beat him cruelly. Some unfortunate victims of those beatings remained crippled for life while others did not recover at all and died as a result.

Mama did not let me leave the house alone. When she had to go somewhere I accompanied her, together with the eldest Wurtzberger son. We, two women, were afraid to walk alone.

I could rarely visit my friend Rochel anymore. Only on infrequent occasions, Mama let me walk to my friend with customers who were going in the same direction—and only if they agreed to walk me home as well.

Every time I did go to Rochel and her grandmother, I brought them food. They were in terrible shape. During war time, no woman in her right mind would pay for embroidered linens so the two women had no work, hence no livelihood and no food in their house.

"Maybe you should do some Hungarian embroidery on shirts for the *goyish* farmer's wives?" I suggested to Rochel, on one of my rare visits. "I'm sure they would buy them from you happily."

Rochel thanked me for my suggestion and said she would think about it. And just a few days later, Rochel knocked on our door. She was dressed in her best clothes and carrying a suitcase. I looked at her in astonishment.

"I embroidered a whole pile of shirts as you had suggested, Leichu, and now I'm on my way to try to sell them in the villages," she cried excitedly.

Mama was shocked. "You're not going anywhere the way you are dressed!" she told Rochel decisively. "You are dressed too nicely and are likely to arouse suspicion. You don't want to be robbed." Mama took Rochel's suitcase and transferred all the shirts to a simple rucksack. She gave Rochel a simple skirt and blouse of mine and told her to change her clothing.

Rochel didn't argue; she changed into my clothes and took the rucksack. "That's much better. Now you look like a simple peasant girl, and there's a chance that no one will rob you this way," said Mama approvingly.

That night, Rochel returned from her trip and stopped at our house to change back into her own clothes. She told me excitedly that she had sold all her embroidered shirts, and had even received orders for more! Rochel was happy, and Mama and I were overjoyed as well. She had found a promising source of income for herself and her grandmother at last.

✦ 54 ✦
The Sewing Machine
[SEVLUS]

SOMETHING ABOUT Sevlus's human landscape had changed. At first we couldn't place our finger on what was different, but soon we realized that all the young male Jews had disappeared from view. Not only had young men disappeared, but fathers of children were gone as well. All these men had received draft notices to the military labor battalions (*munkatábor*). Some of the young men ran away and disappeared while others were drafted. So the town was left with older people, women and children.

At the same time, shortages and privations grew from day to day and became permanent fixtures of our very existence.

And then came the terrible decree of deportation in 1941. Anyone who could not prove that his family had been Hungarian for many generations was expelled from the country. Luckily, Mama had the correct documents so we personally were spared. Some people were able to buy forged documents and they were able to remain. Others, who could not obtain the proper documentation, were expelled. We did not know where they were being sent and what would happen to them, but Mama sat and cried on that terrible day of the expulsion and said that this did not bode well for the expellees. There were many people whose parents and grandparents had lived in Hungary for many years but lacked the right documents. These unfortunates were thrown out of their homes, torn from their extended families and deported from the town in which they had been born, raised and married—together with their children and grandchildren.

Not long after the deportation came another decree: a curfew. From seven in the evening until six in the morning, it was forbidden to leave our homes. Anyone caught during those hours in the street would be shot. Tension and terror increased and letters stopped arriving. I did not know if that was because Anya and Apa were going through hard times like us, or because the post offices were not operating properly.

Mama did not want me to leave her side. But I was almost twenty years old and hated being cooped up in the house, despite the dangers that lurked outside. True, we lived with daily fear but I became accustomed to the fear. This might sound strange—becoming accustomed to fear—but such was the case. And therefore, despite the fear and the dangers, I wanted to visit my friends, to spend time with them. I continued to do so, without thinking too much or too deeply about the risks I was taking or about the worry I caused my mother.

Then one day, after I had been gone a few hours, I came home and found Chungarabi sitting on the porch, crying as she washed our clothes. Mama was standing next to her and crying as well. When Chungarabi saw me she raised her tear-filled eyes and spoke to me. "You must not stay away from home for so long and worry your mother this way!" she chastised me. Immediately I regretted how my rashness had caused my mother so much sorrow. I hugged Mama and promised that I would not leave again for so long. "If I had some real work at home, I would find it easier to stay here," I told Chungarabi. "I just can't sit at home all day and stare at the four walls and the empty shelves of the store. If only I could help and do something!"

Chungarabi looked deep into my eyes and asked me if I really wanted to help. "Yes, of course," I answered excitedly. "With all my heart! If only I could."

Then Chungarabi told me that she continued to come to us only because of me. Mama no longer could afford to pay her for her work, so lately I had started to do the washing. Of course I was not as good as Chungarabi, but my laundered clothes were clean enough.

"We have Jewish neighbors who had a sewing factory," Chungarabi told me thoughtfully. "They had to close the factory because of the edict forbidding Jews from running any kind of store or workshop. However, they still have sewing machines and material and they are looking for someone to borrow a sewing machine from them and do piecework sewing; that is, to sew shirts for men out of pieces of material that were cut according to patterns."

"I only know how to sew sheets and pillowcases," I told Chungarabi regretfully. "I only know how to sew straight lines, not shirts."

The gypsy laughed and told me I was speaking foolishness. "They will give you material that is already cut to size, and all you have to do is assemble the pieces and sew them together according to a pattern. I am sure that if you think it through, you will realize that it's not so difficult: You have an innate sewing ability, Leichu, and you are not stupid. I am sure that you will succeed!" Chungarabi cried. "Even if you don't succeed on the first or second shirt you try, you will get the hang of it soon enough."

The next morning, a horse-drawn wagon stopped outside our house. It was just after six a.m., immediately after the curfew had ended but so early that no one was outside on the street. Eshto the gypsy, Chungarabi's husband, lowered a sewing machine from the wagon and quickly ushered it into our tiny room. Then he returned to the wagon, took out a package wrapped in brown paper and placed it on the table. Now there really was no room to move in our little cubicle.

Mama apologized that she did not have money to pay for anything; she hadn't even been able to pay Chungarabi yesterday for her work. But Eshto said that was okay; neither of them wanted money from us, not Chungarabi nor himself.

And then I remembered that somewhere in the house was a piece of checkered fabric. I didn't know where it came from, but it was likely that one of our customers had given it to Mama in lieu of money for foodstuffs in the store. I decided that once I would learn how to sew shirts, I would sew Eshto a new shirt from that material.

After we examined the machine, Mama and I decided that I would sew during the hours that the store was closed so that no one would know of my new occupation. After all, it was forbidden for Jews to open a workshop and there was no need for people to know that I was sewing to earn money.

On that very morning, I sat down to sew a bit. I opened the package which was full of pieces of material that were cut according to a pattern. Each piece of material was labeled with a number, and I had to match the numbers together. At first it didn't seem too complicated. I attached the front of the shirt to the back, and that was not difficult. Now I had to attach the sleeves—and I realized that I did not have the slightest inkling of how to attach sleeves to a garment!

I turned to Rochel for help, and again she was the one to come to my aid. We sat together and I watched how Rochel attached the sleeve to the shirt. At first the sleeve-shirt connection looked very strange; after all, Rochel was a first-class embroiderer but not very skilled at sewing, and it seemed that joining a sleeve to a shirt properly demanded special skill. So we sat together and used basting thread to sew the sleeve to the shirt time after time, until the shirt finally looked presentable. Then Rochel taught me to how to sew buttonholes for buttons, and she gave me a large stock of buttons from her own supply.

I sat with Rochel almost an entire day until I learned to connect sleeves to shirts, and until I succeeded in making more or less exact buttonholes. Rochel dedicated her precious time to me, time she could have used to embroider more shirts to sell, but she left her own work to help me. I was truly touched.

After about a week I had finished a number of shirts and Chungarabi came to take them from me. Afterwards she returned and brought me money for payment, and told me that my shirts had passed approval. I could now continue to sew the entire stock of piecework shirts.

I was very happy to be able to help earn some money to contribute to the household expenses. The truth was that Mama and I needed the very minimum to survive, but Mama gave away as much as she could to people in need. The money that I earned, gave her the ability to continue her acts of *chesed*.

Mama had to list the grocery store under the name of a non-Jewish neighbor, Mrs. Pickar, because Jewish merchants were no longer allowed to run any kind of store or business under their own name; not even a permanent stand in the weekly market. We were fortunate because Mrs. Pickar was a good woman who loved Mama very much. After the store was listed in her name, Mrs. Pickar did start to take foodstuffs from the store without paying but she also did very big favors for Mama. For example, she told Mama where she could get hold of certain foodstuffs to sell her customers according to the rationing system. She saw to it that all the neighbors in the area were listed in "her" store—and they had to buy in the place they were listed. The rationing coupons for food were only honored in the specific store that a family was listed.

Non-Jews never liked Jews and over the years, I had heard many stories about what the *goyim* did to the Jews. But from the day that the Germans started to disseminate their racial doctrine, the non-Jews in all the surrounding countries joined in their hatred for Jews, with all their heart and soul. I have no explanation why Mrs. Pickar was not anti-Semitic and in fact, helped Mama.

The situation continued to be gloomy, oppressive and frightening, yet life somehow continued. Some of the men who had been taken to the military labor camps returned, and they had horror stories to narrate. They were taken for hard labor such as laying railways, digging ditches and removing mines. That last assignment was most dangerous of all because one imprudent split-second motion could cause a mine to explode. In fact, the Jews were the only ones sent for this task because many of the mines did explode suddenly, killing or maiming the Jewish men. In addition to the harsh work, the men had received endless beatings and were given the scantiest food. The men who scrupulously avoided non-kosher food were truly hungry as they could only eat a small part of the already-skimpy food portions. When food packages were sent to them, they arrived open and torn. The contents were stolen shamelessly, and no one even bothered to hide the thievery.

Yet despite what the Jews of Sevlus and the many refugees hidden in the town had experienced, no one wanted to believe the refugees' stories. No one wanted to believe the horrible rumors that arrived from Poland. Everyone said that this was nonsense; it's impossible that the situation could really be so terrible. Human beings were simply incapable of acting that way.

True, the same stories were repeated by refugees who came from different places and regions. Still, none of us believed them. I guess it was a form of self-protection that is innate in human nature: If you refuse to believe, then nothing can happen.

❧ 55 ☙
The Most Painful Farewell
[SEVLUS]

THE EVIL DAY arrived. Despite all the *tefillos* and fast days that the *rabbanim* had decreed; despite all the *Tehillim* that was recited in shul for three consecutive days and nights; despite all our deeds of *chesed* and charity—the terrible blow fell on us as well. The Germans invaded Hungary.

The invasion took place on Sunday, 24 Adar 5704, March 19, 1944—just ten days after Purim. As soon as the invasion became known, a great silence descended on Sevlus. Every-one—Jews as well as non-Jews—shut themselves up in their homes. There was not a soul on the streets; Sevlus looked like a ghost town. Mama didn't let me stand next to the win-dow, even though the shutters were drawn. Fear was so thick you could cut it with a knife, and it seemed to be contagious as well: It traveled from house to house, and neighborhood to neighborhood.

Despite Mama's prohibition, I did approach the window a few times — but only when I was barefoot so that not even the rustle of my footsteps could be heard outside. Although the shutters were closed, I could still peek out between the slats, which could not be shut completely.

Desolation met my gaze. Not a soul could be seen on the street. I could not even discern figures near the windows of the houses. All the shutters were closed, the doors were locked and the streets, empty.

I sat with Mama on the bed in our tiny room, and we recited *Tehillim* together. Afterwards Mama opened her *sefer kinos* of Tishah b'Av and quietly chanted the horrific, awesome words in the traditional mournful tune. Tears streamed from her eyes.

I sat next to my mother, my very being permeated with fear. After some time, Mama stopped her prayers and whispered to me that it was time to eat. I was hungry too, but I hadn't said anything. Perhaps, on this terrible day when fear alone ruled the streets—perhaps it was inappropriate to eat?

We had a little bit of water left in the house, and we used it sparingly. True, no one had forbidden us from leaving the house, but we were too frightened to leave the house to fill the near-empty buckets with fresh water.

Amazingly enough, I ate everything. At first I thought that I'd have no appetite, but as soon as I started eating I couldn't stop until I finished everything on my plate. Mama also finished her portion and after we ate, we both felt better. Then even Mama went to peek out the window, but she didn't see a thing. It looked like a ghost town.

By the next day, people started to venture outside their houses, little by little. A few neighbors came to the store to buy groceries, and Mama asked me go outside to bring water. I filled all the pails and barrels. Who knew what would be on the morrow; who knew when we'd be able to go outside again? After I finished that task, I went to empty the special pail in the outhouse in the courtyard.

I was afraid to operate the sewing machine — it thundered so loudly, so I sat down to sew buttonholes and buttons by hand. Usually, I saved this kind of work to do when there were customers in the store, and when the store was closed, I would use the machine. But on that day, even when there were no customers in the store, I was afraid to sew with the noisy sewing machine.

It was only on the following day that we saw soldiers outside. A few people went outside. The neighbors spoke about giant posters pasted up on billboards throughout the town, and I slipped outside to see them.

The notices were there, in black and white: Jews were obligated to sew a yellow badge on the left side of their clothing, both on the front and back of every garment. The posters also listed the stores where the yellow badge could be obtained. All the stores on the list were owned by gentiles.

The notices also said that it was forbidden to "congregate": That meant that it was forbidden for more than two people to be together. *Tefillah* in a *minyan* was out of the question. A third clause on the list stated that all the Jewish residents in our neighborhood were required to go to Roghor Street No. 10, where a temporary office had been opened, in order to register ourselves.

When I returned home, Mrs. Weinberg was waiting for me. She had brought me a pile of coats: Warm winter coats, raincoats and Shabbos coats of her entire family, so that I could sew a yellow badge on each one of them. She also brought the yellow badges and paid me five pennies for sewing each one. I didn't want to profit from the degradation of Jews, and I told her this. But Mrs. Weinberg simply forced me to accept payment.

After her, more and more neighbors arrived. Some of them did not have stars and I promised to walk over to Mr. Berlig's store and buy a stock of yellow badges from him, enough for ourselves as well as the neighbors who were reluctant to purchase the badges. I wanted to leave immediately, but Mama insisted that I first sew stars on my coat. I reminded Mama that the decree would only go into effect in another three days, but Mama insisted. She was very afraid because the punishment for disobedience was death, and we all knew that Germans were notoriously trigger-happy.

However, we did not register ourselves at Roghor Street No. 10.

Mama decided that nothing good could come from the registration. True, we would not receive food coupons because we were not listed, but Mama claimed that she was listed by *HaKadosh Baruch Hu* on the Heavenly list, and He would take care of our sustenance.

Purim had passed in dreadful silence. We all had known that the invasion was imminent. We had listened to the Megillah behind closed doors and shutters, in a neighbor's house. Two of our neighbors had been taken to the military work battalions, leaving their wives and children without a penny in the house. Mama had sent cooked food and basic foodstuffs to them as *mishloach manos*. I had also brought *mishloach manos* to my friend Rochel because I knew that she and her grandmother were in dire straits. Instead of rejoicing on Purim, a happy and joyful holiday — we had spent the day crying.

Shortly after the invasion, though, I started to operate the sewing machine again and Eshto the gypsy brought me more piecework shirts. I told him that instead of paying me with money, he should bring me basic foodstuffs: flour, beans, oil, kerosene, soap, sugar and any other food.

A week before Pesach we started cleaning. Rav Kleiner, one of our customers, promised to bring us a bit of his matzos, and Mrs. Weinberg managed to convince Mama to agree that we'd join them for both Seders even though Mama had originally decided that we would not go anywhere.

A few days before Pesach, Mama sent the Weinberg family a small jar of honey that we had received from the David-owitz family; they had given it to us for sewing yellow badges on the family's coats. We also sent a quantity of oil and kerosene to the Weinbergs.

∾   ∾   ∾

On *Motza'ei Pesach*, before sunrise, Mama and I were awoken by a faint, rhythmic knocking on the door. It was pitch black outside, and fright gripped us. Mama hugged me tightly with her one hand, and burst into tears. The knocking continued and after I listened intently, I whispered to Mama, "It can't be Germans knocking at our door; the Germans pound with all their might and they shout and scream. Mama, these knocks are quiet and genteel."

We got up quietly and approached the door in bare feet. It was then that we heard Chungarabi's voice. "Mrs. Fruchter, it's me, Chungarabi," the gypsy whispered. "Please open up! I am alone; do not be afraid."

Mama opened the door a crack and the gypsy snuck quietly inside. Mama hurried to lock the door after her.

Chungarabi waited until I brought both my slippers and Mama's, and then she started to whisper quickly and incomprehensibly. It was clear that she was tense and emotional, and she kept lapsing into the gypsy language, Romany. Mama, of course, did not understand a word but I understood everything she said and I started to cry. "Please be quiet, please don't tell Mama!" I cried. "I don't want to hear! Please leave us alone, Chungarabi." Chungarabi was also crying, but she stopped and composed herself. She saw that I simply refused to translate her words, so she wiped her tears and determinedly went back to speaking in Hungarian so that Mama could understand.

"We have found out that in the morning, in a few hours, all the Jews will be forced to leave their homes," said Chungarabi clearly. "You will all have to meet in the *Scheilhoiv*, near Hungarian Street where the ghetto is being set up. The announcements are already hanging on the billboards, Mrs. Fruchter."

Then Chungarabi did something unusual: She hugged Mama and burst into terrible tears. "Mrs. Fruchter, they will kill you! They will kill Leichu! They are gathering all the Jews in order to kill you!" she cried.

The three of us sat and cried while Chungarabi continued to talk, though she kept lapsing into Romany. "I am risking my life by coming here today," she said. "When Hitler finishes murdering all the Jews, he will murder the gypsies as well. Everyone knows this. He is already seizing them and imprisoning them in special camps...But I am willing to do everything to save you.

"I truly love Leichu, just as I love my only daughter, Lula," continued Chungarabi. "I am here because I am willing to risk my life in order to try to save you. Don't believe them, the Germans; come with us. We are planning to run away to the forest today, and I have worked very hard to convince my husband to let you join us." Chungarabi continued, pleadingly, trying with all her heart and soul to explain to us how her plan would help us survive. "We will escape to the forest where there are some caves that my husband is familiar with — we will hide there." Precious time was passing, dawn was approaching, and Chungarabi started to hurry us. "Get dressed already and take only what you really need and all the foodstuffs you can carry. We must hurry, before the sun rises."

We went into the room and Mama started packing all sorts of things inside a large rucksack. I didn't even see what she was packing because I deliberated over what to wear. Chungarabi came in to help me. "Wear layers of clothing, one over the over, as the gypsies do," she whispered.

"Mama, you must get dressed too," I told my mother.

To my horror, she shook her head. "No, my dear Leichu, I am not coming with you. I am a disabled woman and am not agile and quick as you are; I will only slow you down. Leichu, you must go with Chungarabi."

She must have seen the horrified look at my face, and she added, "I will wait for you, Leichu! I will wait in the cellar. Remember that we did not register, so no one will come looking for me. Don't worry about me, Leichu, but now, you must hurry. Don't stay here; go with Chungarabi and I will wait for you here. When the war is over, come back home, Leichu. I'll be waiting for you."

And I actually believed her! Everything happened so quickly that I had no time to delve into matters deeply, no time to think clearly. I simply believed my mother that she would hide and that they wouldn't look for her; after all, we had not registered. The Germans would never know she was missing.

After a heartbreaking farewell, I left with Chungarabi. I was sure that after the war, soon, I would, indeed, find my mother waiting for me in the cellar of our house.

◇◇◇

How could I have done such a thing? I have asked that question of myself many, many times since that fateful morning, the last time I saw my mother. Why didn't I insist that my mother come with us?

It is because of this that I have not slept entire nights. It is the reason that I still wake up from nightmares crying out. Though dozens of years have passed since that fateful morning—I still search

*for my mother in my dreams, the mother who waits for me in the
cellar of our home.*

*I cannot write too much about my parting from my mother, Hy"d.
It is still too painful. The emotional torments I suffer as a result of
leaving her are terrible.*

*The truth is, though, that Chungarabi's husband Eshto had
refused to take Mama with him. Chungarabi had argued with her
husband all night long; it was only just before sunrise that he agreed
that she could bring me.*
*She didn't dare discuss
bringing my mother, and
only hoped that when she
would surprise him with
Mama, he would have
no choice but to take her
to the forest as well. But
Eshto made the situation
clear to me with his un-
equivocal words to his
wife. "I only agreed to
take Leichu, whom you
love so much. If you had
brought her mother, I
would have left both of
them behind. It's a good
thing you didn't bring her
here and put me in such
a difficult position."*

I believed that Mama would hide in this cellar.

*Then he softened, and
turned to me to explain.*
*"Don't think I am a cruel person, but we are endangering ourselves
with this escape. You, Leichu, can dress up as a gypsy and we can
pass you off as our daughter, but what would I do with an older
Jewish woman who is missing one hand?"*

I know that this was Hashem's will, this was the decree from

Shamayim. But I have never ceased to grapple with this painful decree.

When I first returned to Sevlus after the war, a gentile woman from one of the villages had taken over our house. Still, I was convinced that Mama was alive and hiding in the cellar, waiting for me. I asked some Jewish men who had returned from "there" to threaten the woman until she allowed me to enter the house and cellar—and we saw, with our own eyes, that Mama was gone.

Yet somehow I continued to believe that Mama was waiting for me somehow, somewhere, on the face of the earth. When my eldest daughter was born I could not bear to give her my mother's name, because that would make it final. I didn't want to be the one to say, "It is definite: I don't have a mother anymore." But when my second daughter was born, I did give her my mother's name, Sheina Rochel. May Hashem lengthen her years with goodness and happiness, as well as the years of her brothers and sisters, and may we all have real Jewish nachas from them.

Only my children can comfort me over the sorrow of my mother who was separated from me forever.

❦ 56 ❦
Daughter of Gypsies

[SEVLUS]

L ET ME RETURN to the fateful moment when I left my home, after parting from my mother.

Mama handed Chungarabi two bags: The large rucksack, and another, smaller bag with some foodstuffs we had from Pesach — matzos and a jar of schmaltz. I left the house, kissed the mezuzah, and promised my mother over and over again that I would return to the cellar the minute the war was over.

At first I followed Chungarabi reluctantly while walking backwards, facing the house. But Chungarabi wouldn't allow me to walk like this. Instead she gave me the rucksack to hold with one hand and held my other hand with hers. The darkness started to brighten, the horizons turned grey and the stars slowly disappeared. I could see that Chungarabi was very agitated; she knew that sunrise was approaching and realized that we were in real danger if someone would see us. She prodded me to walk as quickly as possible and in fact, we ran together holding hands. The streets were so familiar to me that I recognized them despite the darkness. I was short-winded and found it hard to breathe because of the running and my silent sobbing.

We ran down Hungarian Street (Magyarsor utca) and approached the braided wooden fence alongside the Klar courtyard. The Klars had not lived there for some time, of course, but seeing the banister evoked so many memories. I withdrew my hand from Chungarabi's, leaned on the fence and silently signaled Chungarabi that I must stop to rest a minute. I simply could not breathe any longer.

The shutters of the house were closed. Another family lived here; *Baruch Hashem*, the Klars had left in time for Eretz Yisrael. But for me, it would always remain the house of the Klar family, the wonderful people who had been our closest relatives, who had supported my mother throughout her most difficult times.

I stroked the braided fence and remembered how Bácsi Klar had made it himself. He had set up sharpened wooden planks at a distance of half a meter between then, and then wove long, thin and dense wooden sheets between the boards. This created a very special fence for the yard, and we all marvelled at Bácsi Klar's skill. Somehow, touching that fence gave me strength to continue to run with Chungarabi.

Beyond the Klar's street was the end of the *eiruv*, which was also the end of *t'chum Shabbos*, beyond which it was prohibited to walk on Shabbos. We continued running until we reached the neighborhood of the gypsies, a foreign and strange place that I had never in my life ever considered approaching. Chungarabi slowed her pace a bit, though she still walked briskly, and I followed her toward a very long house with many entrances.

Meanwhile, dawn had broken. I continued walking automatically like a blind person, my head bent and tears streaming down my face. We walked the length of the house. At its end was a high wooden fence and in the middle of the fence

was a clapboard door made up of small planks that were connected together by wide boards. Chungarabi pushed opened
the door with her shoulder without releasing her grip on my
hand.

We entered a very large courtyard. At the edge of the yard
stood a shack that was not very large and next to it was a
gypsy wagon harnessed to a horse. We entered the shack. A
kerosene lamp stood on the table in the middle of the room.
Eshto, who looked extremely tense, sat hunched over the table. His face was illuminated by the lamp's bright light. As
soon as he saw us he started shouting angrily in Romany.

"What took you so long? How long does it take to run
back and forth to one house in the Jewish neighborhood? I
thought I would never see you again! I was sure that the Germans had caught you with the Jewish girl and taken you off,
together with the Jews!"

Chungarabi did not answer. She bit her lips and did not
say a word.

Then I turned to Eshto and began speaking to him in his

The last street; from behind you catch a glimpse of the Carpathian Mountains.

language. "Please don't shout at your wife," I implored. "It was my fault that it took so long; it was hard for me to part from my mother."

Eshto was taken aback. He never dreamed that I could understand, let alone speak, the difficult gypsy language. And in general, gypsies train their children to treat their elders with great respect and never interfere when adults speak. Even when someone is wrongfully rebuked, it is forbidden for children to interfere. It's no wonder that Eshto was dumbfounded. Luckily he had no time to dwell on my behavior because of his haste to prepare to leave as soon as possible.

Chungarabi pointed to a wide black skirt on a chair and told me to quickly put it on over the clothes I was already wearing. Under that skirt, a colorful head scarf was waiting on the chair. Chungarabi wrapped it around my head the way the gypsies do. Then, from the table, she took a long chain with two coins and tied it on my forehead under the kerchief.

Eshto examined me critically, and then pointed to a small coal stove in the corner. "Take some of the cinders and spread them on your face and palms," he commanded.

Chungarabi and Eshto started to move some objects from the house outside. They also took my rucksack and bag. Finally Eshto decided enough was enough and it was time to leave. Chungarabi was surprised.

"You said that we would leave toward evening," she said. "The streets are full of German soldiers, Eshto."

"Yes, I know," he answered testily. "But they are busy with the Jews so let's hope they don't notice us. There's no time to lose; we must leave right now, in the early morning hours."

The three of us left the house. Eshto took the kerosene lamp with him and locked the door. Then he barred the door from the outside by nailing three long wooden poles along the width of the door. Then he went to work on the windows; he closed the shutters and then nailed long wooden poles to them, as well. Chungarabi giggled to herself as she whispered to me, making sure that Eshto was not in earshot, "Do you really believe that a few wooden boards and some nails will stop people from breaking into our home?"

Chungarabi and I sat down in the laden gypsy wagon. Eshto climbed on the platform at the front of the wagon, grabbed the reins and goaded the horse to a fast gallop.

The closed wagon looked like a little hut on wheels. It had four small windows, but the shutters were closed and the curtains were lowered so that no one could see inside.

And that's how we started on our way as we fled Sevlus for the Carpathian Mountains.

ॐ   ॐ   ॐ

After some time of traveling, the wagon started to jounce and shake terribly. Even though we could not look out the windows, Chungarabi and I sensed that the wagon was leaving Sevlus's black paved road behind, for an unpaved dirt path. It seemed that we were now traveling on an obstructed, less-traveled path that was littered with many obstacles.

It seemed that we drove on and on without end. Chungarabi took advantage of the long journey to talk to me and describe gypsy life in detail. From now on, I was to live as a virtual gypsy; I was supposed to be their daughter and hence, must be closely familiar with their lifestyle and customs.

The fact that I spoke the gypsy language turned out to be a real boon and facilitated my "crash course" in gypsy life. I remembered the days as a child in Budapest when I loved those precious hours with my gypsy laundress! I had been extremely bored in the Feldman household and took special delight in learning the strange gypsy language that the gypsies

called "Romany." Perhaps, deep inside, I had also felt a measure of revenge against Anya and Apa, who would have been
scandalized if they had known of my relationship with Chungarabi. Though I loved my proper, genteel Budapest parents
very much, I still took a measure of satisfaction in surreptitiously learning the ways of the gypsies. "The gypsies steal
children"—that was a sentence I had heard over and over
from Apa and Anya since I was a little girl, and here I was, a
child myself, learning the language from a gypsy whom I was
not even allowed to speak to!

Everyone accuses gypsies of stealing children, but I had
been stolen by a Jew! At the time, though, I had no way of
knowing this. I believe that Anya did not know that I had
been stolen; she thought I had been sold by an unfeeling,
poverty-stricken mother. But even though I had not known
the true circumstances of my adoption, I believe I revelled
in learning the gypsies' language as a subconscious revenge
toward my adoptive parents — the "kidnapped" child learned
the language of the "kidnappers."

Chungarabi always told me that gypsies do not steal children. "We gypsies have our own children," she would repeat
over and over, "and we do not steal other people's children."
At the time, I did not know whom to believe—Chungarabi
or Anya. I loved both of them, and each said the opposite of
her counterpart. But then, in my childhood, I did not dwell
on the issue.

Now I raised the topic to Chungarabi again. Again she
insisted that it was a ridiculous accusation. "Gypsy life is very
difficult, Leichu. We must work at the most menial, wretched
jobs to eke out a living, and that is the reason that some gypsies steal," she sighed.

"Gypsies don't steal gold and diamonds; they only steal
things to help them survive. They can remove clothing from

a clothesline in seconds: Before the housewife even realizes that there are gypsies in the neighborhood—all the clothes are gone from the line. They can steal roosters from a henhouse or even a sheep from a pen; they won't hesitate to take cows or horses, either."

Chungarabi closed her eyes and smiled to herself. Then she opened her eyes and gave me a long, hard look. "You know," she continued in a very quiet voice, "the gypsies are a boldfaced nation. Their hard lives have caused them to be what they are. If a gypsy sees a kitchen door open to the outside with no one in the immediate vicinity, he will go into the kitchen, and fill his hands and utensils with any food he finds." She chuckled a bit, then added, "He will even take the pot off the fire and whisk it off with him!

"But it is important to me that you know, Leichu, that I, Chungarabi, have never stolen. That's why people allowed me to enter their homes in order to clean and launder. If I had stolen, even one time, only one item from one of the women I worked with, it would have ruined my reputation and I would have lost everything as a result. News of thievery spreads very quickly, like fire in a thorn field, and then no woman would have let me into her house afterwards.

"Eshto also did not steal when he built houses. If he had stolen something, even something small, he would have found himself out of work. Then he would have had to make a living like the other gypsies — by cleaning out stinking cesspits and other menial, contemptible jobs where no one would worry that he would steal something.

"We have self-respect, Eshto and I!" Chungarabi's eyes sparkled. "We worked at good jobs, and were not tempted to ruin our reputation and our pride."

I tried to talk to Chungarabi about right and wrong. We Jews know that it is forbidden to steal because that's what

Hashem commanded us. Theft is forbidden even to the non-Jews — it is one of the seven *mitzvos* they are obligated to fulfill. Did Chungarabi refrain from stealing because it was forbidden, or only because of her pride and the importance of "dignified" work? Chungarabi shrugged her shoulders. For her, principles of right and wrong were very different than the principles I was brought up on.

The non-Jews in Budapest as well as Sevlus hardly stole because they realized that in order to live peacefully with your neighbors, you must refrain from stealing from them. Fear of the police was strong in the big city as well as the small town, thus everyone tried to avoid doing anything that would get them in trouble with the law.

But the gypsies had a different worldview and a different value system. They didn't think there was anything wrong with stealing; if they needed clothes that were hanging on someone's clothesline, they would take them without giving it a second thought.

Chungarabi laughed to see my concern. "We're escaping to the forest now, Leichu; don't worry, we won't have anyone to steal from! Let's not discuss this now; it's more important to take advantage of this time for me to teach you how to live as a gypsy. Remember: If we are caught, you must never let on that you are Jewish. You are our gypsy daughter from now on."

The horse slowed down and the wagon swayed danger-ously from side to side. I grabbed Chungarabi's hand out of fear, and she immediately explained to me that Eshto had probably abandoned the path we had traveled until now, and perhaps was starting to lead the wagon up the Carpathian Mountains. Then Chungarabi stood up and started to make her way to the front of the wagon.

I was amazed. How was she able to balance herself and

walk so agilely when the wagon swung crazily from side to side? She reached the front of the wagon and opened up what had seemed like the side of the wagon to reveal a kind of door. Behind the door was the bench on which Eshto sat.

Chungarabi turned to her husband and spoke quietly and quickly to him, so that I didn't hear a word of their conversation. After a few moments she closed the door and returned to me.

Now the wagon really started the ascent up the mountain. "It is still a long way to go," Chungarabi explained to me. "Eshto is still afraid to stop. He wants us first to reach the forest where we will be safe.

"We have enough cooked food for today and tomorrow," said Chungarabi. "I know that you can't eat from my cooked food. I think that your mother put some cooked food into the bag for you. Even if not, I know she put your 'Pesach bread' into the bag. But we will only stop to eat when we reach the forest."

Chungarabi told me about gypsy bonfires: how to kindle a bonfire, where to collect fuel, and how to prepare a special stove for cooking on top of the fire, or, how to insert a pot inside the fire. She also explained the types of vegetables that the gypsies put inside the fire in order to produce the smell they like so much—the scent that other people shrink from, calling it "gypsy smell."

"The smoke from these vegetables also protects people from all kinds of ailments," she said. Chungarabi told me about kinds of vegetables and medicinal herbs that are capable of curing disease, but also warned me that there are grasses and mushrooms that are poisonous.

"I am familiar with them all," she remarked. "When we get to our destination in the forest, I will teach you everything I know, Leichu, and show you how to find wild grasses and vegetables that are safe to eat."

I told her about Bubby Shapiro's story of her friend who died as a young bride from poisoned mushrooms. Chunga- rabi nodded her head and added, "Yes, you must never take a chance and eat anything that you don't recognize to be safe. There are also plants that are poisonous and many people are not aware that they are dangerous. On the other hand, there are plants or roots that are very nutritious, and when you are familiar with forest vegetation, you can subsist and even be satiated on this vegetation without eating dangerous or harmful plants."

"But—I am afraid of living in the forest," I whispered. "I am afraid of getting a foreign object in my hand. That's ex- actly what happened to my mother, and because of that, they had to amputate her arm." I burst out in bitter tears at the mention of my mother whom I had left behind.

❦ 57 ❧
No Wasting Tears
[CARPATHIAN MOUNTAINS]

MY BELOVED mother! I saw her image clearly when I was reminded of the story of the splinter and her amputated hand. My dear mother! I wondered what she was doing at that very moment. How was she managing? True, she was very composed when she talked about hiding in the cellar, but who would bring her water? She had enough foodstuffs in the cellar, but how would she cook? And what about the other Jews? Were the Germans stupid? Didn't they know that every house had a cellar where people could hide?

I cried bitterly. Chungarabi hugged me and cried with me. I found out later, that she and Eshto had known the truth all along but they had resolved not to tell me. They knew exactly where "they" were taking the Jews. After the war, Chungarabi told me about the cattle cars that transported the Jews to Auschwitz. Yes, they even knew about Auschwitz, which had a special section for gypsies. When she and Eshto found out the truth about that accursed place, they decided to flee.

After I had calmed down somewhat, Chungarabi started to tell me gypsy folktales. Later on I was to hear these tales over and over again. This is how Chungarabi tried to divert my attention during the many long hours of travel.

It was evening when we entered a very large forest on the peak of one of the Carpathian Mountains. Eshto said that there were supposed to be caves in this area in which we could hide, but since it was already getting dark, we would sleep in the wagon and search for the caves in the morning.

Eshto opened the door and set up a miniature, three-step staircase that was used to climb up and down from the wagon. After we had entered the wagon, I hadn't even noticed that he had removed the steps; I didn't imagine that such a thing was possible. Chungarabi explained to me that when they travel somewhere, they remove these steps so as not to interfere with the wheels. They hang the steps outside on the wagon platform, near the laundry buckets. All the pails and things were arranged in such a way that they did not touch the wheels, of course.

I descended from the wagon. My body was rigid from sitting so long without movement. How good it was to stretch! Chungarabi had taken care to walk around the wagon every once in a while during the long journey, but I hadn't left my place. Now my entire body ached.

Eshto released the horse from the shafts connecting it to the wagon and led it under a huge tree. Then he took a thick,

A gypsy wagon. Notice the pails hanging and the decorations near the roof. Note also the curtains in the windows.

large piece of material and started to scrub the horse's skin; Chungarabi explained that this was to absorb the horse's sweat so that it would not catch cold. After Eshto scrubbed the horse in all directions, he took a pail and filled it with water from the barrel of water in the wagon. (That was the water we had drunk on the way.) The horse was chewing on grass when Eshto offered it the water, and it then proceeded to lift its head onto Eshto's shoulder, as if saying thank you. Then it lowered its head and started to drink with gusto, making loud, gulping noises.

I looked around. We were on the top of a mountain within a forest. Giant trees rose majestically, close together, and masses of shrubs and bushes grew between the trees. We stood in a spot where there was space between the trees—like a small clearing in the forest—and that was the spot where Eshto parked the wagon. Now I could see the path on which we drove: It ran between the trees but was not a real path at all. It was covered with shrubs and you could see signs of the wagon wheels between the shrubs.

I sat on a log that lay on the ground; part of the log was burnt while the other part was covered with leaves. It looked as if it had fallen from a tree when hit by a lightning bolt. I breathed deeply. The air was damp, with a tantalizing sweet fragrance. The fresh air was a welcome blessing — with my many layers of clothing I was feeling increasingly uncomfortable as the minutes passed. I thought I would faint if I didn't remove some layers quickly!

Eshto was still taking care of the horse. Chungarabi, meanwhile, was busy taking out pots and dishes and preparing food. I surreptitiously removed some layers when I thought that Chungarabi wasn't watching me. However, I had only managed to take off the black skirt she had given me, and two dresses and a sweater that I had put on at home, when

Chungarabi called me over. She asked me to put on the black skirt, and I did as she said. I folded the two dresses I had removed and walked over to the wagon to put them back into my bag. Then Chungarabi offered me a red bolero, decorated with colorful ribbons. "Wear this as well," she instructed.

"What for?" I asked. "We are only planning on going to sleep after we eat and anyway, no one is around here."

But Chungarabi was adamant. "Leichu, you must remember: Whenever we are outside the wagon, you must look like a gypsy. Yes, we are alone here in this remote spot, but you can never tell who might surprise us, no matter how isolated we think we are. We just can't take chances." I knew that she was right, and I did as she said.

I was terribly tired. I took a bit of food from my sack and ate without even paying attention to what I was eating. After I finished I started to walk around a bit just to do some physical exercise. Meanwhile Chungarabi and Eshto finished their meal, and Chungarabi set up the wagon for sleeping and called me to come inside. The wagon was transformed: A large bed was already set up near the invisible door that opened to the direction of the horse's shafts, and near the opening of the wagon, my bed was set up — it was two benches pushed together. Actually I was too tired to notice what I was sleeping on; as soon as I lay down, I fell asleep.

A strange noise woke me up. I looked around and didn't remember where I was—everything was very dark and very strange. Slowly I noticed that I was sleeping on a sack.

The strange noise came from outside. Were those birds chirping? It sounded as if thousands of birds were twittering away. But then there was another loud noise that was totally unfamiliar to me. Fear gripped me, and I felt paralyzed.

Suddenly I felt a hand stroking my arm and a gentle voice that whispered, "Leichu!" Then, all at once, I remembered. I

am in a forest, a wagon, and this was Chungarabi. I opened
my eyes and was relieved to see that the darkness was not as
terrible as I had thought just a moment ago. I saw the gypsy
standing before me and made out the outlines of the wagon
in which I slept. I took Chungarabi's hand and whispered,
"What is that terrible noise?" She answered, "Don't be afraid,
Leichu, there are gusts of strong winds outside; you are hearing the leaves on the trees that are fluttering in the winds. In
addition, you are hearing the songs of the birds and all the
animals of the forest in honor of the new morning."

I had not prepared water for *netilas yadayim* near my
bed, and neither Mama nor Anya was here to do it for me. I
got up and went out of the wagon. Eshto stood outside, offering water to the horse from a pail. I put my cup into the water
barrel, filled it and then washed my hands—one, two, three.

Suddenly I heard Eshto shout, "How much water do you
intend to waste this way, young lady!" I acted as if I didn't
hear him and continued. I decided that first I had to do the
right thing and remove the *tum'ah*; only afterwards would I
deal with Eshto. Meanwhile he had approached me, probably
out of curiosity.

I smiled broadly and said, "Good morning, Eshto. I hope
you have a good day."

He stopped in his tracks, smiled back at me a bit suspi-
ciously and said, "You should also have a good day, Leichu,"
and didn't say another word about the water.

"Can I help with something?" I asked.

Eshto waved his hand and said, "First things first: I must
find the caves that I know should be here, in this area. Once I
find them, I will definitely need your help."

"At your service," I said and curtsied gracefully, just as I
had learned from Anya. From now on I would be living with
the gypsy couple, and who knew for how long. I should not

give them any reason to get angry at me or have any complaints against me. I would look for an appropriate opportunity and a relaxed moment to explain to Eshto about *netilas yadayim*. Now he was too tense and edgy. I suspected this was because he was worried about having to find the caves.

I looked around me, examining the breathtaking landscape with great interest. The forest surrounded us on all sides. Giant trees rose above us, their wide leaves draping the forest in lush green. The leaves were actually only green on one side, and their underside was greyish-whitish. The wind shook the leaves and branches, which seemed to be in constant movement. The leaves—they were the ones that had made the noise that so startled me before sunrise. The trees were extremely tall and their trunks were completely smooth; each trunk branched off into branches only at a great height. Between the leaves and branches, I could see snatches of a blue sky.

I sat down on the same log I had sat on yesterday. Now I saw that it was partly covered with a climber plant. I could see that same climber plant on most of the trees around me. It was dark green, a much deeper green than the leaves of the trees. Around us were numerous raspberry shrubs and currant shrubs, all of them laden with fruit. The earth was barely visible because it was completely covered with flowering plants and black leaves that had fallen. I sat quietly and took in the beauty of creation.

Ribbono shel Olam, what a beautiful world You have created! A forest full of plants, whose names I do not even know; all types of birds flying from place to place; bushy-tailed squirrels that scamper quickly up trees. But Hashem, human beings are also Your creations. Why, then, are there such wicked people among them? Why do they harbor murder in their hearts? Aren't all people the work of Your hands?

It was terrible to think of such things in the midst of the beauty that surrounded me. Then I thought about Eshto and Chungarabi, who had invited me to escape with them. These gypsies — people who were societal outcasts themselves, people who were considered to be disreputable and contemptible — were willing to risk themselves to save me, even though their lives were in danger as well. How could this be?

I felt tears well up in my eyes and I remembered what Mama used to say: "Leichu, don't waste your tears!" When I sliced onions and my eyes filled with tears, Mama would say, "If the onions cause you to cry, then think about the *Churban Beis HaMikdash*." And now I wasn't cutting onions; the air around me was sweet and perfumed, the view was spectacular, and yet — the tears were tears of pain and longing. "Don't waste tears; pray to Hashem instead," I heard my mother's voice speaking to me.

I got up from my place and walked over to the wagon. My sack of belongings stood near the door and I opened it to take out my siddur. Chungarabi was busy organizing the wagon, but though she saw that I had been crying she did not say a word.

"I only want to daven," I told her in a whisper, and she answered me, "Pray to your God, Leichu; pray. Maybe your God will come to your aid and ours, by virtue of your prayers."

I returned to my tree stump and started to daven. I immersed myself in my prayers and ignored everything around me. It was a *tefillah* from the bottom of my heart, like my *tefillos* on Rosh Hashanah. I cried a lot and when I finished, I felt myself to be cleansed. I truly felt that Hashem heard my prayers. The crushing burden that had filled my heart from the moment I parted from my mother had dissipated. I knew, somehow I knew, that Hashem was going to help me.

❧ 58 ❧
The Ducks
[CARPATHIAN MOUNTAINS]

I COMPLETED MY *tefillah*. I was still in the forest, near the tree stump on the ground. I was surrounded by plant growth, birds and small forest animals. A green lizard scampered on the giant tree next to me. Two red-breasted birds skipped on the ground near me and every once in a while they would lower their heads, snatch a worm or berry from the ground, swallow, then resume their mischievous hopping. From afar I could see something white moving; the shrubs concealed some kind of animal from my view. I got up from my place and slowly approached the strange sight, until I was able to discern what it was: A father duck and mother duck were slowly walking through the forest, followed by four rather large waddling ducklings.

At that moment, Chungarabi approached me. I put my finger over my lips to show her that I wanted to keep silent, and pointed toward the ducks. Chungarabi saw them and laughed. "Don't be afraid to speak in their presence, your words won't scare them away," she told me. "You like to watch them because they are so adorable, right?" I nodded my head. "And I am happy to see them," said Chungarabi, "because their presence indicates that there is water nearby. Try to follow them, Leichu, and see where they go. I hope that they will lead you to water in the vicinity."

Chungarabi's words shook me out of my reverie a bit; I had been busy contemplating the beauty of the forest while the ever-practical Chungarabi was busy thinking about how we could obtain the basic necessities of our existence in the forest.

Then I noticed that Eshto and the horse were missing. Chungarabi told me that Eshto was riding around the area, looking for the caves. "We won't feel completely safe until we make our home in a cave," she explained.

I let my eyes follow the ducks. They waddled slowly from side to side while pecking the ground. From time to time the ducks scattered to the sides, then one of the parents would make a special noise and the ducklings would fall back into line again, one after the other. In Budapest I had owned a book about animals with a picture just like this: a mother and father duck leading a whole line of baby ducklings. I loved that book, but I had always assumed that it was just a fairy tale. And here, opposite my very eyes was a picture right out of the book, and this was the way they actually lived!

I followed the ducklings from a distance so that they wouldn't notice me. As I walked I picked some raspberries from the bushes and berries that grew abundantly all around me. I walked and ate, so wrapped up in what I was doing that I forgot to keep track of my direction. After about an hour I finally found a spring of water that was surrounded by a miniature pond. The ducks jumped into the water and I turned to call Chungarabi and tell her that she was right—I had found water! This was good news indeed.

But I turned around to see that Chungarabi was nowhere in the vicinity. I was surrounded by tall trees and shrubs, there were birds that flew from place to place, but there was no sign of our familiar wagon. I began to realize that I was lost in the forest, and my heart pounded with fright. I calmed down after a few minutes, though, when I looked around and realized that I had inadvertently left a trail behind me: Without any conscious intentions of doing so, I had broken branches as I'd followed the ducks and now I was easily able to retrace my own trail back to the wagon. It only took a few minutes of fast walking to retrace my steps, while it had taken the ducks a full hour to cover the same distance! Time is so relative, I smiled to myself.

I excitedly told Chungarabi about the small spring and pond around it, and she was overjoyed. "That is a sign that we are very close to the caves. Eshto will be very happy to hear that, he has been worried." Chungarabi had never been inside the caves herself, but Eshto had grown up in this vicinity and had told her about the caves a number of times.

Eshto returned much later. He had not found the caves anywhere, nor had he found any clues at all to lead him in the right direction, and he was tired, dejected and worried. That's when Chungarabi told him about my discovery, and he brightened up right away. He wanted to head to the spring immediately, but Chungarabi insisted that he eat first. The three of us sat on the felled tree stump. The gypsy couple ate some kind of concoction out of one plate while I ate bread with *lekvar*, a jam that Mama had made. Eshto finished eating quickly and waited impatiently for his wife and myself to finish our meal as well. But when I finished eating, I started to recite *Birkas HaMazon*. Eshto didn't say a word but paced back and forth around me with overt impatience. I appreciated that he waited silently and I *bentched* quickly. When I finished, I got up and led them to the spring.

The ducklings were nowhere to be seen. We approached

the spring and I filled my palms with water and drank; the water was cold and wonderfully delicious. I washed my hands and face and Chungarabi followed suit. Meanwhile, Eshto left us. After a few minutes we heard him call us, and we followed his voice.

We found Eshto near a large boulder near the side of the mountain. Only bushes surrounded the boulder, not trees. We got closer and then noticed that there was a small opening near the boulder. "Crawl inside," Eshto commanded us and we did as he said.

We entered a dark cave. It took a few minutes until our eyes became accustomed to the dim light inside as opposed to the strong light outside and we started to make out our surroundings. The cave was so large and wide that we could see neither its ceiling nor its end.

Eshto took out a large candle from his pocket and lit it with his flint stone. Immediately, a wonderful light filled the cave. We walked around the inside perimeter of the cave, round and round until we returned to the opening.

"Such a large cave with such a small opening!" I marveled.

Eshto laughed. "Originally, there was no boulder in the opening of the cave," Eshto explained. "I, together with other members of my tribe, placed the boulder there many years ago. Meanwhile, so many bushes and shrubs have grown around that boulder that it almost looks as if it's been here forever."

We went outside to the light of day. Eshto extinguished the candle and went to bring the horse and wagon. Chungarabi and I remained near the spring.

The spring flowed on a kind of stone terrace in the mountainside. The entire mountain was a series of flat terraces. Even the place we had slept the previous night was on a terrace in the mountainside.

Yesterday, when we had traveled in the wagon, we had ascended a very steep mountain. Chungarabi and I both re-marked how lucky we were that the benches, and other items in the wagon, were tied to the floor or the walls because the wagon tilted so precipitously from side to side. At the time I was wrapped up in thoughts about Sevlus and my mother whom I had left behind, and had not paid much attention to the trip. A short time before we stopped, we felt that the wagon had straightened out and that was when Chungarabi had told me it was a sign that we were close to our destina-tion.

Now I sat on the stone near the cave. Again and again, I reconstructed my terrible departure from my mother; the early-dawn flight from Sevlus with Chungarabi, the wagon and the journey to the magnificent forest in the Carpathian Mountains.

❧ 59 ❧
A Cave Becomes a Home
[CARPATHIAN MOUNTAINS]

E SHTO AND CHUNGARABI were working hard and I could see that they were very busy. But I sat wrapped up in my own world, thinking about my mother, tears streaming from my eyes.

Suddenly I felt a hand on my shoulder. It was Chungarabi who stood next to me and said, "Enough, Leichu. You can't continue this way. You must trust in your God and pray that your mother will manage to pull through this terrible period as best as can be expected. But now we have a lot of work to do, and we need your help."

I lifted my eyes and saw, to my surprise, that our belongings and furniture had been removed from the wagon and placed outside. Chungarabi didn't waste a moment and handed me a large sack.

"Fill this up with grass so that you'll have a mattress to sleep on," she instructed me. Then she also took hold of a sack and the two of us went to work.

"But be sure to pick only grass," she warned me. "If you let some stones or even leaves slip in, you will find it hard to sleep at night."

I plucked more and more grass until I thought that I had finished, but Chungarabi encouraged me to stuff my sack as much as possible until it was totally full and inflated. By the time I stuffed my sack, Chungarabi had already filled a sack for herself and was in the middle of filling a second one for Eshto. I helped her so we finished quickly. We tied the three sacks closed and left them near the other furniture items and belongings near the opening to the cave.

Meanwhile Eshto was busy cleaning the floor of the cave from rocks, leaves and soil. Chungarabi turned to help with the cleaning; she took some branches, tied them together and used that as a makeshift broom to energetically sweep the floor. The pile of dirt collected at the cave's entrance, and I removed it some distance away. When Eshto came out of the cave he did not like my neat pile of rocks, dirt and branches and showed me how to scatter it instead. "This way, no one will suspect that people were here," he said.

I went back to helping Chungarabi. I carried the lightest belongings and placed them close to the cave entrance. The opening was narrow and it was not easy getting the belongings inside. I pushed from outside and Chungarabi pulled from inside until together, we succeeded. Meanwhile Eshto took apart larger items, such as the kitchen cupboard, into smaller pieces and after we inserted the pieces into the cave, he reassembled the cupboard.

Eshto left the cave, distanced himself for some time, and then called us to help him. He had found a spot where the trees were very dense and the shrubs also created a dense thicket. That was the perfect place to hide the wagon. The three of us pushed the wagon into the middle of the shrubs, and Chungarabi and Eshto went round and round the wagon and cleverly organized the shrubs to hide the wagon from view.

That's when I realized why they didn't just uproot the bushes, as I had thought they should do. If they had done so, the shrubs would eventually dry out and leave the wagon uncovered. This way, the bushes were still connected to the ground and would continue growing over the wagon so that it would remain hidden from view even after time. It was very clever indeed.

Then Eshto went to look for additional caves. He remembered that although there was only one large cave—the one we had found, in which we would live—there were also other, smaller ones.

Chungarabi and I went into the large cave and started to organize it. Chungarabi patiently explained to me what to do and how to do it. There were a few sunken niches in the walls of the cave, in which Eshto had placed logs and kindled them. These lamps gave us light, but also filled the cave with smoke.

Slowly, the cave became more hospitable. The dish cupboard stood in one corner with all the kitchen utensils. In another corner, Chungarabi placed a rug on the floor with two of the grass-filled sacks and next to it, a large crate for clothing. In another corner she placed another rug and sack with my two rucksacks; this was my "bedroom." In the center she placed a crate and some folded mats. "This is our dining room, our guest room and our special Shabbos room," she smiled.

I began "unpacking" as well. I emptied the rucksack Mama had packed. There were a few sets of clothing, my siddur, *Tehillim*, Mama's *machzorim* and her *Tzena U'Rena*. Then my hand bumped into something hard. I pulled out two tablecloths rolled together — one of Mama's hand-embroidered pieces and one of mine — and out rolled Mama's brass candlesticks! I was shocked! What would Mama use for lighting candles herself? I shared my concerns with Chungarabi, who assured me that Mama probably couldn't take the candlesticks with her into the cellar. Chungarabi figured that Mama was concerned that the candlesticks might be stolen, so she sent them, and the tablecloths, along with me for safekeeping.

In addition to all those precious items, Mama had also packed candles, matches, needles and thread, scissors, and assorted kitchenware. And of course — she sent food: flour, oil in a tin can, homemade jam (*levkar*) and matzos. There were also some large paper bags filled with beans and legumes, salt, paprika, cinnamon and brown sugar. I was profoundly grateful — my Mama had thought of everything!

The cave became filled with smoke and the two of us started to cough. Chungarabi urged me to go outside. Then she extinguished the fire that burned in the three niches and also exited the cave. The two of us waited outside for Eshto and it was not long before he returned, sans the horse. He looked gratified at last.

"I have found the two caves I was looking for," he said. "One of them is small, close to this cave, and the other one is bigger, and also not far away. I put the horse into the bigger one, and left it with a nice supply of cut grasses as well as a bucket full of water. I hope it will be happy there."

When Chungarabi told Eshto about the smoke, he went in to check it out and came out with a furrowed brow.

"You're right," he said. "There is no place for smoke to exit that cave. We won't be able to light a fire there at all."

We ate some dry food outside, and then went to sleep in the cave. I was so tired that I didn't delve into thoughts of whether I was comfortable on my grass-mattress or whether sleeping in a cave was spooky. I just slept like a log.

I woke up the next morning and was pleasantly surprised

to find a bucket full of water waiting for me. Eshto had prepared it for me even though he did not like the idea of me "wasting" water near the cave instead of going to the stream to get washed.

I found the two gypsies already hard at work outside. They had decided to move the kitchen to the small cave. "That cave has only a thin layer of dirt covering it," Eshto explained. "I will be able to dig a hole as a chimney to allow the smoke to escape, and you'll be able to cook there."

Eshto was also confident that the tall trees surrounding the cave would conceal the smoke coils. So Eshto took apart the kitchen cupboard, Chungarabi transferred the dishes, and they moved it into the small cave.

Then Eshto took his ax, examined the ground above the small cave, and started to break the ceiling of the cave. After about an hour of strenuous work, sprinkled with sounds of the breaking of the ceiling, Eshto came out.

"You now have a hole in the ceiling!" he announced.

Chungarabi and I entered the small cave and started to clean it. For some reason there was much more to clean in the smaller cave than the larger one, and we worked until evening without taking a break.

In the afternoon Eshto took his horse out of the cave and disappeared. He said that he had to buy a new ax because his work in the cave had ruined his old one. At night, when Chungarabi and I went to sleep, Eshto still had not returned. I was amazed that Chungarabi was not at all worried. "He'll be back, don't worry; he knows the way," she assured me.

And in fact, when I got up in the morning Eshto was already outside as usual, giving his horse water. He had returned late at night when I was sleeping and I hadn't even heard him enter.

I sat barefoot next to the small pool and put my feet inside. It was soothing to splash my feet around in the water. On the previous day, after Eshto had left us and Chungarabi and I had finished cleaning the cave, we had bathed in the pool. But I didn't know when Eshto could come to the pool in the morning so I just washed my hands, face and feet. I knew that I should return and help, but it was so wonderful to dangle my feet in the water that I just didn't feel like getting back to work just yet.

It was then that I noticed that the bottom of the pool was very soft and comfortable to the touch of my bare feet. What could it be? I bent down and removed a fistful of white, pure sand from the floor of the pool.

I started to dig with my hand and slowly I filled my skirt with sand. I turned back to the cave and spread out the lovely sand in the entrance to the cave. Then I took a small enamel bowl and a large wooden basin and headed back to the pool. I used the small enamel bowl to dig and poured the sand into the large basin. Then, when the basin was full I carried it back to the cave and poured the sand on the floor. I did this all day, and by evening the entire floor of the cave was covered with soft, white sand that was comfortable to the touch. I placed the sack mattresses and "furniture" on the sand. This was a definite improvement over the mud and stones that had made up the floor of the cave, and I was very proud of my achievement.

"Tomorrow," I told Chungarabi, "I will bring sand to the small cave as well."

The next day I was true to my word and "paved" the floor of the small cave as well. Since it was so small, it didn't take long. I only needed a few basins of sand to cover its floor. Then Chungarabi said to me, "See, this side will be my kitchen and you can set up your kitchen on the other side." I went to my sack and took out a milchig pot and frying pan, as well as both fleishig and milchig bowls, silverware and plates. I set up my dishes and foodstuffs on a shelf that Eshto built for me, and Chungarabi taught me how to prepare a small oven from rocks.

Then we collected dry branches which we divided into our two ovens. Both Chungarabi and I stood and cooked our food, each of us in her own corner. This was what we did the entire time we lived in the caves.

The truth is that Eshto did not stay with us most of the time. It seems that he simply could not sit still in one place for long. The first time he disappeared for a few days, I was afraid that he wouldn't return. But Chungarabi was calm. "He will return," she said, over and over. "Please don't worry." But although Chungarabi wasn't worried I was, though I was embarrassed to say so.

Then Eshto returned after a few days, leading his horse as well as a cow. "This is a cow that belonged to Jews," he told us. "The Jews in the house were deported to an unknown place, and all the surrounding farmers stole everything. There were a few cows there and I took one. I decided that if the farmers made up their minds to inherit the Jews' possessions, then our Leichu also deserves milk from this Jewish cow. I brought you the cow as well as some other staples I found in the same barn."

Then Eshto removed bags of beans, onions and potatoes from the horse's back. Chungarabi and I were overjoyed at the opportunity to add variety to our meals.

Chungarabi milked the cow twice a day into a tin pail that Eshto had brought with him from the same cowshed. I explained to Chungarabi that I had to be present at the milking anyway, so she taught me how to milk the cow myself. At first I was afraid even to get close to that cow, but after some time I learned how to milk.

Eshto continued to disappear frequently, reappearing with foodstuffs and other things we needed, and then vanishing again. Sometimes he went with the horse, sometimes without it. Our menu improved greatly due to the milk, the onions and potatoes as well as other foodstuffs that Eshto occasionally brought.

I learned not to ask too many questions. If not for Eshto's foraging, we would have starved.

❀ 60 ❀
Secrets of the Forest
[CARPATHIAN MOUNTAINS]

I SPENT ENTIRE days with Chungarabi and she often entertained me by telling me *swatura*, folktales about the journeys of the gypsies. These folktales are not recorded anywhere in print, as the gypsies have no written language and no alphabet. Instead, the stories are transmitted by word of mouth, from generation to generation.

Thus I learned that the gypsy nation is divided into tribes and each tribe has its own special features and characteristics. Usually the nomadic tribes called *kumpania* wander in groups comprised of numerous brightly painted wagons, one wagon to a family. They travel by day; at night they stop and park their wagons. Sometimes they stop for only one night while other times they remain for many weeks in one spot. At night the members of the *kumpania* sit and tell folktales. These stories are repeated over and over so that the children will also learn the history of their tribe and the history of the gypsy nation.

Sometimes in the evenings, the adults would tell special tales — not exactly folktales, but simple stories told for enjoyment. These narratives are employed to teach children the gypsy language, business acumen and how to cope with emergency situations. But of course, the stories' essence lies in capturing hundreds of years of memories of the no-madic gypsies. These stories also portray the weaknesses and characteristics of the *gaje*—all foreigners or non-gypsies are called *gaje* —as well as their prejudices and the methods to cope with them.

I think that I'm probably the only *gaje* in the world who knows so many of the gypsy folktales even though I am not what they call a *"romany gaje"*; that is, a foreigner who signs a pact with the gypsies over holy water. The gypsies had a number of these foreigners who had signed pacts with them, a pact that is forbidden to violate even under threat of death. The gypsies sometimes looked for such foreigners to be their ally.

Sometimes, Eshto sat with us while Chungarabi told me gypsy folktales and he would play his instrument. This gyp-sy musical instrument was an interesting combination of a string and percussion instrument that resembled a harp to-gether with a xylophone. The strings were made out of metal and the pieces of the xylophone were made of thin metal as well. Eshto held in each hand a small, thin leather-covered mallet, and used these to extract very unique tones. At first the music sounded very strange to me, I had never heard anything like it before, but I slowly became accustomed to the tones and the rhythm and I learned to enjoy the unusual melodies.

Once, Eshto was able to convince Chungarabi to dance the special "chingarabi" Hungarian dance. That's when I learned that Chungarabi was named for the dance, and that her very name meant "dancer."

But that was the only time that Chungarabi agreed to dance. And it took a while until I learned the real reason for her sadness and reluctance to dance.

∾ ∾ ∾

One day, Chungarabi and I sat together on the stone near the pool and I reminded her that once, in our far-off days together in Budapest, she had promised to teach me to read palms.

"Do you remember the fortune-teller Anya took me to in Budapest?" I asked Chungarabi. "I realize how her words turned out to be so true: She had told me, 'Little girl! You will live! You will reach some kind of mother, afterwards a forest. You will live in a sunlit land.' Here we are in a forest, and you Chungarabi are really a kind of mother to me. But how did she know that?" I stopped for a minute, then continued. "Remember how Anya got so angry? I guess that she lived in fear that I would have to leave her one day, and that is exactly what happened in the end. But how did the fortune-teller know this?"

"I guess that the woman you went to was really a witch or magician who knows how to interpret what the cards say and what one sees in the crystal ball," said Chungarabi.

Chungarabi used the gypsy word for fortune-teller, but the woman I went to was Hungarian. The fortune-teller had talked to me about a forest, and Basya Leah's children had laughed and said that I could never live in a forest because I didn't know how to climb trees. Well, I still don't know how to climb trees, but what they really had meant was that I was a Budapest city child who didn't know how to do a thing for myself. I had been really spoiled in those days.

And it's a good thing I didn't come to the forest straight from Budapest; I never could have coped. Instead I went from Budapest to Sevlus, and it was in Sevlus with my mother that I grew up and matured in so many ways. I learned to sleep in the dark there, to peel vegetables and bake bread. I had also learned to clean and do the laundry on my own.

These tasks did not fall on me in the forest out of the blue; I had become accustomed to doing them with Mama out of my own volition, with joy and love, and now I saw that I really needed those skills.

I was even managing to cook on my own, under Chungarabi's tutelage, though I hadn't really learned to cook even with Mama. I didn't have a kashrus problem because I didn't have any fleishig food at all, and anyway I cooked for myself.

Chungarabi cooked for herself and for her husband. Eshto often brought rabbits or other game that he caught in the forest, and Chungarabi cooked them. The gypsies were very considerate, however, and tried not to tempt me by eating in front of me. But they needn't have worried; I was not tempted at all. I knew that I, a Jew, was forbidden from eating such foods while they, the *goyim*, were allowed, and that was that! I didn't suffer from hunger either, as I had enough food of my own, and I didn't miss the *fleishig* food. We had plenty of milk and it was my job to churn the buttermilk into butter. Eshto had crudely carved out a tree trunk with his hatchet, and then I scraped it until a bowl was formed. I used this bowl for churning the butter. Eshto also carved a kind of flat spoon with a long handle from a branch. I spent hours with that spoon, endlessly churning the buttermilk until it turned to butter. Chungarabi and Eshto said it was the best butter they had eaten in their lives. It was really delicious and high quality, and I added a bit of it to everything that I cooked.

I also made my own cheese. Small, tart berries grew near the cave and I used to crush them and mix them with milk in the morning. By evening, the milk turned into a very delicious block of berry-flavored cheese.

Sometimes I cooked porridge for myself from flour, milk and butter. I would add some salt or a bit of jam that I cooked from the raspberries that grew around us in abundance. This porridge was a real treat, and Chungarabi really liked it. Eshto, on the other hand, didn't like my porridge, so I cooked it only when he was not around. It was more fun to cook for Chungarabi and myself, than just for myself alone.

Mushrooms also abounded in the forest, but I could not bring myself to eat them. Bubby Shapiro's story about her friend who died from eating poisoned mushrooms was so engraved in my mind that even today, I simply cannot eat mushrooms. And this is despite the fact that Chungarabi assured me many times that she knew which mushrooms were safe to eat and indeed, nothing happened to her or her husband from eating them.

But I simply could not touch them.

∾   ∾   ∾

I found life in the forest to be very interesting, and each day was different from the next—though each day the trees continued to rustle, the birds chirped, the waters in the spring murmured and the animals made various noises. We spent our days in the forest and the evenings sleeping in the cave. Under Chungarabi's directives, I continued to dress like a gypsy before leaving the cave; even though no one discovered our hiding spot in the Carpathians, we always remained on guard. Our isolation from the world was the biggest boon of all, though we were only to find out much later exactly how lucky we really were.

I learned how not to fear the small animals and insects that filled the forest. I recognized the sounds of the different lizards; I noted the screeches of the squirrels and learned to distinguish between the sounds of the various frogs. There were a multitude of birds of every sort; and each bird had its own cry.

The forest rustled with insects and reptiles both small and large; ants of all types and butterflies that fluttered among the plants. The lizards were always trying to trap the butterflies with their long tongues. At first, I got very angry when I saw an ugly lizard eating a beautiful butterfly but Chungarabi explained to me that this was the way the world was created. Even the lizard has its natural enemies that eat it, and the lizards' predator also has its natural enemies and so on. If not, then the world could not continue; animals of one type would multiply endlessly and overrun the world, not allowing any other beings to exist.

This was how I learned a chapter in *emunah* from a gypsy. Indeed, I saw examples each and every day of Hashem's greatness; as we say in *Tehillim* (104:24), "How manifold are Your works, O Eternal! All of them with wisdom have You made them."

ख़   ख़   ख़

One day, Chungarabi decided to tell me about her role in returning me to my mother. I had heard the tale many times from my mother, but it was fascinating to hear it now from Chungarabi's point of view. It truly shed a different light on the events.

"Your mother was reluctant about hiring a gypsy laundress, Leichu, and wanted to meet me personally," said Chungarabi. "I don't blame her; as you know, there are many gypsies that steal. So one day, her former laundress brought me over to meet her.

"She looked me over from head to toe while I stood silently. But I don't think she realized that I, too, was secretly looking at her! And I had to control myself to conceal my amazement at what I saw: The similarity between the two of you took my breath away.

"I knew that your real mother had some kind of disability, Leichu, though I didn't know what it was. When I saw her and her artificial hand, I felt intuitively that she was your biological mother. Remember how you came and cried to me when you found out that you were adopted? Well, Sheina Ruchel Fruchter looked like an adult version of you, as you will probably look at her age.

"I almost wanted to shout, 'I, Chungarabi, know where your daughter Leichu is!' But I controlled myself. After all, I wasn't supposed to know anything about the adoption.

"I felt, at that moment, that it was up to me to reunite you with your biological mother. I didn't know how, but I vowed to find a way to bring you two together — somehow.

"As I worked for your mother, week after week, my mind worked feverishly trying to think of a way to get your mother to open up to me about losing her daughter. This was no easy task; after all, Jewish women don't usually confide in their gypsy laundresses. Then, one day, I saw your mother crying with Néni Rivka Klar, and I realized this was my opportunity. I felt that she was crying because of you—from longing, pain or fear—and I gently convinced her to tell me, the gypsy laundress, about you.

"And that is how Sheina Ruchel Fruchter was reunited with her lost daughter, Leichu Fruchter."

I sat next to Chungarabi and listened intently to her story. Everything seemed so dream-like; the waters of the spring rustled pleasantly as they flowed into the small pool, and the green waters of the pool rippled occasionally when a branch or bud dropped into it. The silhouette of the trees was reflected in the waters, tinting the pool a pleasant shade of green.

We sat on one of the large rocks on the bank of the pool. A multitude of plants and shrubs grew around us, among them yellow and purple plants that were splendid in their beauty.

I plucked some flowers and brought them to the cave to decorate it. But when Chungarabi saw the flowers, she explained to me that gypsies never pick flowers. "We believe that plants should be left in nature as they grow, and should not be plucked from their roots; this kills them."

This is probably the reason that I do not pick flowers until this very day and do not buy flowers for decoration. Instead I enjoy cultivating planters in flower pots. On the ledge of my bedroom window are two window boxes in which I plant seasonal plants. But to pick flowers is to cut something off from its roots, to kill — so Chungarabi taught me — and I simply can't do this. It even pains me to see when others pick flowers.

We sat, Chungarabi and I, surrounded by beauty. The light that filtered through the branches was soft and magical. Chungarabi spoke quietly, with her musical voice, and everything was so lovely and marvelous.

If only Mama could be together with us, and not alone in a dark cellar.

❧ 61 ❧
Estranged Children

[CARPATHIAN MOUNTAINS]

THE LOVELY SUMMER days in the forest started to shorten and the weather got colder. Although none of us said anything out loud, we all worried about the same thing: How would we survive the fall, then the winter, in the forest?

Some days continued to be pleasant while others were overcast and grey, days that sent dark shadows into the forest. When it rained we sat in the small cave and tried to warm ourselves by the fire in the stoves. However, the small cave had a very wide entrance, open to the winds, so we shivered from cold. The large cave was colder though, even when the sun shined outside because we could not light a fire there. At night we wore all our clothes to bed, covered ourselves with our coats and with additional sacks that we had filled with grass. Yet all this was not enough to keep us warm.

One day when the sun shone, Eshto decided to take matters into his own hands to solve the problem. I have no idea from where he got hold of the various tools he brought. He went up to the mountain above the cave and spent several days digging and hewing. Finally, one day we heard someone calling us from above. We lifted our heads and looked for him.

Chungarabi was sure that the voice emerged from the cave, though we knew that Eshto was on the mountain above the cave! We entered the cave and there, on the roof of the cave, we could see Eshto's head. He had succeeded in creating a hole in the roof of the cave by digging out a pit in the mountain above the cave. Eshto built a chimney around the hole which extended very high and protruded from the mountain. However, the cave, and thus the chimney, was situated in such a way that the trees of the forest still concealed the smoke. Afterwards, Eshto collected the stones he had hewn from the mountain and built us a real fireplace in the cave, directly under the chimney. This fireplace was made of rough, unchiseled stones so it looked a bit strange, as did the chimney made from these stones, but they served their purpose. We were overjoyed; finally we would be able to light a fire to warm up the cave.

Some time later, Eshto came riding up on his horse, bringing red sand. I had no idea where he got it from. He mixed the red sand with water and then coated the inside of the fireplace with it as well as the chimney. I told Eshto that I was worried that the red sand would disintegrate and fall into the fireplace when it dried out. Eshto laughed.

"This is not regular sand like the sand you used to carpet the floors of the cave," he explained. "This is special sand that the local people call 'red cement.' When it dries it becomes strong as iron — even fire can't breach this cement when it hardens. The red cement will also keep the chimney from disintegrating, and allow the smoke to leave smoothly. It is the same sand that is used for making bricks for building houses."

Eshto let the cement harden for a few days and then he

brought logs which he had cut from fallen tree trunks. He scattered small, dry branches among the logs and lit the fire. The smaller branches caught on fire right away, and afterwards the thicker logs did, too. Finally, tongues of red and orange fire danced happily in our new fireplace. It was wonderful.

Now we brought our mattresses closer to the fireplace. Chungarabi and Eshto took their places on one side of the fireplace, and I took mine on the other. The cave warmed up within a short time and we enjoyed sitting there cozily. The fire also lit up the cave, and we were able to see better. However, we continued to cook in the small cave. We were satisfied with this separation; cooking and sleeping were not in the same place.

On cold or rainy days we sat next to our fireplace in the cave and talked. That is, mainly Chungarabi talked, or Eshto — on the days that he was "home." Eshto's stories were very interesting, about battles and wars, while Chungarabi told stories about the gypsy lifestyle or stories about different people.

One cold day, Eshto headed to the forest with his horse and Chungarabi and I remained near the fireplace. Finally, I got up my courage to ask her a question I had restrained myself from bringing up, even though I was very curious.

"Chungarabi," I turned to her, "you once told me that you have a daughter called Lula. Once you told me that she is my age, another time you said she is a few years older than me. What is the truth? Where is she? Why don't you ever mention her?"

Chungarabi started to sob bitterly. When she calmed down a bit, she finally told me her sad story. "When Lula, my only daughter, was eleven years old, I made the mistake of my life. Lula was a wonderful dancer; no one else in our *kumpa-*

nia could dance as well as her.

"I requested a *kris romany*, that is, a council of Rom elders of the tribe. They are our supreme authority that determines everything for our community. At the *kris*, I asked permission to send Lula to study dance at the Georgio School of Dance. I received their permission, and I sent her to study there.

"The Georgio school is in Rumania, and the dance teacher was also Rumanian. That was my big mistake: I should have asked a good gypsy dancer to teach Lula the gypsy dances, and satisfied myself with the dance traditions of my own nation. Instead, my Lula learned the way of the *gaje*, the foreigners, and ultimately left us for foreign ways.

"How many times did I cry and plead with her: 'Lula, learn from them what they can teach you about dance, but don't learn their customs or lifestyle. Never forget that you are a gypsy. Remember, we have our own customs, our own traditions and it is forbidden—absolutely prohibited — to abandon your own traditions for someone else's.'

"I will never forget the day that Lula came home and proudly showed me the dress in which she was going to perform. At that moment, I realized that I had lost my only daughter. It was a white dress. To us, white symbolizes death and that dress symbolized death. In addition to the terrible color, the dress was short and sleeveless, with no collar. Female gypsies are expected to dress modestly; skirts must extend until the soles of the feet and sleeves must cover at least half of the arm. We don't exhibit our bodies shamelessly, and our necks must also be covered. And in a white dress, no less!

"But Lula had learned in Georgio that she did not have to listen to us, her parents. 'They are old-fashioned, primitive people who don't understand a thing,' they told her. 'You can't allow the previous generation to interfere with your artistic development. You are an artist!' That's what they preached to her, over and over. 'Art has no borders and no religion; it does not matter what ethnic group you belong to,' they would say. 'Art is universal; it is a gift for the entire world.'

"And that is how we lost her.

"My Lula danced in that white dress, and afterwards she married someone who came from a distant country. A country called Australia. She betrayed her nation—the gypsy nation—and followed that man. Lula was already engaged at the time. When she was twelve, Eshto announced her engagement to a young man from a good gypsy family; Eshto and the boy's father had agreed upon the match when both of them were still babies. Why, Lula already wore a gold necklace with gold coins that her fiancé had given her. Then she rebelled and removed that chain with the gold coins!

"The fiancé's family called a *kris*, and the elders considered the case. They investigated and discussed the issue and asked Lula to reconsider, but she refused. She even claimed that she was no longer a gypsy! She said that as soon as she married the Australian, she herself had become Australian.

"They had no choice but to banish and excommunicate her. That is the worst possible punishment for a gypsy, and is only inflicted on those gypsies who dare to violate the vow of the *kumpania*.

"In addition, the elders also cast upon her the oath of the curse. She can never return to the gypsy nation; not only our *kumpania*, but all other gypsy tribes as well. And we, her parents, were forbidden to see her again, or even to speak about her. Lula is excommunicated and never mentioned, as if she had never been born, as if she never existed. The white dress brought upon her death in our nation. For us, she no longer lives.

"I do know that she reached Australia. She wrote letters

to our landlord in Budapest, not because we couldn't read—both of us know how to read. She knew that she was not allowed to write to us, and we would have been obligated to destroy her letters without even reading them if we had received them directly. So our landlord received the letters and then told us what she wrote; he stood behind an open window and read the letter out loud. He couldn't read it directly to us, that was forbidden, but he read it out loud and 'unintentionally'—we heard.

"She wrote that she was doing well in her new country. She was dancing in magnificent halls and she had a good professional reputation in that faraway country called Australia.

"Perhaps there, in that faraway place she has a good name, but in our circles — her parents, her *kumpania* — she does not exist at all."

After Chungarabi finished her tale, she asked me not to mention her daughter Lula again, and especially not near Eshto.

"I try not to cry," said Chungarabi, "but during sleepless nights, when no one in the world sees me—I let my tears flow. And now you, with your question, caused me to talk about her and cry, and that is forbidden. Please don't ask me again."

I did as she asked. I did not ask about Lula again.

I told Chungarabi about my half-sister Caroli whom I had seen only a few times, on her rare visits to Sevlus. I had received some letters from her, and heard a lot about her from my mother. When Mama went to Caroli's wedding I had rejoiced, but mainly on Mama's behalf.

To me, Caroli was a stranger. Mama had been so happy when Caroli married, especially to a Jewish man from a good Jewish home. Mama felt that since she had married such a fine young man, eventually the two of them would return to their

Jewish roots. Yes, she thought, when they themselves would be parents they would return to their heritage and bring up their children as good Jews. That's what Mama would say every now and then. Then, when Caroli did give birth to a daughter, it was wartime and Mama could not travel to visit them. But Mama rejoiced from afar at being a grandmother.

I had met Isidor and Ari as well. They came to visit me, about three weeks after I first came to Mama. They came for Shabbos, to see their little sister, and both of them burst into laughter when they saw me. They started calling me "little Caroli," saying, "Now we have a big sister and a little sister who look exactly the same!"

On Shabbos they slept on benches in the store, and it was a very joyous time. But early Sunday, at the morning's first light, they left.

Isidor and Ari came a second time after I announced to the judge that I was staying with my mother. They said that they came to congratulate me on my decision and my kind treatment of Mama; they said, "Now our mother has at least one dutiful, respectful, respectable daughter." But every time they talked about "our mother," my whole body trembled.

When I lived in Budapest, I prayed that Anya would have another child. At the time I didn't know that I was adopted, and it was hard being an only child. I always envied all those other children who had brothers or sisters. Only I was alone, though I yearned to be one of a large family of sisters and brothers.

When I reached Sevlus I discovered that although I did have a sister and two brothers, they were far away. Though I had siblings, I was still alone. When I first met my two brothers, shivers gripped me. They looked nothing at all like sons of my pious, righteous mother who observed each and every mitzvah, down to the last detail. Isidor and Ari did not observe the commandments. They were good-looking, tall and dignified and treated Mama very graciously and politely; they even went to shul on Shabbos morning. But Mama did not allow them to make Kiddush. They themselves were aware of the *halachos* and were careful not to touch the wine.

How many tears did my mother cry because of them! She prayed constantly that they would marry upright, Jewish girls who would return them to their traditions. She herself admitted that it was unlikely for upright, good Jewish girls to marry men like them, but she still continued to pray that it should happen.

The accursed Germans did not care if a Jew was *shomer mitzvos* or not. They murdered all kinds of Jews, including Caroli, Isidor and Ari—my half-siblings.

✦ 62 ✦
Alone in the Cave

[CARPATHIAN MOUNTAINS]

ONE DAY, THE cow became ill. Its breath became labored; the cow gasped and wheezed as it tried to breathe. It refused to eat and was only willing to drink a bit. Furthermore, the restless cow would not stand in one place but walked around feverishly.

I was afraid to get near the cow and even Chungarabi had great difficulty milking it. "We must milk it," she explained. "If you don't milk a cow, it will get even worse." However, she was afraid that the milk was infected with whatever disease the cow had, and it would be bad for our health as well. So Chungarabi spilled out the milk after each milking — in a place where neither the horse nor the cow grazed.

After a number of days in which the cow's condition did not improve, Eshto reluctantly decided to bring the cow down from the mountain and sell it to one of the farmers in the area. "Farmers know how take care of their animals," he explained. "They will bring a veterinarian to heal the cow. If we keep the animal here, it will die."

Eshto tied the cow to the horse and tried to lead the horse. But when the horse started to walk, the cow stubbornly refused to move. The more the horse tried to pull it, the more the cow planted its feet firmly in the ground. Chungarabi cautiously approached the cow from behind and started to push it while trying to avoid being kicked. Eshto held on to the horse's halter and encouraged it to continue pulling slowly. At a certain stage this maneuver succeeded, and the cow started to walk.

Chungarabi informed me that she absolutely had to accompany Eshto and the cow; there was no way of knowing when the cow would decide to balk and refuse to move again. She asked me to stay in the cave until her return, and I promised her that I would do so.

I sat near the fireplace with my book of *Tehillim*. Ever since I'd been in the forest, I had davened and recited many chapters of *Tehillim* every day. Unfortunately I couldn't say *Tehillim* with the same *kavanah* as Mama because I didn't know the meaning of the words, but I was able to daven with *kavanah* because Mama had taught me the meaning of the *tefillos*. This time, though, I recited the entire *sefer Tehillim*, and continued reading the *Tzena U'Rena*.

Did Mama have something to read in the dark cellar, now that she gave me her precious *Tzena U'Rena*? Can she light a candle there, or perhaps light the tiny stove in the cellar that we had never used? I always wondered whether it could be lit. Did Mama have proper fuel for the stove?

Every single day I thought about Mama in the cellar, wondering how she was faring. I fretted over whether she had enough food; how would she be able to take the pail with dirty water out of the cellar; how could she draw water from the pump without being seen? Ever since I returned to Mama and learned how to draw water, I had taken that chore upon myself and Mama had not drawn water herself for many years. It must be hard for her to do all that again, with her one hand, by herself. I imagined that she must wait until the late night hours to sneak out and take care of these errands. How I wished I could help her!

When I bathed in the small pool, I wondered: Is Mama able to bathe as well? When Chungarabi washed our clothes, I thought of Mama. Laundry had been the only chore that Mama was not able to do by herself. This was the most difficult job for her, and my immaculate mother simply could not bring herself to wear dirty clothes.

When I churned the milk into butter, I thought: What is Mama eating instead of butter? I remembered that there were some jars of jam in the cellar. Here I was drinking milk. Did Mama have anything to drink other than water? Here I had learned to bake delicious bread for us. In fact, baking bread was my job and Eshto and Chungarabi complimented me on my delicious bread. I knew that a compliment from them was not just to make me feel good. If they said that the bread was tasty, then it truly was.

I had removed a large piece of tin from the plating of the wagon and this became my baking pan. I baked bread once a week, always taking care to save a piece of dough for the next week's baking. This piece of sourdough served as a makeshift substitute for yeast, and caused the dough to rise. I had no real way to measure quantity but every time I prepared dough, I assumed that it was sufficient quantity for *hafrashas challah*. I would take a bit of the dough and burn it in the fireplace; after it turned into charcoal I would remove it from the fire and bury it in the ground. Each time I did that, I would pray for my mother's welfare. Every time I baked, I thought to myself: What would I do to be able to send my mother some loaves of bread! She certainly would not be able to bake in the cellar.

I did not doubt that Mama was in the cellar, not even

once. I don't know if I would have remained in the forest with
the gypsies if I had known that Mama was long gone from
the cellar and from this world. It was the belief that Mama
was alive and well in the cellar that strengthened and shel-
tered me psychologically; it imbued me with optimism and
hope in our forest sojourn. That hope was what allowed me
to continue my life in tranquility with Chungarabi and her
husband, isolated from the rest of the world.

I have often thought back to those moments of parting
from my Mama, and of her last words to me. I understood,
much later, that when she realized instinctively that I had a
chance to escape, her only desire was to save my life. I don't
think she really intended on hiding in the cellar at all. But she
must have known that I would only agree to flee, if I thought
she was safe. She knew that I would never have left her otherwise.

My mother spent years of her life searching for me, her
lost daughter, until I returned to her at the age of twelve. In
the end, it was she herself who sent me away from her, in order to save my life. As a result, I was not at her side when the
Nazis came to take her away, and I was not with her when her
pure soul was taken to *Shamayim*.

I was frustrated that I knew nothing of what was going on
in the world. When Eshto returned from his forays, I would
ask him what was going on in Sevlus and the world. He insisted that he had no idea and did not want to endanger himself by making inquiries. The only thing he knew to tell me
was that the war was not yet over, and he promised that he
would tell me immediately when that would come to pass.

Still, I could not resist asking him time after time about
what was happening "outside," and each time I got the same
angry answer: "This is unacceptable behavior, Leichu. You
don't pester a gypsy man with unwanted questions." Yet he

also seemed to understand me, and I could see a glint of sympathy in his eyes each time.

But where were Eshto, Chungarabi and the sick cow? It was late that night when I finally heard the neighing of Eshto's horse, and then Chungarabi calling my name. They were riding on the horse with a sack of potatoes slung on one side and a sack of beans on the other. That was what they had received from a farmer in lieu of the cow.

Only then did I breathe a sigh of relief, and notice that I had been sitting motionless for hours. I had to struggle to stand up and straighten out my legs and back. Chungarabi hugged me and when she asked why I was so cold, I burst into tears. She realized that I had been afraid to be alone, and she sat next to me to comfort me and raise my spirits.

She told me about their "adventure" that day with the farmer. "After we saw the village in the distance," said Chungarabi, "we turned the horse and cow around to make a large detour in order to reach one of the houses via the field and not go through the village itself. Eshto knocked on the door of one of the houses and asked the farmer to meet him in the field. When the farmer saw our cow and horse, he said, 'You know, I could turn you over to the Germans. If you were Jews I would not hesitate for a minute to inform on you, but I have nothing against gypsies so I'll buy the cow and horse from you. You don't have to tell me where you came from or where you are going.'

"Of course we were not prepared to sell the horse, only the cow, and the farmer was sorry to hear that. But he said that he was familiar with the gypsy proverb that a gypsy without a horse is not a real gypsy. Afterwards he gave us the sacks of beans and potatoes in exchange for the cow, but was not prepared to give us anything else.

"After the farmer left, we tied the sacks on the horse's

back and left. But Eshto did not trust that farmer; maybe he planned to follow us to our hideout and then turn us in to the Germans, after all. Even after we made a very big detour, Eshto decided that we'd best not head toward the mountains yet and found a concealed place between the trees to rest for a few hours until nightfall. Only after darkness fell did we ride the horse, with our sacks, and head back up the mountains.

"We were a very heavy load for the horse—the two of us as well as the sacks—and it walked slowly. But Eshto relied on the horse's sense of direction to find its way to the cave even in pitch darkness, despite its very slow pace. So here we are, Leichu, safe and sound!"

The next day was baking day and I decided to celebrate by making a Hungarian specialty, *aranygaluska* — a sweet yeast cake eaten warm, straight out of the oven. I still had a little bit of the brown sugar we had tried not to use, jam that I'd prepared from the raspberries, and a lot of nuts. We had found the nuts under tall, beautiful walnut trees one day when we roamed in the forest.

That morning at breakfast, I proudly distributed the fruits of my labors—the sweet, warm cake instead of regular bread. "Why, it was almost worth that fright you had yesterday, to get such a delicious breakfast today," Chungarabi said.

I took a closer look at the sacks they brought. The big sack was full of potatoes and the smaller one had yellow beans! I started laughing.

"Now that we have beans, we don't have milk. I would have liked to make *zild bub libsh*, Mama's meal of beans in soured milk," I said. How I missed that delicious and nourishing dish that Mama used to cook for me!

⚜ 63 ⚜
The Tallis

[CARPATHIAN MOUNTAINS]

"**H**AS ANYONE else noticed a strange sort of growling noise all around us?" asked Chungarabi one day. "Sometimes it is fainter and sometimes stronger; almost like lions roaring all the time, though there are no lions in the Carpathian mountains."

"I was wondering when you would notice," said Eshto. "And in addition to the noise, haven't you noticed that I've stopped roaming the forests with the horse, and I've been sitting around?" Eshto sat on the adjacent clothes crate while leaning his back on the wall of the cave. We looked at Eshto, surprised. Of course, he was right; he had spent the last few days at "home." Most of the time he played the cimbalom and sang gypsy songs.

We hadn't connected this sudden homeboundness to the rumbling noises.

"There haven't been lions and tigers in the Carpathian forests for years," said Eshto, "and the roaring is not from animals; it is the thunder of cannons. Meanwhile we have nothing to fear as the cannons are very far away. We can continue our daily routine, but we should try not to distance ourselves from the caves. That's why I told you to pick a large supply of forest fruits for us and grass for the horse. That's also why I brought a large quantity of nuts the other day."

Chungarabi and I exchanged looks of fear.

"The cannons are still far away," Eshto repeated, "but we should take precautions for the future. That's why I intend to leave tomorrow to renew our food supplies."

Almost every time Eshto ventured out, he returned with supplies. Frequently he brought potatoes or onions, and we had plenty of these. Sometimes he brought ears of corn, and we ground them to make cornmeal.

When we had had the cow, we used to eat *mamaliga*, a kind of porridge from cornmeal in milk. After the cow was sold, we ate our *mamaliga* cooked in water. I had salt from the bag that Mama sent with us. When we lacked wheat flour, I baked our bread from cornmeal. That was less tasty, but definitely edible. In general we didn't have to scrimp on food. Since Chungarabi and I didn't have much to do, we cooked frequently; we cooked and ate, then cooked and ate again, over and over.

But the thunder of cannons kept getting louder each day and sounded like a distant thunderstorm. At first the noise made the horse nervous and it would neigh all the time, but eventually it, too, became accustomed to the sounds. However, even the horse stopped trotting around the perimeter of the caves as it used to do, limited by the rope to which it was tied, and now started to stand quietly, close to the cave. Eshto only dared to venture out with the horse once a week to stock up on food staples.

Chungarabi said that a gypsy with a horse who sits in one place and doesn't ride his horse is liable to go crazy. There is a gypsy proverb that says that a gypsy who sits on the grass day after day next to his horse, will eventually grow grass on his body and the horse will develop warts instead of a saddle.

∾   ∾   ∾

As the days passed, the rumble of cannon became louder. Eshto began to leave his horse behind during his forages because he was afraid that people would kill him in order to take his horse. One day, when he returned to the cave, he told us that he had seen a great army camped on the other side of the Carpathian Mountains. "I was still very far from the action," he said. "I could see very little from where I was; I mainly saw tanks and their dust. But there was tremendous noise.

"It was frightening to see the battlefield, despite the distance," Eshto admitted. "I knew that the soldiers could not see me as I stood somewhere safe, but even so—it was definitely terrifying."

After a number of days, Eshto decided to descend to one of the villages at the foot of the mountain and there he heard more detailed news. The farmers told him that the Russians were shelling constantly from their position on the Carpathian Mountain line. The Russian army did not advance from their position but instead, dug trenches in which they felt safe and evidently decided not to move from there. In addition they wanted to first "soften the sector" by inflicting casualties on their opponents and demoralizing them. This way, it would be easier to mount an offensive later on to conquer the Carpathian Mountains and the countries at the feet of the mountains. The farmers were certain that the Russians would continue their bombardments without moving from their position until the end of the winter.

Eshto was heartened by the news. "If that is the case," he said, "then we don't have to worry as much about soldiers approaching our hideout here. We are freer than I'd thought to

move, to cook, to heat up the caves. It is unlikely that someone will come here, and in any case the top of our chimney, as
well as the opening of the cave, are well-hidden by the trees."

One day Eshto came back with only a small amount of
foodstuffs, since he couldn't carry as much without his horse.
But he had something for me. "I think this will cheer you up,"
he said, and handed me a package wrapped in a dirty paper
bag.

I opened the package. There was a tallis inside.

I started to tremble. I spread out the tallis and saw that it
was in good condition; even the *tzitzis* strings were long and
seemed intact and *mehudar*. As I started to stroke the tallis,
my weeping intensified.

Both Chungarabi and Eshto were dumbstruck. Eshto had
been sure that his "gift" would make me happy, because he
knew that it was some kind of Jewish garment. Even Chungarabi, who had seen me cry many times ever since I was a little
girl, was also taken aback.

It took a long time until I calmed down enough to speak
to them and explain myself. "This tallis is a sign that there
are no more Jews. The Jews must have all been murdered because a Jew will leave behind all his possessions — everything
he has accumulated in his lifetime — but will always take his
tallis and tefillin with him wherever he goes. Under normal
circumstances, a Jew is buried with his tallis. If Eshto found
a tallis, that is a sign that its Jewish owner was murdered together with other Jews, and that he wasn't even buried properly with his tallis."

Eshto was so embarrassed and discomfited he didn't know
what to do with himself. "I thought that this present would
make you happy," he kept repeating. "I saw this material used
as a tablecloth on the kitchen table of a farmer's house. I
was standing in the doorway, about to beg for a bit of beans,

groats, rice, wheat — anything the farmer could offer—and then instead, as soon as I saw this Jewish fabric, I asked him for it. I told him that I wanted to wear it like a robe because I was cold. The farmer laughed and said that it really was a warm material.

"The farmer told me that after the Germans came to take away the three Jewish families in the village, all the townspeople plundered the Jewish houses. But since all three families were poor, they hardly had any valuable possessions at all. He, the farmer, grabbed a parcel made out of velvet, and inside was this strip of material. His wife made a nice pillow for the sofa out of the velvet, and this material served as a tablecloth. But the farmer had no problem giving this to me, I think he really didn't like it very much."

"Where did they take the three families?" I asked.

"I asked the same question myself," Eshto responded. "The farmer told me that all the Jews were rounded up from all the villages in the area and taken to a large city where they were all housed in the same place. All three families were taken by one horse-drawn wagon and they had no room for any suitcases at all, there was barely enough room for the people and their children. I suppose, Leichu, that if a Jew had to choose whether to take this material that you call a tallis or instead take his child, then the child has priority?"

I calmed down a bit at Eshto's words. From his story, it seemed that the tallis bag did not include tefillin. If a Jew had to decide between his child or his tallis, then he would certainly take his child. The man could have worn his tefillin — that way they wouldn't take up room. But why did they have to crowd so much? Why couldn't they bring three wagons for three families to take them to the big city?

Eshto could not answer me. He also didn't know to which big city they were taking the Jews.

We went into the cave. I sat on the crate next to my bed while I stroked the tallis and cried. I cried for a long time, until I fell asleep.

In the morning I found myself rolled up in the sand, near the crate, while hugging the tallis with all my strength.

All the possessions that Mama had packed for me were kept in that crate: In addition to my clothes, my siddur, *Tehillim*, Mama's *machzorim* and *Tzena U'Rena*, were Mama's brass candlesticks and the two tablecloths. I also kept my sewing notions there.

When I had first unpacked the sack that Mama had prepared for me and had seen the candlesticks and the tablecloths, I had been very disturbed. If I had noticed while Mama was packing, I wouldn't have agreed to take those precious candlesticks that she lit every week. And the tablecloths—why, they looked like a farewell present to me. But Chungarabi had said that Mama must have realized that she couldn't take her candlesticks with her to her cellar hiding place. She was probably worried that they would be stolen from her, and had decided that the safest place for them was with me.

In the end, I appreciated Mama's wisdom because those candlesticks and tablecloths helped me to create Shabbos and Yom Tov for myself throughout my time in the cave with the gypsies. I polished the candlesticks every week and took them out every Friday. I spread the precious tablecloths on the crate and on that I placed the candlesticks. How I yearned for Shabbos with Mama in the tiny room that she and I had shared, when her tablecloth and candlesticks so magically transformed us both! Every Friday night in the cave, I recalled those magical Shabbosos that Mama and I had shared.

I had cut up the wax candles Mama had sent along, so that I had many tiny candles. When the tiny wax pieces almost ran out, Eshto showed up one day with more candles for me. I was extremely grateful. His candles were very big and thick, the type that the gentiles used to light at weddings. I didn't cut them into such tiny pieces, because I knew that Eshto would bring me more of them when I ran out. These pieces burned for at least an hour. I didn't worry any more.

Now I opened the crate to place the tallis inside. I simply couldn't bring myself to do it; I placed it in the crate and took it out again a number of times. Finally I folded the tallis and placed it on my bed. This way, I could feel it every time I went to sleep.

ॐ　　ॐ　　ॐ

Life in the forest passed slowly. We spent more time in the cave, now, as the fall season came upon us, and the weather became considerably chillier. Each day was much like its predecessor. The constant cannon explosions echoed menacingly.

Every night, I thought of Sevlus. The situation there had been terrible when I had left, no different than the rest of Europe. Each day brought new, crushing decrees. It seemed that everything was forbidden. And thus, when I was in the cave in the forest, every night I reviewed the terrible situation of the last few years, all the terrible decrees, the extreme poverty and hunger, and the intense fear that was our constant companion. I cried uncontrollably; even when I tried to control myself and remember the good times, my tears continued to flow.

I had never been a particularly weepy child, though when I had discovered that I was adopted, I cried at night wondering who I really was and to whom I belonged. I also cried a lot when Anya had taken ill. On the other hand, I had never cried over silly arguments at school, as had other girls. I didn't cry when I wanted something, either. Anya had bought me everything I wanted, and with Mama—well, I knew her limitations and never asked for things that she could not afford to give me. I never felt that I was missing something with Mama; I had had everything in Budapest. In Sevlus I only wanted to be with Mama.

I was careful to cry quietly because I did not want the gypsies to hear me and feel sorry for me. I fell asleep while crying and I often had nightmares. I never remembered what I dreamed but I always woke up in panic, trembling with fear and dripping sweat, despite the chilly weather. I could not explain those terrible crying fits, even to myself.

I became extremely pale and developed dark circles around my eyes. Chungarabi tried to calm me as much as she could, but I couldn't even explain why I cried so much.

Frequently, Chungarabi would examine different types of leaves or take bulbs out of the ground and cook them in a kind of vegetable soup. Then, one day, she found a small bush with round leaves and she was thrilled. She picked some leaves and then dried them on the fire, on a screen that she had prepared by herself. After the leaves dried and turned brown-grey, she ground them between two stones.

That night, before we went to sleep, Chungarabi prepared a kind of tea with a bit of the crushed leaves and gave it to me to drink. It was so bitter that I wanted to spill it out after one sip, but she forced me to drink every drop in the cup. That night I fell asleep calmly, and did not wake up until morning. In the morning, Chungarabi explained to me that the leaves contained a sedative that caused me to sleep well all night. From then on, I drank a cup of the bitter, grey tea every night, and my crying ceased.

❧ 64 ❧
Bomb Shelters
[CARPATHIAN MOUNTAINS]

THE CANNON THUNDER intensified. Every day, Eshto would steal over to a spot from where he could watch the war from afar. He hardly told us anything when he returned to the cave, he only sat silently by the fire. He didn't even agree to play his cimbalom. "There are many, many dead," he said tersely one evening. "I have seen them evacuate the corpses." But he would not elaborate.

He would not take out his horse to ride. "If soldiers from either side see the horse, they will kill me and take the animal," he said. On the days that Eshto did not leave our site, he sat all day next to his horse that grazed near the opening of the cave. On the days that Eshto did leave, the horse remained in its cave and Chungarabi and I gathered large quantities of vegetation to feed it.

At first when we arrived at the caves, I kept my distance from the horse and then from the cow. But as time went on I learned how to approach the cow and milk it, though I didn't get too close to the horse. True, I was not afraid of it; I knew I had nothing to fear since the horse recognized me and would not harm me. Still, I preferred to keep my distance.

As time went by, Chungarabi and I had to gather food for the horse and also bring it water, and I simply had no choice but to become accustomed to the animal. In fact, I reached the situation where the horse ate from my hand, and I grew fond of it. I was not afraid to stroke the horse's face and nose, as it liked. A horse may seem intimidating due to its large size, but in fact it is a good-natured, quiet animal that doesn't cause harm; it only assists and performs many tasks for its master. Eshto's horse didn't have a name but I called it "Wonder." The wondrous thing was me — that I was willing to get near it!

Eshto went down to the village in order to get updated about the general state of affairs and to bring more provisions. The villagers told him that Budapest was being bombed by airplanes and people were spending most of their time sitting in bomb shelters. When I heard this, I immediately thought of Anya and Apa. I wondered how Anya was faring, sitting in a shelter with all the "common folk." I imagined that it must be very hard for her. After all, she looked down on "common people." She always said that a large portion of them are not at fault; they have no money and therefore must live on a low standard. Since they lack funds, they cannot study, and people who are not educated cannot raise themselves from their lowly status. True, Anya had a few dear friends who were "common." She loved talking to them and always said that they had more life experience and wisdom than her other friends. But to sit with them in a shelter? I couldn't even imagine it.

It was also hard to think of Apa sitting in a shelter together with all the *goyim* in the area. I could imagine him sitting stiffly in his chair and learning from one of his *sefarim*. Yes, it must be very hard for them.

And what about Zaidy and Bubby Feldman? They were elderly and Bubby had long suffered many diseases common to the elderly. How would she be able to sit in a shelter for days and nights? Even sitting for extended periods was enough to cause her to become even more ill.

And Basya Leah, how was she managing with all her little ones in the shelter? After all, they were young and mischievous. How would they be able to sit quietly in one place? It's true that Suri and Reizy help her, but still, it must be difficult. Zaidy and Bubby Shapiro must be together with them, and Bubby was presumably helping Basya Leah. But what was Zaidy Shapiro doing? Was there enough light in the shelter for him to learn the *heiliga Torah* that he loves so much?

I visualized the beautiful city of Budapest in my imagination: the lovely homes, the streets, the elegant squares, magnificent gardens, and lovely bridges that cross the Danube. What was the aerial shelling doing to the city?

I shared my thoughts with Eshto and Chungarabi. They, too, thought about the beauty and splendor of Budapest and about the destruction that the bombing was likely to cause. And then Eshto stood up and started speaking emphatically. "What a pity! Just destruction, murder and destruction— that's what wars cause. Destruction of homes, of things that people work and labor to create, to preserve, in order to enjoy. And murder. Killing of innocent people, slaughter of children, old people and women and also of soldiers who are forced to fight, to kill and be killed. What a waste! What lunacy! In the end, when the sides can no longer continue to fight, the war ends, but the anger remains. Then the anger gains momentum until the next war.

"Each time 'they' say, 'This is the last war. Now we will correct all the injustices of the previous war, and will not have to fight again.' But these are baseless claims because even if you correct previous injustices, you create new ones. People who are not satisfied with what they have, they are the ones who wage war. People who are satisfied with what they have, like us, the gypsies—they are the ones who never engage in battle!"

And then Eshto stopped speaking, just as suddenly as he had started. He shook his head as if to say, "There's no use wasting words," and sat down.

I looked at him in shock. It was the first time I had ever heard Eshto make a speech; he was always a man of few words. I had never heard him speak that way, out loud and with such intensity. Even when he told the gyspy folktales, he narrated them quietly while squatting on his heels. I had never seen him so animated.

Chungarabi looked at her husband with amazement. Even she never imagined that Eshto was capable of delivering such an impassioned speech. But, like a good gypsy wife, she kept her peace.

Only the next day, when Chungarabi and I walked toward the spring, she told me that it was the first time she had ever heard her husband speak this way. She hadn't even imagined that those were his thoughts. And she added, "Of course, he is right."

❧ 65 ❧
Winter in the Cave

[Carpathian Mountains]

THE FEARED winter arrived.

It was bitterly cold, and everything around us was frozen. The pool became a glistening sheet of ice and snow covered the entire forest. There was no place to pick greenery for the horse. Eshto went to the village again, this time with the horse. He returned with two large sacks of oats for the horse, a small cask of pickled cabbage and another small sack of semolina flour.

Chungarabi looked at all the abundance of foodstuffs and then looked at Eshto in amazement. Where had he acquired all this?

But Eshto shook his head and did not answer. Only later, in the evening, he said shortly, "Everyone, everyone has to eat. It's impossible to allow some people to hoard enormous stocks of food in their granaries and cellars while others go hungry."

Eshto pulled out from his pockets two jars of homemade jam, and said, "Leichu can eat from this too. This was in a kitchen that belonged to Jews who had moved to the city and left all their foodstuffs behind, as well as furniture and other items." Eshto told us that the gentiles in the area stole every-thing and the farmer from whom he received the jam told him it was from the Jews.

"How was it that the farmer gave you all this, when you don't have money to pay him?" I asked in amazement. But again, Eshto did not answer.

It is not polite to ask a gypsy male how he supports his family. Chungarabi had taught me this a long time ago, so I did not ask again. What was the purpose of asking? We had no food left, not for us or the horse, and would starve other-wise. Evidently Eshto was correct; it is not fair that one per-son has everything and another has nothing.

The Jews give *tzedakah*, and perform acts of *chesed* to help others in need. It seems to me that the *goyim*, on the other hand, don't even understand this concept and there is no point in trying to explain it to them. Apa had once ex-plained to me that observing *mitzvos* causes us to refine our nature and to become what we are but also brings anti-Semi-tism upon us. It is because of our superiority that the *goyim* envy us, hate us, and do terrible, evil things to us.

However, we know that there are some non-Jews who do perform *chesed* or good deeds for their fellow man; we call them *chasidei umos ha'olam*, righteous gentiles. I don't know if Chungarabi and Eshto fell into this category, but they did risk their lives to take me with them into hiding. They brought me food to keep me alive, and treated me almost like a real daughter. I will always remember, and be grateful for, this.

The more that I pondered the issue, the more I was satis-fied with my conclusion. True, the *goyim* cause us great hard-ship during all the long years of *galus*, but we are superior to them by virtue of observing Hashem's *mitzvos*. That is what arouses their anti-Semitism and causes them to inflict so much evil on us.

But I never even imagined the real evils. I knew about the refugees that had been expelled from their homes; about the men in the military labor battalions and work camps where they performed hard labor under torture; I was well aware of all the calamities inflicted by the Hungarians on the Jews. But I knew nothing about the deeds of the Nazis, about the terrible mass murders, the *churban*, the dreadful Holocaust.

The events that actually transpired were inconceivable to me. What sane person could ever imagine Auschwitz? I remembered how the Polish refugees in Sevlus tried to tell us, but everyone discounted their words and said they said such terrible things due to their troubles, or because they wanted others to take pity on them. It never crossed anyone's mind that they spoke the truth. We had been deaf and blind.

Evidently it was decreed from *Shamayim* that we would not believe them, that we would not accept the unbelievable.

෨ ෨ ෨

And that is how I spent my time in the forest. The living conditions were not ideal and the extended leave from my mother was difficult, but I always thought of her as "Mama in the cellar." I imagined how hard it must be for her, especially with her one hand; but I never considered that perhaps she was not in the cellar at all, that something far more terrible had happened to her. Even when I was informed that Budapest was bombarded, I only thought that it must be hard for the people I loved to sit in shelters. Those were my concerns.

"Ghetto." I had never even heard that word before. I had barely even heard of the S.S. I knew that the Nazis—Germans—hated the Jews, but nothing beyond that.

I lived in the forest, in a bubble of naivety, protected from the venomous hatred and terrible cruelty that was inflicted on the rest of our nation. The truth, when it became known to me much later, literally threw me into a state of shock.

∾   ∾   ∾

The winter became even colder. Snow fell constantly and the winds gusted fiercely in the forest. The branches swayed and creaked, as if they, too, cried from the cold.

We sat in our cave all day and even cooked there, too. It was simply too cold to cook in the small cave because its large entrance allowed the bitter cold to penetrate.

We could no longer bring water from the frozen spring, of course. We had to collect snow and warm it in order to create water. But a large pail of snow yielded only one cup of liquid. So when we wanted to bathe, we had to fill the pail as well as a large basin with snow to their very brim, and after the snow melted—we had a small amount of water to wash ourselves. That meant that we had to brave the bitter cold several times a day, to bring snow for drinking water, for cooking, for bathing and for *netilas yadayim* for me. In order to go to the bathroom we also had to venture out, some distance from the cave. And we were always supposed to cover up our footprints in the snow so that no one would discover our existence.

Eshto simply could not sit in the cave for such long time periods so he sometimes left us to sit in the other cave with the horse. He also was careful to take the horse out of its confinement, though he made sure it stayed nearby. Eshto claimed that a horse must run a bit, otherwise it is likely to deteriorate and become sick.

When Eshto would take the horse for a run, Chungarabi and I would clean the horse's cave. We would rake the dirt and spread out new straw from the straw bales that Eshto had brought from the village. Then we would run back to our cave to warm up next to the fire. After we warmed up, we cleaned our own cave. Of course we could not bring clean sand from the pool during the snowy days, so we covered the floor of the cave with a layer of straw. We also filled our sack-mattresses with straw — there were no grasses anymore to renew our grass fillings. I actually preferred to sleep on straw, as Mama's mattress had also been filled with straw; I had slept on a "real" mattress only in Budapest. Chungarabi and Eshto did not especially care for straw mattresses, they much preferred grass that was always fresh and sweet-smelling. During the warmer months, we had changed our grass filling every week so that it would always be fresh and fragrant.

❦ 66 ❦
Palm Readers
[CARPATHIAN MOUNTAINS]

ONE DAY, when we were sitting by the fireplace, I reminded Chungarabi again of the fortune-teller incident from Budapest.

"Everything that fortune-teller said, turned out to be correct," I said. "I did return to a 'new mother,' to my real mother—just as she said. Anya knew that I was adopted even though I didn't at the time, so evidently that was why she was so alarmed. In my heart, I thought her crying was ridiculous. The fortune-teller also said that I would live in a place with a lot of trees, and here I am—in a forest!"

Chungarabi smiled and reminded me that at the time, she had told me that the fortune-teller's "prophecy" was nonsense. I had told Chungarabi that the woman didn't even look at the palm of my hand, and she said that she imagined as much. Then she sat down to explain to me about fortune-tellers.

"I was never a gypsy fortune-teller, a *dukkerin*; neither were my mother nor her mother before her. Still, I know a little about it," Chungarabi said.

"Many *gajes*, foreigners, come to a gypsy *dukkerin* to have their palms read. Let me tell you that every *dukkerin* always says the same things, more or less. She tells everyone that they will have troubles or calamities but that they will overcome them. Let me ask you—how many people live in this world and do not undergo troubles or calamities? Everyone has some kind of trouble in their life, and survives. That's just the way of the world."

"We Jews say that *HaKadosh Baruch Hu* gives each person his or her *nisayon*, ordeal or trial, according to his abilities," I said, "but together with the *nisayon*, He bestows on us the strength to cope with it."

Chungarabi nodded her head in agreement. "That is exactly the case," she concurred. "Each person has his trials and tribulations in the world, and that's what the fortune-teller tells everyone. However, she modifies the same message according to internal and external signs she receives from the person coming to hear her advice. For example, she always promises each girl that she will marry the man most suited to her and that she will have children—that's what every girl wants to hear! If an older woman comes to her, she will tell

The Scheilhoiv. Sevlus's Jews assembled there before they were sent to the ghetto.

her that her children will marry and she will have grandchildren.

"The fortune-teller also knows what we call psychology. She knows how to read body language and learns a great deal about a customer via the way he stands or sits and other movements. She examines his eyes, whether they are tranquil or not; his hand movements; his steps when he enters the room; how he sits on the chair. You'd be surprised at how much you can learn about people from their body language and movements. Usually, a gypsy *dukkerin* is the daughter, granddaughter and even great-granddaughter of *dukkerin*, and the knowledge of human psychology is passed down from mother to daughter. This is how they learn to say what people want to hear.

"Let's say that the fortune-teller somehow knew that you were adopted. She also told you that you will live in a place with many forest trees, but this is something that can be interpreted in many ways. Since it did happen that you went to live in a forest, it seems to you that the fortune-teller knew to foretell the future. But remember — even if you had never escaped with us to the forest, there are many trees in Sevlus!" Chungarabi concluded her discourse.

And she was right. Sevlus was a village of grapevines. Dense vineyards grew just behind the city, almost like a forest.

"Only after we went to the fortune-teller," I said, "Bubby Shapiro told Anya and myself that it is forbidden, in Judaism, to go to fortune-tellers and others who claim to see into the future. Now I know why it is forbidden; it is just deception, sleight of hand."

After we had concluded the subject of fortune-tellers, Chungarabi took my hand and said, "Now that I've just told you that much of the fortune-teller's words are just hocus-pocus, I will teach you the principles of reading palms because there is some truth to it."

Chungarabi showed me the line that spans the length of my palm. "This is the lifeline," she said. "Look at that blueish spot in the center of the lifeline. Here your lifeline was supposed to end, as if there was great danger at exactly this spot. But your lifeline continues from the same spot, traverses the length of your palm and reaches the wrist. This shows that you have the potential to live a long life.

"It is possible, though, that that will not happen in the end," Chungarabi explained. "It could be that something will happen and you will not live a long life. The palm-reading only shows that the probability or potential exists. Of course, the gypsy fortune-teller who reads your palm will tell you with great assurance that you will live a long life.

"This line here," she continued, "shows wisdom. One glance at your palm tells the fortune-teller that you are intelligent and educated; they may tell you that you will always have work and also succeed in it because you also have a line of diligence and quickness. However, you should know that although the lines in your palm demonstrate that these traits exist, they exist only in potential. For example, if you do not continue to study, your 'wisdom line' can be wasted. The fact that it exists only means that your brain is capable of learning. If you take advantage of this and acquire a good vocation, it is likely that you will always find work. And since you also have the line for diligence and quickness, then it is also likely that your employers will be happy with your work and pay you well. And so the gypsy fortune-teller tells you that you will never be poor!

"The lines in the palms of your hand never lie. As you can see yourself, these strengths exist in you. However the question is whether you will take advantage of these potential strengths — and no palm-reader can ever know that, because it depends on you alone!" concluded Chungarabi triumphantly.

I sat with Chungarabi for a long time while she explained to me all the things "written" in my palm and to what extent the realization of my potential is dependent on me.

◇◇

Many years later, I spoke to Rav Shpielman and told him about the significance of palm-lines as Chungarabi the gypsy had explained to me. The rav said to me, "There is a lot of truth to this. HaKadosh Baruch Hu has given us a great many strengths, but it is dependent on us if we take advantage of these gifts, as our Creator wants, or we squander them. That will determine the length of our lives. Even if our life-line is long, if we do not fulfill Hashem's expectations then it does not matter how long we live. What matters is, how we fill the years that Hashem gives us with mitzvos, middos and meaning.

"We can learn from anything — if we only know the right perspective from which to view it," concluded the rav.

After I found out about the great catastrophe that befell our People as a whole and me in particular, I realized that the length of our lives is certainly not dependent only on ourselves. So many of our brethren murdered in the Holocaust were good, God-fearing Jews. Mama was a true tzadekes, as were many others like her. But as Jews, we know that each one of us is held responsible to a certain degree for his fellow Jew's behavior. "Kol Yisrael areivim zeh la-zeh" — this, too, influences a Jew's life, both in actual years and quality.

It is our duty and privilege to pray that the Angel of Destruction will never again be allowed to annihilate us without distinguishing between tzaddik and rasha. Indeed, tefillah is what remains as our legacy. It is what strengthens us, and what will deliver us.

◇◇

It was very cold. Eshto left, and was gone a long time, much longer than usual. We were happy that he took the horse with him so that we didn't have to venture out in the cold to clean the horse's cave.

We carried a great supply of timber from the small cave into our cave. True, there was a pile of logs not far from our cave (hidden under grass and snow, and covered with a large piece of tin) but it was so much easier to take the logs from the small cave, even though we had promised Eshto not to.

Chungarabi and I rested on our respective straw mattresses without speaking. This was the first time that we had reached the point where we had so little food that we were hungry and weak, and had no strength to converse. The truth is that although Eshto took care to stock us up before he left, we hadn't noticed that our stock of food was dwindling until all the foodstuffs ran out. The forest was still covered with snow so we could not pick the various forest fruits and satisfying roots.

The only thing we could do, was wait for Eshto to return with more food—and pray.

Using the last of our flour, I made bread and I also cooked some porridge from groats. We ate the small portions of porridge, but Chungarabi said to put aside the bread for even harder times. She insisted that we not touch it yet.

"Let's lie down to conserve energy, so we'll need to eat less," she instructed. So we lay down, both of us in our separate corners, without further ado.

I was glad that at least we had fire. We could never have made it this far in the bitter cold, without the fireplace. At least we were warm.

As I lay down, I closed my eyes and reviewed the long months that we had been hiding in the forest. At first it had seemed like a lovely, fascinating excursion; everything was new and interesting. We had prepared the cave as a "home," enjoyed our lives near the tiny pond, prepared the small cave for cooking, and spent time listening to gypsy stories, mainly from Chungarabi, about the lives, wanderings and wars of the tribal gypsy life. Eshto would return from his forays with new stories and Chungarabi tried to organize activities so that we wouldn't sit idly during the days. She said many times that sitting idly only causes misfortune. Bubby Shapiro had also quoted *Chazal* in saying that idleness breeds all sin. It seemed that in all the nations and languages, idleness leads to sin!

In general, I had discovered many sentiments in Chungarabi's quotes of gypsy sayings that were analogous to Jewish or Hungarian proverbs that I had heard in my youth—both in Budapest as well as Sevlus. Though I am not familiar with sayings of other nations, it does seem that there are parallels between the moral proverbs and folk wisdom of all nations and in all languages. However, I believe that all the wisdom of the world emanates from *Toras Yisrael*. Just as Christianity has its roots in Judaism, I'm sure that many other religions are rooted in Judaism. All of them drew from the Godly wisdom that was given to us. All of them copied, with various changes, what we alone received on *Har Sinai*.

And eventually, as a gesture of their "appreciation" for everything they received from us, the Jews—the nations of the world aspire to destroy us.

As I lay on my mattress I thought about my hard life: Leichu in a cave in a forest, surrounded on all sides by bitter cold, frozen forest and snow. I thought about Mama hiding in a cellar, and about all the ghastly rumors that had reached us from the beginning of the war, rumors we had refused to believe. But there were many terrible things we could see with our own eyes: the horror stories of the men taken to the military labor battalions; the impoverished refugees who flooded Sevlus with endless stories of those who had been killed or murdered on the way. Every time that I davened, and after every chapter of *Tehillim* I recited, I added a few words of my own:

"Merciful Father in Heavens, avenge us! The *goyim* have done us so much evil; don't let them emerge victorious from this war. Wreak vengeance on them, and bring upon them what they justly deserve."

Chungarabi always used to say that hatred harms the one who hates, and not the object of hatred. But she, too, hated the Germans who caused us to escape to the forest, to live in fear without knowing what happened to her daughter. Despite the fact that they banished Lula from the tribe, she still remained a mother and could not renounce her one and only daughter. Chungarabi had no way of knowing that Australia was far from the Germans' reach —it's probable that she didn't even know where the country was located.

Every day Chungarabi cursed the Germans who harmed the gypsies and scattered the tribe, and she always added, "the Jews as well." She meant what she said — it was not just lip service in my honor. I knew that she loved me very much, and she also loved Mama and Anya. In her eyes, it did not matter that we were Jews. "I love human beings who act like human beings, and detest those who act lower than animals," she used to say, time and again.

❦ 67 ❧
Noises in the Snow
[Carpathian Mountains]

T
HE DAYS PASSED very slowly. In addition to my
thoughts of revenge, the worries of our immediate
predicament also filled my heart. I remembered how
when Eshto left us for the first time in the cave, Chungarabi
had assured me over and over that he always returned from
his forages. I had learned to trust him, as she did, and did not
fear. But these were not regular times. Even Eshto himself,
who generally avoided telling us about the war and terrible
scenes he witnessed "outside," did tell us that conditions were
so terrible that people were desperate enough to try to kill
him for his horse. And yet he had taken his horse with him,
this time.

Eshto had never been away from us for so long. We had
never reached this stage before, with no food at all. Had
something happened to him? How long could we survive
without food? What if he would never return?

I didn't dare say a word about my fears, but suddenly I
heard Chungarabi calling me in a weak voice. I approached
her and saw that she looked terrible. I quickly prepared a cup
of water for her and added a bit of the sugar we had set aside

for an emergency. I brought it to her lips and forced her to drink it. After she drank it all up, she inhaled deeply and told me to open a bag in her crate. I did as she asked, and saw that the bag contained various dry leaves and grasses. Under her direction, I filled the teakettle with water and placed the leaves inside. Eshto had arranged iron grates over the fire so that we had a sort of stove. After the water had come to a boil, I poured her a cup of the "herbal tea," and added another piece of sugar that I broke off from the sugar cone. (In those days, white sugar was sold in a kind of round, solidified cone of sugar, like a large, round sugar cube. One broke the cone to eat the sugar inside [about two pounds worth], and the cone was edible as well.

Chungarabi agreed to drink only after I also took some of the tea with sugar. When she got a bit of her strength back, we each took a piece of bread from our emergency supply and sat down to eat.

"Leichu," said Chungarabi softly, "we must think positive thoughts, constructive thoughts. If we allow ourselves to think bad, negative, angry thoughts, our bodies and souls will suffer as well. Especially when you're hungry and weak, you must force yourself to think only of good things. That is the only thing that can strengthen us and give us hope!"

I had no idea how she knew that I was, indeed, thinking discouraging thoughts, but she spoke again. "Leichu! We must not allow ourselves to think about vengeance now. We must not think about the past, we must think about the future. You, Leichu, must think about the home you will establish in the future, a family that you and your husband will create on the firm, solid foundations of your faith and your religion. You must think about the wonderful, sweet children you will have someday. They will live in a lovely place, a place without wars and hatred, where only peace will exist between all human beings. That is what you must think of!"

That is how Chungarabi helped me to endure our worst days of hunger in the cave. It is due to her that I survived those days of hunger and fear, those days of inaction, without falling into the abyss of despair.

We continued to lie there for a few more days. Occasionally we drank the homemade herbal tea. Once a day we allowed ourselves to add a bit of sugar to the tea and eat a slice of bread.

One day Chungarabi slowly sat up on the crate opposite the fireplace and weakly inserted the logs I had brought. Suddenly she shouted, "Leichu—I can't believe this!" She smacked her palm against her forehead. "I can't believe we forgot, Leichu. Under this very crate we have a big pile of walnuts and chestnuts!" She lifted the crate and a pile of nuts and chestnuts started to roll down with a most welcome clatter.

The two of us burst into joyous laughter. We had both forgotten! Immediately we sat down to crack nuts. We ate and ate until our empty stomachs were full. We placed the chestnuts on the fire and when their shells split with a happy cracking noise, the entire cave became filled with their appetizing smell. Chungarabi and I then shared a delicious feast of warm, tasty chestnuts.

When I woke up in the morning, I saw that Chungarabi was already busy at work grinding peeled chestnuts. Next to her was a respectable quantity of chestnut flour. Later on, I kneaded dough from the flour and baked chestnut bread mixed with seasoning herbs. The fragrance was wonderful. There we sat, overwhelmed with happiness, when suddenly we heard a shout outside. Immediately, the two of us froze in our spots.

The same frightening thought occurred to the two of us at the same time: Due to our chestnut-roasting activity there was probably more smoke than usual. Someone outside must have seen the smoke and was now approaching the cave. That had always been our fear in the cave—that someone would come across our hideout and betray us—though until now, no one had ever discovered it in the forest. We had grown a bit careless with time and hadn't even bothered to cover the tracks we had made in the snow when we went to bring logs or to fill the kettle and pail with water. Whoever was shouting outside, would have no problem in following our tracks to the cave!

We grabbed each other in great fear. We couldn't move, and barely could breathe.

The shouts from outside became louder and tears streamed from my eyes. I knew that it was my fault, because I was the one who went outside a few times without covering my tracks. I was the one who had encouraged Chungarabi to put more logs in the fire, while ignoring the danger of the excessive smoke. The fear and guilt that gripped me was excruciating.

Then, suddenly Chungarabi let go of my hand, released herself from my grip and ran toward the opening with shouts of joy.

It was Eshto! He returned without the horse. He had a full sack on his back, but he was completely frostbitten. Chungarabi immediately removed his overshoes and shoes, then started to rub his feet with snow that I brought her in a pail.

I was barely able to remove the sack from Eshto's back. Then I went to work, removing his coat and the scarf that was wrapped around his head, his ears, nose and mouth. Chungarabi worked very quickly, while I ran to bring her more and more snow when needed.

Slowly but surely, Eshto started to thaw out. After he drank two cups of our herbal tea, his breath became calmer.

His face, hands and feet that had first looked deathly white as snow, started to gain a pink hue. He moved closer to the fire.

I went out again to fill up the large bowl and pail with snow. Then I returned to the small cave and waited there in order to give Eshto the opportunity to wash himself with heated water in the big cave, to allow his frostbitten body to warm up. When Chungarabi called me, I returned to the big cave. Eshto lay near the fire, covered by a straw sack and my coat as well as Chungarabi's; his head was wrapped up in Chungarabi's scarf. All of his wet clothes were hung up all around us. I noticed that the clothes were so cold that they emitted ice crystals and threatened to cool down our warm cave, so I took them to the small cave, lit a fire there, and then hung up the frozen clothes.

When I returned I found Eshto lying on his side, leaning on his arm and eating chestnut-bread.

We did not ask him what happened and why he was gone so long. One simply doesn't ask a male gypsy about his actions and whereabouts; if he wants, he will tell you, and if not—that is his privilege. I had finally learned that lesson from Chungarabi. We didn't even ask about the horse. We only rejoiced that Eshto himself had returned, and was already to recovering from his frostbite.

The next day, Eshto started to talk. Even then he didn't say much. "Don't worry, " he said, "the war is nearing its end, and the Russians are advancing." In his sack was cornmeal, groats and frozen carrots. We were overjoyed with all the food.

After a while, Eshto encouraged us again and promised to bring us more food when the supply would run out. Chungarabi told him about the nuts that we had finally discovered, and he laughed to hear about our adventures.

"Did I forget to tell you that there is another sack of nuts in the horse's cave?" Eshto said. "Once when I was galloping with the horse I came across a field with tons of nuts scattered on the ground. I gathered them up into the sack that I always carry with me, and placed them in the horse's cave for an emergency."

I made a wonderful soup. The groats and chestnuts gave it a delicious flavor, though the frozen carrots were fibrous and tasteless. However, Chungarabi said that we must eat the carrots even though they did not taste good because our bodies needed their nutritious value.

After a few days of rest, Eshto went out again to bring more staples and return the horse. Chungarabi and I had not dared to ask what happened to the horse or where it was. But we were very happy when Eshto returned with the horse on the following day. We were also happy to see that he had brought a large sack of oats for the horse, and another sack of foodstuffs for us.

"The important thing," he repeated, "is that soon, very soon, the war will end. The war is winding down as the Germans are already defeated on all sides."

This is how he encouraged us, week after week. The weather was also party to Eshto's encouraging words — the bitterly cold weather had started to subside and the snow had started to thaw. The view around us became breathtaking. Under the layer of melting snow, everything was green and blooming. The trees started to grow buds and the grasses started to sprout leaves. White bellflowers blossomed everywhere and the birds that had returned from their winter migration raised their voices in song.

Now we were constantly busy cleaning the cave from the melting snow that penetrated inside. Eshto dug long drainage ditches in all three caves, to carry the water inside the caves toward the pool outside. But Chungarabi and I still had a lot of work because of the water that penetrated the cave from the opening, as well as the melting snow that dripped on us from above. We were constantly busy.

At the peak of the winter, at the height of the rains and snow, no water had seeped into the entrances of the caves because Eshto built a kind of raised step for all the entrance-ways. But now the steps were ruined and the walls themselves started to emit the moisture that had permeated them during the snowy season. Chungarabi said the fire we lit caused excessive dampness.

Now we were able to place the pail and large bowl in certain areas to catch the running water, and did not have to bring water from outside all the time. But despite all our efforts the cave remained uncomfortably damp, not as pleasant as it had been when we first moved in. In order to alleviate things a bit, I lined the floor of the cave with green leaves that gave off a fragrant smell.

Despite Eshto's encouraging words that the war's end was approaching, the cannon thunder intensified even more. In fact, the noise became constant until there was no break at all. The war cannons thundered and bombarded all the time, and the noise became closer and closer.

❦ 68 ❧
Daydreams
[CARPATHIAN MOUNTAINS]

W E HUDDLED together in the cave, day after day. The booming of the cannons came so close to us that the noise sounded as if it originated just beyond the wall of our cave. We became very frightened and worried and decided to be more cautious. We lit only a very small fire, so that the smoke would not be visible. As a result, we trembled with cold even though we dressed ourselves in all the clothes we owned as we sat on our beds. What a shame that now that the forest was so blossoming and beautiful, we had to hide in the cave! Eshto covered the openings of all three caves with branches, as he had done when we first made our home in the cave last spring.

Eshto sat and quietly told us all kinds of very frightening stories about the Russian troops. From my youth, I recalled stories about the Cossacks who had treated the Jews cruelly. Was it really better that the Russians were conquering the Germans? The Russians were also wicked and evil. Who knew how they would treat us?

Chungarabi, however, made a clear distinction between the Germans and Russians. She said that the Germans were especially evil in singling out the gypsies and Jews with the avowed objective of harming them. The Russians, on the other hand, were "just" equally bad to everyone, and greedy. They would attack people in order to rob them, enter houses and create tremendous damage in order to steal, but they had no specific agenda against certain nations or ethnic groups.

Chungarabi and I tried hard not to leave the cave, but Eshto ventured outside once a day with his horse. At first he wanted to bring his horse to join us in our "bedroom cave," but Chungarabi objected vehemently. She said that she was afraid that the neighing of the horse would put us in danger of discovery by anyone walking around in the forest outside. The horse neighed every time Eshto approached it, and Chungarabi claimed that if it would be in the cave with Eshto it would neigh constantly. Eshto, on the other hand, tried to convince her that if the horse would be with him all the time, it would stop neighing. Chungarabi emphatically disagreed, and I did not dare get involved in this argument of theirs.

However, I prayed with all my heart that Eshto would listen to Chungarabi and not bring the horse to join us. As it was, the cave was crowded enough! True, it was better for us to live in the cave than outside in the forest. Here we had a place to sit, to lie down and leave our belongings. We had walls around us and a roof over our heads, we had some heating and the opportunity to cook. But a cave is only a cave of stone and dirt, not a terrific place to live and certainly not to share with a horse.

We left the cave only to take care of our needs and only when absolutely necessary. Even then, Chungarabi always accompanied me. Since the snow was melting, the ground was wet and we were able to dig pits in the ground easily. We tried not to distance ourselves from the cave and were strict about covering the pits. Though we had done this throughout our stay in the cave, now we were especially meticulous to make sure not to leave telltale signs. We also were careful to erase our footsteps by brushing the ground behind us with a large, leafy branch. The cave should not be discovered, *chas v'shalom*!

One morning we woke up to absolute silence. Outside was completely still. Out of habit, we waited for the cannons to resume their thunder. But it remained completely quiet for that day, as well as subsequent days.

The silence that enveloped the forest increased our fear. What could this mean? Perhaps there were soldiers in our forest, and that's why there was no cannon fire? Perhaps the Russians weren't shelling so as not to hurt their own soldiers?

We stopped lighting our fire, talked only in whispers and tried not to make any unnecessary movements. We ate dry bread that we softened with a little water, and didn't even heat up water for tea.

I started crying again: noiseless crying, only the tears streamed down my face all the time. Chungarabi noticed and came to sit next to me, to hug me. We sat together, hugging each other, and after a while, I noticed that she, too, was crying silently.

After a few days of quiet, we saw that nothing was happening around us and did not hear footsteps or voices of human beings. So we allowed ourselves to lower our guard a little and move around a bit. Eshto went out to investigate; he distanced himself from the cave in all directions and still did not hear anything. He returned to the cave and this time, he lit the fire. It was wonderful to warm up by the fireplace and to drink hot tea that also warmed our insides and soothed us. The red-orange flames that danced in the fireplace spread their warmth throughout the cave and also melted a bit of the fear that enveloped us. Finally, we allowed ourselves to talk normally.

The sun was shining outside and the forest was blooming. We sat in the entrance of the cave in order to breathe the fresh, pleasant air, but we still were afraid to distance ourselves from the cave. Chungarabi wanted to start to air out our belongings, as everything was damp and wet. But Eshto told her that this was premature; he wanted to investigate the cause of the sudden quiet before doing anything that could draw people's attention to our little corner of the forest.

Eshto left for a few days. Chungarabi and I spent those days quietly, without making unnecessary movements so as not to be detected from afar, just as Eshto had instructed us. When he returned a few days later, he sat next to the fireplace and did not say a word. We could see that he was exhausted. He drank his tea slowly, looking into the cup. He did not raise his eyes beyond the rim of the cup. After he drained the cup he handed it wordlessly to Chungarabi who filled it again for him. He drank about seven or eight cups of tea in this manner, and only after he finished drinking was he willing to eat.

Chungarabi told me that evidently, Eshto had hardly eaten anything during all the days that he was gone. After eating he went to sleep without saying a word, even though he saw how frightened we were and how much we wanted to know what was going on.

Chungarabi and I were left in silence, looking at one another. We didn't know what to think. We realized, though, that if Eshto would not speak or talk at all, that was probably a sign that the situation was so terrible that he didn't dare tell us anything.

The next morning, Eshto told us that he was going out again and would try to return as quickly as possible. Without another word he mounted the horse and galloped off.

Again we were left alone, even more frightened than before Eshto's return and strange behavior.

I went back into the cave, lay down in my bed and covered myself. I thought about Mama hiding in the tiny cellar of our small apartment. Does she still have food? Water? Is anyone taking care of her? How can anyone sit so long in a cellar?!

Perhaps in the middle of the night, in absolute darkness she is able to go out and move around a bit; to empty her pail and fill her water jug, perhaps to get hold of a bit more food? The cellar was tiny and low. You couldn't stand up in it, you had to bend your head in order not to hit the ceiling. There were foodstuffs there, but how would Mama cook them? After all, you can't eat beans, rice and grains without cooking them.

Suddenly I saw my Mama before my very eyes, standing opposite me! I heard her melodic voice telling me, "Don't worry about me, Leichu; you must worry about yourself instead. I am doing very well, *Baruch Hashem*. I am in an excellent place now..." I extended my arms in order to reach out to touch my mother, to hug her—but she disappeared.

I was cruelly disappointed as I lay down and rubbed the tallis on my mattress-sack. I didn't want to get up, eat or do anything else that Chungarabi asked me to do. I wanted with all my very being, to see Mama again, but she did not reappear to me. Instead I thought about her, about everything she had taught me, about her life, about her extraordinary faith in *HaKadosh Baruch Hu*, about her goodness and *chesed* to others, despite everything she herself had endured. I thought about everything she had succeeded in doing with only one hand. But mainly I thought about the efforts she had invested in finding me, to return me to her. And then, in the moment of truth, she had sent me with Chungarabi to the forest, because she knew that was best for me, too.

Then I allowed my thoughts to travel to Anya. How much she, too, loved me and pampered me! She didn't know that I had been stolen from my mother, she wasn't to blame. She and Apa had paid a great deal of money to receive me, in order to bring me up as their daughter. Even Apa loved me very much, in his own way. He was very strict because he believed, honestly and truly, that that was the way to bring up and educate a Jewish girl. He didn't do this because he was an unfeeling person, but on the contrary, he did it out of great love for me.

Mama had explained to me, when I told her about the time that they had locked me in my room, that Anya and Apa were strict down to the last letter of the law because they felt it was best for me. I knew that Mama was right. Apa and Anya were willing to do everything for me. I was very spoiled and very stubborn, and they only wanted to raise me properly.

Where were Anya and Apa now? Our relationship had been severed years ago when the war broke out and we were not able to send letters to each other, let alone visit in Budapest. How were they coping with the war? Did the war also reach Budapest, aside from the bombing that we had heard about? Were they cruel to Jews there too?

I lay quietly, remembering them all, thinking about them, and missing them very much: Mama, and Anya and Apa too. These people were the closest to my heart.

In the background we could hear the constant sound of rushing water. The snow had melted and nothing remained of it except for the sounds of rushing water everywhere. The water flowed into the small pool that had thawed and then the stream continued to flow downward on the other side, creating a kind of mini waterfall, full of foam and flooded with the radiance of the reflected sun. The forest was full of small rivulets that floated and flowed in a dizzying pace. Bright green foliage covering the mountain had replaced the dazzling white snow.

I was transfixed by the sounds of rushing waters that penetrated my agonized heart and brought me tranquility. The waters also soaked the earth and led to its blessed renewal, but unfortunately the rushing waters also invaded the cooking and horse caves so that both of those caves were wet and full of mud. We were very lucky that the water did not seep into our sleeping-cave which had dried out and become more pleasant. Fire still burned in our fireplace. True, sometimes the cave became filled with smoke due to an inadvertent damp log, but it was still usually comfortable. Chungarabi sat near the fire and sang gypsy songs to herself quietly, and I lay on my mattress listening to her songs and the water sounds around me. I felt as if I was drifting cozily in the air.

At night, when Chungarabi rested on her mattress, she started telling me her wonderful stories about the gypsy wanderings. And thus, while I listened to her with one ear and to the flowing waters with the other ear, I drifted off to a sweet, dreamless sleep, as if it was just a continuation of my day-dreaming.

❧ 69 ❧

Liberation!

I GOT UP in the morning full of energy. Enough of this day-dreaming, I told myself; nothing productive ever came out of day-dreaming!

Chungarabi was happy to see me this way. When I lay in bed doing nothing, she could not hide her worry. Now we started to work together — cleaning and straightening up our cave. Then we took our clothes to the pool, where Chungarabi washed the clothes while I hung them up on the branches of the trees in order to dry them. We both hummed as we worked, it was a glorious day. Suddenly, we heard shouts from below, at the slope of the mountain. We looked at each other between the trees, and then all at once we ran back to the cave as fast as we could. There we held each other, trembling with fear.

The shouts outside became louder and louder, and after a few long moments of paralyzing fear, we realized that the voice was Eshto's voice! We burst into loud laughter that broke the terrible tension of the last few minutes. It was not only the laughter of happiness; it was also the release of tension and fear.

We left the cave and squinted to face the bright sunlight that shined on us. Then we saw Eshto. He was galloping on his horse, shouting at the top of his lungs and waving a gypsy neck-scarf excitedly. The horse also lifted its head as soon as it saw us and neighed loudly, as if participating in Eshto's shouts of glee.

We waited for Eshto to dismount the horse and explain the reasons for the shouts. As he jumped off the horse, he shouted in Romany, "The war is over! The war is over!"

The news was stunning! Chungarabi hugged me, then burst into tears and I followed suit. The two of us stood hugging each other and crying. Now these were true tears of relief from worry and release from tension.

Meanwhile Eshto had calmed down from his own shouting and starting talking to us rapidly. Though I had become quite proficient in the gypsy language, Eshto spoke so rapidly and swallowed so many words that I could not understand a single sentence out of his entire speech.

After Eshto calmed down, I quietly said that I didn't understand anything of his speech. "Hungary was liberated two weeks ago, on April 4!" he cried triumphantly, but clearly and slowly. "The Germans have been defeated! They surrendered and have run away from the country. Budapest was liberated a while ago: Buda was liberated in the middle of January and Pest was liberated a month later."

The country is liberated! No more war! We are free!

I sat on a stone and could not move. "We are liberated," I said incredulously. "We are liberated, liberated. The war is over!"

I repeated this over and over, as if under a magical spell. I didn't move from my spot, I only repeated the same words quietly, to myself, again and again— "We are liberated!"

I didn't look at the gypsies nor at the horse that was next

to me, not at anything at all. My eyes were glazed over as I sat and whispered the wonderful words over and over.

After a while Chungarabi came over to me and touched me. I did not respond. Then she grabbed me by my shoulders and started to shake me: "Leichu! Leichu! Do you hear me? Do you see me?" She did not shout, but in her quiet voice was a cry.

I looked at her, and her eyes were full of tears. Then I asked in astonishment, "Chungarabi—if the war is over and we are free, why are you crying? Is it bad that it is over? It's not good?"

Chungarabi hugged me and said, "Leichu, it is wonderful—the best news that we could ever receive, the news that we have been waiting for all these years. But know that there is never good without bad; every great happiness is mixed with sadness or pain. Today we are blessed with great news that brings us joy, but it is mixed with sadness. We are fortunate to witness the end of the war, but there are many who have not lived to see this great day. It is for them, all the victims of this ghastly war, that I cry."

We went into the cave. Eshto took out of his pocket a cone of white sugar and showed it to us proudly. Then Chungarabi extracted a tiny silver hammer from the depths of her crate; this was a special hammer meant for breaking sugar cones.

I had not seen such an elegant hammer since I had left Anya and Apa's magnificent home in Budapest. How did a hammer that usually belongs to rich people fall into the gypsies' possession? I preferred not to ask. Chungarabi broke the cone with the hammer and then gave pieces to us to suck. Eshto was sorry that he didn't have liquor, to propose a toast, but Chungarabi said she was actually happy they had none!

Later on, when Eshto left, Chungarabi thanked me for not asking about the hammer. She had received it as a gift from

Lula just before they parted ways, and had not dared to take it out of the crate since then. She was happy that Eshto did not say anything when she used it and worried that if I were to ask about it, then Eshto might feel compelled to forbid the use of a memento from their daughter, whose name they were even forbidden to mention.

We sat happily sucking pieces of the sugar cone. Then I came to my senses and called out, "One minute! If the war is over, why are we still here? Let's go straight to Sevlus, to Mama! Come with me."

But Eshto shook his head. "No, Leichu. We cannot leave the cave yet, we have to remain here in hiding."

"But why?" I cried. "We are liberated, we are free! You just said so, yourself!"

Then Eshto patiently explained that although the war was over, although we were officially liberated, we would not leave our hideout until he was absolutely sure one hundred percent, that we would not be harmed by anyone we would meet.

"Why would anyone want to hurt us?" I asked innocently.

"During wartime there is a great deal of evil in the world. There is great temptation to kill and murder and even ordinary people do things that they would never allow themselves to do during peacetime," Eshto explained. "This evil does not disappear immediately when the war is over. It takes the evil some time until it sinks into oblivion. During this time there is no rule of law, only anarchy; each person does as he sees fit. It is only after the government gains control and succeeds in maintaining law and order, that people return to acting like human beings. Therefore, this interim period is a very dangerous one.

"We lived here for an entire year and succeeded in eluding the terrors of war. In the entire year, no human being ever entered our little piece of the forest. We lived in relative quiet and tranquility while the whole world was in the midst of chaos, upheaval and terrible bloodshed. Leichu, you have no idea what went on in the world, outside our little hideout. Let's not endanger ourselves now, out of impatience, after all we've been through. It's best that we remain here for a while longer, until I see that everything is quiet and we are not in any danger. Only then will we leave and head straight to Sevlus. Only then, and not a minute earlier!"

I was flabbergasted. "But — Mama," I whispered. "Mama does not know that the war is over and is still hiding in the cellar all this time. I promised to come and get her after the war is over, and I want to keep my promise. What will happen to her if I don't come for her right away?"

"Your mother is an intelligent woman; she, too, would not endanger herself by leaving her hiding place before the coast was clear," proclaimed Eshto. "She, too, would remain waiting for you patiently, despite the difficulties involved, until danger passes completely. You have nothing to worry about, Leichu."

Eshto spoke so confidently that I believed him. I agreed to remain in the cave until Eshto would decide that it was safe to leave.

Then Eshto took out his cimbalom musical instrument from its case and went outside. We followed him and watched as he assembled the cimbalom on the green, budding grass near the entrance to the cave. He worked slowly, taking time to brush the metal bowstrings. Then he smeared the strings of the chords with beeswax and used a special rag to clean the small hammers. He was so focused on his work that he was deaf to the world.

Eshto finished all his preparations to his satisfaction and

then, finally, he started to play. I listened as if hypnotized. I had seen the cimbalom many times and had even heard Eshto play it, but each time I was impressed anew by its very special tones. At first Eshto played quiet tunes but after some time, he abruptly stood up straight, looked at Chungarabi and started to play joyous, festive dance melodies. Chungarabi took a few steps toward Eshto and then started to dance. I realized right away that this was a very special occasion, as Chungarabi usually found it too painful to dance ever since she had lost her daughter. Now she danced very slowly, moving her hands and feet in synchronized movements.

Eshto increased the tempo of the music and Chungarabi increased her dance rhythm as well until she seemed to hover over the earth; she continued to shake her arms in perfect synchronization with her legs as she danced quickly and gracefully. Eshto played and Chungarabi danced harder and faster, while I stood opposite them and clapped my hands in time to the quickening tempo.

Thus we enjoyed ourselves for a long time until Chungarabi suddenly stopped dancing and dropped to the ground, totally out of breath. Eshto also stopped playing and flexed his fingers that had become almost paralyzed from holding the hammers. Even my own hands were red, swollen and painful from clapping! The three of us sat down, breathing heavily and gasping for air while we smiled heartily at one another. The war was over!

The next morning, Eshto left with his horse to see what was happening in the area, as he had told us, to ascertain whether it was safe to leave the cave or not. A day later he returned carrying large quantities of food, really huge amounts. He had never brought us so much food at once before. This was a sign that the war was over, but together with our great glee at such a large quantity of food we also understood that it was not such a good sign—if Eshto was bringing so much food, that meant we would be staying in the forest much longer.

We had lived for almost a year in the cave and during this time, Chungarabi had not brought up Lula's name of her own volition. But now that the war was over, Chungarabi spoke to me about Lula. She nursed the hope that perhaps she would somehow be reunited with her daughter again. She was sure that after such a terrible war, the gypsies would be more tolerant. She decided that she would request a meeting of the *kris romany,* a council of the elders of the tribe, where she would appeal to them to revoke the terrible curse they had inflicted on her Lula for daring to marry a *gaje*—a foreigner.

Chungarabi longed for her daughter very much but almost didn't dare speak about her. The only times she agreed to talk to me about Lula were when Eshto was not around. Eshto had also spoken to me about his dear daughter a number of times when Chungarabi was out of earshot. The two of them loved Lula very much, but had subordinated themselves to the decision of the *kris romany* and justified the verdict of the elders. They knew that it was a correct and just ruling, and they must act accordingly in order to preserve the gypsy nation.

I never told Eshto that Chungarabi told me about their daughter, just as I never told Chungarabi that Eshto had also spoken to me about Lula. I only told both of them that we Jews are careful to maintain Jewish continuity and to combat assimilation and intermarriage. Even if someone wants to convert and become a Jew, it is not easy for them at all. They must first study all the laws and customs, and if they truly desire to be Jewish with all their hearts—the Jews will accept them, but cases like this are few and far between. Once a person does convert, though, we accept him as a regular Jew, and love and respect him very much.

I had told both Chungarabi and Eshto separately about Zaidy and Bubby Shapiro's neighbors who sat *shiv'ah* for their daughter who married a non-Jew—similar to what happened to them with Lula.

❧ 70 ❧
Farewell Cave
[CARPATHIAN MOUNTAINS]

CHUNGARABI AND I were gripped with impatience by our continued isolation in the cave, but it did us no good. Eshto remained completely unyielding to our entreaties. "It is still dangerous," he would say flatly. "We cannot leave yet."

After a few days, we decided to remove the wagon from its hiding place. We took the horse with us. The trees and earth that had covered the wagon over the last year had hardened so much that we had to dig deeply in order to move them. It took us an entire day of work until we succeeded in extricating the wagon from its hiding place.

When we finally did free the wagon and saw what it looked like, Chungarabi burst out in shouts. It looked terrible. It was hard to imagine that only a year ago that wagon had been so clean and pretty that it had been a pleasure to stay inside it. So we harnessed the wagon to the horse and had the horse drag it directly to the pool. Since it was already dark, we decided to return to the pool in the morning and clean it then.

When I awoke, Chungarabi and Eshto were already gone. I found them next to the wagon, trying to whip it into shape.

Eshto had removed the wagon's wheels, replacing them temporarily with large rocks, and was busy washing the wheels in the pool. Chungarabi was inside the wagon, cleaning out the weeds and mud that filled it. I joined her, of course, and the three of us worked all day. At night, when we bathed, Chungarabi said with a groan that at this pace, it would probably take a full month until the wagon would be habitable again.

The next morning Eshto left again on his horse to do his rounds, while Chungarabi and I continued with our scrubbing. Chungarabi smiled at me and said that Eshto ran off because of the cleaning. Male gypsies just don't do this kind of work, and Eshto deserved credit for all his help the previous day. He chipped in then because he knew that no other gypsy would ever find out about it, she said.

For a number of days we scraped and scrubbed the wagon, both inside and out, until Chungarabi was finally satisfied. She kept repeating that it was a good thing she had emptied the wagon of all its contents at the beginning of our sojourn in the forest, because otherwise any belongings that would have remained in it, would have been totally ruined. Who knew, when we first escaped to the forest, that we would be there almost a year!

After we finished cleaning the wagon, we turned our attention to all the belongings we had taken into the cave. Once they were reasonably clean, we returned them to the wagon. Slowly the wagon began to become presentable again and take on the appearance of a real home.

After we finished most of our work, Eshto returned. Chungarabi had even managed to hang the curtains back on the windows of the wagon by then. True, she hadn't ironed and starched then, as she had done to Anya 's curtains, but these weren't supposed to be like Anya's anyway!

The last thing we did was to empty our mattress-sacks,

wash and dry them, and then refill them with fresh, fragrant grass.

That night we slept in the wagon. Chungarabi and Eshto were happy because the wagon, to them, was their home. To me, though, the wagon was just one more stopover before I would finally be able to return to my real home: my mother who was waiting for me in the cellar.

In the morning we cleaned the caves. Eshto said that we must leave them as clean as we found them, ready to welcome other persecuted people who might take refuge within their walls one day.

During our year in the cave we had worked constantly to improve it; we straightened out the floor, removed stones that were embedded in the bottom of the cave, scraped and smoothed the walls as much as we could, and spread sand on the ground to make it more comfortable. Was it my imagination that it seemed to have grown under our attention? The cave had been my home for the past year.

The other two caves—the cooking cave and the horse cave, as we called them —remained exactly as they had been on the day we arrived. That is because we had made no effort to rejuvenate them, though we had been careful to keep both caves clean. It was because we had the use of the two small caves that our large cave had remained relatively comfortable. We didn't have to share our living quarters with a horse or with cooking smells that would have suffocated us in our airless cave. It was only during the most frigid days that we had had to cook in the big cave.

ॐ   ॐ   ॐ

A month passed from the day that Eshto had broke the good news to us about the end of the war. One night, he returned from his foray and told us that we would leave the forest the very next morning, and start on our way home.

I was thrilled—finally, finally we were traveling to Mama! Eshto and Chungarabi were also overjoyed; they, too, wanted to leave the forest and resume their regular lives. To celebrate the occasion, Eshto took out his cimbalom again from the crate, assembled it and played. Chungarabi danced again and I—instead of clapping my hands until they would become red and swollen — took a large spoon and drummed on a sheet of tin. We spent hours this way: playing, drumming and dancing. I will never forget those magical hours, how wonderful the three of us felt. I felt as if the whole world belonged to us! I was happy to be returning to my mother, and I also felt so grateful to Eshto and Chungarabi. That night the three of us went to sleep with great joy and anticipation in our hearts, and woke up happy in the morning as well.

The innocent joy of that special night became etched into my mind with great detail, because that was before all three of us were to uncover the depth and enormity of the *churban* that we were to find when we left the forest and returned to our former homes. It was true that Eshto occasionally told us hair-raising stories he had heard from the farmers about murder of Jews. The tallis he had brought me, also testified to it. But his horror stories of murder of Jews and gypsies never really testified to murder on a large scale.

After the dreadful tragedy became known to me, and after I sank into despair, I was often comforted by my memories of the music and dancing of that night. I was always to remember the innocence of the pure joy and happiness of celebrating the end of the war.

The next morning, we left the forest and the caves. We traveled for two days until we reached Sevlus. The first thing we did was head straight to Eshto and Chungarabi's cabin. Wonder of wonders, the cabin was untouched! The wooden planks that Eshto had used to seal the windows were still in place; even the outside door was locked and barred. Eshto pulled out the nails, removed the planks, and unlocked the door.

I decided to remain in the wagon while Chungarabi and Eshto went into their apartment. I wanted to let them become re-acquainted with their home in private, without me.

The gypsies opened their door, and stood on the threshold. They looked inside, and breathed a sign of relief. Everything was as it was a year ago, when they left. After some time, they called me to join them. I couldn't believe it: My clothes were still hanging over the back of the chair, exactly as I had left them a year ago when we escaped. I was as happy to see my clothes as if they were old friends. After a few minutes Eshto left to check on his gypsy neighbors and see who was still living there. Meanwhile I changed back into my own clothes — only one layer — I no longer had to play the part of a gypsy. Eshto soon returned, and looked shocked. "There's no one here," he exclaimed. "Not a single gypsy is to be found; not in this building nor in any of the cabins in the area."

"They must all be at some kind of central *kris romany*," said Chungarabi thoughtfully. "Once every few years, they hold a council of all the gypsy tribes in all of Europe, and it takes place in the northern plain in Rumania. All the gypsies are required to attend and all the elder councils of the various tribes get together and make decisions that bind all the tribes."

Eshto and Chungarabi were happy that they had not started to unpack their belongings from the wagon, because they decided that they would leave immediately the next morning for their trip to Rumania, for the big meeting.

In their worst nightmare, the two of them would never

ever imagine the real reason for the disappearance of the entire gypsy neighborhood in Sevlus. These gypsies were destroyed by the same agents of Satan who conspired against the Jewish nation. True, the level of hatred and persecution toward the gypsies did not reach the level of their hatred toward the Jews, but the gypsies lost about a third of their nation.

The three of us then headed toward the city itself; Chungarabi and Eshto knew how badly I wanted to go home. I carried my large rucksack on my back and my small bag in my hand. This was the same rucksack that Mama had packed for me the night that Chungarabi came for me: It contained my siddur and *Tehillim*, Mama's *machzorim* and *Tzena U'Rena*, Mama's brass candlesticks and tablecloth, as well as some clothes. Just the thought of the candlesticks and tablecloth made me long for Mama. When we approached Train Street, Sevlus's main street, the gypsies tarried a bit.

"Leichu, you know that we love you very much; you are like a daughter to us," Chungarabi said. "But we know that it is not accepted for a good Jewish girl to walk with gypsies. We don't want to hurt your feelings, but how will the Jews accept you and look at you if you walk together with us?"

This hurt me very much, but I knew that they were right. I told them that I would walk over to them in the evening to say goodbye before they left. Then I walked ahead while they kept a distance behind me, as if there was no relationship between us.

❧ 71 ❧
Goodbye Sevlus
[SEVLUS]

THE ONCE-FAMILIAR streets looked strange and nearly empty. For some reason the city didn't look like my familiar, beloved Sevlus and at first I couldn't figure out why. As I walked, I peered in every direction, but I didn't meet a single familiar soul. The few people I saw on the streets were *goyim*. I peeked into the few stores that were open — all of which were grocery or food stores — but unfamiliar people were working there.

Suddenly, a *bachur* came out of one of the side streets. I was so happy to see a Jew! Out of the corner of my eye, I saw the two gypsies turn back.

As I came closer, I recognized him; it was Yisrael (Srul) Ber Shimonovitz. I was so excited to see someone I knew that I called out his name, but

Yisrael Ber Shimonovitz. He was the first Jew I met when I returned to Sevlus. I told his sister in Eretz Yisrael that he was alive.

immediately put my hand over my mouth, embarrassed. Why was I doing this? A girl doesn't talk to a boy in the middle of the street! But Srul Ber himself turned to me and looked overjoyed to see me.

"Leichu, are you alive?" he called out happily. I didn't understand his great happiness because I did not understand the depths of the tragedy.

"I'm on my way home," I said happily, by way of explanation, and he looked at me warily.

"Why are you going there, Leichu?" he asked slowly.

"To take Mama out of the cellar," I explained to him. "She promised me that she would hide there until I would return after the war to meet her. Now I have returned to fulfill my promise!" I cried triumphantly.

Srul Ber looked at me strangely. He seemed to be weighing his words, trying to decide what to say to me. Then he took a deep breath, and said sadly, "Leichu, I am sorry to be the bearer of bad news, but your mother is not in the cellar. She was with us in the ghetto; she was with us in the boxcar of the train...."

"Ghetto? What's a ghetto? And what train are you talking about?" I was sure that he was confused. And I noticed that he did look different from when I had last seen him—much, much thinner, for one thing.

Srul Ber didn't answer. He looked at me with great compassion, and was silent.

The two of us stood silently on the street in Sevlus, silently looking at one another for a number of minutes. Finally, Srul Ber asked me very quietly, "Leichu, where have you been all this time? We only saw your mother, alone."

"I hid in the forest, with some gypsies."

He was shocked.

"Leichu, why don't you come with me to the Wertzberger's

house? That is where all the survivors are congregating—all the people who have returned," he said.

I followed him and walked through the familiar streets of my beloved city, the city that now was foreign to me. The streets were almost empty and the only people that we did see were *goyim*. It was eerie: We were the only two Jews on a street that had always been noisy and bustling, full of Jewish people.

We reached the Wertzberger home. The house was full of young people; I only recognized some of them, but they all knew me and were overjoyed to see me. I went into the kitchen and there I met Eva Wertzberger and Mathili Rosental. The two of them fell upon me with hugs and kisses. Srul Ber walked into the kitchen and told them, "Leichu hid in the forest. She doesn't know anything about what happened to the Jews in Sevlus."

For the next three days and three nights, we all sat together and each of us told his story. Some of the people spoke for the first time, but most had already told their stories repeatedly — and continued to retell them — as they simply had an inner need to do so. That was when I found out about

A memorial to the Jews of the ghetto

Auschwitz and the terrible tragedy of the Holocaust — my personal tragedy, as well as the tragedy of the entire Jewish People.

They told me that Mama had been brought to the ghetto together with the other Sevlus townspeople. I guess that the Nazis found her right away; I will never know if she really did try to hide in the cellar. She remained in the ghetto for about six or seven weeks with the other townspeople, and then was taken in the cattle cars to Auschwitz on 8 Sivan, 5704/ May 30, 1944. "Your mother was one of the lucky ones," they all told me. "She died on the way, and never made it to Auschwitz. Only her corpse reached that monstrous place."

I had spent the last year thinking that Mama was waiting for me in the cellar, and my mind would simply not accept the truth at first. I wanted to return to the cellar, to rescue my mother. Finally, the young men in the group agreed to accompany me to my old house, which had been taken over by a gentile woman. At first, the woman closed the door on me and refused to let me enter. Only when the men walked up and threatened her, did she relent.

I went into the house that had been our grocery store and into the small room that Mama and I had shared. Memories pounded my mind with great intensity: Mama in her white scarf, lighting candles in her brass candlesticks; Mama davening *Kabbalas Shabbos*; Mama with her one hand, graciously waiting on customers in our little grocery store; Mama performing acts of *chesed* for the needy. Then we went down to the cellar, and the pain was almost too much to bear. It was only then, when I saw the empty cellar, that the truth started to sink in and I burst into loud sobs.

But the night was not yet over. I had rushed to Chungarabi's arms for comfort many times in my childhood and now I was going to her once more, for the final and last time, with my biggest tragedy of all.

I walked like a zombie from the empty cellar in our old apartment to the gypsy compound to say my goodbyes to Chungarabi and Eshto. "My Mama died in the cattle car; she never even reached Auschwitz," I mourned as I cried in Chungarabi's arms. This was the first that Chungarabi and Eshto heard specifically about my mother, though they had already heard what happened to the Jews.

"Gypsy families were also murdered in Auschwitz," Chungarabi and Eshto grimly informed me. "There are only a few of us who have survived, and we will all be traveling to Rumania for the central *kris* for the survivors."

In addition to my heartbreak over my mother, I had to part from the people who had saved my life. Chungarabi and I could not let go of one another; she held me, crying, and kissed me over and over.

They promised me that after the *kris*, they would return to Sevlus to look for me. But somehow I knew, in my heart of hearts, that this farewell was forever. When I had parted from Anya and Apa and my other loved ones in Budapest at twelve years old, I had remained in touch with them for many years with letters and visits. I had even kept contact with the Klars in Eretz Yisrael until the war broke out. But gypsies don't have addresses, and there is no way to contact them.

It was with a heavy heart that I said goodbye.

☙   ☙   ☙

After three days and three nights of horror stories, during which time I hardly slept or ate, I collapsed. I was simply overwhelmed emotionally by the loss of my mother and the murder of most of the familiar friends and faces in Sevlus. I went to sleep in the bed the Wertzbergers prepared for me, and could not get up again.

I became very sick; my temperature climbed to dangerous levels. I was only semi-conscious during this period and Eva and Mathili ministered to me with great devotion. After I recovered they told me that I hallucinated constantly and kept shouting, "I won't let you amputate my arm!" I also shouted strange words in a foreign language that sounded like the gypsy language, though they could not imagine that a Jewish girl would be familiar with that language.

When they told me all this after I was better, I reminded them that a gypsy couple hid me and that I learned a bit of the language from them. They were astounded. I had no desire or strength to tell them about my life-long relationship with Chungarabi, the gypsy laundress who saved my life.

My friends had a hard time understanding how gypsies, who themselves were in danger, managed to save a Jewish girl. But of course, they praised them for their act of selfless devotion.

ભ   ભ   ભ

I spent a full month in Sevlus until I recovered. Afterwards I wandered around the empty streets; even the non-Jews didn't seem to walk around too much on the streets anymore. The market square no longer hosted the weekly bazaar; there were no colorful stalls remaining or merchants' wagons traveling down the square. The peddlers had simply vanished into thin air. Even the farmers' wives, who used to sit on the ground to sell their produce, were gone.

The Jews were the ones who had brought life to the city and gave it its character. Now that the Jews were no more, the town seemed to have withered and decayed. It was like a flower whose petals are brutally plucked; the leaves shed, the stem dries out, and the entire flower shrivels up.

The weekly market

For me—there would never be flowers anymore in Sevlus. They no longer grew in the town of my youth, the town I had loved so much.

For a month's time, more young people returned from their terrible ordeals and made their way to Sevlus. It was mainly young people who managed to survive, a small percentage of those who had been left alive in order to perform slave labor for the Germans. They returned to Sevlus with the hopes of meeting other family members because they knew that anyone who survived would return to their hometown.

There were a few isolated cases that a survivor did meet a brother or sister or other relative. But most were deeply disappointed and walked around like me — without knowing what to do, where to go, and most of all — how to continue to face the future alone, without one's loved ones.

 av   av   av

One night I was awoken by strange shouts. One of the young men was having a nightmare and was calling for his mother in his sleep. His pitiful shouts of "Anya, Anya!" made my heart pound. Anya—I had forgotten all about my adoptive parents in Budapest! In that split second, I realized: It was time to return to Anya and Apa.

When I told my friends that I intended to go to Budapest to seek my adoptive family, they smiled sadly. "The Germans were in Budapest as well," they warned me. "They murdered Jews in Budapest too, so don't get your hopes up." But I was determined to make the trip. There was no point in remaining in Sevlus.

There was nothing to keep me here, and it was also hard for me to walk past the section that had served as a ghetto. I now knew about the ghetto that lasted for less than two months: from after Pesach to Shavuos. It was painful for me to accept the fact that for the last six weeks of her life, Mama had been alone and I had not been at her side. Those who were in the cattle car with Mama on the way to Auschwitz told me that she was fortunate to die on the way, so that her feet never stepped on the cursed land of Auschwitz. If she would have arrived, she would have definitely gone straight to Heaven because Mengele would never have allowed a disabled amputee to live one second longer.

I no longer wanted to see the streets and squares that had once been so full of life and now were dark and desolate. Every time I stepped on the black stones which paved Sevlus's roads, I imagined Mama stepping on them on the way to her death — and my feet hurt. I wanted to run away from this cursed, treacherous place.

I wasn't the only one who wanted to leave. In the end, I departed for Budapest with a group of young people who were left with nothing in the world, whose only objective was to leave this traitorous town. Perhaps the capital city would offer something to hold onto.

As I stood in the train station I turned around to look

behind me one last time at the town of Sevlus. "Goodbye!" I called out. "Goodbye forever—I hope never to return to this place!"

I boarded the train with everything I owned: my large rucksack on my back and my small bag in my hand. I had no other momentos of my mother and my life in Sevlus; all of Mama's letters and pictures had "disappeared" from our apartment. I could feel the weight of Mama's brass candlesticks, her *machzorim* and *Tzena U'Rena* in the rucksack, and thanked Hashem for that.

We reached the big train stop in Budapest and from there we walked straight to Dob Street — the site of the Jewish community center. We were told that that was the meeting place for all the Jews.

The three-storied house bustled with people, all Jews. Some of them looked frightful, like walking skeletons, most of them were wearing strange clothes. The walls were all covered with large sheets of paper, on which were long lists of names. Everyone who survived signed the list, in the hopes that a surviving family member would come across his name. Opposite the lists stood long lines of people who searched eagerly for a familiar name. Everyone hoped to find someone; if not a real family member then at least an acquaintance.

I had intended to move closer to the wall and look for the names of Anya and Apa, and Zaidy and Bubby Shapiro, as well as all the people I had known and loved. But instead, I walked the other way.

I simply could not bring myself to look at that list. I just could not.

✥ 72 ✥
Orphaned of Two Mothers

[BUDAPEST]

OUR LITTLE GROUP from Sevlus was assigned an apartment near the Jewish community center. We walked there with all our packages. It was a large apartment with a number of rooms. The girls—myself and two others—took the small room, and the six boys took the larger room. The two other rooms were already taken.

I got into bed and did not want to get up, to eat or walk around the city. I did not ask for a thing. I only wanted to be left alone. I lay this way for a number of days, and nothing interested me. It was with great difficulty that Eva Wertzberger dragged me out of bed on Friday evening. I showered and went with the group to the nearby shul. During the davening, I could not help but think of Shabbos with Mama: I envisioned Mama's candlesticks on her emboidered tablecloth and her *Kabbalas Shabbos*, and I started to cry. It was the first time I cried since I parted from Chungarabi and Eshto, but I muffled my sobs because there were other women and girls in shul and I was embarrassed. Why was I the only one crying? I didn't go through the tortures that they did! The stories I had heard in the Wertzberger household were so horrible; they were beyond human comprehension. Despite it all, they weren't crying. Yet I who had hid in a warm, protected place with food to eat and people who loved me — I was the one to cry.

Afterwards we sat at a respectable Shabbos table, sang Shabbos songs, told stories from the distant past. Only I could not put on the same brave face as the others. They tried with all their strength to overcome their gaping losses, to recover—to continue to live. Only I, who had not endured the torments they had undergone, was lying in bed surrounded by despair and guilt. On Shabbos I did try very hard to sit with everyone around the table, to act normally like a human being. But it was so very difficult that I soon stopped making the attempt.

On Monday, Mathili Rosental decided she had had enough of this behavior. She simply started to shout at me with terrible screams to get out of bed. Her behavior so alarmed me that I jumped up.

Her tactic worked. I decided that I would not allow the depression to whip me. Mathili was right; despair meant that we were allowing the Satan to win. We must recover and continue to live, to create life and especially Jewish life. Only thus could we show the entire world that stood aside when Jews were murdered, that "Netzach Yisrael lo yishaker." Hashem promised that He will never forsake us. We must show the entire world that Am Yisrael still lives, and will endure forever. No one can wipe all of us off the face of the earth. We, the weak Jews, the few of us who survived—we will outlast them!

Mathili continued talking to me earnestly. "Don't you see, Leichu, that all your 'what if' thoughts — what if I hadn't gone with the gypsies, what if I had remained with Mama 'to help her in her most difficult hours'—all those doubts that gnaw at you are thoughts of *kefirah*, of heresy — you are denying the goodness of *Hashem Yisbarach*!" She stopped to take a breath. "He was the one Who pulled the strings, don't you see? You must believe with *emunah sheleimah*, that every-thing that happened is Hashem's will. Yes, it hurts—it hurts us all very, very much, Leichu. But this is the Godly plan, and we must accept it — even though we don't understand, even though it is very, very hard for us—it was all done for our good, somehow. We must not, *chalilah*, harbor anger. It is not up to us to teach our Creator how to manage the world that He created!"

Mathili's words encouraged me very much. I got dressed, and the three of us — Mathili, Eva and myself—went to walk around the streets of Budapest.

I knew exactly where I was headed as my feet took me to the place in which I had spent my childhood years. We reached Flower Street, and here was our house—why, it looked the same! Eva and Mathili agreed to escort me inside. We walked up the stairs and Eva knocked on the door.

It was Mrs. Kantzuk, the doorman's wife, who opened the door. I trembled to see that face, so unpleasantly familiar to me from my childhood. She didn't see me at first because my two friends stood in front to hide me, but I saw behind her that the whole apartment had not changed. She turned to the girls to ask what they wanted. "We want to see Mrs. Feldman's home," they said coolly. Mrs. Kantzuk started to scream, "What Mrs. Feldman? Who is Mrs. Feldman? This is my home!"

At this point, I pushed Eva and Mathili aside and stood in front of the traitorous Mrs. Kantzuk.

"Mrs. Kantzuk, don't you remember me? I am Leichu Feldman!"

The woman looked at me, turned white and swayed in her

place as if she was about to fall, then started to shout even louder, "Leichu, Leichu — what are you talking about? I don't know anyone by that name. Get out of here right now!"

My displeasure turned to rage. I moved even closer to Mrs. Kantzuk and shouted in her face, "Mrs. Kantzuk, you thieving woman who stole from my parents' home when I was a child — you've taken possession of their home now?!" I couldn't help myself from screaming all sorts of things that I am embarrassed to remember. She tried to close the door in my face but the three of us stood firm and she wasn't able to push us out of the way. Then I tried to enter the house but Mrs. Kantzuk blocked my way. I realized that I couldn't overpower her, so I turned to the two girls. "Let's leave and call all the young men. We'll come together, and then she'll see." We walked out of there with pride, our heads held high.

After we walked down the steps, I looked back into the Kantzuks' apartment on the ground floor. It was empty, dark and neglected. The Kantzuks had taken over our lovely home, and the import of that sunk in at last: Apa and Anya were no longer alive.

We returned to our apartment. After we went inside, I burst into tears. I couldn't stop crying that entire day and night. It was a nightmare.

Two mothers brought me up with great love. Each one had lost me at a different point in time, each one fought to keep me with her, to return me to her. Both of them acted out of love for me.

I had loved both of them, and lost both of them. And now, I was orphaned of them both.

ॐ   ॐ   ॐ

Someone offered me work in a sewing shop, but even that didn't tempt me. I just had no desire to do anything, and returned to the depression and hopelessness I had felt just days before. My devoted friends tried, again, to pull me out of the black cloud by shouting at me that I simply must "pull myself together." "Don't let yourself sink into apathy and depression!" they urged. I tried, but did not succeed.

One day, one of the young men knocked on our door with a message for me. He had run all the way to tell me something important, and arrived short of breath and in a big rush. "I was just at the building of the Jewish council," he said excitedly, "and two girls found your name on one of the lists on the wall. Leichu, they were very excited—they are looking for you!"

I was very surprised. Who could be looking for me? Everyone important to me had died; those I had loved, were no more. I told the young man that it must be a mistake; Leah was a very common name.

But he was adamant. "They are looking for a Leichu Fruchter who lived as a child in the Feldman household—and you know that there is only one person like that in the world." He paused to take a deep breath, and then continued forcefully: "It's you, Leichu, and you must come with me right now!"

Reluctantly I went with him to the building of the Jewish council.

Two girls were waiting at the entrance to the building. As soon as they saw me, they fell upon me with hugs and kisses. "Leichu, it really is you! Our beloved Leichu is alive!"

They were Suri and Reizy, the oldest daughters of Basya Leah, Anya's sister. *Baruch Hashem*, they told me, their whole family survived. All of them were alive — Basya Leah, her husband Aharon Dovid and all their children!

My whole body trembled. They had to literally pull me to their house, the same house I remembered, the house that they lived in from before the war. I walked with them like a zombie and asked one question in a trembling, frightened voice. "What happened to Zaidy and Bubby Shapiro?" They stopped and bowed their heads. "Bubby and Zaidy are gone," they said. "They were taken."

I, too, stopped walking. The three of us stood at the edge of Dob Street and cried.

Zaidy and Bubby Shapiro, my grandfather and grandmother. I was orphaned of them as well. Suddenly I saw Bubby's compassionate eyes looking at me and her lips were whispering, "Leichu, I love you. It doesn't matter to me whose daughter you are, or how our relationship is defined by the law. It doesn't matter to me if you are smart in school or successful in life; I love you as you are. Always remember that, Leichu."

Bubby Shapiro always said this to me, in different variations. It didn't matter if I told her that I got the highest grade in the class on a test, or if I complained to her about an argument with a friend, or even confided in her that Anya was angry at me for something. Her love for me was infinite and unconditional.

In my heart of hearts I already guessed at the truth. The few survivors were almost always young people, not older grandparents. Thus the bad news did not fall upon me as a shock. In fact, the surprise was that Basya Leah and her family survived.

I had put off the real question long enough.

"How did Anya and Apa die?" I dreaded asking this, but I had to know.

"Apa was killed in his clothing store, together with his father, Zaidy Feldman. The murderers then stole the material and robbed everything they could find from the store. We would only realize later on that Apa and Zaidy Feldman were the lucky ones: They were *zocheh* to be buried as Jews.

"Bubby Feldman died the day after she got up from sitting *shivah* for her husband and son.

"Anya went to live with her parents, Zaidy and Bubby Shapiro, after her husband was killed. She was taken with them to Auschwitz."

My sobs just burst from my throat, and Suri and Reizy joined me. That's how the three of us stood on the street: holding each other's hands, and crying. All the people who passed us by on Dob Street, the Jewish street, were all Jews. No one was surprised by our weeping. In those troubled times, it was the most natural thing to do.

❧ 73 ❧
Together with Family
[BUDAPEST]

BASYA LEAH WAS overjoyed to see me. They all survived, their whole family remained intact! That was a very rare thing. At first I thought that this was the only family in Budapest in which everyone survived, but they told me that there were others.

After Zaidy and Bubby Shapiro were taken, one of the policemen who was an acquaintance of Aharon Dovid Shapiro whispered to them that they were next on the list, and urged them to run away. They took him up on his suggestion, and escaped to a place nicknamed "The Glass House" — a Swiss-protected house that housed offices of the unofficial Swiss embassy in Budapest. This was the largest of the buildings under protection of the Swiss Legation; it housed over three thousand Jews. Artur Weiss, a Jewish man, owned the building and the entire surrounding premises. The building was called the Glass House because it belonged to a glass factory.

Although the site was large, it was not meant to house three thousand people and thus was very crowded; there was barely room to move. There were great logistical problems involved in housing such a large number of people: feeding and clothing them, as well as providing bathroom and bathing facilities. However, with great effort and much goodwill, they were able to cope with the challenge. During the time they spent there they established a bakery and Artur Weiss, who had his own connections, managed to provide them with bread. So they had, at least, enough bread, and water from a well in the area.

The weeks dragged by slowly, each day and its difficulties. The different groups of Jews had different customs and behaviors which necessitated a large measure of patience and tolerance, and not everyone had the necessary emotional stamina.

Unfortunately, Artur Weiss, who succeeded in saving three thousand people in his Glass House, was murdered. It happened when Hungarian Arrow Cross hooligans burst into the building and started to drag Jews outside. Artur Weiss ran after them into the street, shouting, "This building is under the protection of the Swiss Legation," he yelled. "This is Swiss territory, and Hungarians have no right to enter here!"

The Arrow Cross murderers grabbed Weiss and forced him onto one of the trucks they had brought, and sped away. Before they left, they threw seven hand grenades into the building. Seven people who were still hiding inside the building were killed, and the rest of the Jews—who were standing in the enormous yard, trembling with fear — were saved. Artur Weiss never returned. The rest of the three thousand people in the Glass House survived.

This was an amazing true story. Three thousand Jews hid in a glass factory, of which a few rooms just happened to be rented to the Swiss embassy, and almost everyone was spared. A true miracle!

After the war was over, the Glass House was converted

into an apartment building. A memorial plaque was erected on the building's façade, listing the names of the seven people who were killed by the grenades. The plaque also cited the rescue story of the Jews who had hidden there. I am told that the sign exists to this day, and another sign above it was added that says, "Satan has not created an appropriate retribution for avenging the spilled blood of a small child." This, of course, refers to the murder of Budapest's Jews.

Despite the wonderful news that Basya Leah's entire family was alive, I could see that all was not well—the harrowing period had left its mark. Basya Leah had aged terribly since I had last seen her and her husband Aharon Dovid had turned completely white. But the major, worrisome change was in Aharon Dovid, whose temperament had completely changed. He sat next to a table with a *sefer* and learned, but barely lifted his head to speak a few words. He was a man who had once been full of energy and joy, and now seemed a ghost of his former self who avoided any kind of communication with the world.

I couldn't understand this. Bácsi Aharon Dovid's wife and children were all alive and well; his entire family had been spared. What had happened to him?

Finally, Suri told me the story. "At one point, the Arrow Cross murderers forced all the men from the Glass House to line up on the banks of the Danube River," Suri whispered. "The Germans waited there for them, and intended to shoot all of them into the river. Luckily, people from the Red Cross showed up. After a long argument with the Germans, they ushered the men — one thousand in all — into trucks and returned them to the Glass House. It turned out that the Germans received a thousand trucks from the Swiss in exchange for "their" Jews—the Jews living in Swiss territory, so to speak. Thus they were spared. (This was not the well-known arrangement of Dr. Kastner; it was a private agreement between the embassy workers and the local German officer in the area.)

"My father was spared physically, but he became a broken shell emotionally," said Suri sadly. "When he stood with all the other men facing a machine gun aimed at them, he said *viduy* out loud with all the others. They did real *teshuvah*, as a person does before he dies. From then on—he lost his joie de vivre. Every day he sits and learns, but his vitality and spirit are gone."

Their mother Basya Leah encouraged them. "Time will heal him," she insisted. "Remember that he lost his parents, brothers and sisters and the rest of his family, his friends, and neighbors. His whole world has changed, and it is very difficult for him." But they prayed that *be'ezras Hashem*, he would recover someday.

And now the entire family was sitting and waiting for a certificate to Eretz Yisrael. "We have a good chance of receiving a certificate soon, because families have preference over singles," said Basya Leah. "Hashem has decreed that our entire family would survive, and we need only one certificate. We hope we won't have to wait long."

Aharon Dovid went to the Jewish Council building and added my name to the list of his own children. "Leah is our niece, the daughter of my wife's sister," he explained. "We have adopted her as our own daughter." The Council people were ordinarily strict—not because they were hard-hearted, but because of constraints—but this time, they did not object. They simply added my name to the other family members, and repeated their promise: The certificates would arrive soon, no need to worry. A family with seven children, now eight, would receive certificates much faster than singles.

After I had become reunited with my long-lost Budapest

cousins, they wouldn't let me leave them to return to the apartment I shared with other survivors from Sevlus. Suri and Reizy walked over with me to help carry my belongings, and I moved in with them. This was a very good thing for me, to become part of a family again. I felt that I belonged, and this was my cure. The despair and depression dissipated and, *Baruch Hashem*, I returned to myself—to being Leichu.

The pain of my loss remained with me, and will remain with me forever; but I learned how to live with the pain. I learned to live without parents and grandparents during times of *simchah* as well as times of trouble, when the ache of the loss grows sevenfold. Yes, I learned to live without a mother.

I, Leichu Feldman-Fruchter who was raised by two mothers, felt doubly orphaned. Yet I merited a dear aunt and uncle, who were true family. My cousins and their families were like brothers and sisters in every way. Until this very day, they welcome me, my husband and our children as family. I pray that *HaKadosh Baruch Hu* grant them all the best, that they will be *zocheh* to see true Jewish *nachas* from their progeny. It is hard to appreciate the extent of the miracle for me: I found that I was not alone in the world, as I had thought. I had a warm, supportive family—and that, for me, was everything.

Basya Leah's family was in difficult financial straits. Now I knew how I could help them: I accepted a job in a small sewing factory to help support the family. This was the same work I had turned down earlier, out of despair and hopelessness, but now I belonged and was part of a family and was able to accept responsibility on myself. I presented myself as an expert sewer of shirts, in light of my experience in sewing shirts in my mother's house in Sevlus—those shirts that Eshto the gypsy brought me.

Every day, I worked on a sewing machine from early morning until the late night hours. I sewed and sewed, and enjoyed each and every day. At first I sewed only shirts, but as time went on I learned to sew dresses and other women's clothing, according to need and demand.

Luckily, the head cutter in the sewing workshop liked me. She showed me how to adjust clothing to fit, how to prepare a pattern and all the little tips of the trade that ensure professional sewing results.

During that time period, I remained in close contact with my group from Sevlus. On my way home from work, I would step into their apartment and spend some time with my friends. It was good for me to have family as well as friends, and I well appreciated my good fortune.

I was finally able to face the future.

✤ 74 ✤

Oceans of Tears

[BUDAPEST]

ONE DAY, I received a message from the Jewish Council that they had received a sewing machine addressed to me. I had no idea what they were talking about, but when I went over to see it I was amazed. The machine looked remarkably like the one that Apa had bought for me so many years ago; it had the same decorations, even the same grooves and notches I had made with a needle when I was still struggling to sew a straight line as a young girl. I was delighted to see my old sewing machine! But how it had mysteriously appeared was a mystery to me.

After a few days, I received an explanation. It turns out that the fellows who had come with me from Sevlus to Budapest, heard from Eva and Mathili about the Mrs. Kantzuk story and how she had taken over my parents' house. So a group of young men went together and expelled the people who had taken over Apa and Anya's home (including the Kantzuks), and settled in their stead a rabbinical family from Rakospalotai, a suburb near Budapest. The family had survived by hiding in the cowshed of *goyim* who protected them, real Righteous Gentiles. So it was only fitting that they be the ones to reside in Apa and Anya's home now.

The fellows from Sevlus knew that I liked to sew and had heard stories about my sewing machine from Budapest. So they decided to surprise me and bring me my old sewing machine, which was still in the Feldman home. In order to doubly surprise me, they sent the machine to me via the Jewish Council.

My beloved sewing machine, such an integral part of my childhood, had returned to my possession. Out of all the clothes and toys that the Feldmans pampered me with in Budapest, that machine was the only possession I had truly missed in Sevlus. I thought I'd never see it again, and here it was! I was truly grateful.

I still own that sewing machine to this very day. It doesn't look exactly the same now because I removed the wooden housing before we left to Eretz Yisrael and only took the machine itself. Then here, in Israel, I installed a new cabinet for it, though without the lovely decorations. But inside is the sewing machine of my youth.

I don't use it anymore, of course; today I have an electric, state-of-the-art-machine. Nowadays, no one turns a wheel with their feet in order to power the machine, as we did in those days. But the sewing machine of my childhood, that served me well for so many years, is the apple of my eye. I guard and preserve it, and I will always love it more than the most modern and efficient of machines. Yes—it is the only trace I have of Apa and Anya.

As soon as I received my machine back, I left the sewing factory and set myself up as an independent seamstress. I advertised myself mainly in Buda, where the wealthier people lived, and it was not long before I developed a very good reputation as a high-quality seamstress. Respectable women flocked to me to sew dresses and suits for them, and I made a very nice living. Thus I was able to support Basya Leah's entire family, and their financial difficulties eased. I was truly grateful to be able to assist the wonderful family that had done so much for me.

Suri and Reizy, even little Shifra'le, worked with me and assisted me in my sewing. We sat together in the room set aside for us, sewing and singing, stitching and laughing. We made a pact not to allow sadness, depression and despair to enter the walls of our sewing room. We were young and energetic, and forced ourselves to resume the joy of our youth.

But at night I allowed myself to cry. I would visualize the image of my mother, her words of sage advice and wise counsel, and her many stories about overcoming her disability. I also visualized Sevlus as it had looked before the war: a district town teeming with precious Jewish life. Apa and Anya's images also arose, as well as Zaidy and Bubby Shapiro. Only at night, when I was alone in my bed, I allowed myself to mourn the past, the people I had loved, and everything I had lost. But I did not allow myself to fall into despair — among the tears I shed at night, I cried and prayed to Hashem to bless my future.

The truth is that we wanted to leave Budapest and Hungary as soon as we could and were eager to begin new lives in Eretz Yisrael. We used to talk a lot about the certificates that we needed to enter Palestine. Periodically we would go to Dob Street and investigate the delay in the arrival of the certificates; the Council people promised, again and again, that they were on their way. Soon, soon, be patient! they'd say. Then a few weeks would pass and the story would repeat itself: another vist to Dob Street, and more promises. It wasn't their fault — the British still limited Jewish immigration to Palestine, even though there were tens of thousands of survivors of the camps who wanted leave Europe and go to

Eretz Yisrael. But the British authorities only allowed a small number of certificates, so the Jews in the Council had their hands tied. Many survivors remained in Europe after the war, eager to leave the blood-stained continent but with nowhere to go.

We spoke a lot about Eretz Yisrael. We knew that there were a lot of non-observant Jews there, especially in a city called Tel Aviv. We knew about the kibbutzim of HaShomer HaTzair, where religion was trampled on and violated in public view. I told them about Haifa as well. That was a lovely city in which Bácsi Nachman Klar had found work and could have supported his family well, but he left because he worried about his children's *chinuch* in such a secular city. There, in Haifa, Shabbos was publicly desecrated. So they left Haifa and moved to *Yerushalayim Ir HaKodesh.*

For me, Yerushalayim had a very special place in my heart because I knew that the Klars lived there, somewhere. I knew from them that even in Yerushalayim not everyone was *shomrei mitzvos*, and in Tel Aviv there were religious Jews too. But it seemed that Yerushalayim had large neighborhoods where only God-fearing Jews lived.

In my mind's eye I could see the old Klar house in Sevlus: the small home with the unique woven fence. I visualized the children of the family playing in the yard, just as I remembered them. Somehow I didn't take into account the fact that many years had passed since I had last seen them. Time seemed to have stood still for me when it came to the Klars: Children grow up and change, and even Dovid'l—the child I had loved so much, who was named after my father—was no longer a small child.

Rosh Hashanah arrived, and we were still in *galus*, still waiting. Day followed day and our lives were on hold. Nothing changed except for the impatience that gripped us and wouldn't let us live ordinary lives — especially not on Yom Tov.

On Rosh Hashanah, the shul was full to capacity. Even the women's section was so crowded that there was no room to move. Although most of the city's Jews were no longer among the living, only a few of the pre-war shuls in Budapest still existed; most had been desecrated and destroyed by the Nazis. Almost all of those Jews who had survived, came to shul that Rosh Hashanah — including those who were not mitzvah-observant. Everyone cried, everyone said *Kaddish Yasom* (Kaddish for deceased family members). In the entire giant, packed *Beis Knesses*, there was almost no one who didn't have to say *Kaddish*.

During shofar blowing, the cries soared though the roof. It was a truly awesome scene, full of majesty and splendor. Anyone who participated would never forget it.

In the afternoon we went to the Danube River for *Tashlich*. About a hundred Jews congregated near the river, and one woman screamed, "How can we cast our sins into the Danube? Our family members and friends were shot into this river, and the Danube churns with Jewish blood!"

I remembered *Tashlich* from my childhood years, when most of Budapest's Jews, about four hundred thousand, would stream from all over the city to say the *Tashlich* prayer. I remember how both banks of the river, all along the river's length, were packed with Jews. I was not the only one to reminisce; one look at the faces of the people around me, showed me that many were making painful mental comparisons with the joyful *Yamim Tovim* of the past.

One of the *rabbanim* got up and spoke. I will never forget what he said. He mentioned the *Tashlich* prayers from before the war, and added, "All the *kedoshim* who have been murdered, are with us now in spirit. We must gather our strength; we must rebuild our lives; we must re-establish *Beis Yisrael*—this is the way we avenge our oppressors. This is the only way to defeat the accursed ones—by re-establishing everything that they tried to destroy. Every one of us who has survived is an emissary of the Jewish People, to spread our message through *Beis Yisrael. HaKadosh Baruch Hu* punished us because we abandoned the Torah's path of life, and went to drink from foreign wells. And now we must do *teshuvah*, we must return to the path of Torah, of life, and rebuild our lives again."

I remember how the *rav* spoke at length in front of the crowd that congregated there, on the banks of the Danube River. His words on that Rosh Hashanah came straight from the heart, accompanied by tears streaming from his eyes, and everyone who heard took upon himself to do as the *rav* instructed us: to vanquish Amalek and his henchmen by rebuilding *Beis Yisrael.*

If Rosh Hashanah roused so much emotion in us, then Yom Kippur that followed was seven times full of awe and majesty. If there had been a few Jews who did not come to shul on Rosh Hashanah or say *Tashlich* with the rest of Budapest's Jews, then they heard from others about the *tefillah* and the *rav*'s speech. In short, when Yom Kippur arrived, all the Jews flocked as one person to the shuls of Budapest.

The large Taback shul had been desecrated but the evil ones had not opened the *aron kodesh* and had not touched the *sifrei Torah*—a true miracle. These *sifrei Torah* had remained intact, and now were distributed among all the shuls in the city. Many apartments were transformed into temporary shuls for Yom Kippur, and these smaller *minyanim* also received *sifrei Torah.*

Another place in which some *sifrei Torah* were saved was Aui Pest, a small village near Budapest. Before the shul was destroyed, a priest by the name of Matthias hid these precious scrolls in his house that was inside a church. In fact, in addition to the *sifrei Torah* Matthias saved, he managed to hide the *paroches* and the shul's other religious articles in a room he set aside for this purpose. It was also in this room — the room of the "Jewish books" as he called them—that Matthias hid the shul's *gabbai*, Mr. Yehuda Leib Klein, his wife Martha and their children. Matthias took care of all their needs, and no one dreamed of searching for Jews in the home of a priest. Thus an entire family was saved.

∞∞∞

There were, indeed, a few gentiles who saved Jews. Though these were a small minority of isolated individuals—we must show our gratitude. They risked their lives to do so and even if they acted out of greed for money, they did a great deed. May Hashem remember them for blessing.

After Hungary was liberated from the Communist yoke—about forty-five years after the end of the war — the Klein family brought the aged Priest Matthias to Eretz Yisrael. They planted a tree in his honor on the Righteous Gentile Boulevard in Yad Vashem in Jerusalem, and hosted him with great respect. Even the Chief Rabbi of Israel met him and thanked him in the name of the Jewish people. The priest explained that the sifrei Torah he saved were taken to Eretz Yisrael after the war, and distributed among various shuls.

Matthias, who was an old man when he came to Israel, said that all the risks he took on himself were worth the chance to come visit the holy land. He said that all his prayers after the war were for the re-establishment of the Jewish People, for peace in Israel and between the Jewish nation and the nations of the world. Then he spoke of his great shame regarding the acts of Christians in Europe during the war.

∞∞∞

The *tefillos* of Yom Kippur in all the shuls—as we heard from friends afterwards — were accompanied by terrible crying

and weeping. The Yizkor prayer in our shul was especially accompanied by rivers of tears.

I remembered how as a child in Budapest, I would go outside during the Yizkor service together with most of the congregation. Anyone whose parents were alive always left the shul during the Yizkor *tefillah*. When I came to Sevlus, I found out that I was orphaned from a father whom I never had the privilege to meet. It was then that I started to say Yizkor for my father, but the truth is that I never cried during Yizkor in those years, even though there were many women around me who did. I suppose that's because I had never known my father.

For the first time, in that first post-war Yizkor, each one of us had a long list of loved ones to cite in the Yizkor prayer. And for the first time, I cried together with the orphans, widows, widowers and other bereaved souls who survived the Nazi oppressors. It was a cry that rent the very heavens.

Three weeks after Sukkos, we finally received the long-awaited certificate. I had worried until the very end that perhaps my name would not be included. But with Hashem's help, I was, indeed, listed as a daughter and not a niece.

❧ 75 ❧
Farewell, Traitorous Homeland
[BUDAPEST/ERETZ YISRAEL]

WHEN BASYA LEAH and her family returned from the Glass House, they found their home exactly as they had left it. It was a miracle that no one had broken into it and plundered it, as had happened to the home of Zaidy and Bubby Shapiro who lived right next door — and most of the homes of the other Jews. Perhaps it was because it was a back apartment so no one noticed it despite its size. In any case, nothing was robbed. And now, ironically, that led to another problem—they had to decide what to pack with them and what to leave behind.

I had my large rucksack, my smaller bag and my beloved sewing machine to take. Safely wrapped up in my rucksack were Mama's precious brass candlesticks and my cherished *sefarim*—my siddur and *Tehillim*, Mama's *Tzena U'Rena* and *machzorim*. That was all I owned, and all I needed to start my new life in Eretz Yisrael. These took up my entire weight quota, though, so I couldn't help Basya Leah's family.

There were a lot of arguments and agonized discussions about what to take. Basya Leah cried about all the things that they didn't have room for, until Bácsi Aharon Dovid said he was almost sorry that their possessions hadn't been stolen from them, as had happened to the others! Finally, they divided up their things so that each family member had a large pack on their back and a suitcase to carry in their hands. The parents took two large suitcases each, and Suri and Reizy carried especially giant packs.

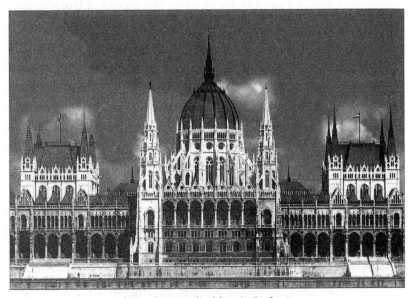

The Parliament building in Budapest

Mr. Arzo Wilhelm bought their house from them for a ridiculously low price and in return he promised to ship them their possessions and furniture that they prepared, as soon as they were settled in their new home. Then the family would inform him of their exact address, and he would ship the boxes. But, unfortunately, these were false promises and the crates with the belongings never arrived. I was secretly happy that I hadn't given in to the temptation to leave behind my sewing machine with the rest of the family's furniture. Instead, I had removed the machine from its heavy wooden housing so that I could take it with me, and that proved to be a very wise decision. The wooden housing never arrived, just as the rest of the furniture never materialized either, despite Mr. Wilhelm's promises.

Before leaving Hungary, we decided to take one more stroll around the streets of Budapest. We walked slowly and headed toward Parliament Square. We gazed at the statues of Kossuth and Rákóczi in Kossuth Square and the magnificent Parliament building. We walked past the ornate benches, and continued for hours along Budapest's main streets until we reached the passageway decorated with the giant arch. We stopped under the arch and reminisced about the stories our teachers had told us about Budapest—the most beautiful city in the world. We crossed the Chain Bridge in the direction of the palace at the top of the mountain, which looked as if it was taken straight out of a magical fairy-tale book. Next to the palace rose the Fisherman's Bastion and lookout terrace on Gellert Hill, and next to that—was the giant Matthias Church — where the *sifrei Torah* and the *gabbai*'s family had been hidden by the righteous Matthias.

We walked quietly without speaking, just contemplating the beauty surrounding us.

We reached Vorosmarty Square. A large portion of the stores there had belonged to Jews who were murdered, and they remained empty and ruined now because they had been plundered during the war. Wealthy women from this street, and the neighboring streets, came to my house to order dresses. If only Bubby Feldman and Anya could see how well I'd learned to sew, even they would want to use my services, I thought.

We returned to Pest via Elizabeth Gate. We walked from street to street until we reached Zaidy Feldman and Apa's material store. The store was in shambles and emptied of ev-

erything; the murderers killed Zaidy and Apa in this place and then stole everything they could. Even the large wooden table and shelves had been plundered by people who used the wood to heat their homes. We glanced into the store, and I ran out immediately. I didn't want to continue to walk toward the house of Bubby Feldman, who had died one day after she got up from *shivah* for her husband and son.

We turned to take a different route home. We walked even more slowly than before, each of us deep in her own thoughts and emotions. We did not speak.

The next day, we left Budapest, then Hungary. Farewell, homeland. Farewell to you, the disloyal homeland that betrayed my people.

In you I was born and grew up. You were my father and mother's homeland, and had been home to many generations of Jews. They loved you, Hungary, they built you; they knew your history, and were familiar with the songs of your poets and singers who lauded your beauty. They narrated the stories of your wars, they identified with your pain and were happy with your joys.

But you, Hungary my homeland, you betrayed us, your Jews. The Germans alone could never have killed the hundreds of thousands of Jews in Hungary, without the willing aid of the Hungarian citizens themselves. There were many who volunteered happily to join the Arrow Cross Fascists, the right hand of the Nazis who shot the Jews into the Danube and packed the Jews into cattle cars to Auschwitz. Then there were the others who collaborated willingly, who informed on Jews in hiding, who persecuted their former neighbors and friends and even killed them with their own hands.

Cursed be you all, murderers of the Jewish People. Hungary, your land and your river are red with the blood of the unfortunate victims. Earth, cover not their blood!

Farewell, traitorous homeland, forever. I will never return here.

～   ～   ～

We traveled to Rumania in a large truck together with the Shimons, a large family, who also accompanied us on the same ship to Eretz Yisrael. At the beginning of the war the father and his two brothers were killed, but the rest of the family hid in a large bunker they had dug under their home in their village. Their gardener had worked for them his whole life, and in their time of need he took care of them and supplied all their needs.

After the war they moved to the city of Mishkoltz, close to their village. But there were many anti-Semites in the city and they felt so threatened that they fled to Budapest. They had a married daughter in Eretz Yisrael who promised to arrange for certificates for them, and they wanted to leave the country as soon as they could.

It turned out that the Shimons were correct in their suspicions of Mishkoltz, and they were wise to leave when they did. A year after the war there was a pogrom in the city. The gentiles pulled the Jews out of their homes, tied them to wagons and sent the horses to gallop on the road until the Jews died. Those who did not die in their agony were murdered in cold blood. It was a miracle that the Shimon family managed to leave that evil city in time.

We waited about another two weeks in Rumania until the Pamia ship arrived. It was a small boat full of Jews who were eager to immigrate to Eretz Yisrael. Our family was assigned a large cabin.

Our ocean voyage was in the winter, with strong winds and a stormy sea. Our seagoing trip was difficult as we all got sick and seasick in the shaking, jiggly boat. But we comforted ourselves: It was going to be worth it, we said—we were on our way to Eretz Yisrael!

After a week, on 18 Kislev 5706/ November 23, 1945 we reached the Haifa port. We all stood on the deck of the ship, watching as the mountain opposite us slowly emerged from the water. Suddenly, the entire city of Haifa appeared opposite our very eyes. In the center of the mountain, on its incline, shined a large gold dome, and the entire mountain was covered with trees. From between the trees peered many houses below us, all of them white.

As we slowly approached the bay, we noticed a number of boats anchored there. I stood on the deck and cried. Around me, everyone else was crying too as we were overwhelmed with emotion to see the Promised Land, at last.

The ship entered the bay. The waters were blue, and relaxed—not the angry blue-green they had been during the past week of sailing when the fierce waves sprayed their salty droplets all over the people standing on the deck. Now we could stand quietly on deck as the ship slowly docked. During our week-long journey, we had to climb up to the deck occasionally in order to breathe fresh air and refresh ourselves. While we stood on the deck, we had to hold onto the ropes with all our strength; the boat rocked so dangerously. Even when we sat on the floor, we grasped the ropes to avoid sliding from side to side. But now, our small boat glided quietly and gracefully, as if it hadn't been lurching from side to side like a drunken *goy* on holiday, the entire week!

Proud and silent was our boat when it glided into the place reserved for it in the port, with its mast erect. All of us on the ship, though, were crying from excitement and overwhelming emotion. We had arrived at Eretz Yisrael, our very own land.

The passengers lined up impatiently, eager to disembark.

We had to wait though, until they finally connected a long wooden ramp from the ship to the dock. Finally, it was our family's turn. We walked slowly, each of us holding onto his or her packages, trying to be careful not to fall or lose our grip on our luggage. We kept an eye out on those ahead of us on the gangplank and those behind us, to make sure that everyone else was okay. We advanced slowly, until finally, the whole family gathered below and then we walked together toward a pavilion on the shore.

As soon as we reached the sandy shore, we bent down and kneeled—all of us, survivors who had reached the Holy Land—and kissed the sand. This was the land of *Eretz Ha-Kodesh*, Eretz Yisrael.

❧ 76 ❧
Welcome Home!
[ERETZ YISRAEL]

W

E WERE SENT to a transit camp called Sha'ar HaAliya. I don't even remember how much time we spent there because the days and weeks passed as if in a dream; we were finally in Eretz Yisrael! However, we insisted that we wanted to live in Yerushalayim, and it was not long before we left Sha'ar HaAliya. During the entire trip to Yerushalayim, Bácsi Aharon Dovid talked about the *kedushah* of Yerushalayim, about our great *zechus* to live in Eretz Yisrael, in Yerushalayim.

The aliya representatives took us to what they told us would be our new home. First we had to descend a very long staircase of broken steps that led from the road to a large courtyard, and in the center of that yard was an ancient, dilapidated and tiny house. There was only one room in the house, and the bathrooms were outside. In the entrance to the house was a tiny, dark corridor without a window. That was the "kitchen."

They told us that we were in a neighborhood called Romema Elite. Bácsi Aharon Dovid was so happy that he started to sing from Hallel: "*Yemin Hashem romema, yemin Hashem osah chayil.* How fortunate we are that we merited living in Yerushalayim!"

But he was the only one who felt fortunate. This was not a house that could gladden our hearts, that was for sure. Aharon Dovid scolded us, "Don't pay attention to the dilapidated status of the house, it's not important at all what it looks like. We'll clean it and fix it up, you'll see. The important thing is that we are in Eretz Yisrael."

The house was in terrible shape. The floor was uneven, bumpy concrete; the roof leaked; the yard and street were full of mud and every foray out of our one room to the outside world was a muddy and difficult experience.

Of course, we were happy that we finally arrived in Eretz Yisrael, to *Yerushalayim Ir HaKodesh.* But the physical conditions and crowding were terrible. It looked like the place had previously served as a goats' pen — it was not really habitable for human beings. I was very worried. I knew that when people live in unsuitable conditions and are too crowded together, there is no way to prevent arguments and friction. We didn't even have enough room for the ramshackle beds they gave us.

I loved my aunt, uncle and cousins and they loved me very much as well. But I wasn't really a member of their immediate family, and my presence made it even more crowded for them. It wasn't fair to them, I decided; I would try to find another place to live as soon as I could.

After a few rainy days, during which we tried with all our strength to impart a more human touch to the terrible dwelling, the sun finally shined. The sky was blue and everything around was blooming. That's when I decided I would go in search of the Klar family. I knew they lived in Yerushalayim and although I didn't have their address, I was determined to look for them come what may. I didn't know Hebrew yet at the time and found only one neighbor who spoke Yiddish.

"There is one very religious neighborhood in Yerushalay-im," he said. "It's called Meah Shearim. I will explain to you how to get there."

I followed his directions, but I walked slowly. I wanted to take in the view on the way, to absorb everything. I realized that this was the first time since our aliya that I had a chance to take in the sights. Around me, all the people were speaking Hebrew. It wasn't the *lashon ha-kadosh* that I was familiar with from the Torah and davening. The *lashon ha-kadosh* was the language we used to speak to Hashem, while on the street people were talking the everyday, spoken language of Hebrew. The truth is, that was what they had told us from the day we arrived and now that I was walking around alone on the street, I saw that it was true. I made up my mind to learn the "new" language.

I tried to ask passersby how to get to Meah Shearim. I only approached people who looked like they might understand Yiddish and they were all very kind. I received very detailed directions, but somehow I walked for a long time and then found myself right back where I started.

At this point, I was slightly dispirited, but then I saw a little girl who seemed to have popped up straight out of Sevlus. Her two braids were braided with a blue ribbon that matched her blue checked dress. And it turned out that she did speak Yiddish. She looked up, smiled at me, gave me her hand and started to lead me to Meah Shearim. I asked her where she lived, and the adorable child told me, "I live in *'Ungarische Heizer'* — Batei Ungarin." This excited me: to think that here, in Eretz Yisrael, in Yerushalayim was a place where Hungarians lived, and there even was a neighborhood named after them!

The little girl brought me to Meah Shearim. It looked to

me like a kind of fortress-neighborhood, houses built in a sort of circle, and inside, a large courtyard. A large building stood in the middle of the courtyard. "This is the central shul and the yeshivah," the little girl explained to me, "but there are many other *shteiblach* too." Suddenly she realized that she had to go home before her mother would worry, and left.

I stood on the stone-paved street and looked around me. I didn't recognize any of the passersby, and I didn't know how to proceed. Then the men started to leave the shuls after Minchah, and I decided that I would look for Bácsi Klar or one of his sons.

Almost immediately I saw the familiar tall, erect form of a man hurrying out of one of the *shteiblach*. He was a bit far from where I was standing and I couldn't see his face, but I was sure it was him: Bácsi Nachman Klar, whom I hadn't seen for so many years. It was a miracle!

He was walking very quickly — I had never seen Bácsi Nachman walk slowly. I couldn't catch up with him, but I was determined not to lose him. I saw him turn into a building and I followed him. I found myself in a long hallway, but by now, Bácsi Nachman was nowhere to be seen. At the end of the hallway was a courtyard; on the right was a door to an apartment and on my left were about five steps, a door to another apartment and more steps going up. I looked around me and noticed that the banister of the five steps was made out of thick, strong wood. Why, this was the very kind of railing that Bácsi Nachman would make himself! My mind made up, I walked up the five steps next to the wooden banister, and knocked on the door of the apartment. I was trembling.

The unfamiliar face of a young woman opened the door. She looked at me, and started shouting, "Fruchter! Sheina Ruchel Fruchter!" Then an older woman entered the room — Néni Rivka Klar. My heart was ready to burst from happiness.

After all these years! She grabbed me and hugged me, and wouldn't let me go. We stood there, hugging each other, for a long time. Finally, she loosened her grip though she didn't let me go completely. She stood back to look at me, examine me while still holding my arms, and kissed me again.

The young woman who had opened the door, stood next to us and followed this scene with amazement. Néni Rivka and I had not said a single word, though tears ran down our cheeks and our hearts were full of joy. We simply could not utter a word from the intensity of our emotions.

Finally, Néni Rivka wiped her tears and turned to the young woman. "This is Leichu, Sheina Ruchel Fruchter's daughter." Her eyes filled again with tears of happiness.

"The one who was kidnapped?" the young woman asked immediately. I smiled.

Néni Rivka introduced her to me. "This is Basya Shimonovitz, the daughter of my good friend Zelda, *a"h*. Do you remember her?" I nodded.

Basya told me how much she had been impressed by my mother, from the efforts she had made to find me and return her stolen daughter. "All of us—all the Jews in Sevlus— admired her for it," she said.

My heart warmed to hear her speak of my mother, and I remembered how all the townspeople had praised my mother when I first came to live with her. That was so long ago. How I wished that my

Basya Eisenman (Shimonovitz), who opened the door for me in the home of the Klar family in Yerushalayim.

dear Mama could be here with me, in Néni Klar's kitchen!

I wanted to reciprocate with some kind words to Basya when I realized that I had something wonderful to tell her.

"I have good news for you," I said. "I have regards to you from your brother, Srul Ber, who is on his way to Eretz Yisrael. He was the first person I met, when I went back to Sevlus after the war. He is waiting for a certificate to come, but he'll be here — with or without the certificate!"

Basya burst into shouts of joy. "My brother! Srul Ber is alive—someone from my family is alive! Thank you, thank you so much for this wonderful news!" She kissed Néni Klar and me and then raced to tell her husband the wonderful news.

Néni Rivka hugged me with one hand while she led me into an inner room with the other hand. Bácsi Nachman Klar sat there, drinking his tea. "Look who has finally returned to us!" Rivka proclaimed.

Bácsi Nachman looked at me, rose and said the words I will never forget, "*Mein teyere kind*, my dear child, welcome home."

Néni Rivka pointed to one of the beds in the room and said, "There is enough room for you, too, in this bed, Leichu..."

I had arrived home at last.

Conclusion

TODAY, BARUCH HASHEM, I am married with six children: three sons and three daughters. Each of them is married with a large, beautiful family of their own, and I am a proud grandmother.

Until this very day I love to sew on my sewing machine. Of course, my daughters, daughters-in-law and granddaughters all proudly wear the clothing I joyously sew for them.

I tried to raise my children in the *derech* I learned from Mama and Anya. To this day, I am happy and content with every little thing I have. When I hear complaints from people about things they lack—a piece of furniture, a new dress for a *simchah* or an appliance—I am reminded of my home in Budapest, where I had everything; and my home in Sevlus, where I had only basic necessities. I also recall the cave, living under the most primitive conditions; while in comparison to the situation of the rest of the Jews at the time, it was the lap of luxury.

Each person and his needs, each person and his concept of what he must have. But I, my husband and children are happy with what we have and say the *berachah* every day with great *kavanah*, "*She'asah li kol tzorchi*"— He Who has fulfilled all my needs.

I lived in one of the most beautiful cities in the world — Budapest. In our house we had running water, electricity— special things for that time period — as well as all sorts of luxuries. I also lived in Sevlus, a relatively primitive district town where we drew water from the well with a pump and carried home heavy pails of water. Our house was lit with a kerosene lamp, and not only that—perhaps unpleasant to say — the "bathrooms" were cesspits in an outhouse at the edge of the yard, which we shared together with all the other tenants. For a year I lived in a cave deep in the forest. We drew water from a small adjacent pool, lit a fireplace in the cave which warmed us up and also provided some light. We took a hoe with us when we had to go out into the forest for our needs; we dug pits and covered them afterwards.

I had two mothers, one father whom I knew and one father who died when I was a baby of six months old, and a gypsy who was almost like a mother to me. I was orphaned of them all.

I have endured much in my life, and I learned that we must be content and grateful for what we have. There will always be people who have more than us, even a lot more; and always people who have less than us, even a lot less. But we always have what we really need because our Creator watches out for us. If we find ourselves lacking something that we think we can't manage without, we must realize that *Hashem Yisbarach* did not provide us with it—and that means that it is not a necessity for us.

I have never returned to Hungary and I have no intentions of doing so. For what? Yes, I know that some people travel on "Back to Our Roots" trips. But not me! The people who were important to me are gone. The house in Budapest is not my house. Today Sevlus is a village in the Ukraine and its name was changed to Vinograd, but I understand that it remains the same district village with water wells and horse-drawn carriages. The house there is no longer my house, either.

Yes, I would love to have seen or heard from Chungarabi. But she and Eshto disappeared behind the Iron Curtain for many, many years, and I had no way to contact them though I did try. I always prayed that Hashem would recognize the *chesed* they did by saving my life.

The caves?—I could never find my way to them by myself, and in any case—they are not my home.

It is here, in Eretz Yisrael, that I have made my true home. It is here that I have continued the legacy of Dovid and Sheina Ruchel Fruchter, my real parents, as well as Yehudah Leib and Mina Feldman, my adoptive parents who were unable to have children of their own. In my home I am continuing the golden chain of *beis Yisrael*.

And with it, I offer my prayer—that this house will continue forever and merit greeting *Mashiach tzidkeinu*, speedily, in our times.

Postscript
Néni Leah's Breakfront

AFTER THIS BOOK was first published in Hebrew, I was flooded with telephone calls from curious readers. Most of them asked the same question: What is your relationship to the protagonist of the book, Leah-Leichu Fruchter? And I confess: Although the book is written in first person, Leah-Leichu Fruchter is no longer among the living. This book is based on facts and true stories that I heard first-hand — from Leichu, and from other characters in the book as well. After Leichu's passing, I took it upon myself to document the story of her life, as she had requested of me years earlier.

Who am I, you ask? My name is Miriam Cohen, daughter of Fanny Klar, and granddaughter of Rivka Klar, Sheina Ruchel's dearest and closest friend. When Leichu came to Eretz Yisrael after the war, she was re-united with the Klar family, as narrated in the last chapter of the book. She remained with the Klars as part of their family until she married Bácsi Chaim Hirsh about two years later. It was my Bubby Rivka and Zaidy Nachman who walked her down the aisle and escorted her to her *chuppah*, as parents do.

As an older, married woman, most people called Leichu by her given name, "Leah," and to me, she will always remain "Néni Leah." She was some years younger than my mother Fanny and was like an aunt to me; it took many years until I discovered our exact relationship. One of my earlier childhood memories is of the special glass-encased display cabinet in Bácsi Chaim Hirsh's bookcase. Actually, Néni Leah and Bácsi Chaim Hirsh had two glass-encased shelves. One proudly displayed their silver candlesticks and *becher*, kiddush cup, which they used every Shabbos. But it was the other shelf, the higher shelf that piqued my curiosity. On that shelf stood two brass candlesticks that were never used, as far as I could tell, but they always sparkled and gleamed. A neatly folded tallis rested behind the candlesticks and next to the tallis was a very peculiar black wheel — the kind they used to have in old, non-electrical sewing machines that one operates with a foot pedal.

Finally, I turned to Néni Leah one day. "What are these brass candlesticks in the display shelf?" I asked. "You never light them, yet they are always so beautifully polished — they shine like gold."

I was shocked to see a tear in Néni Leah's eye. She was always such a happy, cheerful person. "They belonged to my mother, Sheina Ruchel Fruchter, who died in the Holocaust," she said quietly.

I, like so many of my generation, was all too familiar with relatives who had perished in the Holocaust, so I understood immediately why those candlesticks must be so precious to her. But I persisted in my questions; this time, I turned to Bácsi Chaim Hirsh. "Why do you keep your tallis on a display shelf? Why don't you keep it in one of those special velvet bags that all men have?" I asked. Bácsi Chaim Hirsh and Néni Leah exchanged looks, and it was Néni Leah who responded. She removed the old tallis from the shelf and spread it out on the table.

"I don't actually know who the owner of this tallis was," she sighed as she stroked the old, faded material. "He probably is no longer among the living, Miriam. Eshto the gypsy brought it to me when we hid in the mountains during the Holocaust, and that was the first time I realized that something very terrible must have happened to the Jewish People. You see, Miriam, a Jewish man will never abandon or sell his tallis; he will be buried in it, when the time comes, if he is *zocheh* to a Jewish burial. So when I received this tallis, I knew—I knew in my heart."

It was then that I asked Néni Leah to tell me her life story, to tell me about her two "lives," with the Feldmans, her adoptive parents in Budapest; and with Sheina Ruchel Fruchter, her widowed mother in the town of Sevlus. And, of course, there was Chungarabi the gypsy washerwoman, who loved Leichu like her own daughter and persuaded her husband Eshto to allow Leichu to flee with them to the Carpathian Mountains during the Holocaust.

After I heard some of her stories, I begged Néni Leah to write a book about her life.

"Néni Leah, you absolutely must write your life story. Miraculous things have happened to you," I would say, time and again.

"No, Miriam," she'd answer. "My story is too unusual, too strange. People would talk — they'd call me a 'stolen girl,' or a gypsy; or they simply wouldn't believe that it happened at all... No, I won't write it, but after *me'ah v'esrim*, when I am no longer among the living, I want you, Miriam, to write my life story."

I laughed at the time, mainly because Néni Leah was so full of life that it seemed she would live forever. Yes, Néni Leah used to tell story after story, until I could envision myself in Budapest, sitting in young Leichu's beautiful carpeted room, admiring her elegant, enormous wardrobe. I could visualize the small grocery store in Sevlus and the tiny room with one bed that Leichu and her mother had shared, and the brass candlesticks that had lit up the tiny room like a palace on Shabbos. My Bubby Rivka and my mother also told me stories about Sevlus, Sheina Ruchel and her years of searching for her lost daughter; they helped round out the picture.

I was transfixed by Néni Leah's personality and the lovely family that she raised, three girls and three boys; theirs was a home of laughter and wellbeing, of joy and light, one that I enjoyed visiting. When Néni Leah recounted her story to me, it was with happiness and laughter, despite the difficult experiences she had undergone. She never complained or blamed anyone, she judged everyone favorably. She even forgave her father's relatives who had given her up for adoption, and had sold her as a baby for a great deal of money. "It was *Yad Hashem*, the Hand of God, which sent me to Mina and Leibu Feldman, a childless couple in Budapest," she'd say. "That's also where I became so close to Chungarabi, and was probably the reason that she saved my life later on."

Once, I made a disparaging comment about Apa, Leibu Feldman. Néni Leah did not let it pass, though.

"True, he was very pedantic and meticulous, but he felt that was the best way to raise an upright, God-fearing young daughter," she explained gently. "He and Anya loved me; they, as well as most parents of that era, believed that was the way to bring up children—to be seen and not heard. Anya especially was always buying lovely things for me: clothing, toys, anything I ever wanted or asked for. In fact, they bought this sewing machine for me when I was just a young girl."

Néni Leah always treasured that sewing machine — even after she bought a modern, electric machine, she saved the old-fashioned wheel that had been used together with a foot pedal. That wheel was the third item in the breakfront, together with Sheina Ruchel's candlesticks and the tallis. "This is the only item that I have from Apa and Anya Feldman," she would say sadly.

Néni Leah always regretted that she was not able to make contact with "her" gypsies throughout all the years. She had heard that the surviving gypsies congregated in Rumania after the war, but the Iron Curtain separated them from the rest of the world. She prayed that Chungarabi and Eshto would merit being re-united with their own daughter Lula in reward for all they did for her, Leah-Leichu.

"I hope that the war softened the intransigence of the gypsy leaders; I hope they received permission to see their daughter," she would say. Néni Leah planted a tree in their memory in the Righteous Gentiles Boulevard in Yad Vashem in Jerusalem. "That Chungarabi must have had Jewish blood," my Bubby Rivka Klar always used to tell me. "Kind-hearted, wise Chungarabi was so very different than the rest of her people! Maybe she, her mother or grandmother had been a Jewish child who was stolen and raised by the gypsies. Who knows?"

Néni Leah also mourned the loss of her half-sister Kreindy-Caroli and her half-brothers Izzy and Ari. After the war, Néni Leah tried to investigate what befell them but never found out. She always hoped that perhaps one of them survived and emigrated to the United States or some other country; that would explain why she never found them in Eretz Yisrael. But the truth was that many survivors never did track down their family members after the war, as many of them perished without a trace in the Holocaust.

My grandparents, Zaidy Nachman and Bubby Rivka were *zocheh* to move to Eretz Yisrael with all their children even before the war. My mother and Bubby Rivka Klar told me how the Zingers (Chana Malka was Zaidy Nachman's sister) used to joke that in the *zechus* of all they did to help Sheina Ruchel track down her long-lost daughter, Hashem would also take mercy on them some day. And, indeed, Reb Shia and Chana Malka Zinger and their three children survived the Holocaust, each one of them separately and miraculously. They, too, met in Eretz Yisrael after the war.

Of all the people in Néni Leah's life it was her Mama, Sheina Ruchel, that she mourned the most. Sheina Ruchel was the mother who spent years searching for her missing daughter and after she had finally found her, she sent her away again with kindly gypsies to save her daughter's life. She was the mother who promised to wait in the cellar, a promise she knew she could not keep, but one she made nevertheless, in order to convince her beloved Leichu to flee and save herself.

"It was from her, from my Mama that I learned about *chesed* to other Jews; no matter how poor we were, there was always enough to help those even poorer than we. It was from my Mama that I learned about *emunah* in Hashem; no matter how perilous the situation was during the war, her faith never faltered.

"My beloved mother taught me how one can live a life of Torah and self-respect despite an amputated arm and very little money. She opened my eyes to see the world as it is, without the glitter of money and material possessions. It was her teachings, her nobility, and her personal example that taught me the absolute truth — and showed me the path of truth, the path of Torah, to follow for the rest of my life. It was her teachings that enabled me to rehabilitate myself after the terrible Holocaust that befell my People."

I wrote this book because Néni Leah-Leichu had specifically requested that I do so. But her children do not want any kind of publicity, so I was careful not to mention her married name in the book, or disclose any other information that may reveal her identity. Please, dear readers, do not try to pressure me to disclose this information.

I have tried to be faithful to Leichu's marvelous story, a story of *chesed*, of family love, of pure faith in Hashem in the face of adversity. Most of the names in the book are names of real people: Leichu's friends and acquaintances, both in Budapest as well as in Sevlus. Most of them were tragically murdered in the Holocaust *al Kiddush HaShem*; may their memory be for blessing.

And with this, I offer my prayer that I did not hurt anyone through my stories, and that I succeeded in creating a memorial for all the upright, innocent, God-fearing Jews who were killed *al Kiddush HaShem*. May Hashem avenge their blood, *Amen*.

Miriam Cohen